# The History
## of Horse Racing

Roger Longrigg

# The History
# of Horse Racing

Foreword by Paul Mellon

STEIN AND DAY · Publishers · New York

First published in
the United States of America by
Stein and Day/*Publishers* 1972

This book was designed and produced by
George Rainbird Ltd, Marble Arch House,
44 Edgware Road, London W2

House Editor: Peter Faure
Designer: Gwyn Lewis

The text was phototypeset by
B.A.S. Printers Ltd, Over Wallop, England
Monochrome origination, printing and binding
by Cox & Wyman Ltd, Fakenham, England
Color origination and printing by
Jolly & Barber Ltd, Rugby, England

ISBN 0-8128-1488-6
Library of Congress Catalog Number 76-190373

Stein and Day/*Publishers*/
7 East 48 Street
New York, N.Y. 10017

# Contents

# List of Color Plates

# Foreword by Paul Mellon

It is impossible in the brief space afforded by a foreword to describe the comprehensive sweep of this book, or even to indicate dimly the infinite variety of interesting information that Mr Longrigg has assembled. Although he calls it a *history*, it could more accurately be described as an *encyclopedia* of racing and used as such, for it is world-wide in scope and limitless in chronology. It is quite evidently the result of immense and patient efforts of research, together with the most painstaking labors to achieve accuracy. It is almost as though a prehistoric racing enthusiast, having been divinely granted omniscience as well as immortality, had witnessed every race from the dawn of time through the Arc de Triomphe of 1971, and in describing them had achieved total recall.

And yet it is far from pedestrian. What keeps it from becoming dull, from offering merely a devastating array of dry historical and technical facts about racing, training, and breeding, is Mr Longrigg's method of interspersing his narrative with many fascinating and delightfully human anecdotes about past personalities of the Turf, about their triumphs and their defeats, their accomplishments and their failures, their ingenuities and their stupidities, their eccentricities, their vanities, and their humor. In addition, all the great horses themselves stand out in bold and bright relief, from Matchem, Herod, Eclipse and Highflyer to Man O'War, Hyperion, Ribot, Kelso, and Mill Reef, with many interesting sidelights on the ingredients of their breeding.

One also finds odd bits of curious information throughout: where and when starting-stalls were first used, or a horse was first vanned to a race, or the first racecourse was artificially watered, or racing plates were first used, or the first silver trophies were offered. We learn that in 17th-century France horses were given 'biscuits and Spanish wine' while rubbing down after a match, that both in England and France they were regularly fed 'bread made of beans', and that it was not unusual to feed a horse two to three hundred fresh eggs for several days before a race!

This is a book of men and manners as well as of horses, training, racing and breeding. We see the gradual suppression of the worst kinds of excesses, chicanery, and scandal of the early Turf and the constant (and to a large extent successful) efforts of men of good will, who loved racing, to bring the sport under sensible discipline and control. We follow the physical development and refinement of the thoroughbred from its misty origins among native British and European mares crossed with Eastern importations, down to the modern racehorse with all his ability, beauty and symmetry, but also with an eye on his decline in stamina and his increasing fragility. We follow the history of racing and racecourses from Greek and Roman days, from those early two-horse matches in England and France (owners, trainers, and the unruly public riding and crowding in with the contestants at the finish) down to the most glamorous, regulated, sophisticated, irrigated and automated racecourses of today.

It reminds one of a sort of *mille fleurs* tapestry; but the flowers and their background are vivid men and women, great horses – deep bay, bright chestnut, and grey, racing down long green sweeps of grass, multi-colored gay silks, flashing whips, a shine of golden guineas, silver bells and silver plates.

This is Racing – from Achilles to Arcaro, from Osiris to O'Sullevan.

# Acknowledgments

My particular thanks are due to Mr Paul Mellon for writing the Foreword to this book, for his generosity in making his superb collection of pictures available to us and his helpfulness therewith, and for valuable suggestions about the text and corrections to it. My thanks are due also to the staff of the London Library, always as helpful as they are kind, and to the memory of the late Charles Higginson, whose unique collection of sporting books they house; to Mr Robert Fellowes, Agent of the Jockey Club at Newmarket, for allowing me to use the Club's library; to Mr Robert Way of Burrough Green, most knowledgeable of sporting booksellers and most affable of all booksellers, who even lent me a book which was too expensive for me to buy; to Mr Peter Willett for valuable advice; to the late Lord Astor, the late Sir Jack Jarvis, and my late great-uncle A. C. Macnab of Macnab for giving me unpublished information I could never otherwise have acquired; to Mr Roger Mortimer, Mr and Mrs John Oliver, and my father-in-law Mr Marcus Chichester for lending me books for unconscionable periods; to my father Brigadier S. H. Longrigg for correcting my Arabic transliteration; and to Mr John Hadfield and his colleagues at George Rainbird Ltd., especially Mr Peter Faure, for meticulous editing which they contrived never to make burdensome.

I am indebted to Miss Vivien Jarvis and Michael Joseph Ltd for permission to quote from *They're Off* by Sir Jack Jarvis; to Mrs George Bambridge, Macmillan & Co. Ltd and Doubleday & Co. Inc. for permission to quote from *The Broken Link Handicap* from *Plain Takes from the Hills* by Rudyard Kipling; to J. A. Allen & Co. Ltd for permission to quote from *Men and Horses I Have Known* by the Hon. George Lambton; to Methuen & Co. Ltd for permission to quote from *The English Turf* by Charles Richardson; and to Mr Eric Rickman for permission to quote from the late Tom Jennings's memoir of his father quoted by Mr Rickman in *Gladiateur and the Jennings* in *The British Racehorse* Vol. xvii No. 2. To all these I am most grateful.

# 1  The Ancient World

## Enter the Horse

The horse and chariot arrived in Eastern Europe and North Africa a little before 1500 BC. They came with the Hyksos, the mysterious conquerors who held brief sway over the Eastern Mediterranean. In the 18th Dynasty the horse-drawn chariot appears in Egyptian monumental art. The Linear A tablets of Knossos, horseless, give way to the Linear B, which abound in horses' heads, chariots, wheels, yokes, and whips. The Greeks of Mycenae had two-horse chariots for war.

The Hyksos and their horses are important not only from the fact of their arrival, but also for the quality of the animals. All subsequent history attests their superiority to the hairy ponies of the North and the thick-set beasts of the further steppes, the Mongolians. Their descendants are the horses we race today.

But Mongol horses also became dramatically important. In India they arrived with their invading Aryan masters. They went south from Mongolia into China. From Egypt to the Yellow Sea the horse was the basis of military power.

In civilized societies riding remained a junior partner to driving, at least until the middle of the last millennium BC, because it was less useful in war. (The Assyrians were an exception.) The horse also had an important ceremonial role, and chariots were more dignified. Finally, it was chariots that people raced in Homeric Greece and the India of the Rig-Veda.

## Homeric Greece

By Homer's time the Greeks were breeding on a large scale, especially in the Peleponnese. The horses were small. They were ridden, but only exceptionally. Homer speaks of riding as a gymnastic display of no practical value.[1] The war-machine of his day was the two-horse chariot; so was the racing-car.

When Patroclus was killed by Hector under the walls of Troy, Achilles organized a race as part of the funeral ceremony. The prizes were: first, a lady; second, a mare in foal; third, a cauldron; fourth, two talents' worth of gold; fifth, a cup. The runners were: King Eumelus; Diomedes, driving captured Trojan horses; Atrides, King of Lacedaemon, driving Podargus and swift Aethe; Antilochus, son of Nestor, driving a Pylian pair; and Meriones, driving fair-maned horses.

Nestor gave his son long pre-race instructions. Antilochus had been taught horsemanship by Zeus and Poseidon, but his horses were slow. He must win by guile, going closest to the corners. The near horse must be reined in until its head touched the chariot-wheel. But it was vital not to hit the corner or the chariot would go over.

Achilles drew for the starting positions. The field went away fast, manes streaming like flags. The chariots sometimes grazed each other so that they bounced in the air. The cheating now began. Apollo knocked the scourge out of Diomedes' hand, so that he wept with frustration. Athene gave it back to him, then flew at Eumelus and broke his harness. His mares shot away, the chariot-pole ploughed into the ground, the chariot went over, and the driver was injured.

The field disappeared into a dust-cloud. The crowd was agog to see who led when they came into view. Ajax and Idomentus had a side-bet on this, the stake being a cauldron or tripod.

Diomedes was leading. (In fact he was flying: Athene was lifting him along.) He finished well clear, and the first prize was led to his tent. Antilochus was second. Third, on his heels, came Atrides, the mare Aethe finishing with particular courage. Menelaeus, owner of the third horses, objected to Antilochus for crossing; the objection was over-ruled. Afterwards Nestor reminisced at length about other races when he was young.[2]

Apart (perhaps) from the intervention of the gods, there is no reason to suppose that this is not a reliable picture of racing in Homer's time. Evidently such races were familiar and long-established.

It is significant that Trojan horses won as expected. Troy was nearer the southern sources of the best stock; its horses were better than anything the Greeks bred.

## The Greek Games

For some time racing was confined to the two-horse chariot. Then the Greeks, buying horses from the Libyans, learned from them how to yoke four horses abreast[3] and in 680 BC the quadriga race was added to the Olympic programme.

The Olympics were the oldest and greatest of the Greek devotional games. They had been founded in 776 BC in honour of Zeus. They were held every four years, at the first full moon after the summer solstice. At their most elaborate they lasted five days. There were up to eight judges, chosen from the local Elians, called the Hellanodicae. The prize was a wreath of olive.

Pindar, laureate of the games, addressed his odes to winners at the Pythian, Nemean, and Isthmian games as well as the Olympic. The main Pythian games were held near Delphi, in honour of Apollo, but there were others in the same cause at 26 places, includ-ing several in North Africa. The Nemean games were held every two years, in the winter; here the olive-garland prize was replaced by a crown of parsley. The Isthmian games, in honour of Poseidon, were every other year in alternation with the Nemean.

The first 17 Olympics were confined to foot-races. Then wrestling, boxing and the pentathlon appeared, and, in the 25th games, the four-horse chariot. Thirty-two years later the first ridden race was added. It is reasonable to assume North African influence here too. Certainly African horses made this departure possible. Whereas horses derived from the Mongolian breed needed ferocious piercing and squeezing bits, the Africans, then and later, were ridden with halters. The Greeks used bits for race-riding, but they only had the savage kind for schooling, and for the occasional rogue. They rode races bareback, although they used saddle-cloths with a girth for hunting and war.[4]

A mares-only race, the Calpe, was added at Olympia in 496 BC; and then a race for colts of the same age. There were also at various periods races for four-wheeled carts, two-horse chariots, boy riders, and mule-carts.

Horses and their riders or drivers had to come to Elis thirty days before the games, and there undergo special training. There were heats and a final, each race lasting twelve laps. The winner was given a fantastic civic welcome by his own city. When Exaenetus came back to Acragas after winning a chariot-race in the 92nd Olympiad, 'he was led into the town in a chariot; the procession included three hundred chariots, every one drawn by two white horses.'[5] Victors at the other games were similarly celebrated.

QUADRIGA. Greek technique, learned from Libya, was evidently quite different from that of the Romans 500 years later (see p. 14). This driver (500 BC) controls each pair separately, reins in each hand in the American style. He does not have the draught-reins and coupling-reins of a modern coachman: he can turn his chariot but not his horses' heads.

Amid his convoluted metaphors about the gods, Pindar lets fall a few revealing details about the races. At Delphi in 466 BC Arcesilaus of Mycenae won the chariot-race: 'Amongst forty fallen charioteers you kept yours whole and entire, and won.' Victory recompensed Arcesilaus for the vast expense he had been put to. The race was the normal 12 laps, in a hippodrome about 1000 feet long.[6]

The most vivid account of a race occurs in the *Electra* of Sophocles, written about 15 years after the victory of Arcesilaus. The race, at Thebes, was described to Clytemnestra by the tutor. There were 10 starters. Lots were cast for places, and the chariots were lined up. A trumpet sounded. They went off fast, the drivers wielding their goads furiously. An Aenian's horses bolted; they caused a multiple crash which left only Orestes and an Athenian running. These two had a furious battle, lap after lap, Orestes taking the corners with perfect judgment. In the last lap he misjudged the turn and smashed his hub on the post. He was thrown over the rails entangled in his reins, and dragged by his maddened horses across the arena. The Athenian stopped and extricated him, but he was dead and dreadfully mutilated. He was burned at once on a pyre.[7]

The sport was enormously popular. Enthusiasts spent fortunes. The glamorous Alcibiades 'was famed for his breed of horses and the numbers of his chariots. For no-one besides himself, whether private person or king, ever sent seven chariots at one time to the Olympic games. The first, the second, and the fourth prizes, according to Thucydides, or the third, as Euripides relates it, he bore away at once, which exceeds anything performed by the most ambitious in that way.'[8] At the same time (about 430 BC), in the

*Clouds* of Aristophanes, a wild young man called Pheidippides ruined his father, Strepsiades, by the money he spent on racing. Twelve *minae* for a starling-coloured horse was the last straw, and the father was sued by a money-lender.[9]

Not everyone approved of these excesses. Xenephon's friend King Agesilaus 'persuaded his sister Cynisca to breed chariot-horses, and this showed, when she gained a victory, that the breeding of such animals was a proof, not of manly desert, but of wealth.' And later: 'Did he not also show clearly, in conformity with the nobleness of his disposition, that if he conquered private persons in a chariot-race, he would not be at all more worthy of honour?'[10]

Races were not confined to the official structure of the games. On one occasion Plato and his friends were beside the sea at Piraeus:

' "Have you not heard," said Adeimantus, "there is to be a torch-race on horseback this evening, to honour the goddess?"

"On horseback?" I said. "That is a new idea. Will the riders carry torches in relays and hand them to one another?"

"Just like that," said Polemarchus.'[11]

When Xenophon's Ten Thousand arrived at the sea, they celebrated with an impromptu point-to-point. They had to ride down the cliff, turn in the sea, and climb back to the altar. On the way down most of them rolled over. Coming up the horses could hardly walk. There was tremendous noise and laughter.[12]

The Olympics kept their glamour after the rise of Macedon. Philip II was an enthusiastic and successful racehorse owner, with many victories in ridden and driven events. In 356 BC he took the city of Potidaea; his troops defeated the Illyrians; his wife Olympias gave birth to Alexander; and his horse won at the Olympics: all on the same day.[13]

But when Greece became a Roman province the Olympics were reduced to minor status and ultimately, by Nero, to farce.

## The Greek Racehorse and its Training

From the 8th century BC the Libyans sent both horses and horsemanship to Greece. The best horses continued to come either directly or indirectly from Africa. Of the 14 surviving odes of Pindar which celebrate horse races the winners of no less than 12 come from Cyrene or Sicily. Thessaly and the land of the Veneti (modern Salonika and Venice) were the two other cradles of winners. To them new blood came direct from Cyrenaica by sea.

The Greeks documented not only their racing and their horses, but also their training methods. Xenophon urges the stirrup-less and saddle-less jockey to hold on to the mane while jumping; otherwise his instruction might be modern. When buying a horse, look for high, thick-walled hoofs (shoes came much later), moderately sloping pasterns, solid cannon-bones, strong hocks, and plenty of heart-room. Insist also on a high-set neck, small dainty head, small ears, and broad quarters. The horse should be broken gently, and accustomed to noise and crowds. Food and exercise are not a matter of rigid formula, but must be adjusted to the needs of the individual. Look after your horse's feet, and make the stable floor of well-drained cobblestones. Train your lad to groom, bridle-up, and lead. School your horse to turn fluently both ways, and in all training use patience and gentleness.[14]

## Asia Minor and the East; Racing in India

Early in the last millennium BC Egypt began to export the naturalized North African horse back along the route of its arrival. 'Solomon had horses brought out of Egypt.'[15] One of the Bedouin traditions (there are several, which conflict) is that from certain of Solomon's mares all desert Arabs descend.

TWO-HORSE RACING CHARIOT. The driven pair was raced in Greece from about 1000 BC (possibly much earlier) but from the 7th century it was less important than the quadriga. Like the ridden race, it survived as a regular event throughout the history of the Greek games and into the Roman circus. This posthumous coin of Philip II was struck in Macedonia in 325 BC, and celebrates an event at the Olympics. By this date chariot and harness were purely sporting, their military relevance having long disappeared.

Further East another kind of horse had been flooding in from the remoter steppes. The Assyrians had a great horse army, ridden and driven, copiously depicted in the carvings at Nineveh. They hunted lions and wild bulls on horseback; their competitive chasing of this game had something in common with 17th-century hunting-matches.

Assyrian horses were inferior to the famous Nisaeans, 'the largest and best; some say they come from Media, some say from Armenia'.[16] These were the horses of the Persian kings – charger, polo-pony, chariot-horse, and racehorse. They combined the speed, stamina and docility of the African with the hardiness of the Mongolian, and in these qualities could be compared only with the horse of Spain.[17]

The horse that went down into North West India with the Vedan Aryans seems to have been unmixed Mongolian: it was tough but not fast. It was never ridden. 'The Indian horse cannot be controlled by everybody. They are not schooled and driven by the reins, but by spiked muzzles.'[18]

The North West was the only part of India where horses could be bred. In, perhaps, 1000 BC the Sanskrit poet of the Rig-Veda hymned the sacred river Indus, which was 'rich in horses and in chariots'. He goes on to present us with an isolated, unique, and unambiguous reference to racing: 'The Sindhu has yoked her easy chariot with horses; may she conquer prizes for us in the race. The greatness of her chariot is praised as truly great – that chariot which is irresistable, which has its own glory, and abundant strength.'[19]

In 480 BC Xerxes' army included Bactrian cavalry and Punjabi charioteers.[20] Two centuries later, King Porus took 'all his cavalry, 4000 horse' against Alexander.[21] Better horses had come down from Afghanistan, and ultimately from Persia, and cavalry had in consequence replaced the chariot. Ridden races are a probable, but unrecorded, result.

## Gaul and Germany; the Iberian Horse

In Northern Europe the remoter Gauls had horses which were 'shaggy all over the body, to five fingers in depth of hair; they are small, flat-nosed, and unable to carry men; but when yoked to chariots they are very fleet, therefore the natives drive chariots.'[22] German horses 'are undersized and ugly, but by constant exercise they develop in them extraordinary powers of endurance.'[23]

But the Southern Gauls, long in contact with Italy, were avid for the better horses of the South, and would go to great expense to get them. Cavalry therefore gradually moved North and East, replacing the chariot. The military effect was spectacular. A Rhineland tribe called the Tencteri did what had been reckoned a six-days' march to a place where the river could be crossed, and back, in a night, and fell upon their enemies. This was possible entirely because they had got better horses.[24] The horses of the Tencteri were also raced, supplying 'rivalry to their youths'.[25]

At the Western end of the civilized world, in Spain, horses were imported from Morocco from about 400 BC. They were crossed with the little native animals, the proportion of imported blood diminishing with latitude. The result was a bigger, faster, handier horse, ancestor of the Lusitanian and Andalusian. Hannibal brought both Spanish and Numidian cavalry over the mountains. The Spaniards had bridles, the Numidians only their plaited halters. At the Battle of Ticino (218 BC) they outclassed not only Scipio's Gauls but the superior Roman cavalry too.[26]

The Spanish horse was the wonder of ancient writers: 'Celtiberian horses are like the Parthians. They are faster and also run more smoothly.'[27] 'The Jennet in swiftness passeth the Parthians and all other horses whatsoever they be, even so far as the Egle exceedeth all the birds in the aire, and as the Dolphin passeth all the fishes of the sea.'[28] There was one way to account for this: 'In Lusitania the mares turn to the west wind; they become impregnated by it, and the foals so conceived are amazing for speed.'[29]

# THE HISTORY OF HORSE RACING

## *Origins of Roman Racing*

From Sicily, love of horses and racing spread North. A notable centre, as might have been expected, was Sybaris. The Sybarites trained their horses to rise on their hind legs and dance to certain tunes.[30] In 510 BC spies from their enemy Crotona discovered this. Enemy flute-players struck up one of the tunes before battle. The Sybarite horses obediently reared up, off fell the knights, the horses danced over to the enemy, and Sybaris was destroyed.[31]

According to tradition, the city of Thurii was founded on the ruins of Sybaris in 443 BC. The citizens revived the racing and breeding tradition, and from Thurii the Romans learned horse racing.[32]

The first race in Rome was run immediately after the founding of the city. Romulus, in order to have loyal followers, settled a rabble on the Capitoline Hill and declared them all citizens. 'But he was unable to secure the right of intermarriage for his followers; consequently he proclaimed a horse-race, sacred to Neptune. When a crowd, mostly of Sabini, had arrived, he told all his men who wanted a wife to seize the girls who had come to the race.'[33] Neptune, as Poseidon, was the deity celebrated at the Isthmian Games, tutor of the great whip Antilochus, and sire of the winged Pegasus (foaled, significantly, in Libya, out of the Gorgon Medusa).[34] Few paintings of the rape of the Sabines give much idea of the racecourse.

ROMAN QUADRIGA. The chariot is racing along the *spina* in the centre of the circus on one of its seven laps; the driver is about to turn left-handed round the turning-posts. His reins are Y-shaped, the two ends meeting at the withers. The charioteer thus holds a single rein for each horse, whose head he cannot turn. The reins are wrapped round his waist so that he can slow or stop his team by leaning back.

The kings who followed Romulus raced occasionally. Under Tarquinius Priscus the races became annual, and this king founded the Circus Maximus.[35]

## Circus Racing; Charioteers and Factions

The Maximus, greatest of the many Roman circuses, was at first rudely constructed of timber. It was enlarged and improved in the last years of the republic: 'The Circus Maximus, that was constructed by the Dictator Caesar, one *stadium* in width and three in length, and occupying, with the adjacent buildings, no less than four *jugera*, with room for 260,000 spectators seated.'[36] A *stadium* was one-eighth of a Roman mile, and so a little under a furlong. A *jugerum* was a little over 3000 square yards. It is extraordinary that four-horse chariots could gallop in such cramped conditions: the more so as almost all other circuses were smaller, as the number of competitors rose from four to six, and as even in the time of Augustus there were six-horse chariots racing.[37] Caesar's safety precautions sound needful: he surrounded the circuit with canals ten feet deep, to protect the spectators from the chariots.[38]

The Circus Maximus was square at one end, round at the other. The chariots started at the square end: 'In the Circus, the place where the horses start is now [45 BC] called the "prison stalls", *carceres*, because the horses are kept there until the moment the official gives the sign. They used to be decorated with pinnacles and towers.'[39] The gates had hinged doors which opened at the same moment.[40]

Augustus added an 85-foot obelisk, brought from Egypt. Constantine (son of Constantine the Great) installed another, no less than 112 feet high without base or pedestal. This was examined by the studious John Evelyn: its inscription established that it came originally from Thebes, and reached Rome via Alexandria and Constantinople.[41]

The start of the race was given by a dropped napkin or the sound of a trumpet. The course was left-handed. There were six turning-posts[42] straddling the central *spina;* Claudius made these of marble and gilded them.[43] The chariots ran seven laps. Eggs were placed on pillars as each circuit was completed so that spectators and drivers knew how far they had gone.[44]

In the late republic and early empire the sport was amateur. In Caesar's games 'several of the young nobility drove chariots, drawn some by four and some by two horses, and likewise rode races on single horses.' 'High-ranking youths' were the riders and drivers under Augustus. By Caligula's order 'none drove in the chariot-races who were not of the senatorial order.'

But the professionals came in at about this time, and were at once the darlings of the crowds. They were usually of humble origin. They got out of hand. Nero 'forbade the revels of charioteers, who had long assumed a licence to stroll about, and established for themselves a kind of prescriptive right to cheat and thieve, making a jest of it.'[45]

The chariots were skeletal, built for rigidity and lightness. Later they were sometimes of basketwork. The reins went back from the bit to a loop over the withers: they there joined, forming a Y, so that the charioteer had one ribbon for each horse. The driver could not, like a modern coachman, turn his horses' heads; he turned his vehicle by reining in the nearside and giving rein to the offside horse, as Nestor instructed Antilochus under the walls of Troy.

The charioteer wrapped all four reins round his waist, so that he could lean back to steady or stop his team. He held the bunched reins in his left hand, and a whip or goad in his right. He braced himself with his knee against the front of the chariot, and leaned out from the turns.

The sport was wildly popular. 'To these diversions there flocked such crowds of spectators from all parts, that most of the strangers were obliged to lodge in tents erected in the streets, or along the roads near the city. Several in the throng were squeezed to death, amongst whom were two senators.'[46] Juvenal looked sourly at empty streets: 'today the circus takes the whole of Rome.'[47]

This popularity was both a cause and an effect of the factions, to one of which every citizen was fiercely loyal. These were the *Veneta, Prasina, Albata*, and *Russata* – the Blue, Green, White and Red – whose teams were identified on the track by the drivers' colours.

## Racing Emperors

Another factor in the popularity of racing was the participation of the emperors, which did not have the modern effect of increasing the seemliness of the sport.

Caligula was the first royal fanatic. His races in the Circus Maximus went on from dawn until night. He built other circuses in several places, and himself drove in races. He backed the Greens. He 'supped and lodged for some time constantly in the stable where their horses were kept. At a certain revel, he made a present of two millions of sesterces to one Cythicus, a driver of a chariot. The day before the Circensian games, he used to send his soldiers to enjoin silence in the neighbourhood, that the repose of his horse Incitatus might not be disturbed. For this favourite animal, besides a marble stable, an ivory manger, purple housings, and a jewelled frontlet, he appointed a house, with a retinue of slaves, and fine furniture, for the reception of such as were invited in the horse's name to sup with him. It is even said that he intended to make him consul.'

Claudius inaugurated many more races, in honour of his ancestors and family. There were no ridden races in his time; the chariots alternated with gladiators and wild beasts, which he preferred, having a great fondness for violence and death. He was a gambler. 'He even used to play as he rode in his chariot, having the tables so fitted, that the game was not disturbed by the motion of the carriage.'

Nero went further still, in all directions. He instituted four-camel chariot races. He invented the *Neronia* – a triathlon event involving music, wrestling, and horse racing. 'He had from his childhood an extravagant passion for horses; and his constant talk was of the Circensian races.' As a boy he played with toy ivory quadrigas. He doubled the number of prizes, and racing went on into the night. Like Caligula he took to driving a chariot himself, first in his garden, then in public. He showed off his charioteering and his singing all over the Empire. When he announced his entry at Olympia the town was alarmed: rightly: he caused the statues of all previous winners to be pulled down and thrown into the sewers. 'He drove the chariot with various numbers of horses, and at the Olympic games with no fewer than ten. . . . Being thrown out of his chariot, he was again replaced, but could not retain his seat, and was obliged to give up, before he reached the goal, but was crowned notwithstanding.' Like Claudius he was a furious gambler.

The Flavian emperors were initially more respectable. Vespasian cleaned up Rome. He started the Colosseum, which Titus finished. But Domitian recalled the excesses of the earlier period. He held one hundred races a day in the Circus Maximus. To the four factions he added two more, the *Aureata* and the *Purpurea*. He also introduced women gladiators.[48]

## The Roman Racehorse

The best Roman horses came from the same places as the best Greek. Bits of inscription built into the wall of the Castello San Angelo add up to the biography of a charioteer: Avilius Teres, who raced about AD 75. Legible fragments list 42 of his winners. Of these, 37 are *Afer* – bred in Roman North Africa. One is Moorish, one Spanish. Only three are Italian. None is Venetian.[49] The eclipse of the once-great Venetian horse is inexplicable, but it was total. Perhaps political ferment destroyed their 'obsession with horse-breeding, which has now [AD 1] quite disappeared.'[50]

ROMAN QUADRIGA. This would appear to be a winner's lap of honour, since the charioteer has dropped his reins and holds a palm. Visible behind him are the starting-stalls, an aid not re-invented until the 1920s. Three-horse chariots did not race; the off-side wheeler in this team has dropped his head.

ROMAN QUADRIGA. There are differences of harness and technique between this later mosaic and the 1st-century terra-cotta relief on p. 14; each pair is here controlled by a single rein. The horses, as always, have bandaged legs; these carry an unusual quantity of ornament, with fronds in the brow-bands and ribbons streaming from the tails. This chariot is made of woven reeds for lightness.

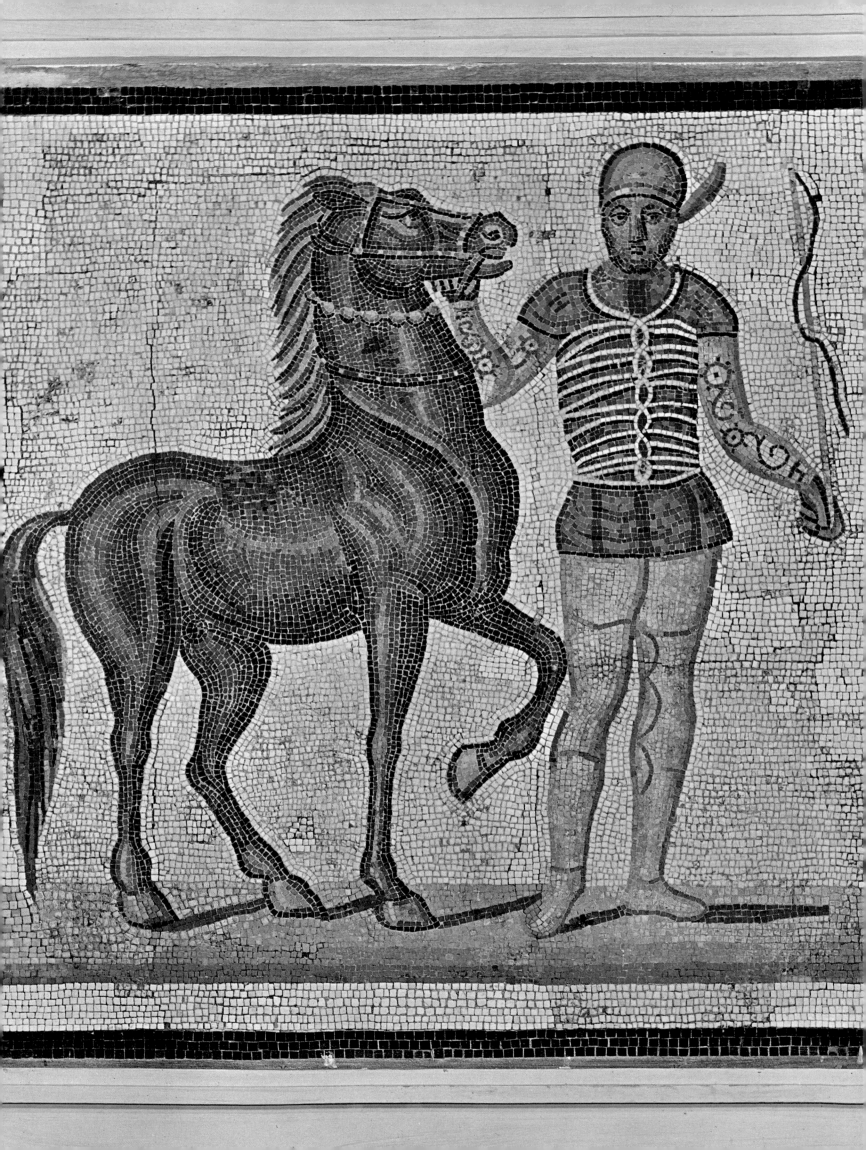

Roman art confirms the Southern provenance of Roman racehorses. They have flying legs, starting eyes, distended nostrils. They also have high-set necks and tails, elegant hairless legs, and dainty 'blood' heads. Rome bought the best, at whatever cost, from anywhere. The North African horse, with the Spanish and Sicilian horse of North African blood, was still the aristocrat.

Some of these horses enjoyed their racing. 'The horses that are yoked to the chariots in the circus, beyond doubt, display remarkable proofs of how sensible they are to encouragement and glory. In the secular games, which were celebrated in the circus, under the Emperor Claudius, when the charioteer Corax, who belonged to the White party, was thrown from his place at the starting-post, his horses took the lead and kept it, opposing the other chariots, overturning them, and doing everything against the other competitors that could have been done, had they been guided by the most skilful charioteer; and while we quite blushed to behold the skill of man exceeded by that of the horse, they arrived at the goal, after going over the whole of the prescribed course.'[51]

## Racing in Byzantium

The first hippodrome at Byzantium was built by Septimus Severus before AD 200. Much of it was held up on vaults. Its design followed the Circus Maximus but it was slightly smaller. Constantine finished it. The starting-stalls, spine, and turning-posts were copied from Rome; but Constantine introduced something new, the *Kathisma*, the royal box. This innovation had a good deal to do with the character of Byzantine racing.

The four original factions were all represented at Byzantium, but the Red and White shrank into insignificance. Everyone was a Blue or a Green. The Blues sat on the emperor's right, to the West, the Greens on his left, to the East.

The sport went on, luridly, for 400 years. In the 5th century the charioteers were still making fortunes. Neither Christian bishops nor satirical writers repressed them. (The 4th Canon of the Council of Arles excommunicated charioteers at the public games.) Passionate partisanship went right down society, from emperor to artisan. Theodosius backed the Greens, Marcian the Blues, Leo and Zeno the Greens, Justinian the Blues. These loyalties were not only rabid; they were also specifically political. The point has been made that the circus was the only place where public demonstration could be held.[52]

If the sport was fiercer, it was also more lavish. On the *spina* Justinian and his predecessors placed ornaments of a scarcely credible richness.[53] Justinian also made arrangements to get direct from his palace, by covered passage, to his royal box. At his appearance flags were raised, and the factions sang antiphonal hymns.

Every other big town in the Eastern Empire had a similar circus, with the same factions. The crowds were so dense that every pinnacle and rooftree was occupied by clinging enthusiasts.

Not much is on record about the horses, but an assumption can be made. The factions, backed by the bottomless royal coffers, would have imported the very best available horses, and in large numbers. Asiatic Turkey must by 600 have been well stocked with Libyan racehorses.

Meanwhile murder as a racing tactic became normal instead of exceptional; and in one riot after the races 30,000 men lost their lives. Classical racing stumbled to a bloody end.

ROMAN RACING COLOURS. This is one of four matching mosaics, in which charioteers pose with single horses. Their garb is identical – crash-helmet, reinforcement stitched over the rib-cage, and leather leggings – except for the colour of the tunic. This is the livery of the *Prasina*, the green faction, to which one quarter of Rome, and one half of Byzantium, was fervidly loyal. Caligula, least balanced of all the racing emperors, espoused this faction, and it was in these colours that Incitatus ran.

# 2  *The Middle Ages*

## *Goths, Franks and Anglo-Saxons*

Europe was taken over by waves of uncouth invaders, themselves being pushed by the mounted Huns. All inherited the Roman horse.

The new masters of Rome sat on the marble seats of the circus. No doubt they watched racing, but they did not have the habit of literary record. When the Franks conquered Provence in about AD 500 they found the horses of the Camargue and the arena of Arles; they naturally raced the one in the other.[1]

In Britain there had presumably been racing under the Romans. At Netherby in AD 200 the racehorses are said to have been stabled separately from the others. There is also said to be evidence for racing at Caerleon, Silchester, Rustborough, and Dorchester.[2] A 4th-century mosaic in Lincolnshire shows two-horse chariots racing, but everywhere else the evidence is very thin. Much more convincing is the presence of racing in Britanny, evidently brought by those refugee Romano-British who crossed the sea to Armorica. A Breton poem said to be of AD 500 describes a race for which the prize was the hand of the Princess Aliénor, daughter of King Brodrick.[3]

The Anglo-Saxons arrived without horses, but they took to the British ones. In 642 King Oswald achieved a posthumous miracle by curing the sick horse of a traveller. The Anglo-Saxons always rode, never drove.[4]

In 686 there was a race of a kind. Herebald, later a monk, was travelling with a party led by Bishop John of York (later, uncanonically, known as St John of Beverley). 'We came to an open place, very suitable for racing our horses.' The bishop allowed them to race, but forbade Herebald to take part. Herebald, 'not yet having quite restrained myself from youthful diversions,' watched as long as he could bear it, and then joined in. 'But at once my impetuous horse made a great leap over a ditch. I fell, and lost all consciousness, as though dead.' He came to the following morning, revived by the bishop blowing on his face. He ascribed both accident and recovery to divine intervention.[5]

More formal racing has been inferred in the 10th century. This is because in about 900 King Athelstan received a present, from Hugh the Great of France, of *equos cursores plurimos*: Hugh being after the hand of Athelstan's sister Ethelswitha.[6] *Cursores* is generally rendered 'running horses', and racing thus inferred. This is improbable. From its earliest use the English word 'courser', and its Anglo-Norman cognate, meant a warhorse 'able to indure travell, and to bear the weight of Armour.'[7] The picture of Anglo-Saxon kings at the races thus hangs, it seems, on a mistranslation.

## *Racing in Ancient Ireland*

Ireland, on or beyond the fringe of civilization, had by far the most racing of the Dark Age world.

RACING IN ROMAN LINCOLNSHIRE. This 4th-century mosaic from Horkstow almost certainly depicts racing, since only one man stands in each chariot. In battle an archer or spearman would be beside him, if the Romano-British still used war-chariots, itself most doubtful. The saddled horse being led by his reins has a distinctly Arab look, which lends a small amount of colour to the tradition that the Romans imported specialized racehorses to Britain.

IRISH RIDING. This is one of the many decorations in the Book of Kells (*c.* AD 700) showing horsemen, clearly not warriors, riding bareback but with bits and bridles. This continued to be the Irish method for centuries; after the Anglo-Norman invasion the English were forbidden by law to ride in the improper Irish fashion. The Irish also mounted on the wrong side of the horse. Ridden horses were in this period raced on the Curragh, but it is clear from the Brehon Laws that there were still chariot-races in other parts of Ireland.

In AD I Ireland, like Britain and Germany, had little native horses which were driven. Queen Mebd had a chariot worth 21 bondmaids; a good horse was only worth one bondmaid. The Irish fought exactly like the Greeks: two-horse chariots, driven by a charioteer and carrying a spearman.[8] There is no hint of the Red Branch Knights riding.

Cuchulain was the most famous general of this military brotherhood of Ulster, the army of Conchobar mac Nessa. Chariot-racing was their greatest diversion. This was also true of the similar military organizations of Munster and Connaught.[9]

Even in this dim and savage period things were beginning to change. Cuchulain had a grey or roan horse, and Conchobar's horses had dappled heads. If these were correctly described they must have been imported. There is no difficulty about believing that the Irish imported horses from the European mainland, as well as from Britain, as early as AD I: the clothes, jewels and weapons described so interminably in the Saga of Cuchulain are of the familiar Late Celtic type known as La Tène.[10]

The change shows dramatically by the mid 3rd century. The Fena (*Fianna*) of Erin were another celebrated army, serving Finn in Kildare, and most powerful about 260. They hunted from May until October; they always rode. They neither fought nor raced in chariots. Their horses were obviously imported or bred from imported stock. They were exceptional in their own time, which accounts for the power of the Fena.

By the 7th century, however, the Irish horse had improved enough to be ridden in peacetime as a regular thing. The decorations which illuminate the Book of Kells (about 700) include many horsemen, riding with bridles but without saddles or stirrups.

By 800 the Brehon Laws (properly *Fénechas*, the laws of free farmers: *brehon* means 'judge') were fully authoritative; they insist that every man, of every rank, be taught to drive. They also confirm that many horses were imported.[11] Later Irish tradition is emphatic that the best horses came from Spain, which, of the early centuries AD, is speculative, though not incredible.

Ireland's racing took place at an *Aenach* (or *Aonach*), a fair, the most sporting of the various kinds of gathering. The most important of these were at Tlachtga, Ushnagh, and Tailten: the last now Teltown, between Navan and Kells. Its *Aenach* lasted for several days each side of 1 August. The whole of Ireland came, as well as visitors from Scotland. At the *Aenach* of Carman in Leinster, held every three years from the 1st to the 6th of August, a day was given entirely to ridden and driven races.

The greatest centre of racing, from the time of the Fena of Erin, was the Curragh of Kildare. Its annual fair was the *Aenach Colmain* (or *Aenach Life*, the fair of the Liffey); it lasted several days. From the mid-3rd century races at the Curragh were ridden.[12]

# THE HISTORY OF HORSE RACING

Both law and folklore show the importance of racing in ancient Irish society. According to the Brehon Laws, an established fair-green, a racecourse, could be used for horse racing without fine or charge, regardless of anyone's rights over the land. No penalty or compensation was payable for damage by a flying horseshoe. The sons of kings and chiefs in fosterage had to be supplied by their foster-fathers with horses on race-days.[13] Most significantly, the pagan Irish heaven promised unlimited racing.[14]

## Arab and Barb

Arabia was not the cradle of the horse. In Xerxes' army 'the Arabians all rode camels not inferior to horses in speed.'[15] They still had no horses at the birth of Christ,[16] but soon afterwards they began to acquire them, from Egypt via Sinai, perhaps from Turkey via Syria, perhaps from Mesopotamia. The North African environment had improved the breed to a point. The Arabian improved it further. It is not at all clear why. What Arab horses ate was a mystery to Marco Polo and is a mystery still.

According to Sahara tradition, Isma'il ibn-Ibrahim (Ishmael) was the original horse-tamer. The Ishmaelites had a mare who foaled on a journey. The foal, a filly, was unable to keep up with the caravan; she was accordingly wrapped in a goat-skin and carried, which left her with deformed legs. This filly was the great tap-root mare. Her descendants were *Benat el-A'waj*, Daughters of the Crooked. The *A'waj* breed, under that name, survived in the Sahara. An early sub-breed – or the *A'waj* under a new name – was the *Kehila* of Arabia, contemporary with the Prophet.[17]

Arabian tradition is a little different. The tap-root is *Kehilet el-Ajuz*, the Mare of the Old Woman. The families that descend from her are *el Khamsa*, the Five, of which the noblest is the *Kehila*. The tribe who bred the finest *Kehilan* were the Aniza, and the Darley Arabian is said to come from them.[18] (Mr Darley said himself the horse was something called a Manicha.)

Pedigree was held in far higher esteem than either conformation or ability. The Arabs inbred recklessly, generation after generation, so as not to adulterate their noblest blood. They particularly valued bays. Greys were frequent; chestnuts despised. Like the North Africans, the Arabs rode without bits; they used instead a fine chain over the nose.[19]

Islam took about 60 years to conquer North Africa. In 710 the army of the Prophet crossed into Spain. It is reasonable to guess that very few Arab horses made so long a journey, over two generations, under Berber masters; they took Barbs.

Was there any significant difference between Arab and Barb? The horse of North Africa may have received injections of genetic impurity from the North, from which the desert Arab was safe. Although documentary evidence (the little there is) combines to suggest that the Arab derived from the Sahara, it may have come partly or even primarily from the Euphrates, in which case it had a difference of environment over an immense period. There are said to be clear differences of bone-structure between Barb and Arab: the Arab has a dished (concave) face, the Barb a Roman (convex) profile; the Arab has a triangular eye-socket, the Barb a round one; the Arab has a flat croup, the Barb a sloping one.[20] There is no evidence that these differences affect performance.

## Horses and Races in Medieval Britain

William the Norman won the Battle of Hastings not so much by dint of arrows shot in the air as by more heavily armed men on more powerful horses. But the Normans also valued horses of a different stamp. Hunting was the Norman passion. The New Forest and other large areas were strictly preserved by William the Conqueror for deer, boar, and hare, which was extremely unpopular with all classes of the English.[21] Hunting was part of the reason for the development of a special breed. Giraldus, touring Wales in

NORMAN KNIGHTS. This detail from the Bayeux tapestry shows the horse and the school of horsemanship which dominated European warfare from the 8th century. The horse is a big weight-carrier, a natural trotter, whose development began in Roman times and from which derived the Great Horse breeds such as Percheron and Courser. The high, heavy saddle and long stirrup-leathers developed with the horse; they survived in warfare until gunpowder caused the re-invention of light cavalry, and in the *manège* long afterwards.

1188, noted: 'In this third district of Wales, called Powys, there are most excellent studs put apart for breeding, and deriving their origin from some fine Spanish horses, which Robert de Belesme, Earl of Shrewsbury, brought into this country; on which account the horses sent from hence are remarkable for their majestic proportions, and astonishing fleetness.'[22]

There is a firm (if frankly incredible) record of an 'Arab stallion' in Britain early in the 12th century. King Alexander I of Scotland gave it to the Church of St Andrew in 1121. It is not known what the church did with it, nor what effect this exotic had on the Scottish breed which, under the generic name Galloway, later became an outstanding racehorse.

Fifty years later a sudden, undoubted, contemporary spotlight is turned on racing of a kind. This took place at Smithfield Market, among 'hackneys and charging steeds'.

'When a race is to be run by this sort of horses, and perhaps by others which, in their kind, are also strong and fleet, a shout is immediately raised and the common horses are ordered to withdraw out of the way. Three jockeys, or sometimes only two, as the match is made, prepare themselves for the contest . . . The horses on their part are not without emulation; they tremble and are impatient, and are continually in motion. At last, the signal once given, they start, devour the course, and hurry along with unremitting swiftness. The jockeys, inspired with the thought of applause and the hope of victory, clap spurs to their willing horses, brandish their whips, and cheer them with their cries.'[23]

The race was a trial among horses brought to Smithfield to be sold. It seems that they were racehorses, and were put up for sale as such. Clearly it was a regular event.

The Crusades are always assumed to have educated Western Europe in the merits of the Eastern horse. This seems probable. According to quite credible legend, Richard I bought two horses in Cyprus:

> Two stedes fownde kinge Richarde
> Thatt von Favell, thatt other Lyard;
> Yn this worlde, they hadde no pere;
> Dromedary, neither destrere,
> Stede, rabyte, ne cammele,
> Goeth none so swyfte withoute fayle;
> For a thousand pownde of golde,
> Ne sholde the one be solde.[24]

The metrical romance of Sir Bevis of Hampton, though not written until the early 14th century, deals largely with the Crusades and its period is the late 12th century. It describes a race:

> In somer about wytsontyde,
> Whan knyghtes most on hors ryde,
> A cours they cryed on a day,
> Stedes and palfraye to assay,
> What hors that best myght ren;
> Thre myle the cours was then.
> Who fyrst came to the ende, sholde
> Haue twenty pounde of redy golde.[25]

Two of the knights got a start of 'a large halfe myle and more', unknown to the other competitors. But Bevis spurred his great horse Arundel, overtook them half way, and finished before the rest thought he had gone a mile. He refused to sell Arundel to the king's son, who therefore went to the stables in the middle of the night and tried to steal him. Arundel kicked him in the head and killed him. Edgar the king was very angry, and Sir Bevis had to hurry into exile.

This legend has given rise to marvellous confusion. At one extreme we are asked to imagine Anglo-Saxon racing for a thousand-pound prize, two hundred and fifty years earlier; at the other a royal match won by a man called Arundel two hundred years later. These minefields negotiated, we are left with a credible report of 12th century racing between knights, on good horses, for good prizes which were probably given by the king.

King John imported many Eastern horses for the hunting he loved, and founded the important royal stud at Eltham. Henry III is supposed to have liked racing. Edward III bought coursers; these, like Athelstan's, have often been miscalled 'running horses'.

In 1377, when the Prince of Wales was knighted and just before he succeeded, there is supposed to have been a match sponsored by the old king between the prince and the Earl of Arundel. The story goes that Arundel won, and immediately after his accession Richard II, as the prince had become, bought the winning horse for a large sum. The contemporary account on which this story is based seems, however, to be a French version of Bevis of Hampton:

> Ce fut Arondel le courant;
> N'est meilleur au firmament.[26]

'Arondel' is a legendary 12th-century horse, not the actual 14th-century earl (who was later beheaded).

Richard did, however, have many good foreign horses at Eltham and the other royal studs. The most famous was Roan Barbary. The usurper Bolingbroke upset Richard terribly by riding Roan Barbary to the Abbey for his own coronation.[27] This horse was doubtless roan, but it is difficult to say what they meant by Barbary.

## Medieval France

Racing was an occasional public amusement in Brittany and Burgundy. In 1370, under Charles V, races were held at Semur, Côte d'Or. They became annual, at the fair held on the Thursday after Pentecost. 'Artisans mounted on very bad horses' were the contenders. Entries had to be made at the Mairie. The race started at 2 p.m. The first prize was a gold ring, the second a white taffeta scarf, the third a pair of gloves.[28]

Nobles also rode matches as a change from tourney and chase. One of these took place in 1389. Froissart, who was contemporary, tells the story. King Charles VI, then 21 years old, was in Montpelier with his brother the duc de Touraine. They missed their wives. Yearning to be in Paris, they made a match to race there for 5000 francs. They started together the next day, each with a knight. They rode all day, and slept in carriages, still travelling. It was a rough and rigorous business for princes. The duke took four days and a third, the king four days and a half. The duke made better use of the Seine, getting a skiff from Troyes to Melun and there remounting for Paris. The duke was delighted to win so much money. He was paid the same evening. The king was very sporting. The two young wives, the queen and the duchess (Valentina Visconti) were deeply impressed. They turned their husbands' return into a wild and prancing revel, but they said it must have been hard work.[29] There is no doubt that the story is true, although the starting-point was Bar-sur-Seine, not Montpelier.[30] The account is unique, the event not apparently unusual.

The nobility were mostly concerned with the hunting-field and the lists. For the one they developed a horse, for the other a style of horsemanship.

The horse was the Limousin, the pre-eminent French saddle-horse, and particularly the hunter. Traditionally, it was said to descend from Barbs left behind by the Saracens after their defeat in 732, crossed with other Barbs imported from Morocco to Marseille. Ultimately the breed was destroyed, by stupidity and socio-economic pressures, but throughout the Middle Ages, and into the 17th century, it was the horse ridden by the

French noble for his amusement, and certainly the one he rode in his matches.[31]

All Europe (except Spain) rode in armour with fairly straight legs: but French legs must have been distinctly the straightest. Marco Polo, in the late 13th century, said of a people called the Shans that 'they ride long, like Frenchmen.'[32]

## Italy: the Races for the Palio

Italian racing was the worst, but the best documented.

The earliest recorded races for the *palio* – a valuable embroidered banner, originally a cloak – were run in Siena. A man was fined 40 *soldi* in 1238 for misbehaving while riding. In 1262 the Council announced that riders in the race were not to be held responsible for killing or wounding any citizens.[33] These two earliest references establish the character of the *palio* for all time.

Italy was a country of exceptional violence, even in a violent age. *Palii* were often held by besieging armies under the walls of enemy cities, after the manner of the Greeks outside Troy. The corpses of donkeys would afterwards be hurled by catapult into the city, by way of insult. The Perugians, besieging Arezzo in 1335, held a parody of a *palio* among their female camp-followers, to the scandal of the defenders.

The formal *palio* was contested between the wards, *contrade*, of each city. That of Siena was in August, part of the lavish celebration of the Feast of the Assumption. Originally it was run outside the city. It moved within the walls (for security, or for fun); it there initially took the form of *palio alla lunga*, round the streets. The animals were the city's worst, and were distributed to the riders by lot.

Dante mentions the annual sports of Florence;[34] they were well established by 1300. The most important race was the *palio* of St John the Baptist, on 24 June, 'unique in all the world'. This event was described in about 1400: 'Thereafter, dinner being over, and midday being past, and the folk having rested awhile, according to the pleasure of each of them; all the women and girls betake themselves whither the horses which run the *palio* will pass. Now these pass through a straight street, through the midst of the City, where are many dwellings, beautiful sumptuous houses of good citizens, more than in any other part thereof. And from one end of the City to the other, on that straight street, which is full of flowers, are all the women and all the jewels and rich adornments of the City; and it is a great holiday. Also there are always many lords and knights and foreign gentlemen who come every year from the surrounding towns to see the beauty and magnificence of that festival. And there, through the said *Corso*, are so many folk that it seemeth a thing incredible, the like whereof he who hath not seen it could neither believe or imagine.

'Thereafter, the great bell of the Palazzo de' Signori is tolled three times, and the horses, ready for the start, come forth to run. On high, upon the Tower, may be seen, by the signs made by the boys who are up there, that that is of such an one, and that of such an one. And all the most excellent race-horses of the world are there, gathered together from all the borders of Italy. And that one which is the first to reach the *Palio* is the one which winneth it.'

The *palio* itself was made of brocade, gold, ermine and miniver 'whereon are spent six hundred florins or more.'[35]

The Florentines ran other *palii* celebrating saints or victories: for example, from 1331, the *Palio de' Tintori* in honour of Sant' Onofiro, patron saint of dyers. The dyers' races were notable for the brutality of riders and crowd and the misery of the ancient and worn-out horses.

The Veronese held horse-races for a red *palio* (the usual colour), foot-races for a green one. Both were run outside the city.[36] Verona varied her programme with donkey-races, buffalo-races, and chariot-races. At Pisa, a month before the sports, 50 boys blew trumpets to announce them. Huge crowds assembled, and 20 prisoners were released. Besides *palii*, the prizes included an ox, a ram, a cock, a goose, and a pig. Ferrara's *palio* celebrated St George, Padua's the defeat of a tyrant. Bologna had fanciful prizes for races run in honour of St Peter and St Bartholomew.

As the Renaissance developed, the festivals of which the races formed a part became, in all the cities, extremely lavish. They included processions of allegorical figures, orchestral concerts and dancing, and rituals, some of a religious and some of a neo-classical character.

Besides spending a lot of money on his parties, the Renaissance Italian was, according to Burckhardt, 'the first gambler on a large scale in modern times.'[37] Franceschetto Cybo lost 14,000 ducats in two games to Cardinal Raffaelo Riario, and afterwards complained to the Pope that the cardinal cheated. There was heavy betting on the *palio* races, which were often consequently fixed.

*Above*

BERBER HORSEMANSHIP. These equestrian gymnastics were made possible by handy, docile desert horses as well as by the style of riding *a la gineta* which the Berbers brought to Spain. This agile, bent-legged style may be contrasted with that of the Normans (p. 22), which was the horsemanship of all European chivalry, and known in Spain as riding *a la brida* or *estradiota*.

## The Barb Horse in Spain

The Berbers arrived with their Barbs in 710, with a few Arabians possibly on Arabs. They found Spaniards on Andalusian horses riding *a la brida* – the normal European fashion of proto-chivalry, with long stirrup-leathers and saddles high back and front. The Moors rode quite differently. Their saddles were lighter and further forward, and their knees were well bent. A Berber tribe of famous horsemen called the Zenete gave their name to this style of horsemanship, which became Zenáta and then, in Spanish, riding *a la jineta*.[38] In 15th-century English and French the word was further transferred to mean a light Spanish horse, the celebrated jennet. The Spaniards learned to ride *a la jineta*, and their horsemanship was unlike English or Italian, and completely different from French. But an accomplished Spanish horseman rode both *a la jineta* (later *gineta*) and *a la brida*.[39]

The agility of the horses, and the desert style of riding, made possible horse-games quite unlike the ponderous clashing of the tilt-yard. In *juego de cañas* the competitors were armed with light canes which they threw at each other. The object was to catch the cane before it hit you. This was an ancient Arab game, adopted by the Berbers and brought by them into Spain: adopted in time by the Spaniards and taken by them to the New World: and adopted there by the Indian *vaqueros*.

It is clear that from an early date the Spaniards (perhaps the Moors too) bred distinct types for different purposes, and that one of these was racing. A French traveller described racing in Spain about 1400.[40] One hundred and fifty years later racehorses, so defined, joined the horses for battle, parade, and draught in America.[41]

## The East in the Middle Ages

By the 13th century the Arabs had thousands of horses to spare. Marco Polo reports: 'There are despatched from the port of Aden to India a very large number of Arab chargers, and palfreys, and stout nags adapted for all work, which are a source of great profit for those who export them'[42] These horses were of various types, for various purposes; some of them were described by Ibn Batuta in the next century as 'thoroughbred'.[43]

It was and remains amazing that the country could sustain the stock. 'All their cattle, including horses, oxen, and camels, live upon small fish and nought besides, for 'tis all they get to eat. You see in all this country there is no grass or forage of any kind; it is the driest country on the face of the earth.' The fish were caught in the early summer, dried, and eaten the year round. The animals also cheerfully ate them alive, when fresh caught.[44] Ibn Batuta identifies the fish as sardines.[45]

*Below*

PERSIAN POLO, 14TH CENTURY.
After racing and hunting, polo is the
oldest of all sports involving the horse.
It was probably invented in Persia, and
possibly in the time of Darius. From
the beginning the game made great and
special demands on the pony and its
training. 'Their horses,' said an
English traveller in 1613, 'are so well
trained to this that they run after the
ball like cats'. They must have been
predominantly Arab.

Palestine and Syria were now full of horses, the best of which were Arab. The Franks
of Syria lived side by side with the Moslems, intermittently fighting. On one occasion
in the late 12th century Tancred admired an Arab horse he saw in battle. During a truce
a race was arranged between this Arab, ridden by a thin young Kurd called Hasanun,
and the Frankish horses. The Arab 'outran all the horses which were in the race,' and
Tancred gave Hasanun a robe of honour.[46]

Persia was laid waste by the Tartars in the 13th century, but the Persians still had 'a
great supply of fine horses; and people take them to India for sale, for they are horses of
great price.'[47] The Persians were probably racing at this period, and certainly playing
polo: the game may have been as old as Darius, although it was not described in English
('pall-mall on horseback') until 1613.[48]

The Crimea and Ukraine were conquered by the Comans or Qipchaqs; they had
many horses, but used them to draw their big four-wheeled wagons. In the far Eastern
Ukraine and Turkestan horses were reared like sheep; they were exported to India in
herds of 6000.[49]

Mongol-ruled North China was thronged with horses. In the South, however, there
were no horses in the 13th century. The king and all his people were only interested in
women; they were thus easily conquered by a general of Kublai Khan's.[50] The nomadic
Mongols in the great spaces to the north-east of Kublai's new capital at Peking had
enormous herds. These were of pure Mongolian blood, and remained so. They almost
certainly raced them. Those herdsmen changed little over the centuries, and a description
of their racing in 1904 can probably stand as a fair picture of their sport in the middle
ages. If so, they raced bareback over extreme distances.

From 1188 North India was ruled from Delhi by a Persian-speaking Moslem king.
The kingdom of Hind was never able to conquer the mountainous North or the Hindu
South, and its hegemony over the lower Ganges was at best partial. But it was immensely
rich.

Horses were still carefully and successfully bred in Sind – an area covering the whole
valley of the Indus and south to Cambay – as they had been for more than 2000 years.
According to an Indian source, pure-bred horses were given royal treatment.[51] The
horsemen performed military exercises like those of 17th-century France.[52]

The rest of India had an insatiable appetite for imported horses. They came from
Arabia, Persia and Turkestan in the West, from the Shans and Anin in the East. 'This
king [of Madras] wants to buy more than 2000 horses every year, and so do his four
brothers who are kings likewise. The reason why they want so many horses every year
is that by the end of the year there shall not be one hundred of them remaining, for they
all die off. They feed their horses with boiled rice and boiled meat, and various other
kinds of cooked food.'[53]

It is impossible to say to what uses all the very different kinds of imported horses were
put. Certainly the Turcoman – big and hardy – was for war and ceremony; comparable,
in use and type, to the Great Horse of contemporary Europe. But the best Arabs, which
cost twenty times as much, were bought specifically as racehorses. In about 1310 the amir
of the Arabs in Syria, who had settled in India and married the king's sister, sent Shaikh
Sa'id to Arabia to buy thoroughbreds; he took 50,000 dirhams. The scale of the traffic, and
the prices paid, indicate plenty of racing at Delhi, and probably Calcutta, Madras, and
Bombay, as well as in Sind where it was traditional.[54]

# 3 The Sixteenth Century

## Henry VIII's Horses and Racing

In 1486 Dame Juliana Berners listed 'the propretees of a goode hors':

'A Goode hors sulde haue XV propretees and condicions. yt is to wit III of a man. III of a Woman. III of a fox. III of an haare and III of an asse.

Off a man boolde prowde and hardy.

Off a Woman fayre brestid faire of here & esy to lip uppon.

Off a fox a faire tayle short eirs with a goode trot.

Off an hare a grete eygh a dry hede and well reunyng.

Off an asse a bigge chyne a flatte lege and goode bone.'[1]

But after the Wars of the Roses England was short of horses, with these or any other qualities. The drab but provident Henry VII forbade the export of horses in 1496[2] and Henry VIII began a considerable programme of importing. In 1514 he was sent brood-mares, Barb stallions and jennets by Francesco Gonzaga, Marchese di Mantova. He was lyrical in his praise and thanks. In 1515 Ferdinand of Aragon sent him two Spanish horses, valued at 100,000 ducats. Contemporaries thought Ferdinand must have gone mad to part with them. His insanity was ascribed to an aphrodisiac dinner given him by his new young wife Germaine de Fois two years earlier, from the effects of which he never recovered. (He ultimately died of 'hunting and matrimony'.)

In 1517 more horses arrived from Italy. The next year the king sent two agents there to buy horses, and the year after another agent to Italy and Spain. Later in the reign more horses arrived from Mantua and from the Emperor Charles V.[3]

The result was a roster at Eltham of 'coursers, young horses, hunting geldings, hobbies, Barbary horses, stallions, geldings, mail, bottle, pack, Besage, and two stalking-horses.'[4] These were not kept separate at stud, but cross-bred: 'King Henrie the eight created a noble studderie and for a time had verie good success with them, till the officers waring wearie, produced a mixed brood of bastard races, whereby his good purpose came to little effect.'[5]

Henry used some of his own horses for racing. A separate establishment was kept for this, under the Master of the Horse, at Greenwich. There were two, three, or four stable riders; they were paid (like pages, gardeners, gamekeepers, and jester) directly from the Privy Purse.

Towards the end of every month, in the Privy Purse Accounts, there is an entry like this of January 1530: 'Item the XXVI daye paide to Thomas Ogull, for the bourde of III boyes that rynne the kings gueldings by the space of a monethe at IIs. the woke: — XXIV s.' Various tradesmen are regularly paid for the boys' colours: Mr Pyne for 'a paire of quarterd hosen for the boyes of the stabull'; John Scot for 'III doublettes of bruges satin and for III doublettes of fustian wt. the makyng and the lynyng for the III boyes that Rynnes the gueldings'; 'xpofer the Milloner for III Ryding Cappes of blac vellute and XXII botons of golde to garnisshe them'; 'the showmaker for showes and boots for the saied boyes'; 'stephen the hardewareman for III night cappes for the boyes of the stables and one for Sexton'. Sexton was the king's 'fole'.

The horses raced are called simply the 'gueldings', although on 16 April 1530 a white nag was run, and in June 1532 'a couple of hobyes' direct from 'my lord of Kyldare'. One Barb at least ran. This horse is first mentioned in May 1531. It was in the care of a Signor Pollo, who must have come with it, and who is variously called 'powle', 'polle', and 'poule the ytalian'. The horse is described as the 'barbary', 'barbaristo', 'barra', and 'barbare'. On 17 March 1532 'polle that keepeth the barbary horse' and the 'boye that Ranne the horse' were each paid 18s 4d., and Thomas Ogle, Master of Horse, 20s.

A 'dyatter' is once mentioned – a trainer. Veterinary expenses include £8 18s. to 'hanyball zinzaro for drynks and other medicynes for the kings horses.'[6] There is also a bill for oil which was needed for the legs of a horse which ran 'agaynst Mr Karey's gelding for a wager.'[7] This – from a different source – is the only undoubted reference

HENRY VIII PROCEEDING TO A TOURNAMENT. Tudor interest in horse-sport put hunting first, tourney second, and racing third. Henry was also interested in scientific equitation, and imported a pupil of Grisone. The horses for these activities were quite distinct: hunting-gelding, courser, and running-horse or gelding. The animal here hidden by the caparison is undoubtedly a courser, 'able to indure travell, and to bear the weight of Armour'.

to betting on horses, although the king paid streams of gambling-debts on cards, tennis, dominoes, dice, 'shovilleborde', 'bowles', 'prymero', 'pope Julius game', and 'Imperiall'.

Henry's racing sounds like informal matches among gentlemen of the court. We here see one of the twin fountainheads of organized British racing: the king's patronage of a sport conducted among his friends.

The other, completely different, equally important, was happening at the same time.

## Chester: the Invention of Municipal Racing

On a strip of land by the River Dee outside Chester, known variously as the Roodee and the Roodeye, there had been games and mock fights from time immemorial. In 1511 they decided to try racing instead, although it may have been some years before they actually started. A local antiquarian, later in the century, wrote: 'Alsoe, whereas the Companye and occupation of the Saddlers within the Cittie of Chester did yearely by Custome, time out of memorie of man, the same day, hour, and place, before the Mayor, offer upon a truncheon, staffe, or speare, a certain homage to the drapers of the Cittie of Chester, called Saddlers' Ball, profitable for few uses or purposes, as it were, being a ball of silke of the bigness of a bowle, was torned into a silver bell, weighing about two ounces, as is supposed, of silver; the which said silver bell was ordayned to be the rewarde for that horse, which with speedy runninge, then should rune before all others. This alteration was made the same time, and by the same Mayor, like as the Shoemakers' foote-ball was before exchanged into six silver gleaves.'[8] The bell was worn by the winning horse; its value was 'three shillings and four pence'. The Mayor was Henry Gee; his order in the matter survives.[9]

Some racecourses came into being by virtue of the King's patronage (Newmarket), among local farmers and gentry (Kiplingcotes), or for the benefit of local breeders (Hambleton), but the great majority were started, like Chester, by towns and cities, on land owned by their Corporations.

Elizabeth patronized some of them. She went racing at Croydon in 1574; and in 1585 a special grandstand was built to accommodate her party, at a cost of 34 shillings.[10] She also went to Salisbury, where a bell was furnished as a prize by the city in 1585, and a golden snaffle by the queen's favourite Essex.[11]

Growth took place everywhere, without benefit of queen or court. In the North, Kiplingcotes started about the middle of the century. In the Forest of Galtres (a name spelled a dozen ways) the races were described in 1590 as anciently established. Bells were the prizes; the crowds and betting were enormous.[12] There are two bells from Carlisle dated 1559. One is inscribed: 'The sweftes * Horse * this * Bel To * take * for * mi * Lade * Daker * sake.'[13] Richmond (Yorkshire) had racing by 1576, Boroughbridge by 1595. A map of Doncaster in 1595 shows two courses; and in 1600 a 'stoope' was set up at the west end of the racecourse, presumably for starter or judge.[14]

In East Anglia, '6 April 1602. This day there was a race at Sapley neere huntingdon: invented by the gents of that Country: At this Mr Oliuer Cromwell's horse won the syluer bell: And Mr Cromwell had the glory of the day. Mr Hynd came behinde.'[15] Mr Cromwell was uncle of Cromwell the Protector.

## The Elizabethan Racehorse

Elizabeth maintained her father's establishment at Greenwich and the ill-managed stud at Eltham. In 1575 Robert Dudley, Earl of Leicester, took it in hand and sent to Naples for Prospero d'Osma, a well-known expert. In 1576 d'Osma reported: listing the 'Savoy' and 'Brilladoro' mares, and recommending that they should be bred only to their own kind.[16]

Elizabeth also founded a new royal stud at Tutbury, in Staffordshire, which in the next reign became of first class importance. It is reasonable to assume, first, that the best of Elizabeth's horses were the descendants of those sent to her father from Italy; second, that they went to Tutbury; third, that d'Osma's advice was taken. If so, Elizabeth, Leicester and d'Osma between them may have made a significant contribution to the thoroughbred.

There was still constant importation. In 1586: 'Such outlandish horses as are daily brought ouer unto us . . . as the genet of Spain, the courser of Naples, the hobbie of Ireland, the Flemish roile, and Scottish nag.'[17]

The nag (apparently the same as the Galloway) was an ordinary racehorse; it was beginning to be joined by others: 'Some man perchance would haue a brede of great trottinge horses mete for the war, and to serue in the field . . . Some again would haue perhaps a race of swift runners to runne for wagers.' Of the best of the latter: 'Those horses that we commonly call Barbarians, do come out of the King of Tunnis land, out of Massilie Numidia, which for the most part be but little Horses, but therewith verie swift, and able to make a verie long cariere, which is the cause why we esteeme them so much.'[18]

Thomas Blundeville, who wrote this, admired the Barb as a racehorse rather than as a getter of racehorses. This is a view which subsequent history repudiates. Gervase Markham – eclectic, plagiaristic, repetitive, and contradictory – says: 'Againe for swift-nesse, what nation hath brought forth that horse, which hath exceeded the English? For thereof we have this example: when the best Barbaries that euer were in my remem-brance were in their prime, I sawe them ouerrunne by a black Hobbie at Salisburie of Maister Carltons, and yet that Hobby was more ouer runne by a horse of Maister Black-stone called "Valentine", which "Valentine" neither in hunting or running was euer equalled, yet was a plaine bredde English horse both by syre and damme; to descend to our instant time, whatever men may report or imagine, yet I see no shape which can perswade me that "Puppie" is any other than an English horse: and truly for running I holde him peerlesse.'[19] This said, Markham urges breeders to use Arabians as sires, as their get has 'wonderful speede in both short and long courses.'[20]

There are racing implications, more or less fanciful, in Markham's ways of categorizing horses: for example; by temperature and humidity. 'A horse in his foal-age, which is, till he be six years old, is naturally hot and moist; in his middle age, which is till twelve, more hot and dry than moist; and in his old age, which is past eighteen, more cold and dry, than either hot or moist. So likewise, the Horses which are bred in Southern parts, as either in *Spain*, *Barbary*, or *Greece*, are naturally more hot than those which are bred either in the seventeen lands, *Germany*, or *England*.'[21]

Markham, Blundeville, and Harrison make it clear that 16th-century English horses were a mixed lot, with many useless individuals of dubious parentage. They were often

THE NEAPOLITAN COURSER. Gower described 'A courser, that he sholde ride Into the felde' in 1393, and Caxton's *Chivalry* remarked that 'Knights ought to take Coursers to Iuste and to go to torneys' in 1484. This was the horse on which Grisone in Naples taught his pupils scientific horsemanship. It is not clear how it got its misleading name, nor how, in an area to which the African galloping horse had been imported for a thousand years, it came to be bred.

bred quite haphazardly, with stallions running with all kinds of mares. The result was unpredictable. Horses so bred would never themselves breed true. This genetic muddle provided the 17th and 18th centuries with an urgent motive for importing Arabs, whose get, as more and more travellers were able to report, was consistent.

There were, at the same time, some Elizabethans who went in for careful breeding on fashionable lines, and specifically for the racecourse: enough for Joseph Hall to mock the breeder who thought his useless horse would win races simply because of a celebrated parent:

> Say'st thou this colt shall prove a swift paced steed,
> Only because a Jennet did him breed?
> Or say'st thou this same horse shall win the prize
> Because his dam was swiftest Trunchefice,
> Or Runcevall his sire, himself a Gallaway,
> While like a tireling jade he lags half way?[22]

As well as specialized breeding, there was specialized training for the racecourse. Gervase Markham advises eight to ten weeks strong work for a gross horse, six for a lean one, as the right preparation for a race. Two gallops a week are enough. On saddling up and riding he says: 'Now I shall give you another instruction worth observing, that is, the day you are designed to run the Race when you come within a mile or less of the starting gate or post for that purpose assigned; take off his cloaths, which being done clap your Saddle upon his Back sending some person, with his cloaths to the end of the Race intended, and ride him on gently till you come to the weighing or starting post; show him the post, and make him as far as he is capable, sensible of what he is designed for to be done withal.

'The Signal for the start being given put him on or near three quarters speed, or if his Strength will allow it more, but be sure you put him not to more than he is able to perform, hold the Rains pretty streight in your hand but by no means check him in his Course, but let him run on chearfully, and give him all the encouragement you can, and so let him run the whole Race through.

'If you, during the Course find his strength to fail him, or that he begin to yield, give him what ease you can and do not force him to two [sic] great a swiftness, but use him so that he may be at all times well-pleased with his courses and free to run on.'

This is Markham at his most practical, the jockey and gambler. So is his advice about finding out what going your horse likes, 'whether it be smooth, rough, dry, wet, or a little rising that he most eagerly covets, and for the future chuse it if possible in all your Races.'[23]

On feeding: 'whilst it is sweet, clean and good, as Bread well made and baked, dry Oats, dry Beans, sweet Hay, sweet Straw, or short Grass, so long it nourisheth and preserveth the Horses body: But if it be fusty, raw, corrupt and unclean, or if he eat Tares, Pitches, Rye or Barley, then must he needs be unsound, and full of infirmities.' Racehorses need special additions to this diet: stoned raisins and dates, boiled up, and 'licoras, Anniseeds, and sugar-candy finely fears'd'. You mix these up and make 'round balls thereof of a pretty bigness, roll and cover them all over with sweet Butter, and give so many of them unto the horse as you shall think meet for his strength.'[24]

## Racing in Scotland

On 15 April 1504 James IV paid 18s to 'the boy that ran the king's horse;' and a few days later 21s. 'to Dande Doule whilk he wan frae the King on horse-racing.'[25] At Berwick in July 1549 there was a match between the Earl of Rutland and Sir Francis Leyke. By the end of the century there was regular racing there. Lanark is alleged to have had racing, and a silver trophy, from about 1000, but examination of the hall-mark of the cup sadly dispels the legend.

A firm record (though in almost unintelligible language) shows the Provost and Baillies of Haddington providing a silver bell for their race by 1552. As in many other places, what is recorded is a demand by the Burgh that the previous year's winner return the prize.[26]

Leith had racing on the sands at about this time: people 'wald ryid to Leith, and ryn thair horsis, And wychtlie wallope ouer the sandis.'[27] The same thing happened at Dumfries, well before racing at Carlisle on the English side of the Solway Firth; the Regent Morton presided in 1575 over a race won by Lord Hamilton with a small horse.[28] Stirling had annual racing at Easter. By 1598 there was a silver bell which weighed two and half ounces.[29]

Scottish racing was growing up in another way. David Home or Hume, who died about 1575, was, according to his son, 'a man remarkable for piety, probity, candour, and integrity . . . strictly just, utterly detesting all manner of fraud.' Nevertheless, 'so great a master in the art of riding was he that he would often be beat to-day and within eight days lay a double wager on the same horse and come home conqueror.'[30]

## The Irish Horse

The Irish scholar Thomas Carve said: 'Most excellent horses of a very pure breed are produced termed Hobini by the English, which have a most gentle pace, and on that account are most sought by effeminate persons, and in France and Italy are given as presents to noble ladies.'[31] Blundeville confirms: 'The Irish Hobbie is a prettie fine horse, having a good head, and a bodie indifferentlye well proportioned, saving that many of them be slender pin buttocked, they be tender mouthed, nimble, light, pleasant and apt to be taught.'[32] Harrison, ambiguously, says they are: 'in running wonderful swift, in gallop both false and indifferent.'[33]

The reason for the hobby's excellence was the importation of breeding stock from the earliest centuries AD. Irish tradition was clear that the source was Spain: 'The Island produces a kind of horses which the natives call *Haubini*, whose pace is of the gentlest. They were called *Asturcones* in old times, because they came from Asturia in Spain.'[34] This tradition is confirmed in some eyes by conformation: the Connemara has been described as 'a slightly altered Barb on pony's legs.'[35]

Their reputation being as ladies' hacks, it is surprising to find hobbies on a racecourse. But the 'black Hobbie at Salisburie of Maister Carltons' defeated the best Barbaries Gervase Markham ever saw.

Henry VIII and Elizabeth had hobbies. Their blood may have survived, with that of the Barbs and jennets, into the Tutbury stock and thence into the Stud Book.

If Markham was concerned about feeding horses, the Irish had ideas about feeding horsemen. In 1566: 'If they never lend out fire to their neighbours, they imagine it adds length to life, and much health to their horses. When the owner of a horse eats eggs, he must be very careful to eat an even number, otherwise they endanger their horses. Jockeys are not at all to eat eggs, and whatever horseman does it, he must wash his hands immediately after.'[36]

## Italian Racing, Breeding, and Equitation

The best early medieval Italian horses came from the South. But in the 15th century northern Italy began to import and breed horses of outstanding quality. As Italian horses changed, so did Italian racing, and for the first time good horses were raced by rich owners.

CESARE BORGIA. While still in his teens this unusual prelate became the first identified individual racehorse-owner in Italy, winning the Sienese *palio* in 1492. He was also the first great sporting cleric. In the former regard his precedent was widely followed in 16th-century Italy. In the latter, parsons following his lead became a power on the turf in Georgian Britain, colonial Virginia, and 19th-century Tennessee.

Siena had its own stud at Maremma, and the horses bred there were probably the best that raced in the city until the late 15th century. But at that time the jolly mayhem of the townspeople was subdued into serious racing. Lorenzo de' Medici entered his horses for the *palio*, as well as many prosperous private citizens of Florence, Lucca, Arezzo and Cortona. In 1492, when Cesare Borgia was Archbishop elect, he won the Sienese *palio* by dubious tactics: his jockey jumped off the horse, which finished riderless. The Commune refused to give Cesare the prize, which he angrily demanded by letter.[37] 89 years later, on 15 August, a peasant-girl called Virginia was one of the riders for a superb *palio*. She was the darling of Siena. She came third.[38] Normally the horses were ridden by boys who wore the liveries of their employers (racing colours of great splendour and complexity). Each also wore a card, like a modern number-cloth, but inscribed either with a nickname – *Spron di Vallo, Gativello, Scaramuccia* – or a motto – *Spero in Dio ed in Nostra Donna, Ho Paura d'Esser l'Ultimo.* Some owners had strings of *barberi*, which they toured from city to city. The artist Giovanni Antonio Bazzi owned seven *barberi* which ran in the Sienese races about 1530.

Besides *barberi* of dubious provenance, Italy imported English horses from the royal stud at Eltham; Spanish – in 1514 Mantua had jennets; and Irish – when the Italians sent Barbaries to England, hobbies were the gift they most wanted in return.[39]

Italy made in the 16th century a giant contribution to the science of horsemanship. Early in the century Frederico Grisone started his riding-school in Naples. The horse was the courser, larger than ever, and still a trotter. The methods were crude and severe: but this was the beginning of scientific equitation, and it was immediately influential. Henry VIII got a riding-master who was a pupil of Grisone; and Grisone's book setting out his methods was studied and plagiarized all over Europe.[40]

The popularity of the *cavalerizza* had a curious result. It meant that the Great Horse continued in unrivalled esteem long after its military relevance had gone. In countries where scientific equitation was strongest there was little interest in the galloping horse and little, therefore, in the turf.

This was above all true of France.

## France

Sixteenth-century France inherited no tradition comparable to the *palio* and developed no racing comparable to the British. At the beginning of the century chase and tourney still dominated the noble attitude to horse-sport. Later the *manège*, adopted from Italy and infinitely improved, became the supreme achievement of French horsemen; naturally it involved the big trotting-horse.

The Royal Stud at Fontainebleau concentrated on this high-stepping animal the French admired: but not exclusively. When in 1550 Edward VI of England sent the king of France some Spanish horses he had been given by the Emperor, he received in return 'VI cortales, III Spanish horses, one torke, a barbery, one cowerser, and II lyttel mewles.'[41]

In the 16th century as in the 14th the most fully-described race was run in the country with the least racing. In 1517 the Duke of Suffolk – Richard de la Pole, known as Blanche Rose – was in Metz. He acquired a horse, 'very swift and of extreme value'. He issued a general challenge, which was accepted by a sportsman called Nicolle Dex. The race was 'from the Elm at Avergney to within St Clement's Gate, for eighty crowns.' It was run on St Clement's day, 2 May. For three days before the race Dex gave his horse no hay, and restricted his own diet to white wine. (A misreading of the French account gives the *horse* nothing but white wine for three days.)[42] Suffolk was normally equipped with a heavy French saddle and clothes; Dex 'came into the field like a groom, in his doublet and without shoes, and with no saddle but with a cloth tied round the horse's belly.'

PROCESSION BEFORE THE PALIO, SIENA. All the *Contrade* paraded, magnificently liveried, pulling with them giant effigies of their heraldic badges – respectively eagle, snail, dolphin, panther, rhinoceros, tortoise, owl, unicorn, scallop-shell, elephant, ram, caterpillar, dragon, giraffe, porcupine, wolf and goose. These floats, stoutly made of wood, acted as refuges during the bull-fight that followed. The procession in this form lasted from 1499 to 1597; the one illustrated was on 15 August 1546.

PALIO RACING IN FLORENCE. This is almost exactly contemporary with Goro Dati's description of Florentine racing in 1400, quoted on p. 25. The scene is the finish of the principal race, that in honour of St John the Baptist on 24 June. The best horses in Italy ran for the *palio* which was made of brocade, gold, ermine and miniver and cost 600 florins. The riders carry clubs, which in the rougher *palio* races were used on opponents.

His horse was specially shod with light steel shoes, which is the first recorded use of racing-plates.

The Duke jumped off in front and stayed there for half the race. 'But when they were near St Laidre his horse lagged behind, so that the Duke urged him on with spurs until the blood streamed down on both sides; but it was in vain, Nicolle gained the race and the hundred and sixty crowns of the sum.'[43]

The Duke learned his lesson about putting up a 'feather' in a catch-weight match: but he fell into the opposite trap. Two years later to the day the challenge was renewed. This time the Duke put up a page. But the boy fell, and Dex won untroubled.

## The Spanish Horse in America

Columbus took no horses in 1492. On his second American landfall three years later he had 20 stallions and a number of broodmares. He won an immediate and overwhelming victory with his tiny force, because, as another *conquistador* later said: 'Horses are the most necessary things in the new country because they frighten the enemy most, and, after God, to them belongs the victory.'[44] While they were still rare they were obviously of tremendous value. Robert Burton read and repeated that 'a Spaniard in Incatan sold three Indian boyes for a cheese, and an hundred negro slaves for an horse.'[45]

From 1500, therefore, horses went in every ship. Mares for breeding always came with the cavalry-horses – mostly Andalusian – so that as early as 1500 there was a royal stud on Hispaniola with 60 broodmares. They 'multiplied in the Indies and became most excellent, in some places being even as good as the best in Spain.'[45] Hispaniola at once supplied Cuba and Jamaica, later Puerto Rico and Trinidad. By mid-century 'There are so many horses now it is no longer necessary to bring any more over.'[46]

Hernán Cortés, a successful horse-breeder in Cuba, took his men and horses to Mexico in 1519. His friend Bernal Díaz listed the horses. There was 'a swift grey mare'; 'a dark brown stallion which was fast'; a 'grey mare, a pacer which seldom galloped'; 'a dark brown horse, good, and a grand runner'. Above all 'Pedro de Alvarado and Hernándo López de Ávila had a very good sorrel mare, turning out excellent both for tilting and for racing.'[47]

*Conquistadores* poured onto the mainland, North and South, and they wanted all the horses the islands could produce. De Soto took about 300 from Cuba to Florida in 1539. He perished; some of his horses survived. Menéndez followed in 1565. He took 100 horses and mares, some of which he imported specially from Cádiz. The descendants of these horses were bought and raced by the English colonists of Virginia.

The Spanish horse was also going South. When Pizarro pushed down to Peru, he took horses from Panama and Nicaragua. By mid-century, far south in Chile, there were 300 or 400 mares for breeding  and this although in 1536 Anzurez' men drank the blood of their horses to survive, and finished by eating 220 of them.

On the other side of South America, Mendoza took 72 horses to La Plata in 1535. He had to decamp, leaving five mares and seven stallions. When Juan Garay refounded Buenos Aires in 1582, he found the area swarming with horses. Their number and excellence were the strongest inducement to settlers in the colony.

Horses came to South Brazil from Paraguay, to which they had come from Peru; they came to the North direct from Portugal. The *Crioulo* is consequently a mixture of Andalusian and Lusitanian; although history does not reveal much difference between the two.

The almost miraculous wild herds of the La Plata basin were paralleled in the North. Ibarra took horses up from Mexico in 1562. He was defeated. The next expedition, less than 20 years later, found Indians with immense herds.

This proliferation of the horse is no more amazing than its adoption by the Indians.

THE PALIO AT FERRARA. Most of the cities of Umbria, Tuscany and Emilia had races through their streets from the early 13th century. Those of Ferrara were in honour of St George, and run on his day, 23 April. Like Verona, Ferrara had races for donkeys as well as horses; the artist has here overlapped the two.

37

The first 'centaurs' which climbed down from the Spanish ships sent them scampering. Narváez, singled-handed, routed an army, riding a bell-decked horse. The centaur was more horrible because it could split into two animals – man and monster – without either suffering. But the Indians got over their terror quickly. They began to steal horses. They deified them. They not only rode them, they ate them and wore them. As the feral herds spread, in pampas and prairie, they transformed the culture and economy of both continents.

Undoubtedly most of these horses were top-class Andalusians; to take a cheap brood-mare on so expensive a journey would be foolish. But the Spaniards brought different kinds of horses for different purposes; these included parade-horses which (it has been argued) might have been piebald like modern drum-horses.[48] There was probably also Asturian blood in the North to produce the 'paint' of the West, and Friesland blood from Holland to produce the *tobiano* of Brazil. Certainly the English colonists in Virginia found horses of two quite different kinds, one good-sized and docile, one small and un-manageable.

The Spanish raced in Mexico, which insists that they did in Cuba, and therefore in Hispaniola and the other islands. They raced in Peru, which suggests that they did in Chile, Paraguay, Argentina and Southern Brazil, to which Peruvian horses went, and Central America, from which they came. It is thus probable that the Spanish raced their horses right from the beginning throughout both continents: and if the Spanish, then the Indians too.

CONQUISTADORES IN AMERICA. The literature of the Spanish conquest is full of horses because 'to them, after God, belongs the victory.' North America was probably the cradle of the two surviving species of horse, which crossed into Russia when the Behring Strait was still land, but the many other indigenous American species were destroyed by the blowfly, the carnivores, or the ice. The *conquistadores* brought their Andalusians to horseless continents. These men have heavy saddles and curbs, but they ride *a la gineta*.

# 4 Britain:

## Early Stuarts and Commonwealth

### James I and Charles I at Newmarket

Robert Burton, seeking remedies for Melancholy, approved of moderate exercise – 'as ringing, bowling, shooting, keelpins, tronks, coits, pitching bars, hurling, wrestling, leaping, running, fencing, mustring, swimming, wasters, foiles, foot-ball, balown, quintains, &c. and many such, which are the common recreations of the country folks; riding of great horses, running at rings, tilts and tournaments, horse-races, wilde-goose chases, which are the disports of greater men, and good in themselves, though many gentlemen, by that means, gallop quite out of their fortunes.'

Racing is a normal noble amusement, but as much overshadowed by hunting as it was in Henry VIII's time: hunting is 'the sole almost and ordinary sport of all our noblemen . . . 'tis all their study, their exercise, ordinary business, all their talk: and indeed some dote too much on it; they can do nothing else, discourse of naught else.'[1]

Burton might have been talking about James I. When still only James VI of Scotland the king had been racing there. But his greatest contribution – the establishment of Newmarket as 'headquarters' – happened by accident. He went there to hunt, with his hounds and his falcons, on the great grass plain of the Heath and the game-rich scrub of Warren Hill. He stayed weeks at a time, usually in midwinter, transacting business when hunting permitted. At first he used an inn called the Griffin; later he built a palace on its site. Besides the interminable slaughter of hare, duck and partridge there were hunting matches at which the king was a bad loser.[2]

The extensive royal stables – the king's and Prince Henry's – were primarily for hunting and tilting, but James was a racehorse owner. At his accession there were four 'Riders of the Stable', and, 20 years later, two 'riders for the races'. The Surveyors of the Races were royal officials.

On 19 March 1619 (two and a half weeks after the queen died of a dropsy) there was 'A Horse Race at *Newmarket*; at which the King tarrying too long in his Return from *Newmarket*, was forced to put in at an Inn at *Wichfordbridge* by reason of his being indisposed.'[3]

From 1625, when Charles I presided over the further destruction of traditional government, things went on much the same. He loved hunting and patronized Newmarket, kept up the palace and stables, and maintained the royal racing establishment. In 1634 Newmarket had a race of the kind becoming normal elsewhere: a 'Golden Cup' was run for.

### Growth of Racing: Old and New Meetings

A dozen places had regular racing by the beginning of the 17th century and others had it intermittently. Many of these meetings contributed something of their own to history.

In 1609 Chester, which had changed the Saddlers' Ball into a Silver Bell, gave instead three silver cups – first, second and third prizes. As always they were run for on the Roodee on St George's day. Sheriff Robert Amerye made another innovation which has not won general acceptance: 'he had a poet, one Mr Davies, whoe made speeches and poeticale verses, which were delivered at the high-crosse, before the Mayor and Aldermen, with shewes of his invention.' The inaugural race run under this new dispensation resulted in a dead heat, 'to the great pleasure and delight of the spectators.'[4] In 1623 the Mayor sold the three cups, 'caused more money to be gathered and added, soe that the interest thereof would make one faire Silver Cupp of the value of £8, as I suppose, it may be more worth, and the race to be altered' – lengthened from three laps to five. The object of both these changes must have been to attract better horses and richer owners. In 1629 the Companies of the City put up the money for the prize, which was kept by the winner. In 1640 the Sheriffs gave a piece of plate worth £13 6s. 8d., run for on the Roodee on Easter Tuesday, 'in lieu of the Sheriffs' breakfast of calves'-heads and bacon, which it was previously customary for the two Sheriffs of the city to shoot for on Easter Monday.'[5]

Doncaster had a grandstand by the turn of the century. By 1614 it had a groundsman – Anthony Hogg, paid one shilling and sixpence for 'making the waye at the horse race.'[6]

At Lincoln 'on Thursday, 3rd April 1617, there was a great Horse race on the Heath for a Cupp, where his Majesty was present, and stood on a Scaffold the Citie had caused to be set up, and withall caused the race a quarter of a mile long to be raled and corded with ropes and hoopes on both sides, whereby the people were kept out, and the horses that runned were seen faire.'[7]

In 1619, Kiplingcotes invented comprehensive rules of racing. These covered subscriptions, weights, fouls, weighing in and out, and disqualifications.[8]

Stamford, Lincolnshire, had in about 1620 two 'ancient and public sports . . . The one a sport savouring of manhood and gentry, and of a concourse of noblemen and gentlemen meeting together in mirth, peace, and amity, for the exercise of their swift running horses, every Tuesday in March. The prize they run for is a silver and gilt cup, with a cover, to the value of seven or eight pounds, provided by the care of the aldermen for the time being, but the money is raised out of the interest of a stock formerly made up by the nobility and gentry who are neighbours and well wishers to the town.'[9] (The other diversion was bull-running.) Stamford made another innovation, in the area of rules, less enduring than Kiplingcotes: 'if anye of the matched horses or theire riders chaunce to fall in anye of the foure heats, the rest of the riders shall staye in theire places where they were at the tyme of the fall untill the rider so fallen have his foote in the stirrope again.'[10]

Richmond, Yorkshire, had a new course in 1622: 'A new maid race upon Rychmond Moore of IV myles, set forth and measured.'[11]

Before the Great Rebellion, therefore, a string of important contributions had been made by wide-spread and autonomous English racecourses: cups; bigger prizes to attract better entries, and non-returnable prizes and stiffer tests to the same end; the provision of prizes by subscription or endowment; measured four-mile courses; weighing out and in; systematic and comprehensive rules; roped-off home-straights; course maintenance; heat-racing.

There were also many new courses, some important. Brackley, Northamptonshire, was established by 1612: on 13 July Henry and Thomas Throgmorton arranged 'to meete together the Tuesday after Michelmas next, at Brackley Cwoorse, and thether to bring a graye mare and a gray shorne mane nagg, and each of them to ridde the same coursse upon equal wate in their one persones, for X quarter of oats.' At Harleston in the same county a silver-gilt cup and cover was provided by the Corporation, but paid for by 'William Lord Spencer and other gentlemen of the county'. Racing was annual by 1632.[12]

Hambleton ('Black Hambleton') in Yorkshire may have been much older. It was in

CHARLES I. This luckless king was not as obsessed by the horse as his father James, his brother Henry, or his son Charles II, but he patronized Newmarket and its racing, and maintained the royal stable. It is probable that he gave Newmarket its first Gold Cup, run for in 1634.

the heart of a breeding area, with a straight three miles of magnificent turf. It was a training- and trying-ground for the Yorkshire studs rather than a place of public amusement.

At Woodham Moor, Durham, a piece of plate was provided in 1613 as a 'hunting prize', to be run for annually on the Tuesday before Palm Sunday.[13] 'Hunting prize' does not convey any suggestion of jumps, nor is it to be confused with the hunting matches the king went in for at Newmarket.

There were at least three courses in Cheshire: Tarporley by 1622; nearby Little Budworth in Charles I's reign, with a four-mile course and a £20 prize; and Wallasey Shore, over the Mersey from Liverpool: 'These fair sands, or plains upon the shore of the sea at Walsey, which for the fitnesse of such a purpose allure the gentlemen and others oft to appoint great matches, and venture no small sums in trying the swiftness of their horses.'[14]

In what are now the northern suburbs of London, at Barnet: 'Heere all the countrey gentlemen appoint a friendly meeting . . . some for pleasure, to match their horses.'[15] Nearer Westminster still: 'Shall we take a fling to London, and see how the Spring appears in Spring Garden, and in Hyde Park to see the Races both Horse and foot.'[16] In 1635 a match was run between John Pretyman and John Havers: 'To begin and start together at the Upper Lodge in Hyde Park and to run the usual way from thence over the lower bridge unto the ending place at the Park Gate.'[17] The same year a Mr Michael Hudson brought his nag south from Yorkshire to London, and matched it in the Park. He was an ordinand, only 19 years old. The Lambeth clergy backed against his horse, and there was great ecclesiastical outrage when he won. Hudson became a royalist parson, and was treacherously killed in the Civil War, though not by the Lambeth clergy.[18]

## Growth of Scottish Racing

Scotland was developing her racing at the same rate. Berwick, Haddington, Peebles, Dumfries and Stirling were all going concerns at Elizabeth's death.

The races at Peebles were on Beltane, 2 May; in 1608 the Scottish Government prohibited 'ane Horse-race appointed to be at Peebles . . . whereunto great numbers of people of all qualities and ranks, intends to repair, betwixt whom there being quarrels, private grudges, and miscontentment.'[19]

The same year the Burgh of Paisley 'concluded that ane silver bell be made of 4 oz. weight, with all diligence, for ane horse-race yearly, to be appointed within this burgh.' In 1620 there was an 'Act setting down ane hors raiss . . . bell race and efterschot, quhilk was of auld set doune and not effectuat.' Prize-money was added to the bell, and the second got a double-angel. The Provost and Baillies subscribed double-angels, 'lyikas the noblemen haifand lands within the parochin of Paislay,' Lords Sempill, Rose and Blantyre, 'everie ane of thame ar willing, for the vphalding of the said bell race, zeirlie to give in ane single aingell yairunto.' There was additionally an entry-fee of a single angel from each starter. Horses and riders had to be ready at ten o'clock to weigh out and to cast dice for starting-positions. The 'aftershot' race was for a furnished saddle. It was specially ordered that 'The ryders allwayis of the saides horses keipond their wechts they war weyit of befoir furthdrawing, and na vther wayis.'[20]

The Perth Hunt meeting was first held in 1613; a bell was run for on the South Inch. Two years later the Council provided six stakes to mark the course. In 1631, following what was now general practice, the bells became a cup.

Dunfermline and Cupar Fife races were probably annual by this time. In 1610 at the former David Boswell's black won a three-horse race and he bound himself to return the bell. In 1621 at the latter Lords Morton, Boyd, and Abercorn ran a three-mile race for 10 double-angels a head, winner take all.

Although Lanark's bell was made about 1600 (and was supposed to have been the gift of William the Lion 600 years earlier) the first winner's name – that of Sir Iohne Hamilton of Trabro – was not engraved until 1628.[21] Glasgow started at about this date.

## The Development of the Racehorse

James I's first recorded acquisitions were 'a dozen gallant mares, all with foal, four horses, and 11 stallions, all coursers of Naples' in 1605.[22] His first Arabian was the famous Markham, somehow acquired by Gervase or a relative. The king bought him for £154, with £11 to the groom.[23] The Duke of Newcastle did not admire him, and he was useless on the racecourse. He went to stud, almost certainly to Tutbury, where his descendants were later found.

GEORGE VILLIERS, 1ST DUKE OF BUCKINGHAM. Villiers (1592–1628) went as a young man to France, where Pluvinel was already teaching. His horsemanship explains his extraordinary, unmerited rise to greatness, James I being a passionate if inexpert horseman, and his son Prince Henry a *manège* enthusiast. It equipped him to be Master of the Horse, but not High Admiral, in which role he was assassinated. He imported many African and Spanish horses, but the Helmsley Turk, often credited to him, probably belongs to a later period.

In November 1617 George Digby, an equerry ('one of oʳ. quirries') was given £550 from the Exchequer 'to be imploied and disbursed by him for provision of horses for us for the Race,' ('Race' means breed or family) and sent to Italy.[24] The horses he got were known as the Digby Arabians. In the same month Sir Thomas Edmonds arrived in England with 'half a dozen Barbry horses', which probably came from Italy.[25]

The master of the Horse, the Duke of Buckingham ('reckoned the most accomplished man of his age in riding'),[26] actually sent 'into Barbary' for horses: six, including mares, passed through Exeter in August 1621, on their way from Plymouth to Tutbury.[27] Two years later Buckingham was in Madrid; he received on Prince Henry's behalf 30 or 35 horses, gifts of the Spanish court.

In 1624 there was drawn up 'An Accounte of all his Maᵗˢ. Mares and Colts within the Race of Tutbury, in Staffordshire, and with what Horses the Breeding Mares were Covered in this Yeare 1624'. The stallions were: 'Amblinge Courser Digby' (one of the draft of 1617), an Arabian Colt (Markham?), a dark grey Barbary, 'Potts the white French horse', 'Potts the gray courser', and a 'Spanish Ginnet dapled'. They covered 47 mares, of which many were Italian, a few Spanish, and two Barbary.[28]

Buckingham's own 'Highe Wair Stable' had, in 1623, about 22 mares of which five were Spanish and three Barbary. The stallions were 'Rennets', Barbaries, and a courser.[29]

A courtier of equal importance was the Duke of Newcastle. One of Charles I's most valuable acts was to appoint William Cavendish tutor to his sons in 1628. This outstanding authority criticized, 30 years later, the conformation of the Markham Arabian: but he also stated his conviction about the way to breed racers – the philosophy anticipated by Gervase Markham: cover your English mares with Barb or Arab stallions. His Welbeck stud was undoubtedly run on these lines.

There are several indications from elsewhere that a quiet revolution in horse-breeding was beginning. This has two aspects: careful selection, and the use of 'Eastern' blood.

A WELBECK BARB. Welbeck, Nottinghamshire, was the seat and stud of the Duke of Newcastle. Behind the house were stables hardly less magnificent than those of Louis XIV at le Pin: pillared, heated, ventilated, and sluiced out by a diverted river. Although the records are lost, a number of Eastern horses stood here, making an early contribution to the thoroughbred. Paragon, the Barb shown, was almost certainly a covering stallion, not a 'managed' horse or a racer.

As early as 1605, a treatise on the 'Order and Governance' of a nobleman's household instructed the 'Officer of the Gentleman of the Horse' that he must 'keep a note in a booke when everie mare is coverede and with what horse.'[30] Sir George Reresby of Yorkshire was deeply concerned about 'his breed of horses, in which he was very exact.'[31] Robert Burton took it for granted that 'An husbandman . . . will not rear a bull or a horse, except he be right shapen in all parts, or permit him to cover a mare, except he be well assured of his breed.'[32]

At the same time, Sir William Ingleby, another Yorkshireman, bequeathed a 'baie Barbarie horse' to his nephew.[33] Lord Cranbourne, Sir Thomas Howard, and Sir John Sheffield (Sir Johan Shefillde) each bought 'Barbarye' horses at Marseille, where they had just arrived from Africa, to send to their English stables.[34] The Pelhams (Sir Thomas and his son Sir John) had in 1639 an 'ould barbine mare'; and they had another mare covered by Lord Northumberland's 'barbine'.[35]

## Betting and Gambling

One of the more surprising facets of James I was his passion for high play. On Twelfth Night 1607–8 he gave a party to which no-one was admitted without £300 cash.[36] Sir Christopher Hatton backed his friends with £1000 of his own gold for one night's play; and Lord Pembroke lost £2000 in one evening 'imitating Augustus Caesar's play'.[37] This was 'an exercise of profaneness diligently followed by many of our gentlemen who of their weekly and almost daily meetings, and matches on their bowling-greens, or their lavish betting of great wagers in such sorry trifles, and of their stout and strong abetting of so silly vanaties amongst hundreds, sometimes thousands, of rude and vile persons to whom they should give better, and not so bad example and encouragement, as to be idle in neglecting their callings; wasteful in gaming, and spending their means; wicked in cursing and swearing, and dangerously profane in their brawling and quarrelling.'[38]

Burton, naturally, found here one of the causes of dread Melancholy: 'It is a wonder to see, how many poor distressed miserable wretches one shall meet almost in every path and street, begging for an alms, that have been well descended, and sometimes in flourishing estate, now ragged, tattered, and ready to be starved, lingring out a painful life, in discontent and grief of body and mind, and all through immoderate lust, gaming, pleasure, and riot.'[39]

Racing had been one of the healthy pursuits which (if not too expensive) was a cure for Melancholy, and the growth of gambling was at the expense of racing: 'Hawking, hunting, and swift horse running, Are changit all in wrangus, wynning; There is no play but cartes and dyce.'[40] The achievement of the early 17th century was to bring gambling and racing together. On 8 March 1622 Buckingham lost £100 to Lord Salisbury at Newmarket, and two days later another £100.[41] In 1631 Lord Pembroke made 'extraordinary great winnings at a horse-race at Winchester'.[42]

Betting led, as always, to skulduggery. Lord Herbert of Cherbury deplored 'riding of running horses, there being much cheating in that kind.'[43] Ben Jonson talks of 'Thy rules to cheat at horse-race, cock-pit, cards.'[44] Shirley's play *Hyde Park* revolves largely round a race in the park, which is won by a character called Jockey. 'The odds,' says the hero, 'Play'd 'bout my ears like cannon.'[45]

## Racing and Breeding in the Commonwealth

The Great Rebellion did not immediately kill racing. In Scotland a man 'bursted a poor man's head' at the races at Cupar Fife, and at Peebles they raced for the bell in 1647 and '48. Before returning the prize, winners added 'little bells and pendicles' to the 'great bell'.[46] But in 1649 and every year thereafter the Council of State forbade racing through-

THOMAS, 3RD LORD FAIRFAX. As a young man Fairfax (1612–1671) studied warfare and equitation in France and the Low Countries. He was a Parliamentary leader from 1641 and commanded Cromwell's New Model Army in 1645. He disapproved of Charles I's execution and in 1660 supported the Restoration. In retirement he bred horses and composed a treatise on the subject. His Morocco Barb and other Eastern horses were of outstanding importance, and he seems – exceptionally though not uniquely – to have imported mares as well as stallions.

out Britain. An Order of February 1655 noted 'how great a concourse of People do usually frequent such Meetings, and the evil use made thereof by such ill-disposed Persons as watch for opportunities to raise New Troubles.'[47]

Even so, in February 1650 the City of Salisbury demanded overdue subscriptions for the races from the gentlemen of the county;[48] and in 1654 there was a lot of racing. Dorothy Osborne wrote in May: 'I have the honour of seeing my Lady M. Sandis every day unless some race or other carries her out of town. The last week she went to one as far as Winchester.' Her ladyship stayed for Winchester races with her husband, although they were separated: 'he thought it better than an Inn, or at least a crowded one as all in the town were now because of the race.'[49]

From then until the Restoration coach-racing in Hyde Park was regular and popular; respectable ladies went, but always masked.[50] In 1658 John Evelyn 'went to see a coach-race in Hyde Park, and collationed in Spring Garden.'[51] In 1659 an English writer (pretending to be a French writer) described 'a field near the town which they call Hyde Park . . . the place not unpleasant, and which they use as our "Course".' They raced wretched jades and hackney coaches.[52]

Breeding, meanwhile, both lost ground and gained it.

The parliamentary soldiers sacked the royal stud at Eltham: 'both palace and chapel in miserable ruins, the noble woods and park destroyed'; and that at Woodstock: 'destruction of the royal seat and park by the late rebels'. Private men suffered equally: 'the country was much molested by soldiers, who took away gentlemen's horses for the service of the State, as then called.'[53]

At both a public and a private level, however, the good work went on.

In 1649 an inventory was taken of the 139 horses at the captured royal stud of Tutbury. There were descendants of the Digby and Buckingham imports; a number of Morocco mares and a stallion; an 'Arab' stallion of the Villiers race, and several of Fenwick's 'Arabian Race'. There were two colts by Frisell (by the Markham Arabian), and several Newcastle horses from Welbeck.

The Council of State decided that these were the best horses in England, and should not be dispersed. Six animals were however sent to Ireland. The Lord General got six. Sir Arthur Hazelrigg got several, some of which went to Hampton Court after the Restoration.[54]

Cromwell made importations, from Italy and from the Middle East. In 1655 Longland, his agent in Livorno, was ordered to buy horses of Eastern blood from Naples or the Orient. He got six, for which he paid 2382 piastres.[55] Place's White Turk, named for Cromwell's stud-master, seems to have come from France a little later. Cromwell was not breeding for the turf, but he was breeding chargers as though for the turf.

Private efforts were still more important. Certain parliamentary leaders were shocked by the judicial murder of the king and revolted by extreme puritanism; they returned to their estates and bred horses. The most notable was Thomas, 3rd Lord Fairfax. Parliament gave him the Duke of Buckingham's Helmsley estates, where there were already Eastern horses. Buckingham was the 2nd Duke, son of the murdered Master of the Horse, and brought up by Charles I with his own sons; he was too arrogant to agree for long with the exiled king's Chancellor Hyde (later Clarendon). He made his peace with Cromwell, came back, married Fairfax's daughter and heiress, and thus recovered his estates. They had the Helmsley Turk, Fairfax's Morocco Barb (assuming, as docs the Stud Book, that this is a different horse), and the 'Unknown' Arabian and equally unknown Barb Mare which are sire and dam of Old Bald Peg.

The quality of this North-Country activity is further shown by the Pelham records. In 1650 Sir John had a filly by 'Mr Huetts Barb', in 1653 one by the Earl of Northumberland's 'barbe', and in 1654 a colt by Mr Master's 'barbe'.[56]

# 5 Britain:

## Restoration and Later Stuarts

### Charles II and Newmarket

In Paris in 1650 John Evelyn saw 'a triumph in Monsieur de Camp's Academy, where divers of the French and English noblesse did take their exercises on horse-back in noble equipage, before a world of spectators and great persons.'[1] Newcastle had two Barbs in Paris in the late 1640s, eight in Antwerp in the 1650s, where he published the first (French) version of his book on horsemanship.[2]

Thus the Restoration racecourse saw a higher standard of horsemanship, and a closer knowledge of the Eastern horse, than any previous time. It also had those improved horses which certain studs were breeding. These initial advantages went far to give Restoration racing its character. The rest was provided by Charles II and his friends.

The personal importance of the king can hardly be overstated. He rode frequently and well, in matches and for Plates; he set down rules; he was adjudicator and appeal-court.

He probably first went racing at Epsom (Banstead Downs) in 1661. He intended to go to Newmarket in October 1663. Newmarket racing had restarted in the Spring of that year, a match being recorded between the Duke of Richmond and Lord Suffolk. He did go in 1666, and thereafter two or three times a year, for two or three weeks at a time. The anxious civil servant Pepys deplored this waste of time and money: on one occasion he was dreading a foul-weather journey into the country, 'but the less it troubles me because the King and the Duke of York and Court are this day at Newmarket, at a great horse-race, and proposed great pleasure for two or three days, but are in the same wet.' In the event it was fine at Newmarket. This was the meeting at which, the king being bored on a Sunday, 'the Duke of Buckingham did in the afternoon make an obscene sermon to him out of canticles.' To get to Newmarket for the Spring meeting of the next year (1669) the royal party started by coach from Whitehall at three in the morning. The coach overturned, with king, Duke of York, Duke of Monmouth, and Prince Rupert – 'the King all dirty, but no hurt'.[3]

That summer the Duke of Tuscany visited Newmarket Heath. 'The racecourse is a tract of ground in the neighbourhood of Newmarket, which, extending to a distance of four miles over a spacious level meadow, covered with very short grass, is marked out by tall wooden posts, painted white. . . . The horses intended for this exercise, in order to render them more swift, are kept always girt, that their bellies may not drop, and thereby interfere with the agility of their movements; when the time of the race draws near, they feed them with the greatest care, and very sparingly, giving them for the most part, in order to keep them in full vigour, beverages composed of soaked bread and fresh eggs.' The duke watched a match: two horses were led out 'by the men who were to ride them, dressed in taffeta of different colours'. They started slowly, but 'the farther they advanced in the course, the more they urged them, forcing them to continue it at full speed.' The king and a retinue were watching on horseback; in the closing stages they all rode hard alongside the runners to the finish. 'Trumpets and drums, which were in readiness for the purpose, sounded in applause of the conqueror, which was a horse of Sir – Elliot [*sic*].' Afterwards 'His Majesty, being very much heated, adjourned to his house.'[4]

The king regularly watched training-gallops as well as races, sitting either in his 'chair', a little pavilion on top of the hill, or on his hack Old Rowley, which became his own Newmarket nickname and then that of part of the course. John Evelyn describes 'fast work' of the kind the king watched: 'we returned over Newmarket Heath, the way being mostly a sweet turf and down, like Salisbury Plain, the jockeys breathing their fine barbs and racers, and giving them their heats.'[5]*

In 1670 the king's house was 'new-building' on the site of 'an old wretched house of my Lord Thomond's'.[6] In October of the next year Evelyn visited it; he and his hosts 'proceeded immediately to Court, the King and all the English gallants being there at their autumnal sports. . . . The next day, after dinner, I was on the heath, where I saw the great match between Woodcock and Flatfoot, belonging to the King, and to Mr Eliot of the Bedchamber, many thousands being spectators.' Racing lasted a fortnight. It was at this meeting that Louise de Querouaille was first bedded by the king. Evelyn 'lodged this night at Newmarket, where I found the jolly blades racing, dancing, feasting, and revelling, more resembling a luxurious and abandoned rout, than a Christian Court.'[7]

The king must have had extraordinary energy. 'Yesterday his majestie rode himself three heats and a course and won the Plate, all fower were hard and nere run, and I doe assure you the king wonn by good Horseman Ship.'[8]

Alexander Pope thought all this was dreadful:

> In Days of Ease, when now the weary sword
> Was sheath'd, and *Luxury* with *Charles* restor'd;
> In ev'ry taste of foreign Courts improv'd,
> 'All, by the King's Example, liv'd and lov'd.'
> Then Peers grew proud in Horsemanship t'excell,
> New-market's Glory rose, as Britain's fell.[9]

But in the early 1680s Newmarket's glory was twice in danger of being dimmed.

In 1681 there was an effort to move 'headquarters' to Burford, Oxfordshire. This was because of Parliament's removal from the dangerous volatility of London to the calm of Oxford. The king took great trouble to make Burford a success, bringing all his own horses from Newmarket and getting his friends to do the same. If larger matters had so dictated, Burford could have become the permanent centre of royal racing. But in the autumn the political atmosphere relaxed, Parliament went back to London, and the king and court went to Newmarket for more racing than ever.

Two years later assassins planned to murder the king at Newmarket. But there was a fire in the town. The king left earlier than he had planned, and the assassins missed him. 'This made the king more earnest to render Winchester the seat of his autumnal field-diversions for the future, designing a palace there, where the ancient castle stood; infinitely indeed preferable to Newmarket for prospects, air, pleasure and provisions. The surveyor has already begun the foundation for a palace, estimated to cost £35,000, and his Majesty is purchasing ground about it to make a park, &c.'[10] The Tory Duke of York strongly supported the move, on political grounds: 'there is a faction in this business too, ye Whig party being lords at Newmarket.'[11]

The king died two years later, when the new palace was almost finished. His brother was too pre-occupied to complete it.

---

* This passage is full of semantic interest. *Breathing* means giving a sharp gallop – the opposite of the modern 'giving a breather'. *Heat* here means the same thing, which is Gervase Markham's usage; Evelyn was probably out of date with this usage. *Jockey* is not a race-rider but in this context a training-groom; it also means expert, horse-coper or rogue. *Barb* is difficult; probably Evelyn was speaking loosely.

## Plates and Matches

The plate the king won in 1675 'by good Horseman Ship' was his own, the Newmarket Town plate, predecessor of all the King's and Queen's Plates given by William III, Anne, and the Georges. The races were four-mile heats at 12 stone (168 lb.), and were a specific attempt to encourage the breeding of big, stout horses. The policy worked. Until the last quarter of the 18th century the horse regarded as supreme was that which won races under these searching conditions, and towards this ideal breeders planned the matings. In 1761 John Baylor of Caroline, Virginia, imported a King's Plater, 'as I am in want of strength for our small Virginia mares.'[12] Newmarket's 14 stone (196 lb.) Plate of 1698 'to encourage the breeding of Strong and Useful Horses'[13] was probably going too far.

The Plate had full and formal rules: 'Articles ordered by his Majestie to be observed by all persons that put in horses to ride for the Plate, on the new Round-Course, at Newmarket, set out the 16th day of October in the 17th year of our sovereign Lord King Charles II.'[14] These rules broadly follow those of Newcastle, who had a private race-course at Worksop, near Welbeck;[15] they were in turn based on the Kiplingcotes rules.

At Newmarket, as elsewhere, there were widely-varying Articles for races and matches, but outside the Plate no formal rules. Racing was bedevilled by their lack. 'Here hapned yesterday a dispute upon the greatest point of Criticall learning that was ever known at Newmarket, A Match between a horse of Sir Rob: Car's, and a gelding of Sir Rob: Geeres, for a mile and a halfe only, had engaged all the Court in many thousand pounds, much depending in so short a course to have them start fairly. Mr Griffin was appointed to start them. When he saw them equall he sayd Goe, and presently he cried out Stay. One went off, and run through the Course and claims the money, the other never stird at all. Most possibly you may say that this was not a fayre starting, but the critics say after the word Goe was out of the mouth his commission was determined, and it was illegall for him to say Stay. I suppose there will be Volumes written upon this subject; 'tis all referred to his Majesty's judgement, who hath not yet determined it.'[16]

Even when rules came to exist, matches were normally immune. 'Crossing was understood in every match, unless specifically interdicted in the article, by the words "*no crossing*".'[17]

Matches were often made months before they were run, and recorded in the Match

Book. They varied from £100 to £1000, and were at various weights and distances. Four miles was normal, six and seven frequent. A mile and a half was exceptionally short.

## Epsom and Chester

All over England racing restarted where it was traditional, and started where it had not been.

The first new meeting after the Restoration was near Epsom, on the miles of fine upland turf known as Banstead Downs. If Newmarket owed its start to hare and partridge, Epsom became a place of resort because of a mineral spring. A farmer discovered this by accident in 1618, when his cows refused to drink from a certain puddle. Some labourers presently (less particular) drank the water, and its laxative properties were dramatically revealed. Its celebrity was immediate and widespread. Bottles and extracted salts went all over Europe, and people thronged from London to put right the effects of their gigantic meals. Pepys visited the Wells in 1663; they were doing a booming trade but he was disappointed in the class of patron. Four years later he was there again; he managed to drink four pints. Nell Gwynn was staying in the next house with Lord Buckhurst.

The town's commercial interests added racing to the spa to attract more visitors. The date is uncertain but it might have begun before the Civil War. It was established, or re-established, in 1661. In 1663 'there was a great thronging to Banstead Downs, upon a great horse-race and foot-race. I am sorry I could not go thither.'[18] The races were still no more than side-shows to the main business of Epsom: in 1684 'the post will go every day to and fro', betwixt London and Epsom during the season for drinking the waters.'[19]

Chester, again pioneering, saw in 1665 an early example of a local official using his powers to win himself a race: the 'High Sheriff borrowed a Barbary Horse of Sir Thomas Middleton, which won him the plate; and being master of the race, he would not suffer the horses of Master Massey of Puddington, and Sir Philip Egerton of Outon, to run, because they came the day after the time prefixed for the horses to be brought, and kept in the city; which thing caused all the gentry to relinquish our races ever since.'[20]

The gentry must have changed their minds; Chester remained an important and popular course.

## James II and William III; Continued Growth of Racing

James II liked his hunting and his mistresses, and he raced almost as much as his brother when Charles was alive. But his brief reign was devoted to turning England Catholic, and this pre-occupation kept him off the racecourse. Racing everywhere continued to grow, but without the lurid glamour of the previous reign. It was hardly interrupted by the 'Glorious Revolution' of 1688: the London Gazette advertised Plates as usual.[21]

William III seemed dull to the English—'wonderful serious and silent . . . very intent on affairs'[22] – but he was a deep plunger and he took his racing seriously. Although the court was respectable, the course saw heavier betting than ever before.

There were about two dozen new fixtures in William III's reign. The king revived racing at Hampton Court, as well as the royal stud there. In 1698 Epsom had three meetings. In spite of a bad epidemic of equine 'flu in 1699 – 'a distemper among horses, attended with a running at the nose'[23] – there was more racing that year than in any previous.

Wharton (Thomas, 1st Marquis) started a private racecourse at Quainton, near his Buckinghamshire stud, on the pattern of Newcastle's. Some of the best horses in England ran there, and the meetings were brilliant. In 1698 his Careless (9 stone; 126 lb.) was narrowly beaten at Newmarket by the king's Stiff Dick (a feather); Careless was the best

horse in England – the best since his sire Spanker, the best until his grandson Flying Childers. All Wharton's racing was political in motive to a degree unknown since the days of Philip of Macedon. He was a passionate Whig:

'Sometimes when, in a distant county, it was fully expected that the horse of a High Church squire would be first on the course, down came, on the very eve of the race, Wharton's Careless, who had ceased to run at Newmarket merely for want of competitors, or Wharton's Gelding, for whom Lewis the Fourteenth had in vain offered a thousand pistoles.'[24]

Another racecourse of special interest was Durham. In 1695: 'It is thought fit and so resolved by the justices in open Court, that from henceforth their wages goe and be employed for and towards the procuring a plate or plates to be run for on Durham Moor.'[25]

In Scotland racing revived but did not much expand. Hamilton was added to the short list of regular meetings; otherwise they were substantially those of 100 years before.

Stirling, one of the oldest, broke new ground in 1706. The programme was enlivened not only by a foot-race, which was normal enough, but also a goose-race.[26]

## Queen Anne and Tregonwell Frampton

Queen Anne kept up her Newmarket establishment, and she was the first sovereign to go racing in the North as well as the South. She also kept on William Tregonwell Frampton.

*Left*

'HORSE RACEING.' This is usually alleged to be a match between Charles II and Henry Jermyn at Newmarket in 1684, but this is improbable by virtue of the date, the terrain, and the gypsy encampment. It is surely one of the thousands of unrecorded local events – regular meetings or impromptu matches – which grew enormously between 1660 and 1740. The horses were hunters or Galloways, the riders their owners or grooms, the raceground any convenient piece of common, and the prize a measure of oats or barley.

*Right*

WILLIAM TREGONWELL FRAMPTON. Frampton (*c.* 1641–1727) was Keeper of the Running Horses at Newmarket for four sovereigns, and from Queen Anne's reign 'Governor' of Newmarket. He was an owner, match-maker, coper, and deep plunger on his own account. His first good horse was Nutmeg, which beat the Duke of Albermarle's Black Buttocks about 1687 and won him a lot of money. The horse in the picture is alleged, in the 1790 caption to this print, to be Dragon; the gamecock and greyhound stand for his other absorbing passions.

Frampton was born a Dorset squire; from early youth he devoted his life to racing, coursing, and cocking. Newmarket was obviously his spiritual home, and he was matching horses there, for frightening sums, by the mid-1670s. By James II's time, Frampton was 'of great notoriety on the Turf'.[27]

Soon after his accession William III made him 'Keeper of the Running Horses', an appointment which can be compared to a modern racing manager: 'Tregonel Frampton, Supervisor of the Race Horses at Newmarket, for the Maintenance of 10 Boys their lodgings, &c., and for Provisions of Hay, Oats, Bread, and all other necessaries for 10 Race Horses, £1000 per annum'.[28]

Very many matches were made in his name and recorded in the Match Book. Some of these involved the king's horses; in others he ran his own. He gambled as heavily on his cocks in the main as on his horses on the turf, betting, on both sports, on a scale out of all proportion to his modest salary.

He was eccentric. 'This gentleman (whose picture may be seen in many a house in Newmarket) was as great an oddity as perhaps ever was heard of. He was a known woman hater . . . passionately fond of horse-racing, cocking and coursing, remarkable for a peculiar uniformity in his dress, the fashion of which he never changed, and in which, regardless of his uncouth appearance, he would not infrequently go to Court, and enquire in the most familiar manner for his master or mistress, the King or Queen. Queen Anne used to call him "Governor Frampton".'[29]

In Anne's reign occurred (or did not occur) the two most famous episodes with which his name is linked.

In 1752, in Dr Johnson's *Adventurer*, a schoolmaster called Dr Hawkesworth published a conversation between the shades of a horse and a donkey who met in the Elysian fields. 'I was a favourite,' said the horse, 'but what avails it to be the favourite of caprice, avarice, and barbarity. My tyrant was a wretch who had gained a considerable fortune by play, particularly by racing. *I had won him many large sums*, and being excepted out of every match as *having no equal*, he regarded my excellence with malignity when it was no longer subservient to his interest. *Yet I still lived in ease* and plenty, and he was able to sell my pleasures, though my labour was become useless. *I had a seraglio* in which there was a perpetual succession of new beauties.' This nonpareil was brought back from stud duties for a £1000 match, which he won. The owner of the loser offered a general challenge: his horse against any gelding. The champion's owner accepted, not naming his entry. 'I suffered myself to be bound; the operation was performed, and I was instantly mounted and spurred on to the goal.' He won, and died at the winning-post.[30] Frampton was later identified with the 'tyrant', and the horse with one of several called Dragon. A number of racing historians have unaccountably accepted the identification.[31]

The other episode is of the jockey out-jockeyed. Northern and southern racing were largely separate, so when the Yorkshireman Sir William Strickland challenged Newmarket with his Merlin there was keen interest and unprecedented betting. Frampton accepted the challenge with an unknown horse. Before the match they ran a trial, for purposes of side-betting. Frampton gave his horse a secret seven pounds overweight. It was just beaten. This was good enough for Newmarket. Money poured on the local runner. But Strickland's trainer Heseltine also gave his lad overweight in the trial, and in the match they ran true to the trial form. Fortunes and estates were lost.

The North celebrated its victory in drinking-songs for years, but Strickland was not popular in York. When he stood for Parliament in 1710 'Sir William Strickland was mightily abused, by People crying no Rump, no Whig, Atheist, Presbyterian, Hang-dog, Hare-Scutt, and whatever they could invent, to abuse him.'[32] (His father had been a Cromwellian, which explains these epithets.)

Newmarket's losses on the Merlin match are supposed to have been the reason for the anti-betting legislation which was passed soon afterwards.[33]

CHARLES II AND NELL GWYNN AT NEWMARKET. Charles II first raced at Newmarket in 1666, and thereafter attended nearly every meeting until 1683. Many of his successive mistresses came racing with him here, and his affair with Louise de Querouailles started at Euston, nearby. Of them all Nell Gwynn is most associated with the place. She was here regularly from the early 1670s and had her own house in the shadow of the palace with, allegedly, an underground passage connecting the two.

## York; Ascot; the Isle of Man

One of the important events of Anne's reign was the foundation of formal racing at York.

21 September 1709 'was ye first time that four mile heats were run on Clifton Ings, Sir Willm. Robinson making a large stone bridge, nine yards broad, between Rockcliffe and Clifton Ings att his own proper charge. There was a starting and weighing stoop at this end, and att an equal distance, stoops to ye turning, stoops at ye far end, painted all white.'[34] Queen Anne gave a Gold Cup. In 1713 she was present herself; her horse Mustard was brought from Newmarket, but ran unplaced.

In 1711 racing began at Ascot. Somebody – the queen herself, or her Master of the Horse the Duke of Somerset – decided that this well-turfed corner of the royal park was almost as convenient for Windsor Castle as Datchet Mead, and a much better race-ground. In July 1711 the *London Gazette* announced: 'Her Majesty's Plate of 100 guineas will be run for round the new heat on Ascott Common, near Windsor, on Tuesday August 7th next.' The Master of the Horse's accounts show the making of the course, and the provision of posts and their paint, in July and early August.[35]

On 10 August Dean Swift, staying at Windsor, was riding with Dr Arbuthnot, the queen's physician. 'We saw a place they have made for a famous horse-race tomorrow, where the Queen will come.' The inaugural race was duly held on 11 August, in front of the queen and court. 'I intended to go to the races to-day, but was hindered by a visit . . . I dined at the Green Cloth, where every body had been at the race but myself, and we were twenty in all; and very noisy company.' There was also a race two days later, otherwise unrecorded. Swift 'missed the race to-day by coming too late, when everybody's coach was gone.'[36]

There was a September meeting in the same year, and two meetings in each of the next two years. Then the queen died, the day after her horse Star won a £40 Plate; and so for six years did Ascot.

Another race-meeting of special interest was held, throughout this period, near Castletown, Isle of Man, of which the Earls of Derby were lords. It is possible that these races were started by James Stanley, 7th and 'Martyr' Earl, but the first record is of 1665. In that year Charles, 8th Earl, paid £1 for the 'plate wch was bought at Chester for ye horse race.' The earl declared his intentions in 1670: 'Out of the good affection that I have to every of my Tennants of my Isle of Man to furnish themselves with, and thereby to have a breed of good Horses there: it is my pleasure to allow the sum of five pounds yearly to bee paid out of the Revenues of the Island, to be Run for.'[37] The date was the heir's birthday; the races were made the occasion of his birthday party, which was held in a pavilion built, by a macabre whim, on Hango Hill, the site of the public gibbet. A grander cup than the £1 Plate was made in Dublin in 1701.

These races were at an end by 1736; but for 70 years they were a unique case of a family who were kings in their own realms sponsoring their own races for their own tenants.

## Start of Racing in Ireland

In 1665, at Dublin:

'We have had upon the Strand several races, but the most remarkable was by the Rings and Coaches (which is an odd kinde of carriage and generally used in this country), there were a matter of 25 of them, and His Excellency the Lord Deputy bestowed a piece of Plate upon him who won the race, and the second, third and fourth, were rewarded with money. It is a new institution, and an annual custom, for the humour of it gave much satisfaction, there being at least 5000 spectators.'[38]

In 1673 Sir William Temple visited Ireland. He wrote, as a result, a remarkable letter to Essex the Lord Lieutenant urging the institution of racing. The grazing and climate

FLYING CHILDERS. The first supreme thoroughbred racehorse, bred in 1715 by Colonel Leonard Childers of Doncaster (pedigree p. 59). He raced for the Duke of Devonshire, for whom he won every time he started. In his own time and for long afterwards he was reckoned not only the best horse ever seen, but the best ever likely to be seen: an unrepeatable phenomenon.

were excellent, he said, and the horses already good. He suggested a horse-fair, with races on alternate days, at Phoenix Park. There should be Royal Plates, restricted to Irish-breds. Fairs and sports would divert the people, and the races would improve the breed. The owner of the winning horse should be asked to dine, regardless of rank.[39]

Nothing happened until Clarendon (2nd Earl) was Lord Lieutenant. In 1686 he wrote to his brother: 'The next week there will be a great meeting at the Curragh of Kildare, where will be several horse-races . . . I have resolved to go thither on Monday, and will be back on Friday.'

Three days later he wrote, from Kildare, in these disenchanted terms: '. . . it is, indeed, a noble country; and the common where the race is held, is a much finer turf than Newmarket, and infinitely larger; but it is sad to see the people – I mean the natives – such proper lusty fellows – poor, almost naked, but will work never but when they are ready to starve; and when they have got three or four days wages, with them walk about idly till that be gone . . . Their habitations (for they cannot be called houses) are perfect pigsties.'[40]

The Down Royal 'Maze' was started at the same time in Ulster. Charles II and William III gave Plates to both courses.

## Betting and Gambling

Gambling was heavy on and off the racecourse. 'Strange,' said Pepys, 'the folly of men to lay and lose so much money,' and 'Lord!' he said of the cockpit, 'to see the strange variety of people, from Parliament men . . . to the poorest 'prentices . . . and all these fellows one with another cursing and betting.'[41]

Evelyn saw the heavy play of the court – 'the wicked folly and monstrous excess of passion amongst some losers.' Another time, 'Deep and prodigious gaming . . . vast heaps of gold squandered away in a vain and profuse manner.' 'The ladies also played very deep'[42] – especially Lady Castlemaine, 'so great a gamester as to have won £15,000 in one night, and lost £25,000 in another night, at play, and hath played £1000 and £1500 at a card.'[43] Lord St Albans continued a formidable gamester, though blind, 'having one that sits by him to name the spots on the cards.'[44]

Anne's anti-gaming legislation was anticipated in Charles II's reign as early as 1664. The preamble of his Act says that gambling leads to 'the circumventing, deceiving, conserving and debauching of many of the younger sort, both of the nobility and gentry and others, to the loss of their precious time, and to the utter ruin of their estates and fortunes.'[45]

These excesses were less obtrusive in the last two Stuart reigns, but money poured to and fro on the racecourse and in the mains. 'The Duke of Devon lost £1,900 at a horse-race at Newmarket.'[46] There is no guessing how much changed hands on the Merlin match of 1709.

Heavy betting was by no means confined to the raffish. Evelyn's infinitely respectable friend Sidney Godolphin (1st Earl) was a famous plunger. The letters of the equally worthy Earl of Bristol to both his excellent wives are full of the triumphs and miseries of his wagers.[47]

# 6 Creation of the Thoroughbred

THOMAS 1ST MARQUIS OF WHARTON.
Wharton (1648–1715) was an adroit and
committed Whig politician, and
brought all his skills, as well as his
convictions, to the turf. He had a major
stud in Buckinghamshire, but it produced
nothing as good as the horses then being
bred in Yorkshire; consequently he
bought his best horses from the North.
For a short time his private racecourse
at Quainton was one of the most
important in Britain.

## Conflicting Theories

John Lawrence ('this prosing and argumentative old man')[1] wrote in 1829: 'The species of horse used in Great Britain, for the purpose of racing, was from the beginning, the silken haired courser of South Eastern Europe, the origin of which was African, either Arabian or Barb; and this apparently without any, save fortuitous and accidental admixtures with the indigenous breeds of this country.' Foolish fellows have argued that the English racehorse is so much larger than an Arab that it must be a cross of local and imported blood. They are wrong: 'that advantage has resulted purely from the incrassating and improving nature of our graminerous soil, our superior and more nourishing food, and systematic attention.'[2]

Admiral Rous (then Captain) 20 years later confirmed: 'The English race-horse boasts of a pure descent from the Arabian, and under whatever denomination the original stock of our thorough-breds have been imported – viz., as Turks, Barbs, or Royal Mares . . . and whether they were brought from Barbary, Turkey, or the continent of Europe, they were considered as the true sons and daughters of the Desert . . . The change of climate, the pasture, and extreme care and attention in breeding by the best stallions . . . have wonderfully increased their size, their strength, and their powers of endurance.'[3]

But the thoroughbred is not only larger than Arab or Barb, but also different. For example, a point of the desert horse is the high-set tail; in the thoroughbred ' "high-setting" of the tail is a distinct defect,' according to a Victorian expert writing at the same time as Rous. 'Most of the first-class horses, both on the flat and across country, have their tails set on low.'[4] It has moreover been stated as fact that the thoroughbred is a cross of imported stallions and English mares, these having been improved over decades (or centuries, in some accounts)[5] by Eastern blood.

In order to explore these opposing points of view, it is relevant to inquire who was creating the thoroughbred, how, with what motives, on what theories, and with what results.

## The Early Breeders and their Importations

There were three sorts of men engaged in inventing the thoroughbred: monarchs and their stud-masters; magnates like the Dukes of Newcastle, Buckingham, Bolton, and Devonshire, and Lords Godolphin, Montagu and Wharton; and private men, land-owners – almost all in Yorkshire – whose names are not to be found in the *Dictionary of National Biography*, but are remembered in the beginnings of pedigrees – Darley, Curwen, Croft, Leedes – where they join those of royal servants like Darcy, Oglethorpe, Pulleyne, and Marshall.

Of the magnates, Wharton has been described as the first professional party politician; his son, 1st Duke, died of drink, penniless, at the age of 32. The Godolphin and Montagu families were important public servants in a variety of capacities. Buckingham swung, with drunken arrogance, between favour and disgrace at Charles II's court. Newcastle was not latterly a public man at all; Pepys mentions him only as a playwright (and that disparagingly) with a Duchess of whimsical appearance.[6] The others, the private men, were either moderate Parliamentarians like Fairfax, or the best of the cavaliers who, Pepys remarked, were the ones who ran their estates and stayed away from court.[7]

These men imported foreign horses: a lot of stallions and a few mares.

Kings did this by way of ambassadors and special emissaries. Charles II got horses as gifts from Louis XIV, and as part of Catherine of Braganza's dowry. The king also told Lord Winchelsea, Ambassador to the Porte, to send him mares.[8] It is not clear that they ever arrived.

For William III arrived Pulleyne's Arabian, named for the Master of the Stud; and in 1699 the new stud-master, Marshall, imported nine Barbary horses and five mares from Tunis; of this period are Chillaby, his son Greyhound, Dodsworth's dam, imported carrying her famous foal, and the Moonah Bay Barb. The Marshall or Sellaby Turk belonged to the stud-master's brother.

Private enterprise had imported the Helmsley Turk and the Fairfax Morocco Barb, assuming these to have been different individuals. In Charles II's and James II's reigns arrived, for certain, half a dozen Turks and Barbs, probably many more. Among the most important were the White-Legged Lowther Barb, the Lister or Straddling Turk brought back from the siege of Buda, and the Darcy Yellow and White Turks.

Three other Turks arrived in 1684, captured at the siege of Vienna and brought to England by a German. 'I never beheld so delicate a creature as one of them was . . . beautiful and proportioned to admiration, spirited, proud, nimble, making halt, turning with that swiftness, and in so small a compass, as was admirable . . . Five hundred guineas was demanded for the first.'[9] The whole court saw and coveted them. It seems morally certain that they were Arabs, and that they went to the royal or some other stud.

## The Byerley Turk and his Contemporaries

Shortly afterwards another Turk was captured at Buda, by Captain Byerley. He fought two years later at the Boyne; it is supposed that his Turk carried him. The horse's real work began with peace. He got among others Sprite, Black Hearty, Basto, and Jigg. He was also an early and profound influence on the descendants of the Tregonwell Natural Barb Mare (Bruce Lowe No 1 family),[10] and may have been sire of the Dam of the two True Blues (No. 3 family). Through Herod, he is one of the three horses from whom in tail male every thoroughbred horse in the world is descended. He did all this without covering many good mares. Byerley can hardly have predicted it.

In the first few years of the 18th century the Curwen Bay Barb, Toulouse Barb, and St Victor's Barb (or Turk) were imported from France. The first of these was a gift from Mulay Ismael, King of Morocco, to Louis XIV, and was bought by Mr Curwen from the king's bastard who was Master of the Horse. He was an outstanding sire, mostly of the small animals, between horses and ponies, already called Galloways from their resemblance to small Scottish racehorses. The Toulouse Barb commemorates another royal bastard. Sir J. Williams's Turk arrived, which is the same as Sir C. Turner's White Turk and the Honeywood Arabian. This stallion got the two True Blues. Sir Marmaduke Wyvill (father-in-law of James Darcy the younger of Sedbury) bought the Belgrade Turk from the French. Mr Croft imported Bloody Buttocks (a grey with a reddish mark on the quarters) and Croft's Egyptian, but his Bay Barb was a 'natural', being by Chillaby out of the Moonah Barb Mare.

*Above*

THE BYERLEY TURK. Captain (later Colonel) Byerley's horse was captured at Buda in 1688; it is morally certain that, like the many other 'Turks' acquired the same way, he was in fact a high-class desert Arab stolen or bought by a Turkish officer. His male line descends to the present through Herod (see p. 77); his blood also survives copiously through his female descendants and those of Herod, Highflyer and Diomed.

*Above right*

THE DARLEY ARABIAN. This horse was foaled in 1700; he was about 20 years younger than Byerley's. He was bought by Thomas Darley in Aleppo in 1704, who sent him to his brother Richard at Aldby, Yorkshire. He stood there until 1730, latterly the property of John Brewster Darley. One of his sons was Bulle Rock, the first thoroughbred to go to America. Others were the two Childers, one the first great thoroughbred racehorse, the other the progenitor, by Eclipse, of most of today's thoroughbreds (see pp. 78–80).

This list is not comprehensive. It is intended to give an idea of the kind of horses that were coming and where they were coming from. Most were Barbs, imported via France, and captured 'Turks' from South-East Europe.

## The Darley Arabian and the Two Childers

Also in the first years of the 18th century one of the few horses arrived which was imported direct from the Middle East. Another Yorkshire breeder, Mr Darley of Aldby, had the good luck to have a brother who was a merchant at Aleppo. The latter's membership of a Syrian hunting club gave him horse-trading contacts, and he bought and sent home a four-year-old of, he wrote, 'the most esteemed race among the Arabs.'[11]

He covered Darley's own mares almost exclusively; out of these he got Almanzor and Daedalus, good horses, and a number of moderate ones. One of the few outside mares he covered was Betty Leedes, bought from the breeder by Colonel Childers of Doncaster.

This mating, which was repeated, is of the utmost interest for several reasons.

First, the importers and breeders whose long-term efforts here culminated were: Lord Fairfax, the 2nd Duke of Buckingham, Mr (later Lord) Darcy, Mr Leedes, Mr Darley, and Colonel Childers. Mr Gilbert Routh and Sir Marmaduke Wyvill may also have been involved. Every one of these lived and bred horses in Yorkshire.

Second, the foals of this union were of pure imported blood. Their ancestors were: the Darley Arabian, Darcy's Yellow Turk, Fairfax's Morocco Barb, the Leedes Arabian,

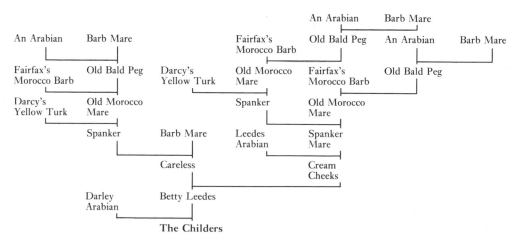

another (Unknown) Arabian; and two Barb Mares. On the assumption that the unnamed Barb mares were imported or natural, there is no native blood here at all.

Third, Betty Leedes's dam, Cream Cheeks or Sister to Leedes, was by the Leedes Arabian out of a Spanker mare, she being out of Fairfax's Old Morocco Mare. This mare was Spanker's dam. He covered his mother: a degree of inbreeding which has been flatly, though wrongly, disbelieved.

Fourth, the matings of the Darley Arabian and Betty Leedes resulted in two colt foals. One was Flying or Devonshire Childers, foaled in 1715, and bought by the 2nd Duke of Devonshire. His maternal grandsire Careless, bred by Leedes and raced by Wharton, was the best racehorse in England at the end of the 17th century. Careless's sire Spanker (to whom Betty Leedes was inbred $2 \times 3$) was the best racehorse in Charles II's reign. To their blood and theirs only were added the Leedes and Darley Arabians. The result was a horse of such extraordinary merit that he was reckoned an unrepeatable phenomenon. In 1722 'Chillders & Fox run over ye Long Course, Chillders carried 9 stone [126 lb.] Fox 8 stone [112 lb.], Chillders beat Fox a distance & half.'[12] Fox was an extremely good horse. Receiving 14 lb. he was beaten by nearly 400 yards. The full brother could not stand up to training because he broke blood vessels. He was called Bleeding Childers. He was bought by Mr Bartlett, yet another Yorkshireman, and given his more respectable name. He covered a daughter of Snake, who was a good racehorse by the Lister Turk. The breeding of this Snake mare is in profound contrast to the Childers', being full of question-marks. The get was Squirt, sire of Marske, sire of Eclipse. From Eclipse derives the fact that the Darley Arabian is, in point of chronology, the second horse from whom all thoroughbreds descend in tail male. In point of numbers he is overwhelmingly the first.

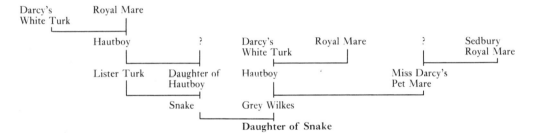

## The Godolphin Arabian

By the end of the first quarter of the 18th century breeders were using English-bred Eastern stallions, as well as a few home-breds of dubious ancestry. But they continued to import stallions in greater numbers than ever.

William III had been prominent among importers; Anne's consort Prince George had a considerable stud at Newmarket; George I never took the smallest interest. Importing was left to private persons. New names enter breeding history – Alcock, Bethel, Johnson, Matthews, Pigot – remembered in the Stud Book by their Arabians, Turks, and Barbs.

The most important of this early Georgian wave was a horse foaled in the Yemen in 1724. He was exported via Syria to Tunis, given by the Bey to the King of France, bought or found by Edward Coke of Derbyshire, and finally acquired by the 2nd Earl of Godolphin for his stud near Newmarket.[13] Stories of his being found between the shafts of a Paris water-cart are attractive but difficult to substantiate.[14]

He was sometimes called the Godolphin Barb, because he came to France from Tunis, and because he had an allegedly Barb look; but more often, and more accurately, the Godolphin Arabian.

In 1731 he covered Roxana (whose two grandsires were St Victor's Barb and the Akaster Turk) and got Lath, the best racehorse since Flying Childers. In 1734 he had

THE GODOLPHIN ARABIAN. This was the youngest of the three stallions from whom all thoroughbreds descend, foaled in 1724. He became the property of the 2nd Earl of Godolphin, and stood at Gog Magog, near Newmarket. Grimalkin, the cat, was his invariable companion; after Grimalkin died, the Arabian detested all cats, and tried to kill any that he saw. He was buried under the stable gateway. Through his grandson Matchem his male line descends, thinly, to the present (see p. 76).

another son out of Roxana: Cade, sire of Matchem. In 1739 he sired Regulus, dam's sire of Eclipse. Through Matchem he is the third tail-male ancestor of every living thoroughbred. In 1850 Rous said 'the blood of the Goldolphin Arabian is in every great stable in England.'[15] Yet he was used sparingly. He only got about 90 foals. Osmer said in 1756: 'It was a pity he was not used more universally for better mares.'[16]

## Ingredients of the Thoroughbred; the Puzzle of the Mares

Spanker, Careless, Childers and Lath each, in his generation, prompted the importation of more Eastern blood. But after the Godolphin Arabian's arrival, new blood lost importance. John Lawrence forbore to list the arrivals after 1730 because of their irrelevance. The job had been done. Arabs could contribute no more. The English thoroughbred existed. It changed a great deal, both by crossing the world to different environments, and by selective breeding over another two and a half centuries: but it was hardly to be infected by any outside blood.

What was this breed? What were its ingredients?

One writer has compiled a list of 178 imported stallions – Arabs, Barbs, Turks, 'Foreign Horses', and one Egyptian – and 31 mares.[17] The Stud Book lists 103 imported stallions. Pick[18] and other sources bring the number up to about 160.[19] The Stud Book finds 78 tap-root mares; Bruce Lowe calculates about 50, of various origin, whose progeny survive in tail female. These figures include many duplications. Several horses had various names. When they changed ownership they changed apparent identity. They often changed breed, alternating between Barb, Turk and Arab, according to whim or commercial advantage. Against this, many horses shared names. Dimple, Cricket, Why Not, Merlin, Careless, Bonny Black – some of the most resounding names of both course and paddock confuse fathers and sons, mothers and daughters, or similarity of choice by different owners. It has been calculated that eight *different* Dragons appear in Pick.[20]

The stallions are either imported or English-bred of pure imported blood, with few exceptions. If imported, they were given descriptive titles purporting to define their country of origin. The titles did no such thing. Osmer said in 1756: 'The name or breed assigned to foreign horses by their importers is not of the smallest consequence. If a horse be purchased in Turkey he is styled a Turk. Amongst us all southern horses are called Arabians.'[21] No wonder. A 1773 advertisement for the Damascus Arabian claimed he was 'of the purest Arabian blood, without any admixture of Turcoman or Barb',[22] which showed, as Lawrence pointed out, 'the fashionable opinion' at that date.

It has been argued that the Turks, if really Turkish, would have been Arab-Mongolian cross-breds – refined Turcomans.[23] It is far more likely that the Turkish commanders from whom they were captured secured good desert Arabs. The three on sale at Whitehall can have had no trace of Turcoman.

The confusion between Barb and Arab is often inextricable. Many Arabians and probably Turks were indeed Arab. The Barbs imported from France came from North Africa; and there were direct importations from Tunis and Morocco. But many horses were incorrectly described.

The female side is more obscure. There are a few Barb mares, *eo nomine*, in the Stud Book. (But 'Layton Barb Mare' does not mean Barb mare belonging to Layton, but mare, quite likely half-bred, by the Layton Barb.) There is an unknown number of Royal Mares: unknown because they were nearly all only so described. There is an even less guessable number of animals described only in terms like 'Dam of Clubfoot Daughter of Hautboy'.

What were these mares?

The Royal Mares have usually been identified with some supposed to have been sent by Lord Winchelsea to Charles II, together with some given the king by Louis XIV, and some which arrived with Catherine of Braganza. The first, if they existed, were Arabs, the second Barbs, and the third Lusitanians of Barb character. But this identification has not stood up to research;[24] it is not disproved, but it is dubious.

Another presumed source of these mysterious matriarchs is the Royal Stud at Tutbury. Some of the mares there were recovered after the Restoration and delivered to the king. They were of the best races in England. The famous Coffin Mare, found hidden in a cellar, was probably one of them.

A third possibility is that Charles II's breeding was not relevant at all: he bought his racehorses. He had a contractual arrangement with James Darcy of Sedbury by which the latter supplied him annually with horses. Possibly the Royal Mares were not royal mares but Darcy mares breeding royal horses. (There was certainly a Sedbury Royal Mare.) Whether from Tutbury or Yorkshire-bred, they could hardly have been of pure Eastern blood.

Most of the other foundation mares are an equal puzzle. Sensible guessing on the subject must take certain things into account. The superiority of the Barb was stated in the 16th century, and its pre-eminence for breeding racehorses at the beginning of the 17th. There were Barb enthusiasts importing privately in James I's reign. The Yorkshire studs, most single-minded about Eastern horses, were also least disturbed by the war. All this suggests a substantial infusion of Eastern blood in the mares covered by the early imported stallions.

But there is extremely little evidence of the importation of mares by individuals. The total number may be under a dozen. The balance of probability is that most of the significant mares were, like the Royal Mares, the best available half-breds.

It is impossible to assess the importance to the thoroughbred of these various contributions, known and unknown. If Eclipse were a bowl of soup, made up of ingredients which combined but did not change, he could be reckoned just under two-thirds definitely imported blood, a little over a fifth absolutely unknown blood, and 15 per cent Royal Mare. Of course genetics does not work in this mechanistic way. Nor can the Darley Arabian, at the top of the pedigree, or the Royal Mare, dam of Brimmer, at the bottom, be given by virtue of their position any more importance than any other individual: nor can the Darcy and Lister Turks, with so many crosses in the pedigree. It could be that the characters of the domestic mares were, over a period, overwhelmed by prepotent newcomers: that the thoroughbred, regardless of ancestry, is genetically Eastern. But the scale is large. The proportion of impure blood may be 30 per cent. Flying Childers was almost the last pure-bred Eastern racehorse; thereafter the thoroughbred was a different animal, a new and distinct hybrid.

THE LEEDES ARABIAN. This is one of the stallions privately imported to Yorkshire before the end of the 17th century which, like the Darcy 'Turks', have left no surviving male line, but are nevertheless as important as the three horses that have. Mr Edward Leedes's stallion has, by Lady Wentworth's reckoning, 112,667 crosses in the pedigree of Bahram (English triple crown 1935).

## Intentions and Methods of Breeding

It would be absurd to pretend that luck did not come into the thoroughbred's creation. It would be even more absurd to underrate the clarity with which his creators saw their objectives and the skill with which they pursued them.

Their intentions must be considered in two contexts: the state of the British horse, and the growth of racing.

Tudor methods had left the horse in a genetic mess. Fifty years later, the better the horses and stud-farms, the more likely they were to have been dispersed by the Great Rebellion, although some serious and successful breeding went on between 1640 and 1660. The light harness horse had not yet been re-invented – coach horses were still Dutch or Flemish heavyweights – but there was an enormous demand for hacks, hunters, *manège* horses, and light cavalry horses. These could not be predictably bred from England's 'bastard races'. Some Arabs and Barbs were doubtless imported partly, even primarily, to improve the breed for a dozen non-racing purposes.

Meanwhile racccourses multiplied their number between 1660 and the end of the century. Breeders needed racing to test the quality of their product; racing also needed breeders. There is therefore no reason to doubt that the primary purpose of most importations was breeding racehorses. Only on the turf could importers recoup their outlay, or breeders advertise their product.

Breeders set themselves to produce a better running-horse, and when they got it they knew what to call it: 'thro'-bred English horses are allowd to surpass most of ye same species,' wrote Lord Bristol in 1713.[25]

There was nothing slapdash about matings. Some Elizabethans tried to breed from the best. In James I's reign farmers knew better than to breed from a faulty animal, and some studs were already keeping meticulous records. There was, in fact, already a tradition of breeding selectively towards an objective. Now practical breeding took a step forward, with new agricultural skills. The Yorkshiremen who bred racehorses also bred cattle, sheep, pigs, and poultry. Soon they grew better feed and looked after their pasture. They went in for close inbreeding on the farm; they did it in the paddock too. Forward-looking farming shaped both the breeding and the care of the thoroughbred; it may also be that the agricultural revolution of the late 18th century owed a lot to the example of horse-breeders.

The early breeders were vividly aware of the racecourse test. Importers of stallions were denied this: hardly any imported horses ran. But the first get were run. Then, if they won, the stallions were patronized.

Some modern opinion would say that the early breeders overused a single stallion. They covered all their mares, year after year, with the one horse they had. The result has been called 'saturation' and even 'congestion'.[26] By the same token they often used the 'nick' – repeated a successful cross of individuals or close relatives. This could be quite deliberate. The Duke of Bolton bred Spark by his Bay Bolton. Spark stood at Ickworth for Lord Bristol. When Bay Bolton died, the duke got Spark back to cover the same mares and thus, hopefully, repeat his sire's success.

Stud-farms and training-stables were commonly combined, both at great establishments and the smaller stables of private men. This enabled horses to go in and out of training – many mares ran after foaling, many stallions after covering. This was thought to be good for them. It also meant that the same groom looked after a horse all through its racing and breeding careers.

In spite of these advantages, it was not easy to be a breeder. Lord Bristol gave it up in 1737: 'I have mett with so many disappointments, besides those commonly attending all studs. . . from the ignorance, carelessness, and drunkeness of grooms, &c., that I am finally determind to carry it on no farther.'[27]

# 7 Seventeenth-Century Europe

## *Italy: Palio Races; Barb Races; Cavalerizza*

In 16th-century Italy some of the ancient races for the *palii* were contested by rich owners with good horses. But in 17th-century Siena they were back to the turbulent townspeople and the broken-down nags.

Certain changes were made. In 1605 they measured the course of the *Palio alla Lunga*, and then calculated how many circuits of the Piazza the distance made. It was three: and the *Palio alla Tonda* was born. It became regular in the middle of the century.

The preliminaries were much the same: the races were announced on their traditional days, officials were named, the *contrade* entered. The city hired horses for eight lire, and they were distributed by lot to the wards. Sand was carried to the Piazza and spread out to make a track. Trials were run, to the peril of the people. There was a lavish procession with floats and allegories. The *fantini*, the jockeys, mounted and were handed whips now of a maximum specified length. They moved to the start. A trumpet sounded. The rope fell.

The *palio* was no longer given to the winning ward, but a silver goblet or its money equivalent. In 1621 a maximum of 10 runners was imposed, because of a fatal accident the year before. (Two or three centuries earlier so trifling a mishap would not have changed the rules.) The *fantini* were no longer members of the wards for which they rode; they were not even Sienese; they were professional riding-boys.

The violence and cheating in the race, and the brutality to the horses, were as great as ever. So was the turbulence of the crowd. It has been relevantly noted[1] that the Sienese had a reputation, unusual in Italy, for drunkenness, and at the running of the *palio* they were drunkest.

The Barb races in Rome were of some antiquity; they were unlike anything else in Europe. 'The most remarkable were the three races of the Barbary horses, that run in the Strada del Corso without riders, only having spurs so placed on their backs, and hanging down by their sides, as by their motion to stimulate them; then of mares, then of asses, of buffaloes, naked men, old and young, and boys, and abundance of idle and ridiculous pastime . . . The streets swarm with prostitutes, buffoons, and all manner of rabble.'[2]

During the 17th century the riderless barbs ran also in the streets of Florence, Bologna, and other cities, replacing the defunct *palio* races.

The *manège* was everywhere in Italy. Evelyn in Florence: 'At the Duke's Cavalerizza, the Prince has a stable of the finest horses of all countries, Arabs, Turks, Barbs, Gennets, English, &c., which are continually exercised in the *manège*.' In Naples: 'At the Viceroy's Cavalerizza I saw the noblest horses that I had ever beheld, one of his sons riding with that address and dexterity as I have never seen anything approach it.' Naples also had the best prostitutes; there were no less than 30,000 courtesans, who displayed 'all their natural and artificial beauty'.

Every major Italian city except Venice had its riding academies. The rage spread also into Switzerland; in Geneva they performed their exercises in the 'Campus Martius'.[3]

## The French Horse; The Manège; the Haras

In 1600 hunting was still 'the sole almost and ordinary sport of all our noblemen in Europe',[4] especially in France. It was restricted to those noblemen, a factor which 500 years earlier in England contributed to the hatred of the Norman lords, and which 200 years later in France was one of the most powerfully emotive causes of the Revolution.

The royal forests of St Germain and Fontainbleau were teeming with game. In the forest at Blois wolves were strictly preserved, but the most esteemed game was the stag.

The horse for forest hunting was still the part-Barb Limousin, and Evelyn noted of Marseille in 1644: 'The chief trade of the town is in silks and drugs out of Africa, Syria and Egypt, and Barbary Horses, which are brought hither in great numbers.[5] Some of these were re-exported to England. Some were raced, without being in English terms specialized racehorses. Most were hacks, hunters, and breeding stallions.

These Barbs, pure-bred imported and half-bred Limousin, were less esteemed than the Great Horse, whose trot was the *grand pas*. The reason for its continued glamour was the *manège*. One of the glories of 17th-century France is the height to which horse-manship was raised. The great master was Antoine de Pluvinel, who ran a riding-school for young nobles at the beginning of the century. Perhaps his greatest contribution was the re-introduction of kindness and patience into training (Xenophon had insisted on these qualities, but the Italians disdained them). In theory all his caprioles and curvettes were training for war. In practice it was peace that made the whole thing possible. The

BARB RACES IN SIENA. From an early period the Sienese sports were varied by bullfights, pageants, tourneys, mock battles, real battles and these races for riderless *barberi* along the streets. Sienese horses were said to be able to gallop *scossi*, without jockeys, as well as mounted; certainly these are not hung about with the Roman and Florentine goads (compare pp. 101, 194).

emphasis could move away from tourney and quintain. As late as 1669 a priest published a book on tourneys and jousts but in it he remarked that 'tourneys are now horse-races, tilting with sticks instead of lances.'[6]

The Great Horse was also the product of modern Europe's first National Stud. In 1685 Colbert founded the *Administration des Haras* and its great headquarters at le Pin, designed by Mansard as '*un Versailles rustique*',[7] not finished until 1730. The objective was a powerful *demi-sang*, largely of Percheron blood. The effect was not only indifference to thoroughbred racing, but enduring hatred of it.

## *Racing in 17th-Century France*

French horsemanship was influencing aristocratic England; English racing began to be popular among a few of the French nobility.

The first inkling of this is from the maréchal de Bassompierre, ambassador late in Elizabeth's reign. In 1626 he said that English racehorses were introduced into France and were highly esteemed. He knew what they were for: he was a gambler to the tune of losing £500,000 in a single year.[8]

A curious match took place in 1651. 'This day after dinner, 15 March 1651, a match for a wager of a thousand crowns was decided in the Bois de Boulogne between prince d'Harcourt and the duc de Joyeuse, both of whom ran horses that had been trained for the occasion in the village of Boulogne, on the Seine, in the same manner as English race horses. They had been fed for three weeks, or thereabouts, on bread made with beans and aniseed, in the place of oats, and two days previous to the contest taking place were each given between two and three hundred fresh eggs. They went the track from the barrier of la Muette, or Meute, and passed along the highroad in the direction of St Cloud. Turning, however, off to the right, they came on at this spot neck and neck. Prince d'Harcourt was attired in a grey overcoat, made exceedingly tight for the occasion, with a round close cap, in which all his hair was rolled up, and carried three pounds of lead in his pockets to weigh as much as Plessis du Vernet, the riding-master, who took the place and rode the horse of the duc de Joyeuse. But upon reaching the Madrid they rode past the Sieur Dauphin, who was awaiting them at that place on horseback. According to their *paction* Plessis took the lead, and coming in about a hundred feet before his antagonist at the barrier of la Muette, was declared the winner. Many of the Court personages were present.'[9]

Although few such matches are recorded, many must have taken place: enough for Cromwell to draw a complacent comparison between the frivolous French, who had races but no religion, and the godly English, who had the Gospel.[10]

A closer imitation of England came in 1683. Louis XIV offered a prize of 1000 pistoles for a race at Achères. Five horses were entered, one English. This belonged to Wharton. At the last moment his rider was revealed to be Charles II's oldest bastard the Duke of Monmouth, a fine horseman, like all his family. He was ambitious, Whig in sympathy, and detested the coming accession of his uncle the Duke of York; he was consequently in exile. Monmouth duly won. Louis XIV offered Wharton 1000 pistoles for the horse. Wharton refused to sell, but offered to give his horse to the king. Louis courteously refused.[11]

The next year the prince d'Harcourt once again 'Loses an important race at St Germain against M. de Marsan.'[12] Perhaps there was another *paction*.

In 1685 at le Pecq, near Vésinet, there was a match between the duc de Vendôme (*Grand Prior*) and M. le Grand (*Grand Ecuyer*). Another specifically English innovation, recognized as such by the French at the time, appeared here: a professional rider (*palefrenier* or *postillon*). Vendôme's horse was ridden by an English groom. He was beaten. People who backed it said the groom had been bribed to lose. Ears were boxed,

FRENCH SCIENTIFIC HORSEMANSHIP.
At the beginning of the 17th century
Antoine de Pluvinel adopted and
immensely improved the 16th-century
Neapolitan techniques of equitation.
His classic *Manège du Roy* was published
in 1623, and republished in 1628 as
*l'Instruction du Roy en l'exercise de
monter à cheval*. He is here (right) in the
middle, instructing Louis XII. The
royal pupil is striking the quintain,
usually a simple wooden target but here
a lifelike enemy. Jumping an obstacle
formed no part of the *manège*; the pupil
(left) is probably learning the capriole.

wigs pulled off, and swords half out of their scabbards before the Dauphin intervened.[13]

In 1692 at the same place Vendôme won a match by two lengths. This race was watched by the exiled James II; the only known occasion when he went racing after Charles II's death. Later the same year there was a race from the Pont de Sèvres to the Porte de la Conférence, between the duc de Mortemart, the marquis de Saint-Germain, and M. de Raré, owners up, 100 louis d'or each. Raré won in under eleven minutes; 'for this,' said a contemporary, 'you need a very fast horse and a very skilful rider.'[14]

In 1694 the king, princes, Court, and town were 'impassioned' by a harness-race against the clock. The duc d'Elbeuf bet M. de Chemeraut 1400 new louis d'or that his team would get from Paris to Versailles and back in under two hours. 'Six black mares ran this course; they were Dutch, and their tails and manes were cut in the English fashion. They had pulled the Prince of Orange's cannon and they were captured at the battle of Steinkerque.' Fourteen such mares were captured and sold; Elbeuf bought six of them. He boasted extravagantly about them; hence the bet. 'The parties asked M. le prince de Conti, whose perfect integrity is known, to do them the honour of being judge of the race and of the wager. M. d'Elbeuf and M. de Chemeraut agreed on a clock placed beside the Porte de la Conférence, where M. le prince de Conti was waiting to see the race start and finish.' Elbeuf took it fairly easily on the way out. 'They reached Versailles one hour and one minute after the start. As soon as they had been turned round the column, where the king sat, M. d'Elbeuf mounted the seat of the coach, and had Spanish wine given to the mares by six grooms who were waiting their for the purpose. He left immediately afterwards, and the whole race, going and coming, only took one hour and 53 minutes. So this prince won the bet, with the applause of the Court and people, who lined the road all the way from Paris to Versailles.'[15]

Spanish wine reappears – a single exotic touch – in the first French attempt at an exact copy of an English race. This was in 1700. 'There has hardly ever been a race like this in France, though they are common enough in England. It is what the English call *courir la vaisselle*. They have horses which they greatly value, which they buy expensively and which are only trained for this. M. le duc de Chartres has one which he bought for 600 pistoles in London. The speed of this horse gave the occasion for the race. The English ambassador has three which he values just as much, and the Grand Prior one which gives nothing away to the others. The idea was to bet on the speed of these five English horses. The great lords of the Court, after the English custom, offered to give something to the jockey who would ride the horse which reached the agreed finish before the others. A trusted man was picked to remember the donors and the sums offered. Then four big posts were set up in a square, a thousand paces apart.' Many grandees were present, of both the French and English Courts, 'with a prodigious concourse of persons of note of the Court and the town.'

'The race is run round these four posts, four laps in all. At the end of each the horses are rubbed down, and refreshed with a biscuit and some Spanish wine, which they are fed. The first post, at the start, is in the form of a gallows; attached to it are scales in which men and horse-furniture are weighed. Lead is fixed to the lightest to bring them all to the same weight. The start given, the five mounted jockeys, handsomely dressed in taffeta and satin, all in different colours, go off like streaks of lightning and come back a few minutes later to the first corner where they started, going always round outside the four posts.' English rules of racing were used. There was heavy betting. The duc de Chartres' horse was favourite but Vendôme won.[16]

This account was written in the same month as the race; the writer assumed total ignorance in his readers. Outside a few Anglophil enthusiasts, racing had scarcely scratched the surface of the French national consciousness.

## English Racing in Holland

In the late 1630s and 1640s a number of British officers served the States under the Prince of Orange. One of these was Henry Verney, whose spelling was uncertain and who turned his coat cheerfully in the Civil War. He was the younger son of a moderately distinguished family; he was, he admitted, 'in love with rasing'.

He seems to have been a typical member of a military-sporting set very similar to the officers of a garrison in British India two centuries later. He wrote to his brother Ralph in 1636: 'I can right you noe nuse but of a horsmache, as is to be run yearely at the Hagge for a cupe of 50 pounds, as every offecer gives yearly 20 shillings toewards the bying of it. I hope to winit afore I die myselfe. I have rod but to maches cince I saw you, and have won them both, I hope likewise to win the cup for the third.'

From other letters it seems that the horses raced were not Dutch; Picardy, Flanders and the Netherlands had specialized for centuries in the trotting Great Horse and the heavy harness horse. Henry and his brother officers imported English horses: in Henry's case, by begging from his family. His brother Edmund consequently wrote: 'I doe not at all wonder at brother Henry lyking a souldier's life, senc he can follow that and horse maches too.'

After the taking of Breda in October 1637 Henry 'rod a mach of six mile with a Dutchman for 50 pounds and won it, but it was not for myself but for a friend.'[17]

Of this flicker of English racing in Holland no trace survived the war between the countries later in the century.

# 8 Georgian Britain:

## Horses and Races

### Transformation of Racing in the 18th Century

When George I came grumpily over from Hanover there was racing all over Britain. Most of the races were four to six miles, and the runners typically six-year-olds. Matches were still in a great numerical majority, but for plates of all kinds there were fair-sized fields. Heat-racing was growing: a well-contested plate required a horse to run sixteen miles, with half-hour rests at the rubbing-house between heats. Training-grooms were humble servants who obeyed orders. Horses were still ridden by the owners or their friends, or by little riding-boys if the weight was a feather. The owners were grandees or considerable squires. Horses changed hands by private treaty. Colours were inconsistent and subject to whim. The sport had no government; each meeting was autonomous; each made its own rules and enforced them according to its taste. Many meetings were tiny, with tiny prizes. There was no record of racing, official or unofficial, except in a few private stud-books; and no central registry of names or pedigrees.

From 1714 the changes were enormous. The races changed: the horses ran younger and the distances grew shorter. The owners changed: the greatest horse of the century was owned by an Irish adventurer who spent a period as the front legs of a sedan chair. The horses changed: by selective breeding, the long-staying weight-carrying thorough-bred developed into the middle-distance horse and the sprinter. A governing body started to form itself, and well before the end of the century it was powerful enough to tell the Prince of Wales to dismiss his jockey. Records began to be kept. By the time George III was mad and his son was Regent, the turf was transformed in practically every detail.

### Frampton and the Royal Stable

George I kept on Tregonwell Frampton and his Newmarket and Hampton Court establishments. There were at least eight running-horses and three boys of the king's at Newmarket, racing in Frampton's name. The Royal Stud had a widely-varying number of stallions, mares, colts, fillies, and 'supernumarys', and the running-horses were regularly boarded there for a month at a time. Six were 'dismissed' at the end of 1718, as appears in the balance-sheet 'sworn to by Mr Marshall, Studd Groom'[1]; this was weeding out rather than closing down, since Frampton was there for many years yet.

Frampton was up to his old tricks under a new dynasty. In 1719 there was a great match on Banstead Downs: Mr Green, a Quaker and vintner, hired a mare called Creeper and matched it against Frampton's Hobler for £400. Hobler won two heats, and the mare went lame. ''Tis computed that in the bets on the Vintner's there was lost £10,000, and a Portugese Jew suffered extremely. The Quaker has since been advised to mind his own business without concerning himself about Horse Races and other ruinous diversions.'[2]

Frampton, Queen Anne's old 'governor', is usually said to have been a kind of royal representative at Newmarket, overseer of the races and arbiter of disputes. This seems likely enough. Certainly George II confirmed him in his position and title, until his death in 1728. He left his horses to his neighbour the Earl of Godolphin, owing to a family quarrel of great antiquity and bitterness[3]: springing unpleasant surprises to the last.

## Legislation and Prizes

The major racecourses in the 18th century can be defined as those at which Royal Plates were run for. George II increased the number from 11 to 16, excluding Scotland and Ireland. The number was later increased again, and the plates turned into their money equivalent, fixed at £100. For other plates at the major meetings the normal value was £50.

An enormous iceberg grew below this glittering tip. In 1736: 'It is surprising to think what a height this spirit of horse-racing is now arrived at in this kingdom, where there is scarce a village so mean that has not a bit of plate raised once a year for the purpose.'[4] In some areas half-bred hunters were raced, in others ponies or cart-horses. A lot of this village racing was rough and dishonest. The prizes were tiny, and the plate unlikely to be worth its putative value. The owners were farmers, inn-keepers, corn-merchants and apothecaries. Races were fixed or foully-ridden, officials bribed or terrorized, and the public swindled.

The only control was legislative. 1740 saw 'An Act to restrain and prevent the Excessive Increase of Horse Races.'[5] The preamble complains of little meetings which encourage idleness, impoverish the 'meaner subjects' of the king, and lead to the deterioration of the breed. No race therefore is to be of less value than £50, except at Newmarket and Hambleton (a recognition of the special role of these two courses). The Act also sets out minimum weights: Five-year-olds 10 stone (140 lb.), six-year-olds 11 stone (154 lb.), seven-year-olds 12 stone (168 lb.). This section sought, like the 12-stone plates, to encourage the breeding of stout horses.

Five years later another Act[6] relaxed the rules of weight, thus permitting the handicap matches which had been frequent for at least half a century; but it reaffirmed the £50 rule.

Some village racing undoubtedly went on, braving the Magistrates' Officers; but the mainstream of racing was unaffected, because the important owners of good horses did not run them for a £6 prize at Kentish Town or Chester-le-Street.

Increasingly during the century, the statutory £50 was cash. But there remained a great deal of plate, for all or part of the value. Another normal prize was hogsheads of claret. The sons and daughters of Herod won £201,505 in stakes, 40 hogsheads of claret, three cups, and the Whip.

This last trophy was a Newmarket eccentricity. It had to be challenged for. It was alleged to be Charles II's, and later incorporated hairs from Eclipse's mane and tail. Its winners included Matchem, Gimcrack, and Pot-8-os. It was imitated in Ireland, by George IV's gift in 1821 – an occasion made memorable by the king's diarrhoea – in Germany, and in America. It can hardly have been worth £50, but that was permissible at Newmarket.

## Developments in Racing: New Kinds of Races

Cash, plate, cup, claret or Whip were run for by the good horses in four-mile heats at level weights. During the century all kinds of changes happened. Four of the most

RICHARD TATTERSALL. 'Old Tatt' (1724–1795) started life the son of a North Country yeoman, and died as head of the world's first and greatest company of bloodstock auctioneers, proprietor of an estate at which he often entertained the Prince of Wales, and owner of Highflyer (pictured behind him), the champion racehorse of his time. Clamped between hand and stud-book is the order 'Highflyer not to be sold.'

important originated in matches: handicaps, weight-for-age, give-and-take, and sweep-stakes.

Two gentlemen at Newmarket who wanted to match two horses of different merit asked a third to handicap them. This was done in the Restoration jovially, after dinner. In George II's reign a curious ceremony was observed, described in Pond's Kalendar of 1751, reproduced by Weatherby, and again by Rous: 'A Handicap Match is, A, B, and C to put an equal sum each into a hat; C, who is the handicapper, makes a match for A and B, who, when they have perused it, put their hands into their pockets, and draw them out closed; then they open them together, and if both have money in their hands, the match is confirmed; if neither have money, it is no match. In both cases the handicapper draws all the money out of the hat; but if one has money in his hand, and the other none, then it is no match; and he that has money in his hand is entitled to the deposit in the hat.'[7]

It ought to have been a short step to bringing a field together by adjusting their weights. In fact the first public handicap for more than two horses was the Oatlands Stakes at Ascot in 1791. The weights ranged from 5 st. 3 lb. to 9 st. 10 lb. (73 to 136 lb.). The winner was the Prince of Wales's Baronet, ridden by Sam Chifney.

The weight-for-age scale of the 1740 Act does not imply fields of different ages: merely the burdens proper to each. Different-aged horses were nevertheless matched together, at weights which made such matching fair. This principle was extended about the middle of the century to fields of horses, at weights still bizarre by modern standards, though more restrained than Parliament's. The Chester City Plate of 1780 was 'for five, six-year-olds, and aged horses; five-year-olds to carry 8 st. 2 lb. (114 lb.), six-year-olds 8 st. 11 lb. (123 lb.), and aged horses 9 st. 5 lb. (131 lb.); mares to be allowed 3 lb.'

The Master of the Horse admitted a weight-for-age scale into King's Plates in 1799.

The theory of a give-and-take race was that a big horse gave weight to a smaller one according to a scale of weight-for-size. This was easier to apply than the agonizing calculations (and recriminations) attendant on handicapping.

The date of the first give-and-take plate is uncertain: it might be the beginning of the century. A race was thus advertised in 1711: 'On the 9th of October next will be run for on Coleshill Heath, in Warwickshire, a plate of six guineas value, three heats, by any horse, mare or gelding, that hath not won above the value of five pounds, the winning horse to be sold for 10 pounds, to carry 10 stone weight if 14 hands high: if above, or under, to carry or be allowed weight for inches, and to be entered on Friday the fifth, at the Swan, in Coleshill, by six in the evening. Also a plate of less value, to be run for by asses.'[8]

Give-and-take weights could be calculated from the bottom – a 12-hand pony was given 5 stone (70 lb.); when they became frequent about the middle of the century, a central mark was taken. The Calendars typically show a 14-hand horse allotted 9 stone (126 lb.); the gradation up or down was 7 lb. to the inch. Thus a 15.2 hand giant carried 12 stone (168 lb.).

This system ought to have been fraud-proof, but it was not. A horse could be taught to stand with its feet wide apart, to reduce its height at the withers and its weight in the race. To circumvent this, courses had stone slabs sunk into the grass, with positions marked for the horses' feet. This was still not good enough. An aged man recalled, in 1827, that he had very long before, as a lad, been a ditcher and repairer on the Knavesmire course at York. He saw many measurings. The trick was to rap your horse sharply over the withers, again and again, in the stable. It learned to shrink down when touched on the withers, as by the measuring-rod, thus losing an inch or two.[9]

Give-and-take races went on longer in the North than in the South; they lasted until the end of the century.

The financing of a match was easy: a given sum put up by each, winner take all.

SIR CHARLES BUNBURY WITH TRAINER AND LAD. Bunbury (1740–1821) was the son of the Rector of Mildenhall. He became M.P. for Suffolk in 1761; in a very long Parliamentary career he made no impression at Westminster whatever. In 1762 he married Lady Sarah Lennox, daughter of the 2nd Duke of Richmond, who had been as a 16-year-old rashly wooed by the Prince of Wales (George III). In 1764 he succeeded as 6th baronet, and in 1768 he was a Steward of the Jockey Club for the first time. His preoccupation with the turf bored his wife, who ran away, but he did racing more good than anyone between Charles II and Admiral Rous. His training-groom Cox (centre) was dying in the spring of 1801, while training Bunbury's Eleanor (by Whisky, a grandson of Eclipse, out of Young Giantess by Diomed). His last words, muttered to the hovering clergyman, were: 'Depend upon it, that Eleanor is the hell of a mare.' A few weeks later she became the first filly to win both the Derby and the Oaks.

Originally an owner who scratched lost his whole stake; half-forfeit became normal about 1700. The trouble was that the winning owner provided half his own prize. An important Georgian invention was transferring the subscription principle of the match to a larger field. Twenty entries at £50 each made a prize worth running for, and the winner only contributed a small percentage. This was called a sweepstakes; it started about 1750.

It grew fast. Admiral Rous computed as follows[10]:

| 1762 | 49 | matches | 38 | sweepstakes | 205 plates |
| 1807 | 189 | matches | 263 | sweepstakes | 269 plates |
| 1843 | 86 | matches | 897 | sweepstakes | 191 plates |

The advantage of sweepstakes to owners was overwhelming; it was bound to grow. This was not altogether welcomed. An anonymous Victorian lamented a development which allowed Mr B, with no land and not much money, to defeat Lord A, whose stud cost him £15,000 a year. And the larger the field the easier for a horse to be pulled, or for foul riding to spoil a favourite's chance.[11]

If sweepstakes grew and grew, matches grew before they shrank. This was a phenomenon of more owners with more horses. Matches were more and more apt to be handicaps or at weight-for-age and sex, less and less likely to be in heats. John Lawrence says that their stakes were reduced in the last quarter of the century as the value of sweepstakes increased.[12]

But matches could still be of great value and great interest. The Hambletonian-Diamond match, 25 March 1799 at Newmarket, was for 3000 guineas. It was a North-South contest. Hambletonian (by a son of Eclipse out of a daughter of Highflyer) had won the St Leger of 1795. He was owned by Sir Harry Tempest Vane and ridden by Frank Buckle. Before and during the race the latter was cool, the former not. Mr Cook-

THE HAMBLETONIAN-DIAMOND MATCH. 'The Famous Match between Sir Harry Tempest Vane's Horse HAMBLETONIAN carrying 8 Stone 3 Pounds rode by Mr Buckle beating DIAMOND, the Property of Joseph Cookson Esqr. over the Beacon Course, Newmarket, on Monday the 25 March 1799 being the Craven Meeting – This race was run for THREE THOUSAND GUINEAS a Side half forfeit. Diamond was rode by Mr Dennis Fitzpatrick and carried 8 Stone. Betting was 5 to 1 on Hambletonian at Starting. The Beacon Course is nearly Straight and is Four Miles and near two Furlongs in Length. The race was run in Eight Minutes and a half.' Another record gives the time as 7 min. 15 secs. The Beacon Course dated from Charles II's time; it became obsolete early in the 19th century and by 1900 was used only for The Whip.

MATCHEM. Matchem (1748, pedigree overleaf) was 'an excellent honest horse'; and although probably short of brilliant speed he transmitted his honesty. It became proverbial among breeders to use 'Snap for speed and Matchem for truth and daylight': Snap, by Snip, being a very fast grandson of Flying Childers. It is interesting that Matchem's few tail-male descendants are notable for exactly his qualities.

don's Diamond was one of the best horses in the South, and he received 3 lb. from Hambletonian. Diamond was ridden by Dennis Fitzpatrick, the first Irish professional jockey in England. Hambletonian won a very hard race by a 'half neck', thanks to Buckle's brilliance. His owner is said to have been rendered so ill by excitement that he left the turf.

Side-betting was estimated between 200,000 and 300,000 guineas. Wagering on this scale invited rigging. Lawrence says that many matches were dishonestly staged by 'partnerships', both stables backing the horse of one of them.[13]

There was also an enduring tradition of bizarre matches. In 1744 'They write from Lincoln, that on Thursday seven night, there was a very extraordinary horse-race on the course of that city.' A six-year-old was matched against a 21-year-old, over 14 miles, for 100 guineas. The race took 39 minutes and was won by the six-year-old by a bare length. 'There were great wagers laid, and the greatest concourse of people ever seen there on such an occasion.'[14] At York in 1788 there was a 30-stone (420 lb.) match. Several people had to lift each saddle on.

The ancient diversion of a match against the clock was still good for public interest. In May 1758 Miss Pond (daughter of the publisher of the Kalendar) betted to ride 1000 miles in 1000 hours, for 200 guineas. She did it easily.[15] The next year Jennison Shafto undertook, for an unknown wager, to ride 50 miles in two hours. He did it in one hour 49 minutes 17 seconds, using 10 horses.[16] Two years later the same Shafto bet Mr Meynell (who was constantly involved in this kind of thing) that a man could ride 100 miles a day for 29 successive days. Mr Woodcock did it, going round and round Newmarket Heath for the whole of May.[17] These are typical examples among hundreds.

## The Great Horses: Matchem, Herod, Eclipse, Highflyer

Between the 1720s and the 1750s there were many excellent racehorses, but no champion of the status of Flying Childers.

Between 1748 and 1774 four horses of supreme importance were foaled: Matchem (properly Match'em) 1748, Herod (properly King Herod) 1758, Eclipse 1764, and Herod's son Highflyer 1774. Only the oldest of these was bred in the North.

Matchem was bred by Mr Holmes of Carlisle, and sold to Mr Fenwick of Bywell, Northumberland. He was a very good racehorse if not a great champion. He went to

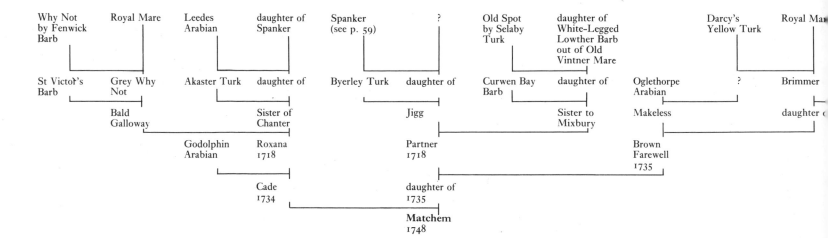

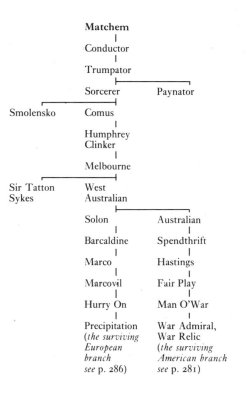

stud at Bywell and stood there until 1781. He is the reason for the tail-male survival of the Godolphin Arabian, and his descendants are the third most important male-line family in the Stud Book.

Herod was bred by the Duke of Cumberland. This was the third son of George II. He had been a successful Commander in Chief in Scotland; his later nickname of 'Butcher' was probably unfair to his treatment of the Jacobites after Culloden. He was unsuccessful on the Continent, for which his father never forgave him. Horace Walpole quotes a friend who said he looked (one night at cards) like the prodigal son and the fatted calf both. Walpole called him 'Nolkejumskoi' and noted his heavy gambling.[18] Immediately after the Rebellion of '45 he was made Ranger of Windsor Park where – the one member of the royal family then interested in such things – he started a stud. This meant enclosing paddocks, and he 'incredibly disgusted the neighbourhood of Windsor by excluding them from most of the benefits of the park there.'[19] He was probably a founder and certainly an early member of the Jockey Club. In 1758 he bred a colt who first ran un-named, was then called King Herod, and from whose name the King was later dropped. Like Matchem, Herod was a good horse but not a champion. He was beaten several times and at least once broke a blood-vessel. After the Duke's death in 1765 he was bought by Sir John Moore. He went to stud in 1768 near Bury, where he stood until 1780. He is the reason for the tail-male survival of the Byerley Turk, and his descendants are the second most important male line.

In 1764, the year of the great eclipse, a chestnut colt with a white blaze and one white leg was foaled for the Duke of Cumberland in Windsor Park. He was by Marske out of

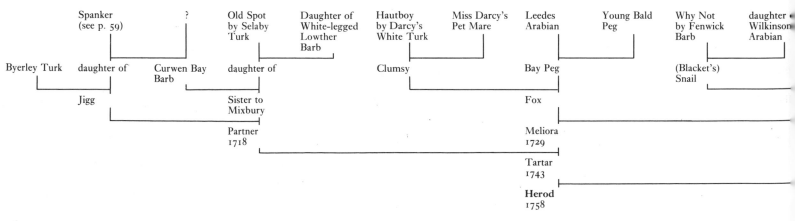

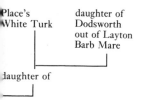

Spiletta: breeding which has not, however, been universally accepted. A doubt, tiny but ineradicable, derives from John Lawrence and Richard Tattersall, both of whom knew the horse and his handlers. Their conviction was that Spiletta was covered not only by Marske but also by Shakespeare. Then Eclipse became undisputed champion. Lawrence says: 'The fact of the double cover seems never to have been disputed, until Eclipse became so celebrated, and that Wildman had got hold of Marske, when doubtless it was a powerful interest with him, to insist on the paternity of his racer for his own stallion. . . . In a conversation on the matter, with Sam Larner, Eclipse's groom, he remarked, "*now* they say the mare was not covered by Shakespeare".'[20]

When the Duke died the yearling was put up for auction. Mr Wildman, a meat salesman and substantial grazier, bought him for £75. He was a difficult colt; he is said to have been disciplined by an Epsom rough-rider, who also took him poaching at night. This is neither proved nor unlikely.

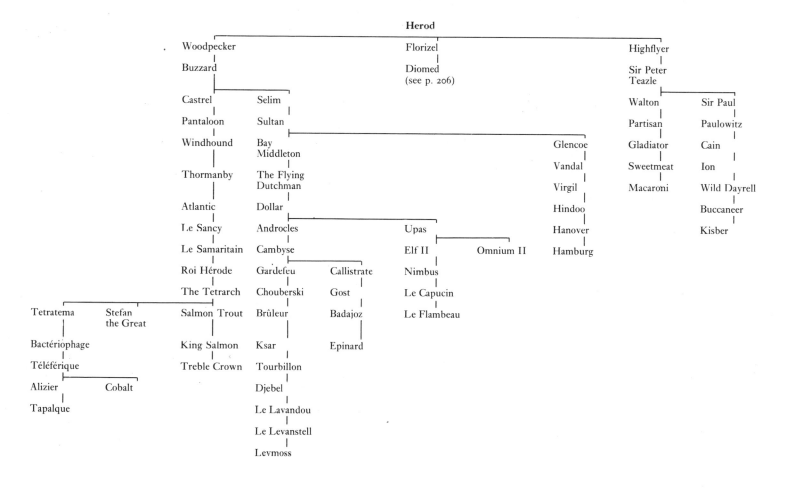

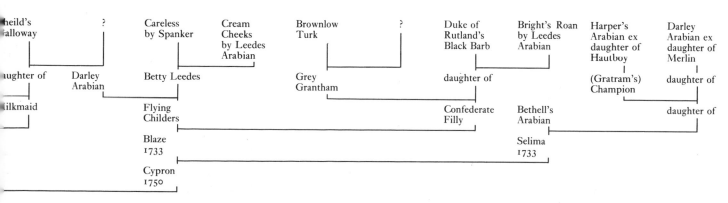

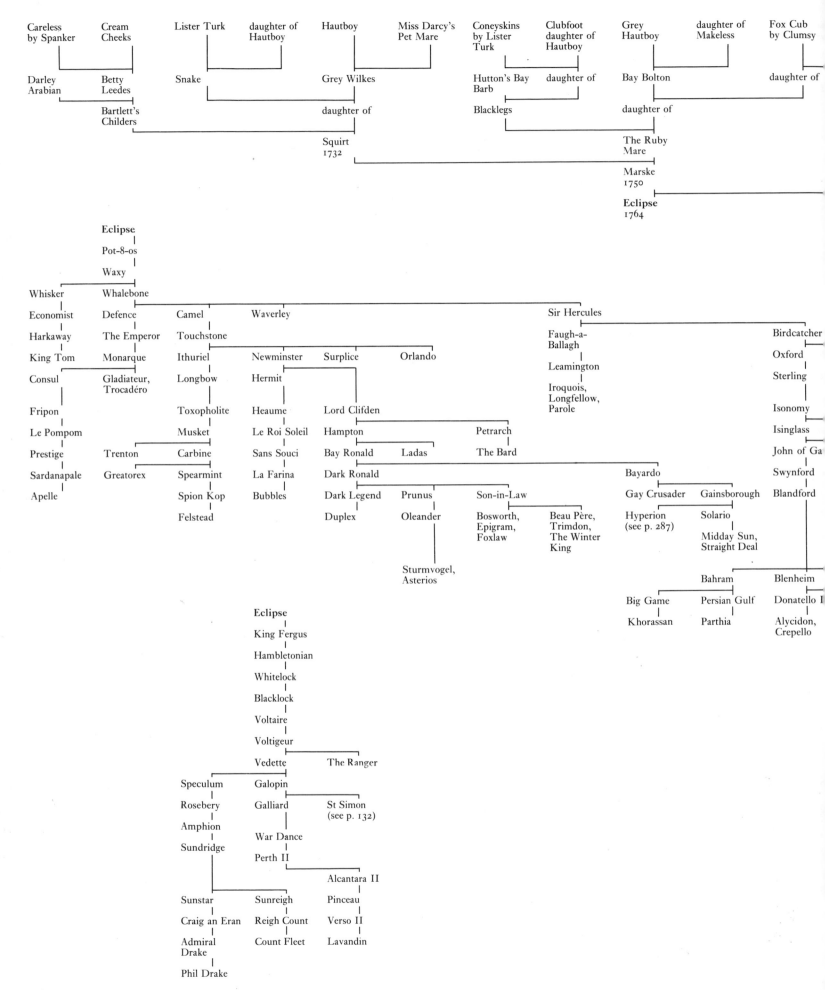

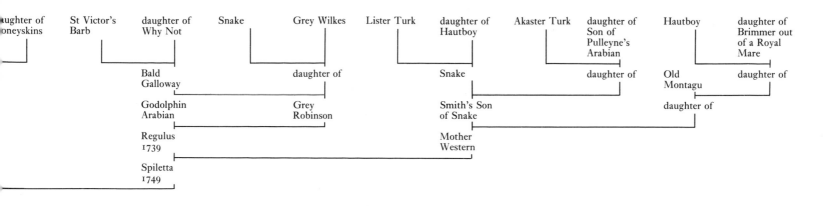

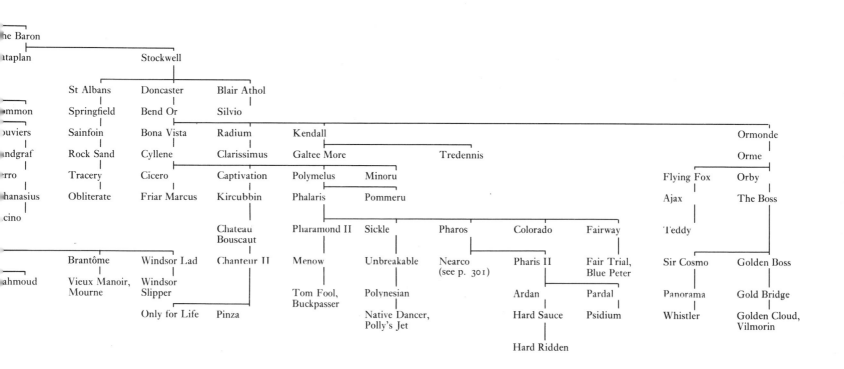

At five Eclipse went into serious training, and in April 1769 he had a secret trial on Banstead Downs. The touts came. 'They were a little late; but they found an old woman who gave them all the information they wanted. On inquiring whether she had seen a race, she replied she could not tell whether it was a race or not, but she had just seen a horse with a white leg running away at a monstrous rate, and another horse a great way behind, trying to run after him; but she was sure he never would catch the white-legged horse if he ran to the world's end.'[21]

Eclipse first ran in public in a race of four-mile heats, for £50, at Epsom, on 3 May 1769. Rumours of the trial made his price 4 to 1 on. He won the first heat easily. At this point an Irish gambler called Dennis O'Kelly enters history. Not liking the odds for the second heat, he offered, for any sum, to name the *placings* of the runners. His prediction is the most famous five-word phrase in racing history: 'Eclipse first, the rest nowhere.' Nowhere meant distanced: which is to say that the beaten horses were too far away from the winner at the finish for the judge to place them. The distance-post was normally

240 yards short of the winning-post: the theoretical limit of the judge's vision. A distanced horse was unplaced and disqualified from subsequent heats. Eclipse won his heat by more than a furlong; O'Kelly won his bet. Clearly he knew all about the trial. He may have been in league with Wildman; he may have been in league with the touts.

Wildman immediately got hold of Marske from the Dorset farmer to whom this unfashionable stallion had gone. (He later went to Lord Abingdon, breeder of Eclipse's greatest son Pot-8-os.) Dennis O'Kelly meanwhile bought two legs of Eclipse from Wildman for 650 guineas. The new part-owner was a cheerful extrovert who had emerged from County Carlow to make his fortune in London. He was reduced to carrying a sedan chair (according to perfectly credible legend) and further reduced to the Fleet. But he was a lucky and competent professional gambler, and by this time he was rising rapidly.

Eclipse had a two-year career of contemptuous wins and walk-overs. At the end of his first season O'Kelly bought Wildman out for 1100 guineas, a steep price for the time and a marvellous bargain. Eclipse won 18 recorded races, including 11 King's Plates. He was never whipped, spurred, or headed. He became, literally, matchless. He went to O'Kelly's stud in 1771. (He is said to have been taken in a cart. If so, he is probably the first thoroughbred ever to be 'vanned' or 'boxed', instead of walking along the road.) He is the reason for the survival of the Darley Arabian male line. He is part of the reason for the extraordinary numerical superiority of this over the other two.

His conformation, even his size, have given rise to much research and dispute.[22] His head was criticized; he was unusually high behind. His action was a revelation. It is impossible to guess by how many pounds he was superior to the best other horse in England; impossible to compare him to champions of earlier or later times.

Herod's most important son Highflyer was bred by Sir Charles Bunbury at Barton. Sir Charles sold him to Lord Bolingbroke, of whom Sir Charles's ex-wife Lady Sarah had said 'Ld Bolingbroke is much the same as mad when he is drunk, & that he is generally.'[23] Like Eclipse he was 'never beaten and never paid forfeit.' He was bought from Bolingbroke by Richard Tattersall, who loved him and named his house after him.

It follows that by 1780 there were two supreme stallions, Eclipse and Highflyer, each owned by a man who was businesslike and knowledgeable. O'Kelly, now Colonel (an authentic rank, though in a farcical regiment of militia) wanted Eclipse to get the best horses possible, in order to increase his value as a stallion. Clearly the thing was for Eclipse to cover the daughters of Herod and Highflyer. Simultaneously, Tattersall wanted to do the best he could by Highflyer. He therefore mated him with the daughters of Eclipse. Both breeders were thus working to the same nick.

Eclipse was young enough to sire Derby winners, and got three: Young Eclipse, Saltram, and Sergeant. The first and third belonged to O'Kelly; the second beat a horse of O'Kelly's, Dungannon, also by Eclipse. The full brothers Dungannon and Sergeant were of typical O'Kelly breeding, being out of Aspasia by Herod. Saltram, out of Virago by Snap, went to America (unless, which is conceivable, he went to Russia). He left no male line, but his daughter out of a daughter of Syme's Wildair was dam of Timoleon.

Eclipse's most important sons were King Fergus, and a colt bred by Lord Abingdon in 1773 and sold by him to Lord Grosvenor. In his stable, for some reason, he was unglamorously called Potato. Lord Abingdon required a stable-boy to paint this name over the stable door. The boy wrote Potoooooooo. This was presently rendered Pot-8-o, and later became Pot-8-os. Some writers still prefer the stable-boy's version.

Pot-8-os' most important son was Waxy, and Waxy's was Whalebone, both Derby winners. These two are the supreme examples of the Eclipse-Herod nick; the male line they founded is the world's most important; this is why Eclipse must share his pedestal.

Another horse of this era demands mention. In 1760 Mr Gideon Elliott of Hampshire bred a grey colt by Cripple out of Miss Elliott. He first ran at Epsom as a four-year-old. He ran nearly 40 races and won nearly 30. In July 1765 Lady Sarah Bunbury wrote:

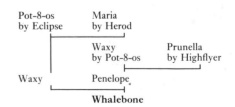

Whalebone is thus not only bred to the nick, but is the product of parents both bred to it. Whalebone is inbred 1 × 2 to Waxy, 2 × 3 to Pot-8-os, 3 × 4 to Eclipse, and 3 × 4 to Herod.

'There was a meeting of two days this time of year, to see the sweetest little horse run that ever was; his name is Gimcrack, he is delightful.'[24] He was barely over 14 hands. He was owned successively by Mr Wildman; Lord Bolingbroke; Lady Sarah's husband; Lord Grosvenor (who when he was ennobled had no idea to what degree, as instead of 'kissing hands' he was watching a trial at Newmarket); and comte Lauraguais, as unpopular in France as at Newmarket. Gimcrack was almost a Galloway; he would nowadays be called a pony. He was not really in the class of the great champions. But he held and still holds public affection, as very few racehorses do. He was perhaps the first horse to carve himself a place in turf history by virtue of his charm.

## Changes in the Thoroughbred; Racing Young Horses

Horses got bigger. Admiral Rous thought the thoroughbred had grown by an inch every 25 years – a hand a century.[25] They got better. In 1850 – 'the form of the best race-horse of 1750 is inferior to that of a common plater of the present day.'[26] And they matured earlier. In 1769 at Epsom, in the four-mile heat race won by Eclipse, the weights were: five-year-olds 8 stone (112 lb.) six-year-olds 9 st. 3 lb. (129 lb), 'aged' – seven-year-olds and upwards – 9 st. 12 lb. (138 lb.). Rous thought this was grotesque. But the Georgians must have been right about their own horses; their seven-year-olds ran and won giving 26 lb. to five-year-olds.

Horses also became shorter runners. A four-mile heat was often a three-and-three-quarter-mile dawdle, followed by a furious quarter-mile sprint in which the mounted spectators perilously joined. But not always. Early Georgian horses must have had bottom-less stamina.

The weight-for-age scale and the distances of Georgian races suggest a racehorse very different from ours, and one which had changed substantially well before the end of the 18th century. There were also changes in taste and in economics. Racegoers wanted more spectacle and more opportunities to bet: more and shorter races. Owners and breeders wanted a quicker return on their capital. Ultimately both desires were satisfied by the deliberate breeding of 'early' horses, which are always sprinters, but it is doubtful if this happened in the 18th century. What they did breed for was speed, and the horses they produced incidentally matured earlier.

The first recorded four-year-old race was at Hambleton in August 1727, and there were others in Yorkshire in the same year. Three-year-old racing also began in Yorkshire, at Bedale, as early as 1731. It was not imitated in the South until 1756, at Newmarket. Pond recorded the latter race as a freak; it was not repeated until 1761.

The first two-year-old known to have been seen on a racecourse was Gibscutski, who beat a six-year-old mare, receiving 3 stone (42 lb.), in the first October meeting of 1769 at Newmarket. This was another freak. The 'two-year-olds' in the Craven Stakes in March 1771 at Newmarket were, of course, three-year-olds, horses' birthdays being 1 May. There was a two-year-old match in 1773, and a sweepstakes (three ran) in 1776. The first known two-year-old race in the North was at Hambleton in 1779, a handicap match over an astonishing two miles.

By the mid-1780s two-year-old racing was established. The July Stakes at Newmarket is the oldest two-year-old race still in the Calendar; in its early days the produce of Eclipse and Highflyer carried an extra 3 lb.

Sir Charles Bunbury was uniquely influential at Newmarket, so the guess has often been made that he invented two-year-old racing. On the other hand Yorkshire pioneered the racing of younger horses; it may be a Northern idea.

Yearlings were raced from 1786. There was never much of it. The 'yearlings' that ran early in the season we should call two-year-olds. A yearling which was a yearling beat a three-year-old, at 3 stone, at the Newmarket Houghton meeting in 1791, over an

DONCASTER RACES. Doncaster racing had a long and patchy history. It became regular early in the 18th century and important in the middle. In 1778 it moved to this new course on the Town Moor. The towering grandstand was started in 1776 by order of the Corporation; it cost £2,637 and the architect John Carr was paid 100 guineas. In 1809, as a private speculation, another stand was built, overlooking the paddock, by a Mr Maw: but it became instead Miss Murphy's School for Young Ladies, then Dr Inchbald's School for Boys, and in 1830 a county school for deaf and dumb children, who watched the racing from their balcony.

85

HIGHFLYER. Highflyer (1774) was named for the trees round the paddock at Barton where he ran as a foal. He first ran, for Lord Bolingbroke, as a three-year-old over two miles at Newmarket (compare Eclipse, who first ran as a five-year-old in four-mile heats). After a triumphant turf career he became, under Richard Tattersall's expert control, a stallion almost as important as Eclipse, his stud-fees financing the rebuilding of Highflyer Hall (above left). When he died in 1793 his tombstone read: 'Here lieth the perfect and beautiful symmetry of the much lamented Highflyer, by whom and his wonderful offspring the celebrated Tattersall acquired a noble fortune, but was not ashamed to acknowledge it.'

extended quarter-mile. Shrewsbury in 1859 ran the last public yearling race; soon afterwards the Jockey Club rules forbade the racing of babies.

## Doncaster and the St Leger; Epsom and the Oaks and Derby

Four-year-old and two-year-old racing grew lustily, but the greatest *réclame* came to be attached to three-year-olds. Nothing illustrates this more vividly than the establishment of three (then five) three-year-old sweepstakes whose prestige became so great that they were given the special title of Classic Races.

Doncaster had racing before 1600. In 1615 racing there was stopped by the Corporation 'for the preventinge of sutes, quarrels, murders, and bloodsheds.'[27] Throughout the 17th century Doncaster racing was intermittent and of minor importance. Early in the 18th century the Corporation backed it: there was a Town Plate in 1716, a Corporation Plate in 1764, and a Gold Cup in 1766.

In 1776 a group of sportsmen subscribed to a new sweepstakes. They included the Marquis of Rockingham and Lieut. General Anthony St Leger of Park Hill. Their race was for three-year-olds, over two miles, at 2 lb. weight-for-sex. It was the first three-year-old race at Doncaster. The winner was Lord Rockingham's filly Alabaculia, ridden by John Singleton. It was run on the old course at Cantley Common.

Next year the event was repeated, still unnamed, with many more subscribers. Early in 1778 there was a dinner at the Red Lion in Doncaster, apparently of the subscribers to the third running. Lord Rockingham was present. The race might easily have been called the Rockingham; it is supposed to have been at his suggestion that it was named instead after the popular St Leger. The 1778 race is accordingly shown in the Calendar as the St Leger Stakes, run for the first time on the new Town Moor course.

The race was reduced to 1 mile 6 furlongs 193 yards in 1813, and from 1814 the Calendar says it was run on the 'St Leger Course'. It grew from a local to a national event.

Doncaster was a broad 'galloping' track, like Newmarket. At Epsom there was a course of quite different character, all up and down and sharp corners.

In 1726 the waters, the parties, and the gaming-houses of Epsom were still much more important than the races, although the downs were 'covered with grass finer than Persian carpets, and perfumed with wild thyme and juniper.'[28] In 1730, 'On the Downs is a four mile course for horse-races from North East to South West, which is much frequented.'[29] Racing became annual for the first time. In 1743 there were good fields and good prizes, and royalty was present. By 1776 Epsom was a major course (though not of King's Plate status) with two meetings: 'this day the October meeting at Epsom begins, at which good sport is expected, many capital horses being gone down there from Newmarket, to run for the different plates and sweepstakes.'[30]

Shortly before this the young 12th Earl of Derby, keen on racing and even keener on cocking, took a converted inn near Epsom called The Oaks from his uncle General Burgoyne. Derby was clubbable and sporting; he filled The Oaks during race-weeks. By the May meeting of 1778 the three-year-old sweepstakes at Doncaster had been run twice: this may have inspired what followed. At a party at The Oaks at this meeting, Derby and his friends planned a three-year-old sweepstakes, for fillies only, to be run next summer and to be called the Oaks. Derby won it himself with Bridget.

At a party attendant on this event, a second three-year-old sweepstakes was planned, to be run the following year, by colts and fillies, over the surprisingly short distance of a mile. (It became a mile and a half in 1784.) Sir Charles Bunbury was present, still in his thirties but an eminent figure on the turf. According to enduring legend, a coin was tossed to decide whether the new race should be called the Derby or the Bunbury. Sir Charles lost the toss, but he won the first race with Diomed, by Florizel (by Herod) out of a Spectator mare.

The next seven Derbies may still have been minor races, but they were contested by beautifully-bred horses. Three were won by sons of Eclipse – Young Eclipse, Saltram, Sergeant – and two by sons of Highflyer – Noble and Sir Peter Teazle. The last of these was Derby's own; it was named in honour of his future second wife, the delightful actress Mrs Farren, who had a particular success in the *School for Scandal*.

The race was Sir Peter's first time out; this was true of many early Derby winners. Like Diomed he was ridden by Sam Arnull. Lord Derby so admired the blood that had produced the horse that he inbred to it to a degree which has astonished posterity.

## Newmarket; Other Meetings; Ascot

Newmarket kept its pre-eminence throughout the century. It was unquestioned headquarters. By the end of George III's reign it had seven meetings a year.

Lord Bath wrote a description of racing on the Heath in 1753:

GIMCRACK. Gimcrack (1760) was a grandson by Cripple of the Godolphin Arabian. At this active period of his racing career he was a very dark grey, but he later faded to an almost chalky white. He was an outstandingly honest and consistent little horse. His stud career is often dismissed as unimportant, but wrongly: his son Medley was immensely important to the American thoroughbred.

'When the horses are in sight, and come near Choak Jade, immediately the company all disperse, as if the Devil rose out of his Ditch and drove them, to get to the turning of the lands, or some other station for seeing the push made. Now the contention becomes animating: 'tis delightful to see two, or sometimes more, of the most beautiful animals of the creation, struggling for superiority, stretching every muscle and sinew to obtain the prize and reach the goal! to observe the skill and address of the riders, who are all distinguished by different colours of white, blue, green, red or yellow, sometimes spurring or whipping, sometimes checking or pulling, to give fresh breath and courage! And it is often observed that the race is won as much by the dexterity of the rider, as by the vigour and fleetness of the animal.

When the sport is over, the company saunter away towards the Warren Hill, before the other horses, left at the several stables in the town, are rode out to take their evening exercise and water. On this delightful spot you may see at once above a hundred of the most beautiful horses in the universe, with the grooms and boys upon them, in their several liveries, distinguishing each person of rank they belong to. This is, indeed, a noble sight; it is a piece of grandeur, and an expensive one too, which no nation but our own can boast of.'[31]

York became the leading course of the North. The racing was helped by the gaiety and importance of the city. Richmond and Doncaster (ancient) and Newcastle and Manchester (new) were the other most successful Northern meetings.

Hambleton (usually called Black Hambleton) was the one major casualty of the century. It was convenient for certain studs, but it was desperately inconvenient for visitors. It was hard to get to; there were no stables and no beds; there were no parties. Its Royal Plate went; its Gold Cup moved to York. After 1776 nearly all the races at Hambleton were matches. By the end of the century the best natural race-ground in Britain was dead as a meeting, and a brief revival was doomed.

In the South there were not many important new courses during the century: there had been plenty at the beginning. Of the established courses, Epsom had the great advantage of being convenient from London, and Winchester and Salisbury kept their traditional standing.

In the Midlands, dozens of respectable meetings, few new, prospered: from Lincoln in the East to Chester in the West. Their race-weeks were the social high time of the year.

Ascot died when Queen Anne did in 1714. It came to demure life in 1720 with a two-day meeting for hunters which had never run in races. Hunters, running under various conditions, all ridden *bona fide* behind hounds in Windsor Forest, were all that ran there until 1740. They ran for tiny prizes, so the Act of 1740 killed Ascot again. Prizes were raised to the legal minimum in 1744, but the racing was still derived entirely from the horses which followed His Majesty's Buckhounds.

Then the Duke of Cumberland started living and breeding in Windsor Park. Under his *aegis*, Ascot racing became conventional and fashionable. The 'stands' were still canvas booths, put up by private enterprise, but dicing, gaming, wrestling and boxing made Ascot at last a normal racecourse. In 1793 there were 12 races in five days, and two years later a grandstand was built. George III had taken to coming, with a train of nurses and children, as to a jolly picnic. Ascot was royal; by 1807 it had a Gold Cup.

# 9 Georgian Britain:

## Controls and People

### Founding the Jockey Club

Charles II was maker of rules and arbiter of disputes. In Queen Anne's reign and George I's, it seems likely that Tregonwell Frampton was Newmarket's court of appeal. Somebody filled this position after his death: at Preston in 1731 an owner disliked a decision of the 'founders', 'declaring he would appeal to the Judgement of Newmarket.'[1] Whose judgment? The Duke of Devonshire? Bolton? Rutland? Was this appeal unique? Occasional? Normal?

Cheny reviewed the state of the turf in his Calendar of the next year: 'The Diversion of Horse-Racing is advanced to such an Hight as to render the Practice of it Intimate and Familiar to almost every Part of the Kingdom: notwithstanding which, the Accidents incident to these Affairs are so numerous; the Conditions of Running so various and different; the Articles, or Advertisement, or both, so often capable of counter Constructions; the Methods of deciding Bets in particular Cases, known to so few, and with such Reluctancy (through Byass of Interest) submitted to by many, who are well acquainted with them, that those Affairs are frequently attended with Disputes and Contentions, too many of which, proceed to expensive Law Suits, that terminate not, but with the additional Evil, of leaving behind them Impressions of Resentment, between the Persons concern'd.'

Two things were needed, both a long time in coming: consistent rules, consistently applied; and an authority to whom appeal could be made and whose decision was final.

There were two sets of rules. One related to King's Plates; it was not intended for other races and was inappropriate to them. There were also the Newmarket Rules, half of which related to betting, published by Pond in his Kalendar of 1751. It seems likely that Pond transcribed a document already in existence; it is possible that he was urged to do this by some elected or self-appointed authority.

In the same Kalendar of 1751 there is a small announcement which casts a large shadow: at Newmarket on 1 April 1752 there was to be run 'A Contribution Free Plate, by Horses the Property of the Noblemen and Gentlemen belonging to the JOCKEY CLUB at the *Star and Garter* in *Pall Mall*, one heat on the Round Course, weight eight Stone, seven Pound'.

It is impossible to say who the members were; impossible to guess if they thought of their meetings at the Star and Garter as anything more than the festive gatherings of like-minded friends. In 1752 they got land to build a Coffee Room at Newmarket; while this was building they used the Red Lion in the town.

Almost immediately this new fellowship made itself felt. In 1757 a dispute at the Curragh was referred to the Jockey Club at Newmarket. The next year Heber published the first general order of the Jockey Club: 2 lb. overweight was the maximum permitted

unless declared, and failure to declare meant disqualification. The second of these events means either that the Club decided to stop being a drinking-circle and become a government, or that it always had the latter intention; the first means that the assumption of power was not only happening but seen to be happening.

In 1762 the second order was published; in it 19 noblemen and gentlemen, being members, registered colours which they undertook to use consistently. The list of members making the undertaking includes a royal duke, five other dukes, a marquess, five earls, a viscount, and a baron. This must go some way to explaining the early authority of the club. No-one has quite defined by what right it seized power even over its limited bailliwick of Newmarket. Perhaps the Duke of Cumberland got some kind of authority from his father or brother.

The rule ends with a reference to the Stewards, to whom the members were already delegating their powers.

THE JOCKEY CLUB. Members of the Club at this period (about 1790) included the Prince of Wales and Duke of York; the Dukes of Bedford, Bolton, Devonshire, Grafton, Norfolk, Queensberry and St Albans; Lords Barrymore, Clermont, Egremont, Foley, Grosvenor and Ossory; Sir Charles Bunbury and Sir John Lade; and Messrs Fox, Panton, Vernon and Wastell. Few of these distinguished persons can be identified with confidence in Rowlandson's lampoon.

An expulsion occured in 1767. 'The Jockey Club met on Saturday last to expel a Mr Brereton for charging Meynell and Vernon with cheating at play.'[2] This is not a warning off the Heath, but an expulsion from the social facilities of the Coffee Room. It is to be contrasted with an actual debarment from the turf in 1770, printed in the Calendar: 'Chester Races. In order to save Mr Quick, Mr Castle, or any of the Ascott confederacy the trouble and expense of training, they are desired to take notice that none of their horses will be allowed to run for any of the above plates, neither will they be suffered to run for any of the plates at Conway, Nantwich, or Holywell; nor will Thomas Dunn be permitted to ride.'

By this time Sir Charles Bunbury's wife, the beautiful Lady Sarah, had run off with Lord William Gordon. The husband she left behind was rich, respectable, hypochondriac ('he loves to be thought ill')[3] and his name crops up in nearly every aspect of late 18th-century racing. He bred Highflyer, owned Gimcrack, and won the first Derby. In the present context he was more important still.

IIe was not among the members who registered their colours in 1762: he was only 22 at the time. He was a member soon afterwards. He was not interested in travel, politics, the arts, or women. Like Tregonwell Frampton he liked coursing. Like him he lived for the turf. Other great racing men of his day had other concerns: Grafton, Rockingham, Derby, and March ('Old Q') who *was* interested in women. Not Bunbury. His single-mindedness, rectitude and courage gave the Jockey Club a moral authority which, in the 19th century, it sometimes conspicuously lacked. He became 'Perpetual President'. He was the third dictator of the turf (following Charles II and Frampton), and the first whose *cathedra* was the Club (preceding Bentinck and Rous).

## Calendar and Stud Book

Control required documentation and communication. Records were needed. A medium was wanted for promulgating rules. The identity of horses had to be established. Calendar and Stud Book both had to be born.

The first attempt at filling this enormous gap was made by John Cheny of Arundel. In 1726 he announced his purpose to publish, annually for seven years, a list of all races. In 1727 the first volume appeared: *An Historical list of all Horse-Matches Run, And of all Plates and Prizes Run for in* England (*of the value of Ten Pounds or upwards*) *in 1727.* His preface said that he 'travelled the Kingdom over, contracting a correspondance in every part with persons who, at the very time of the sport, are to take accounts for me where I do not appear.' He included a large number of pedigrees; he also recorded the principal cock-matches. In 1739 he was empowered, or commanded, by the Master of the Horse to publish revised King's Plate rules. In 1741 he contemplated taking the pedigrees out of the Calendar and putting them in a separate Stud Book; but he had not accomplished this when he died in 1750.

He had not one but two successors: Pond (of the celebrated daughter) who published a Kalendar until 1757, and Heber, who beat him to the normal spelling, and published his Calendar until 1769. Both followed Cheny's format.

After Heber there were again rival Calendars. Mr Walker tried for two years, but he was defeated by the well-entrenched combination of Tuting and Fawconer, the one Keeper of the Match Book at Newmarket, the other Secretary of the Jockey Club.

In 1773 the Jockey Club authorized the new Keeper of the Match Book, James Weatherby, to publish a Calendar. He had heirs, and the Weatherby family gradually became the civil service of British racing.

Cheny took trouble to get his pedigrees right. His success was patchy. Heber rather gracelessly said in the preface to his first volume: 'As to the Pedigrees of the Horses, I have made only a small number of Additions, but most of them from the best Authority, that of the Gentlemen who are owners of them, and who have been so kind as to favour me with their true Genealogy; but as in a Matter of this complex Nature, *Mistakes are almost unavoidable*, I chose to mention those Pedigrees only which might be depended on, for fear of committing suchlike Errors as have appear'd in some former Performances.' Mistakes were indeed unavoidable. Many horses were unnamed, many shared names. Relying on some owners for pedigrees can hardly have satisfied the laws of evidence.

In 1790 James Weatherby announced his Stud Book. The first volume, *Introduction to a General Stud Book*, was published in 1791. For pre-1750 material his principal source was Cheny. In 1793 the Introduction was revised. In 1800 the first Supplement was published, which brought the records up to date. There was a further version of Volume I in 1803, and one regarded as final in 1808.

A Stud Book places breeding on record. It also admits or excludes, qualifying horses as thoroughbred or dismissing them as half-bred. In this task, Weatherby's principle of admission was descent from certain named or otherwise identified mares. This was pretty rough, since a large proportion of the most influential tap-roots are identified only by their produce.

## Indiscipline and Danger on the Racecourse

It was a long time before the Jockey Club had firm and continuous influence outside Newmarket. Not only were there the disputed bets and bent rules deplored by Cheny. There were also completely undisciplined crowds. At Epsom, on the first day of the October meeting, 1776, a horse was winning: 'Just before he came in at the winning post, being crossed by a gentleman on horseback, the rider was thrown; but his leg hanging in the stirrup, the horse carried his weight in, and won miraculously without hurting his jockey.'[4]

Epsom seems to have been unusually casual. Mirabeau about 1785 said 'Horse-racing and cockfighting are carried on here to a pitch of absolute madness. . . . There are neither

BAY MALTON BEATING OTHO, NEWMARKET. This was a match for 1000 guineas, at the Second Spring Meeting of 1766, between the Marquis of Rockingham and the Hon. Richard Vernon. Bay Malton won seven prizes worth £5000; Otho was a successful sire. The galloping mounted spectators were a hazard forbidden, but unsuccessfully, by the Jockey Club in 1838, for reasons here evident.

lists nor barriers at these races. The horses run in the midst of the crowd, who leave only a space sufficient for them to pass through, at the same time encouraging them by gestures and loud shouts. The victor, when he has arrived at the goal, finds it a difficult matter to disengage himself from the crowd, who congratulate, caress, and embrace him with a effusion of heart which is not easy to form an idea of without having seen it.'[5]

The time of the Jockey Club having Inspectors of Courses, and refusing its countenance to those which were dangerous or bad, was far in the future. But the Club did make an occasional attempt, from early in its life, to improve safety. The 1777 Calendar cautions Clerks of Courses to make their posts thin and brittle. This was because, some years before, a boy called 'Little Wicked', the favourite lad of Lord Ossory, 'was dashed to pieces against one of the old immovable posts, in riding a match. I was assured by one present, that the good natured lord "cried like a child at this unfortunate event".'[6]

In a dry summer, with ill-kept grass, the hard bumpiness of a course became a menace. In a drought about 1775 'there was a sweepstakes at Epsom, ridden by officers of the Guards. . . . They went to the expense of daily water carts for the course, from Tattenham's Corner in, but with very little effect.'[7]

## The Escape Affair

ESCAPE. Chifney never used a double bridle; he was an artist with the whip. His horse is hobbled by a banner bearing the royal motto, and the owner, finger to nose, is planning his bet for the following day. This cartoon shows not only that royalty could be thus savagely lampooned, but also that racing was supposed to be honest.

The Prince of Wales began racing as soon as he attained his majority in 1784. He was quite successful, largely because in buying he was advised by Richard Tattersall. His expenses were so great that he had to stop, until Parliament paid his debts. He started again, with the cheerful resilience of a man spending other people's money. By 1790 he had a big string and a lot of winners.

On 21 October 1791 his horse Escape ran in a field of four, for 60 guineas, 'from the Ditch in' at Newmarket. Sam Chifney rode. Chifney later said that Escape had not had a sweat for a fortnight. He was not fit. Chifney told the Prince so. Nevertheless the horse

93

started favourite. Chifney, naturally, did not back himself. Escape finished last.

They decided to bring him out again the following day. Chifney says he said to the Prince: 'I am very glad your Royal Highness does run Escape tomorrow. This sharp rally today will not fatigue him, has sweated him, opened his pores, and lightened his flesh.'[8]

So Escape ran, on the Beacon Course, a generous 5 to 1 in the betting. He won easily, beating two of the horses in the previous day's race. He was backed by the Prince and by Chifney.

The Stewards of the Jockey Club were Bunbury, Mr Dutton, and 'Polite' Tommy Panton. They interviewed Chifney and looked at his betting-book. Presently they told the Prince that if Chifney rode his horses again, 'no gentleman would start against him.'

The Prince left the turf in a huff. He stood by Chifney, loyally and publicly, giving him a pension of £200 a year.

What were Bunbury and his friends about? They were men of honour and they cared about racing. Chifney's apologia *Genius Genuine* is not to be accepted blindly, but it seems possible that Escape had two ways of running, and probable that he needed that first race to run well in the second. There was no firm suggestion that the Prince was dishonestly involved. But the Prince thought rules were made for other people. Charles Greville, his faithful Clerk of the Privy Council, said years later: 'A more contemptible, cowardly, selfish, unfeeling dog does not exist than this king.'[9] Chifney was a known villain and his book reveals him as an egomaniac.

The most likely explanation is that the Stewards were after Chifney, who for all his art was bad for racing. Perhaps they chose the first occasion when they thought themselves justified in acting; perhaps they chose a bad occasion; perhaps they chose just this occasion in order to demonstrate their power. This last they certainly did: which gives the whole scrubby episode its historical importance.

## Tattersalls

Dennis O'Kelly by the end of his life knew all the greatest men on the turf. They drank with him, bet with him and bought and sold with him. It was not to be expected (except by him) that he would be elected to the Jockey Club: but his nephew Andrew was. Dennis did qualify to enter a horse in the Noblemen's and Gentlemen's Plate at Ascot. This is a striking example of the social mobility of 18th-century England. The snobbery of birth is an invention of continental Europe.

An even more striking example is Richard Tattersall. He came from Yorkshire yeoman stock. He came south as a young man at the time of the '45, and got a job at Beevor's (or Beavor's) horse repository in St Martin's Lane. He then went to work for the 2nd Duke of Kingston, a breeding and racing man and an early member of the Jockey Club. His wife was the notorious Elizabeth Chudleigh, later farcically tried for bigamy. As the duke's Master of Horse, Tattersall got to know the great men of racing. He began buying and selling horses for them. This was possible because of his excellent judgment and absolute probity. He may have been involved in some capacity with the Duke of Cumberland's dispersal.

In 1766 he rented a piece of land on the Grosvenor estate, in the uncouth wilderness behind Hyde Park Corner. He established sales twice a week, dealing in horses of all kinds, carriages, and hounds. In 1773 the Duke of Kingston died, and Elizabeth sold up the stable. This was the first of the great dispersal-sales which made Tattersall famous. By 1779 he was rich enough to buy Highflyer, the best racehorse in England, from Lord Bolingbroke.

He was already providing the Jockey Club with a room (and the claret for which he was famous) for its London meetings. In 1780 he opened a Subscription Room, a club with

AUCTION AT TATTERSALLS. Pierce Egan early in the next century described the famous yard where the sales were held as 'the resort of the *pinks* of the SWELLS, – the *tulips* of the GOES, – the *dashing* heroes of the military, – the fox hunting clericals, – sprigs of nobility, stylish coachmen, – smart guards, – saucy butchers, – natty grooms, – tidy helpers, – knowing horse dealers, – *betting* publicans, – neat jockeys, – sporting men of all descriptions, – and the picture is finished by a number of real gentlemen.'

annual paid membership, for the comfortable laying and settling of bets. The committee which adjudicated on betting disputes was therefore called Tattersalls Committee: the governing body of bookmaking.

Highflyer was meanwhile a triumphant stallion, ranking with Eclipse. 'Old Tatt' rebuilt a house on his stud near Bury, and called it Highflyer Hall. He regularly entertained there the Prince of Wales and Charles James Fox, who both got marvellously drunk. A far cry from the Yorkshire cottage, and from sleeping among the carriages in Beevor's Repository.

## Jockeys, Trainers, and Training Methods

From the Restoration some owners employed professional riders, but their names hardly survive.

The first two jockeys of national reputation were John Singleton and Sam Chifney. John Singleton rode the first St Leger winner for Lord Rockingham, by whom he was principally employed. He had a long and respectable career.

Sam Chifney the elder was the first great jockey. He was born about the middle of the century, and learned his trade at Newmarket. 'In 1773 I could ride horses in a better manner in a race to beat others than any person ever known in my time, and in 1775 I could train horses for running better than any person I ever yet saw. Riding I learned myself, and training I learned from Mr Richard Prince.'[10] Chifney commuted the Prince of Wales's pension for a lump sum, spent it, and died in a hovel near the Fleet and 'within its rules'.

Frank Buckle was a Newmarket man, born in 1766, small, tough, durable, and intelligent. He won five Derbies, nine Oaks, and two St Legers for a variety of owners. He based his riding style on Chifney's, but his personality was in sharp contrast. He was honest and provident.

95

The brothers Sam and John Arnull were approximately his contemporaries. Sam was perhaps the more celebrated. They won nine Derbies between them. John's son was later of equal eminence. This sober, neatly-dressed, well-conducted family, with Buckle, made the trade of jockey respectable.

The public trainer was a 19th-century invention. From the beginning of the 18th century there were just a few men, like the Heseltine who brought Merlin south, whose

FRANK BUCKLE, JOHN WASTELL, ROBERT ROBSON, AND LAD. Buckle (left) rode his first race at 17, weighing 55 lbs, for Richard Vernon. He rode for 48 years. He was known as the 'pocket Hercules' and the 'Peterborough screw' – he farmed at Peterborough, and had a distinctive circular action with the whip. He died in 1832. Wastell (second from left) was an owner-breeder on his own account as well as Grafton's manager. He was born in Yorkshire in 1736, educated at Cambridge, and lived and bred horses near Bury St Edmunds. His best horse was Scotia (by Delpini) winner of the Oaks in 1802, with which this picture may be associated. He died in 1811. Robson's father trained for Bolingbroke; he himself trained Waxy (Derby 1793) for Sir Ferdinando Poole before moving to Newmarket. He trained seven Derby and 11 Oaks winners, and started a revolution in training methods.

skill as training-grooms became known. Later in the century there were a number of stables where the training-groom had become respected and consulted. Chifney's master Mr Prince was one such. Another was Lord March's long-time servant Richard 'Hell-Fire Dick' Goodison, father of the Regency jockey Tom Goodison. Robson trained Highflyer for Lord Bolingbroke; his son went to the Duke of Grafton and did remarkable things. But trainers of this status and skill were exceptional.

Training methods were severe. The way to get a horse's flesh off was to sweat it; give it hard work in heavy clothing; and purge it. Horses were also tried over the full distance of a forthcoming race, or further. John Wastell kept a meticulous trial-book for the Duke of Grafton, normal in form but unusual in preservation.[11] It shows that all the stable's runners were given searching tests before their races.

The great menace to trials was touting. From mid-century touts swarmed at training-centres and on private gallops. They were in the pay of gamblers or rival owners – often the same people. It was for this reason that 'The late Sir Charles Bunbury said to me on a particular occasion – "I have no notion of trying my horses for other people's informa-tion".'[12]

Although subjected to purges, sweats and trials, thoroughbreds were thought too delicate to stand even a summer breeze. Racehorses were kept heavily rugged in their stables, and the stables were heated and unventilated. This is why John Wootton could paint owners and grooms from the life, but had to guess at the conformation of their horses, and why James Seymour could paint his horse portraits as well in his studio as in the stable-yard. Only the immense reputation of Stubbs allowed him to insist on the dangerous eccentricity of an unrugged horse out of doors.[13]

This regime produced horses which appeared on the racecourse looking like toast-racks. Towards the end of the century a French visitor said: 'These racehorses do not show their worth by their outward appearance; they are gaunt and meagre, and an awkward manner of stretching out their necks deprives them of all their beauty.'[14]

It seems certain that many horses were broken down at home, by severe gallops over hard ground; and that naturally light-framed horses had their strength sapped before they raced. It seems equally certain that 18th-century tendons were stronger than today's: and that the horses needed more work.

Racehorses look odd in 18th-century paintings not only because they 'stripped' so light; not only because of the convention that excellence consisted of a long back and a tiny head; but also because of cropping, docking, and nicking. Berenger said in 1771: 'the cruelty and absurdity of our notions and customs in "cropping", as it is called, the ears of our horses, "docking" and "nicking" their tails, is such that we every day fly in the face of reason, nature and humanity.'[15]

Timing was occasionally attempted, either as a trial against the clock or in a race. Flying Childers, with 9 st. 2 lb. (128 lb.), allegedly ran the Round Course at Newmarket (3 miles 6 furlongs 93 yards) in 6 minutes 40 seconds. Matchem, with 8 st. 7 lb. (119 lb.), ran the Beacon Course (4 miles 1 furlong 138 yards) in 7 minutes 20 seconds. These times are widely quoted, but not widely believed. Lawrence states a view which is still held in England: 'Timing, of racers does not often take place . . . In fact it can answer no purpose generally, since the horses only make their play on particular parts of the course, and at the run in. The case is different where circumstances lead to the expecta-tion that the race will be run out and out, and that the horses will be urged to the utmost of their ability.'[16]

## Parties and Diversions

Racing remained a party and an excuse for parties. 'Newmarket', said Lady Sarah Bunbury in 1763, 'was charming, all the charming men were there.' Beween the two October meetings there was private racing on a nearby estate: 'The race at Euston was the prettiest thing I ever saw; I doated upon it, for I rid on my beautiful Weazle, who was gentle enough to let me gallop backwards and forwards, so I saw the whole course.'[17]

The 'charming men' gambled on the racecourse and off it. According to Horace Walpole, hazard (which was dicing) caused the deepest play; loo, brag, and gleek were the principal card games.[18] Lady Sarah says quinze was the heavy betting game at Newmarket.[19] Cock-fighting was as popular as ever and the betting was prodigious. Lord Derby's famous black-breasted reds were as important to him as Sir Peter Teazle himself.

The Newmarket habitués raced constantly. In the Provinces race-week came once a year; it was the only diversion of its kind for the local families; they made the most of it. So did the inn-keepers. At Lichfield (an important Staffordshire meeting) in 1776: 'the town was very full of company, who testified the utmost approbation at the entertainment they had each day on the course, and the brilliancy of the balls.'[20] The Perth Hunt meeting in October 1784 lasted two full weeks, with daily 'ordinaries' and nightly balls.

Besides cocking, gaming, drinking and dancing, prizefighting became a recognized adjunct to the racecourse. For the first time it was chic not only to go to the 'mills' but also to make friends with the boxers. The Prince of Wales was an early member of the Fancy. At a race-meeting in 1791 it was a source of astonishment to a newspaper that no fight took place during the races 'notwithstanding Hooper, the tinman, Green, Sale, and several other boxers were present.'[21]

Eccentrics like Lord March and Sir John Lade made wagers also with all kinds of other contestants, such as geese. (March always won money, Lade always lost it.) A more conventional event was a foot-race. Gentlemen matched their running-footmen, as they matched their horses, cocks, and hounds. In 1759 at Northampton 'Lord Northampton had a running footman at the races in white satin and gold lace, his shoes and cap white and the apparel cost four-score pounds.'[22]

## Turf Notables of the Late 18th Century

Towards the end of the century there appears a *Receipt to make a jockey*:

> Take a pestle and mortar of moderate size,
> Into Queensberry's head put Bunbury's eyes,
> Pound Clermont to dust, you'll find it expedient —
> The world cannot furnish a better ingredient —
> From Derby and Bedford take plenty of spirit
> (Successful or not, they have always that merit),
> Tommy Panton's address, John Wastell's advice,
> And a touch of Prometheus — 'tis done in a trice.[23]

March, Duke of Queensberry – 'Old Q' – was probably the most consistently successful big gambler of his day. He was careful and clever. He was also a fine horseman. Once, somehow learning that his jockey had been got at, he arrived on the course swathed in a cloak, peeled it off just before the 'off', revealed that he wore his own racing colours, replaced the jockey, and rode and won the race.

Sir Charles Bunbury's name has already appeared in every connection. Lord Clermont raced from 1751; he was the leading owner in Ireland and one of the mentors of the Prince of Wales. The Duke of Bedford was more successful than Lord Derby – he won three Derbies with horses bred at his great Woburn stud. It is nice to see this appreciation of their sportsmanship. 'Polite' Tommy Panton's address did not stop him, as junior Steward in 1791, from joining Bunbury and Dutton in the ultimatum to the Prince over the Escape affair. John Wastell was the Duke of Grafton's manager and a celebrated expert on breeding.

The greatest spenders were Lords Grosvenor and Egremont. The latter's stud at Petworth was the largest in the country. It was casually run. Horses got mixed. He won five Derbies (a feat not equalled until the 20th century, when it was achieved by the Aga Khan); it is more than likely that some of Egremont's five winners were four-year-olds. He himself would have been appalled at such a thing.

## Crime on the Turf

Early in the century D'Urfey wrote:

> Let cullies that lose at a race
> Go venture at hazard to win,
> Or he that is bubbl'd at dice
> Recover at cocking again;
> Let jades that are founder'd be bought,
> Let jockeys play crimp to make sport . . .
> Another makes racing a trade,
> And dreams of his projects to come;
> And many a crimp match is made,
> By bubbling another man's groom.[24]

A 'crimp' match was fixed beforehand: 'However, there be sharpers at this, as well as at other diversions of England; a groom's riding on the wrong side of the post; or his riding *crimp*, or people's crossing the horse's way in his course, makes a stranger risk deep when he lays his money, except he can be let into the *secret*, which you can scarce believe he ever is.'[25]

Owners and their agents were the biggest cheats, including, in O'Kelly's view, the Jockey Club dukes. Matches were fixed, horses were pulled in sweepstakes, and ringers were run less innocently than by Lord Egremont. By the nature of things these transactions are not much recorded.

The great attracted leeches. The Duke of Cumberland, according to an admirer after his death, suffered 'an incredible succession of losses to the sharks, greeks and blacklegs of that time, by whom His Royal Highness was surrounded; and of course incessantly pillaged'.[26]

In the 18th century, and for long afterwards, the tout was also vermin. His function was to anticipate betting *coups*. Pursuing touts as they pursued poachers, owners were simply improving the odds at which their horses ran. It is not easy to share their moral indignation.

There are a few 18th-century reports of a more odious crime. Tuting and Fawconer record three episodes. In May 1772 a horse called Rosebud was fancied for a race at York. 'Some villains broke into the stable where Rosebud stood and gave him a dose of poison.' In September of the same year at Scarborough, 'some malicious persons got into the stable where Tosspot stood, and gave him a dose of physick the night before he was to run.' In 1778 Miss Nightingale died on the Sunday before the races at Boroughbridge; 'in her stomach about two pounds of duck-shot, made up with putty into balls.'

Sam Chifney reports that the Prince of Wales's training-groom Casborne was 'concerned with those breaking into noblemen's stables, the night before running, to give the horse, as was supposed, opium balls; and it is believed Casborne had done it for many years.' His accomplices were another groom called Bloss and 'a person called Old Tight'.[27]

The races were hazardous not only for betting men. Pickpockets swarmed at them. When they were caught they were ducked, beaten or shaved. At Ascot in 1791 a culprit suffered all three. He was caught again at Windsor later the same week, but got away. He nevertheless died of his Ascot beating.[28] There were E.O. tables at all racecourses: this was a primitive roulette, and usually crooked. At Doncaster in 1793 the tables were all seized and burned in front of the Mansion House. There were also crooked card and dice games.

In justice to the raffish 18th century, it should be added that the blackleg, welsher, nobbler, pickpocket, cardsharp, briber of jockeys and runner of ringers only came to full maturity in the pious 19th.

# 10  Eighteenth-Century Europe
## and Russia

### Italy : the Riderless Barbs

The *palio* races of medieval Italy had been dead for a long time, except in Siena. There they continued much as ever, blazingly heraldic, frequently dishonest, the occasion of broken heads and maltreated horses. Elsewhere the riderless 'Barbaries' galloped through the streets of the cities. Toland, describing Newmarket to Eudoxa in 1724, says: 'The swift running of horses to you may seem insipid, as the races we saw in Bologna in Italy were, where the horses ran through the streets without riders; but here there is something so very noble in the whole pursuit of the courses, that it animates even a by-spectator, or stranger, to share in the pleasure.'[1] We are to take it that there was nothing very noble in the pursuit of the Bolognese courses, and that by-spectators and strangers were not animated to share in the pleasure.

Mirabeau's account of Epsom later in the century concludes: 'these races are not like those of Barbary horses in Rome and other cities of Italy.'[2] This is odd. Mirabeau has talked of dense and unruly crowds, shouts and gestures, passion and ribaldry, and 'thin and meagre' horses. All these seem eminently to belong to the Barbary races.

At the end of the century: 'Some of the Italian races are a disgraceful burlesque on those of other countries. . . . The horses termed Barberi – because the race was at first contested by Barbs – are brought to the starting post, their heads and their necks gaily ornamented; while to a girth which goes round the belly of each are attached several loose straps, having at their ends small balls of lead thickly set with sharp steel points. At every motion these are brought in contact with the flanks and bellies of the horses, and the more violent the motion, the more dreadful the incessant torture. On their backs are placed sheets of thin tin, or stiff paper, which, when agitated, will make a rustling, rattling noise. It is difficult to conceive of the rearing, kicking, pawing and snorting which occurs at the starting-place . . . Many serious accidents are sure to happen.'[3]

The races at Florence were the same. Each riderless horse was goaded by an ivory ball with spikes like a hedgehog. Mrs Piozzi thought it was rare fun: 'it makes one laugh to see that some of them are so tickled by it as not to run at all, but to set about plunging in order to rid themselves of the inconvenience, instead of driving forward to divert the mob, who leap, and caper, and shout with delight, and lash the laggers along with great indignation indeed, and with the most comical gestures. I never saw horses in so droll a state of degradation before, for they were all striped, or spotted, or painted of some colour, to distinguish them from each other.'[4]

### France : the Period of Anglomania

Louis XIV kindled a fitful gleam of English racing. It died, with him, in 1715.

In 1722 there was a match against the clock which aroused keen interest and furious betting. M. d'Estaing, marquis de Saillans, wagered to ride from the Porte Saint-Denis to Chantilly and back twice in six hours – a toal of 36 leagues. He chose from the stables of his friends 16 horses exceptional for their speed, and won his bet with 25 minutes in hand. He then went to the opera.[5]

This event was unique. In the first half of the 18th century the fashionable French were hunting and 'managing' their horses. In the second half of the century two changes occurred.

Voltaire describes the first. 'All these military games begin to be abandoned, and, of all the exercises which in time past made the body stronger and more agile, almost nothing remains except hunting; and even that is neglected by most of the princes of Europe. Revolutions are being made in amusements, as in everything else.'[6] Spectator sports were wanted.

The other new event was Anglomania. Horace Walpole describes the parties of French touring English country houses (including Strawberry Hill) agog to learn how to behave, dress, talk, and amuse themselves. He thought they were ninnies, obsessed by a fad: 'I take for granted that their next mode will be *à l'iroquoise*.'[7] He was wrong. Their mode remained *à l'anglaise* until their heads were chopped off.

It was a short step from Strawberry Hill to Newmarket. For a number of grandees, it was another short step to owning racehorses. The duc de Lanzun ran Taster and Patrician at Newmarket in 1773. The duc de Chartres (later duc d'Orléans) had a Newmarket stable. He ran Cantator in the Derby of 1784. Just before his death he had four horses in training in England.

These pioneers brought their racing home. The comte de Lauraguais – Louis-Léon-Felicité de Brancas, later duc de Brancas – brought Gimcrack from England; he subjected the little horse to a 22½ mile match against the clock. In February 1766 Lauraguais had been involved in another match, twice described by Horace Walpole. 'Today I have been to the Plaine de Sablons, by the Bois de Boulogne, to see a horse race rid in persons by Count Lauraguais and Lord Forbes.' Lauraguais' horse lost, and then died at the finish. Some of the French accused 'others' of poisoning it, but most people thought Lauraguais himself had doctored it. Later Walpole talked of Lauraguais 'quacking his horse till he killed it.'[8]

Racing began at once to flourish, 'Under the patronage of the profligate duc d'Orléans'.[9] There was racing in the Bois de Boulogne, and at Sablons, Vincennes, Fontainebleau, and Chantilly. It blossomed under even more influential patronage than the duke's: that of Marie Antoinette.

With increasing gloom, throughout 1776, Mercy wrote to the Empress Marie Thérèse: 'M. le comte d'Artois, the duc de Chartres, and a number of young people have made horse racing fashionable; the races take place at Paris and the Queen goes regularly. Her Majesty, having been on the night of the 11th [of February] at a ball at the Opéra until five o'clock in the morning, went back to Versailles at half past six and left again at 10 to watch a horse race near the Bois de Boulogne.'

A few weeks later – 'Every week there are several horse races, and the Queen, who has acquired an extraordinary taste for this kind of spectacle, has not missed one.'

In the Autumn the Court went continually to Fontainebleau. 'One of the objects of these outings is to see the daily exercise which the race-horses are given so that they are always fit. The place fixed for the races is a league and a half from Fontainebleau, a big heath, where two tracks have been laid out, each half a league long and joined by a circular section. At the end between the two tracks a wooden building has been constructed, of which the upper storey forms a great *salon* with a curved gallery, where the Queen and all her suite watch the races. The men arrive on horseback, most in a scarcely decent undress. Nonetheless they are all allowed to climb up into the *salon* where the Queen is; this is where the bets are struck, amid much argument, noise, and tumult. M.

RIDERLESS BARBS IN ROME. Horses like these, called *barberi* though unlikely to have been imported from Africa, were raced in the *Corso* from the 15th century. This remained an unseemly part of religious festivals for 400 years, until its abolition in 1872. The horses were induced to gallop by dangling goads.

le comte d'Artois risked pretty considerable sums there, and was greatly put out when he lost, which nearly always happened.'

In November 'These horse-races are odious functions and, I dare to say it, indecent because of the Queen's participation. I went to the first race on horseback, and I was careful to stay in the crowd, some way from the Queen's grandstand, where all the young people went in boots and undress. The Queen saw me, and asked me in the evening why I had not climbed into the grandstand. I replied, loud enough for several wasters who were there to hear, that I was in boots and riding-clothes and I would not dream of appearing before the Queen dressed like that. The Queen smiled and the ones who had done just that looked at me very crossly. I went to the second race in a carriage, dressed properly for the town. I did go up into the stand, and found a great table covered with a copious luncheon, which was pillaged by a gang of improperly dressed young people, who made a noise so that you could not hear yourself, and in the middle of the mob, there was the Queen, Madame d'Artois, Madame Élisabeth, Monsieur, and M. le comte d'Artois, the latter running up and down, betting, despairing when he lost and pitiably radiant when he won, hurling himself into the crowd to encourage his grooms or *jaquets* (this is what they call the men who ride the race-horses) and presenting to the Queen one who had won a race for him. I was deeply upset to see such a thing.'

A few days later Artois ran his 'famous racehorse' and lost 100,000 francs.[10]

There were many matches. There were large fields, too. In November 1777 there was a 40-horse race at Fontainebleau, followed by a 40-donkey race. There were good prizes. On two days in April 1781 there were five races, each worth 100 louis (2000 francs).[11]

The English were there all the time, certain of being welcomed and imitated. In 1776 the duc de Chartres' Glowworm (by Eclipse) beat a horse of Lord Clermont's. In 1783, in the royal park of Vincennes, Lord March, Lord Derby, and Mr Wyndham had runners. 'We have copied the races from the English. The *jockei* who is going to ride is made to fast, to weigh less . . . We go to the Plaine des Sablons to watch skinny animals run covered in sweat.' They went to the races on horseback, riding in the English fashion, on an English saddle, dressed in the English manner in a *redingote*, a riding-coat.[12]

English racing meant English racehorses. As early as 1753 – 'Many thousands are carried out of England every year; so that it is become a trade of great consequence, and brings a vast balance of money to this country annually. The French monarch rides no other horses but ours in his favourite diversion of hunting. You may, at any time, see two or three hundred beautiful English geldings in those great and noble stables at Chantilli.'[13]

In the 1770s they were coming to race and to breed. The duc de Chartes and the comte d'Artois both started thoroughbred studs. They bought or borrowed stallions and well-bred mares. By the Revolution in 1789 French-breds of pure English blood were already running and winning.

Unlike his wife Marie Antoinette (quite unlike) Louis XVI began to disapprove. A contemporary says he saw multiply all the vices which accompany racing and decided to suppress it.[14] The Revolution saved him the trouble.

FONTAINEBLEAU. This is one of the meetings described with such detestation by Mercy to the Empress of Austria in 1776. The grandstand had just been built for Marie-Antoinette and her suite; they ate, drank, and betted on the upper floor. The horses racing at this date were all imported from England, although a few thoroughbred studs were by then established.

## Russia: the Imperial Studs; Racing; the Orlov Trotter

Over a long period, and in a large and heterogeneous country, little had been done to improve the Russian horse. Then Tsar Alexis (father of Peter the Great) started the first royal studs, importing stallions from Asia and the Baltic. Peter the Great extended this policy. He founded new studs round Kiev. He imported mares from Silesia and Prussia. In 1722 he established racing, by edict, with a view to improving the breed.

Things sagged after Peter's death, but recovered under Catherine the Great. The imperial studs flourished. For the first time there were private studs, on many of which the great landowners spent enormous sums. At about the end of the century at least four English Classic winners went to Russia: Noble, Tartar, Daedalus, and Symmetry. These were not quite top-class horses, although the Russians were probably told otherwise. They were not used sensibly, breeding being experimental and haphazard. But Russia went on racing, at least occasionally. Races were recorded in the English Calendar of 1792.

The other Russian 18th-century achievement began with the end of a love-affair. In the late 1760s Catherine the Great's lover was Count Gregory Orlov. She discarded him in favour of Potemkin. Gregory's brother, Count Alexis Orlov, knocked out Potemkin's eye, 'and then sought distraction in breeding horses.'[15] In about 1775 he imported from Greece a pure Arab stallion called Smetanka, with which he covered a Dutch cart-mare. The get was a stallion he called Polkan. Out of another Dutch mare Polkan got Barss. These Dutch mares were Friesland Blacks, of the type known as *hard-draver*, fast trotter. Cart-mare does not mean shire-horse, but light harness-horse. The breed is extremely ancient. 'The Frizeland Horse is no verie great Horse, but rather of a mean stature, being therewith strong and well compact togither, and hath verie good legs. And Vegetius saith that the Frizeland Horses be verie swift in running, and able to maintain a long course. . . . The pace of this horse is a good comely trot.'[16] Crossed with the English thoroughbred, the Frieslands produced the Norfolk Trotter. Crossed with Orlov's Arab they produced Barss.

Barss got three sons: Lubeznoy, out of an Arab-Mecklenburg crossbred mare; Dobroy, out of an English thoroughbred mare; and Lebed, out of a mare of mixed Arab, Mecklenburg, and thoroughbred blood. From these three stallions the whole breed of Orlov Trotters descends. They were typically long, strong horses, about 15.3 hands, with an 'elegant trotting action'.[17]

Orlov's training methods were described by contemporaries. He built a small racecourse in front of his mansion in Moscow, and there gave his horses fast quarter-mile dashes which were carefully timed.[18]

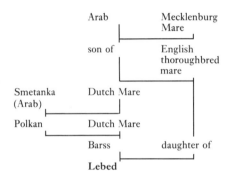

ORLOV AND BARSS. Barss was bred about 1785, by an Arab-Friesland crossbred stallion out of a Friesland mare. This breeding is clearly discernible in the horse's conformation and colour. His descendants were the Orlovs, all natural trotters 'bending the knee when striding'. Count Orlov's two-handed reining resembles the American, not the English, style.

# 11 Colonial America

## Primitive Racing and the Quarter-Horse

In 1607 Jamestown was founded in Virginia. The colonists had no horses with them. The local Indians had none. In 1610 six mares and a stallion were brought, but the settlers ate them that winter. More came in 1611 and 1614. In 1620 the Viginia Company sent 20 mares. All were English saddle-horses of the mixed early 17th-century type. The names of Mr Wood, Mr Sandys, and Mr Gookin survive as the first importers.[1]

The settlers also made contact with horse-breeding tribes to the South – the Choctaw, Cherokee, Seminole and Creek – and bought their naturalized Andalusians, which were known generically as Chickasaws.

There was still a crying need for horses. By 1649 there were only 200 in Virginia. Then they increased rapidly. By 1668 the colony was exporting. Their horses were tough and fast, but smaller than English: so small that in 1686 the colonial government, following Henry VIII, ordered that no stallion under a certain size should run with mares. The size was only 13.2 hands.[2] The 'shrinkage' could hardly have been caused by the climate or grazing of Virginia; it must have been crossing with the Indian ponies.

The settlers were sportsmen. Every member of the first King's Council of the colony had raced or bred horses in England.[3] These sporting squires probably raced in 1620. Their racing was legalized by Governor Nicholson in 1630. Many refugee cavaliers – racing men – arrived about 1650. But there was nowhere in the ordinary sense to race. The country was thick forest. Cleared land was at a premium. Racing had to be done in village streets, or in narrow tracks through the woods. All early Virginian racing was thus of one kind, completely new: a very short dash, two horses matched, in which the start was crucial, and bumping and crossing habitual.

The principal evidence about quarter-mile racing in the 17th century comes from the law courts.

The 1674 Court Records of York County, Virginia, describe two linked convictions: 'James Bullocke, a Taylor, having made a race for his mare to runn with a horse belonging to Mr Matthew Slader for twoe thousand pounds of tobacco and caske, it being contrary to Law for a Labourer to make a race, being a sport only for Gentlemen, is fined for the same one hundred pounds of tobacco and caske.

'Whereas Mr Matthew Slader and James Bullocke, by condition under the hand and seal of the said Slader, that his horse should runn out of the way that Bullocke's mare might win, wich is an apparent cheate, is ordered to be putt in the stocks and there sitt the space of one houre.'[4]

The Henrico (Enrico) County Court Records of 1689 describe an action brought after a race. An agreement had been made, and was produced, that neither horse should cross unless clear. One did, jostling the whole quarter-mile. The same court in 1698 records an action claiming non-payment of a £5 wager on a horse-match. The horse backed by the plaintiff was owned by Thomas Jefferson, grandfather of the future president.[5] The characteristics of the earliest Virginia racing are here displayed: rigid social stratification; wagers made in goods as well as money; rigging matches; the law-courts, as the only available authority, judging racing disputes and enforcing racing debts.

Horses arrived in New England in 1629, soon after the Pilgrim Fathers. They were bred with extraordinary success, so that by 1650 there was a surplus of horses in Massachusetts and Rhode Island. Many of these went to Virginia, Maryland, and South Carolina, including the famous Narragansett Pacers. This breed was always sorrel. It was said to come from the sea (as though bred, like Pegasus, by Poseidon). It was certainly raced in Rhode Island; probably in Carolina too.

In New England, as in the South, physical circumstances dictated the type of racing. In puritan Plymouth a decree of 1674 forbade horse-racing in the streets of the town.[6] Maryland forbade racing 'near the yearly meetings of the people called the Quakers'.[7] But Pennsylvania, founded in 1681, had its raffish element. William Penn's own importation, in 1699, of a stallion called Tamerlaine and two mares was not for the turf, but there was racing in Philadelphia in the next decade. They held meetings in Central Square, where the horses went 'dodging in and out among the trees'.[8] When the square was used for hanging, the horses raced round the gallows. A law was consequently passed in 1710 announcing the penalties for those who 'run races, either on horseback or on foot, lay wagers, or use any gaming or needless or vain sports and pastimes'.[9]

In Rhode Island, Deputy Governor William Robinson was the leading breeder of quarter-horses. His foundation sire was Old Snipe, one of a wild herd found on Point Judith.[10] Old Snipe must have been Andalusian. The Robinsons beat the best of Virginia in an inter-colony match, over the usual quarter-mile; the Virginians were glad to buy some Old Snipe blood.

## Full-Course Racing, New York and Virginia

Ten years before the citizens of Plymouth, to the north, banned racing from their streets, and York County Court, to the south, put a man in the stocks for fixing a match, Sir Richard Nicholls received the surrender of New Amsterdam. He became first Governor of New York. Immediately, in 1665, he laid out America's first full-sized racecourse: on Long Island, near modern Jamaica in Nassau County. He chose a wide-open plain of good grass, on which long races were possible on the English model.

The racing was, the Governor announced, 'not so much for the divertisement of youth as for encouraging the bettering of the breed of horses.'[11] Cups were given to encourage both breeders and importers. The Governor's Cup was contemporary with, and identical in intention to, the Newmarket Town Plate. A silver porringer of 1668 survives, 'wunn att hanpsted plaines, march 25.'[12]

Virginia had meanwhile been clearing land for tobacco. This crop was valuable, but it impoverished the soil, which became useless. On considerable waste tracts, therefore, racecourses were laid out, usually a mile round. Long races began, and there were Governor's prizes for them by 1691.

Virginia was becoming rich. Fine houses were built, roads laid, carriages imported. Society could afford to become wasteful, and for the first time the best horses were kept for racing. Owners had been restricted by law to the gentry, but racegoers were not. In the colony as in England racing grew so fast that it was seen to become a social evil. An Act of 1727 was directed against gamesters, for the protection of the foolish humble who were losing their time and their money.[13]

Racing developed in the same way, on a smaller scale and largely undocumented, in Maryland. Twelve silver spoons were run for at Annapolis in 1712.

NEW YORK RACING TROPHY. Sir
Richard Nicholls instituted his
Governor's Cup races only a year after
Charles II invented the Newmarket
Town Plate, and long before Royal
Plates became the established championship races of Britain. The porringer
shown is dated 1668; it is only three
years younger than the first full-sized
racecourse in America. Virginia had no
equivalent until 1691. New York thus
shares with Newmarket the distinction
of pioneering the kind of race which
dominated the next 100 years.

New York had new courses on Manhattan Island in the early 1720s. There was one
at Greenwich Village, and one on Church Farm, where in 1725 the first New York
Subscription Plate was run. Soon afterwards the farm was owned by Francis Child,
who announced: 'All persons coming into the field, subscribers and winning horses only
excepted, are to pay six pence each to the owner of the grounds.'[14].

There was probably by this time racing over a distance in New Jersey, at Paulus or
Powlus Point (Jersey City), at Philadelphia, and at Charleston.

## Racing and Breeding in Virginia

Racing in Virginia in the two generations before the Revolution was frequent, popular,
gay, and largely unrecorded. There were Governor's Prizes, other plates and purses, and
prizes of various commodities. Throughout the century there were matches. The
population of Williamsburg trebled in race-week.[15]

Hanover, with its Scottish population, had a full-sized racecourse from an early
period. In 1737 the *Virginia Gazette* announced a forthcoming three-mile race for
'20 Horses and Mares at the Old Field in Hanover County'.[16] The races were on St
Andrew's day. The programme included 'a hat to be cudgelled for; a violin to be played
for; a Quire of ballads to be sung for; a pair of silver buckles to be wrestled for; a pair
of shoes to be danced for; a pair of silk stockings for the handsomest young country
maid.'[17]

Alexandria was a third centre, in the north of the colony. In 1761 George Washington
was one of the Managers who accepted entries and adjudicated on disputes.[18] He bred
at Mount Vernon, and raced both before and after the Revolution.

In 1765 an English officer wrote: 'there are established races annually at almost every
town and considerable place in Virginia; and frequently matches on which great sums
depend. Very capital horses are started here, such as would make no despicable figure
at Newmarket; nor is their speed, bottom, or blood inferior to their appearance.'[19]

The scholars of William and Mary College, Williamsburg, were forbidden to keep
racehorses at the College 'under Pain of ye severest Animadversion and Punishment.'[20]

The most important man on the Virginia turf was John Carter, who was educated in
England at Cambridge. He was typical of one type of the pre-Revolution Virginia racing
men: the gentry, the landowners. After him came John Tayloe, second of the name, first

of Mount Airy. These Washingtons, Carters and Tayloes could have dropped into the great houses near Newmarket and no questions asked. But there were also bustling, self-made men on the turf in Virginia: colonial O'Kellys: Scottish merchants from Hanover County, prosperous yeomen who raced only to bet, and professional importers and breeders.

Proper racing required proper horses.

In 1730 Samuel Gist, a tobacco planter in Hanover County, imported Bulle Rock (or Bull, or Bully) by the Darley Arabian but of dubious dam's-side breeding. His sire's reputation had been made by Flying Childers ten years before. He was 21 years old, and had long before won and been placed at York. The fact of his arrival is more important than anything he did.

Between Bulle Rock's arrival and the Revolution, 38 identified horses and 21 mares came to Virginia: as well as others about whom nothing is known. They went to 27 principal studs on the James, York, Rappahannock and Potomac Rivers.

It is surprising that so few followed Bulle Rock for ten years, the new generation of English 'Eastern' horses being so renowned. Then in the 1740s came Dabster (grandson of the Darley Arabian out of a Spanker mare); John Baylor's Crab (Old Crab out of a Counsellor mare); and Monkey (Lonsdale Arabian out of a Byerley Turk mare). The last arrived in 1747, aged 22, and left 300 colts in Virginia.

Beginning in 1750 four horses arrived who are more important than the rest put together: Jolly Roger, Morton's Traveller, Janus, and Fearnought.

Jolly Roger was a good racehorse in England, known as Roger of the Vale. He was by Roundhead (by Flying Childers), out of a daughter of Partner by Jigg. He stood at a number of Virginia studs in the 1750s and 1760s.

Morton's Traveller arrived the same year, by Partner out of a daughter of Bloody Buttocks. Like his horse, Morton came from Yorkshire. He was a commercial importer, who bought principally from Croft's stud which was rich in Byerley Turk blood. Traveller was highly successful; many of his sons, by way of advertisement, were also called Traveller.

Janus was foaled in 1746, by Janus (Godolphin Arabian out of a Bartlett's Childers mare) out of a daughter of Old Fox. As Little Janus he was a successful racehorse, and then stood for two years near Oxford. He was imported by Mordecai Booth in 1757, and then went to John Randolph of Roanoke. He ran the usual English test of four-mile heats: but nearly all his get were very fast short runners, with no 'bottom'. John Randolph had been brought up a quarter-horse man, and had ridden in and adjudicated at quarter-races all over Virginia. He used Janus deliberately with half-bred mares to breed quarter-horses. He also used him with staying mares to get stayers, but for some reason, invisible in his pedigree, they never stayed.

Janus already had a close relation in Virginia: Childers (by Blaze, by Flying Childers, out of a Fox mare). Childers was imported by John Tayloe of Mount Airy in 1751, and he stood there for many years. His significance is that he sired many of the mares which made John Tayloe III the most important breeder in Virginia after the Revolution.

Baylor's Fearnought was the most important stallion in Virginia. John Baylor of Caroline was English-educated (Putney Grammar School); he called his house Newmarket. He had imported Crab in 1746, and had stallions of obscure pedigree called Shock and Sober John. He needed new blood and he wanted the best. In August 1761 he wrote to his agent in Liverpool listing 23 horses, the names from Heber, in which he was interested. In a letter to Thomas Hales he said: 'I should be sorry to see any but a King's Plater come as I am in want of strength for our small Virginia mares.'[21]

The horse he got was foaled in 1755, by Regulus out of Bay Silvertail by Whitenose. He fulfilled all Baylor's requirements. He was big, powerful, and very fertile. Most stallions stood at '15 shillings the leap and 45 shillings the season';[22] Baylor was able to

JOHN TAYLOE II OF MOUNT AIRY. This second-generation Virginia land-owner was one of the most significant of of the founding fathers of the American thoroughbred. His Mount Airy stud was of the first importance from 1750 until 1828. His most valuable importation was Childers (by Flying Childers' son Blaze out of a Fox mare) who sired some of Virginia's best broodmares.

charge £8 for a Fearnought cover, £10 'insured' (no foal no fee). Like Janus he was prepotent, but his stock had plenty of bottom. Thirty-two of his undoubted sons were advertised as stallions in Virginia from 1772. He also got a lot of fillies. He was America's outstanding sire until Medley; perhaps until Diomed. The Fearnought-Janus cross is particularly important, the brilliant speed of the Janus line complementing the stamina and courage of the Fearnought.

Fairfax Harrison's researches have cautiously established 21 imported mares in Virginia before the Revolution. Few are in the General Stud Book. Most pedigrees end on the bottom line with 'imported English mare'. Clarke's Godolphin Mare (imported 1733) was allegedly by the Godolphin Arabian out of a Byerley Turk mare. Duchess (or Diamond) was said to be by the Cullen Arabian out of Lady Thigh by Partner; she belonged to John Spotswood of Spotsylvania, and is an ancestress of Lexington and tap-root of what has been called the most successful bottom-line in America.[23]

But the most important mare in Virginia was Braxton's Kitty Fisher. She was by Cade (Godolphin Arabian) out of a mare by the Cullen or Somerset Arabians. She arrived in 1759 as a three-year-old, and won several matches before going to stud. She then had 13 foals, three by Fearnought. She is one of the handful of supremely important pre-Revolution mares.

## Racing and Breeding in Maryland

There were 20 courses in Maryland before the Revolution. Annapolis had a three-mile Subscription Plate by 1743; the prize was a silver bowl. Baltimore in 1745 had a three-day meeting. A ribboned hat was cudgelled for and a pair of London pumps wrestled for.[24]

The first king of the Maryland turf was the Northumbrian Samuel Ogle, who founded the Maryland Jockey Club in 1743. Of the seven considerable studs before the Revolution, by far the most important was Ogle's Belair, in Prince George's County. Like other Marylanders of his time, Ogle imported Spanish blood: 'Barb' mares from both old and new Spain. In 1735 he sent an imported mare to Bulle Rock in Virginia. They bred Ogle's Bulle Rock Mare. But by 1747 Ogle and his brother-in-law Colonel Benjamin Tasker were converted to English blood, by the example of Virginia breeders or by the new distance racing. Ogle imported Spark, by Young Aleppo out of a Bartlett's Childers mare, and inbred 3 × 3 to the Darley Arabian; and Queen Mab, by Mosco's Grey Arabian out of a Hampton Court Childers mare. These two bred Moll Brazen and Mille.

In 1751 Tasker imported Selima, by the Godolphin Arabian out of a daughter of Flying Childers. She was foaled in 1746. In 1752 (the year Ogle died) William Byrd, owner of the Hanover racecourse, issued a general challenge with his imported Tryall: four mile heats, 500 pistoles ($2000) a side. It was accepted by John Tayloe of Mount Airy with Jenny Cameron and Childers, both imported; by Colonel Francis Thornton with an unknown horse; and, facing these Virginia champions, by Tasker with Selima. The race was run at Gloucester, Virginia, on 5 December, the five entries producing 2500 pistoles ($10,000). Selima won. She went to stud at Belair; after Tasker's death Tayloe got her for Mount Airy. She ranks with Kitty Fisher.

In 1755 Governor Horatio Sharp imported Othello, by Panton's Crab out of a Bartlett's Childers mare. He stood at Belair while Sharp's Whitehall Stud was being built. In the same year Tasker imported Spark's dam Miss Colvill. From this material the first great American-bred racehorses were produced, and the American Stud Book got some of its most influential early blood.

Of the surviving Spanish strain: Ogle's Bulle Rock Mare threw a colt and a filly by Spark and a filly by Othello; these are the reasons for Bulle Rock's survival. Of purely English blood: out of Mille, Othello got True Briton, who was bought by A. W. Waters

JOHN BAYLOR. John Baylor of Newmarket, Caroline County, made it a matter of urgent priority to increase the size and stoutness of Virginia horses, which were small and short of stamina owing to their Indian (quarter-horse) blood. He therefore imported Fearnought in 1764, by the Godolphin Arabian's son Regulus, who as a King's Plater had won four-mile heats under 168 lb. This powerful horse, nearly 16 hands, achieved all that Baylor hoped.

of Long Island and General Nathaniel Heard of New Jersey in the early 1760s. Waters issued a public challenge: 'Since English horses have been imported into New York, it is the opinion of some people that they can outrun the True Briton. This is to satisfy the public, that I will run him with any horse in America; to run on Long Island the four-mile heats, or of one heat, carrying 11 stone, for 300 pounds or more, at any time only to give me one month's notice.' John Leary of Cortlandt Street had just acquired the newly-imported Old England. He said Waters' challenge was in 'most illiterate, unsportsmanlike terms', suggested four-mile heats, 9 st. (126 lb.) at Harlem, and added that if Waters declined these terms for True Briton 'I desire that he will not presume to rank him with any others than the common mongrels of the country, from which he derived, and that he will be forever silent on the subject of matching and racing.'[25] True Briton distanced Old England in the first heat.

Benjamin Tasker died in 1760. His stock was dispersed all over Maryland and Virginia. True Briton stayed in New York. In 1780, when he was an old horse, he was daringly stolen from the rebel-held city by some English officers, and taken to Connecticut. He there sired Justin Morgan, founder of the race of Morgan horses.

## Racing and Breeding in South Carolina

South Carolina racing was of a different, more ramshackle character in its early years: organized by inn-keepers and ferry-operators, with taverns and ferry-landings as the racecourses.[26] Saddles and tankards were the prizes. The horses were Chickasaws or Narragansetts. At Goose Creek there was a place called Newmarket, not to be confused with the New Market at Charleston.

In 1734 there was a Jockey Club at Charleston, which meant that a group of men, of unknown status, operated a racecourse. The races were over a distance. Some were limited to amateur (white) riders; others were open to their Negro grooms.

In 1758 South Carolina had a colonial Jockey Club organized by Edward Fenwick and his friends. Fenwick was a member of the famous English North Country family, owners of Matchem. He had come over with his father; by this date he had several estates and a great many slaves. He kept close touch with England and often went there. The races of which he was founder were at New Market, Charleston. They are more fully documented than any others of the period. There was a Charles Town Plate and a Colts' Plate; there were sweepstakes and many matches. It is evident that imported horses were raced for these principal events, since there were also races for country-breds. Cock-fighting was regular and regularly reported.

The first English horse arrived in South Carolina almost as soon as Bulle Rock: it was owned by Governor Johnson during his term of office – 1730-5. It appears in the pedigree of a horse called Coxcomb. In Coxcomb's ancestry there is also a Chickasaw horse; this is an ingredient as special to South Carolina as the 'Barb' to Maryland or the quarter-horse to Virginia.

South Carolina had one stud as pre-eminent as Belair in Maryland. Edward Fenwick founded it in about 1750, named it John's Island after his father, and attached it to his father's Fenwick Hall. He started with Chickasaws. In 1756 his breeding went English. His family's recent success with Matchem influenced him towards the Godolphin Arabian: nearly all his imported stallions were the Godolphin's grandsons. His first and most important purchase was Brutus, by Regulus out of Lodge's Roan Mare. Brutus was foaled in 1748 and was a good racehorse. His stock was usually roan; racing against each other his sons dominated Charleston from the late 1760s.

Fenwick also imported six mares. The most important was a Squirt Mare (granddaughter of Bartlett's Childers) out of a half-sister to Cypron, dam of Herod. Fenwick's Squirt Mare ranks as a matriarch with Kitty Fisher and Selima.

SLAMERKIN AND FOAL. Slamerkin (1769) was bred by James DeLancey II at Bouwerie, by imported Wildair (by Matchem's sire Cade) out of an imported unnamed mare by Cub. She won the Four Years Old Plates at Newmarket (S.C.) and Philadelphia in 1773 before going to stud, where she became one of the most influential broodmares in American History. Her sire was repurchased by his breeder Edward Leedes in 1773.

GOVERNOR SAMUEL OGLE. Ogle (1694–1752) is said to be descended from an ancient and noble Northumbrian family. Relationship with Henry VIII's Master of Horse (see p. 29) is speculative. He was three times Governor of Maryland, to which post he was appointed by Lord Baltimore. After he turned from Spanish 'Barbs' to thoroughbreds he travelled regularly to England, bringing back, among others, Spark, a present from Lord Baltimore to whom he had been given by Frederick Prince of Wales.

*Right*

JAMES DELANCEY II. Stephen DeLancey, an Englishman of Huguenot descent, arrived in New York in 1666, and became the richest man on Manhattan Island. His son James (1703–1760) was Chief Justice of the colony, and presided over the first Colonial Congress. His son, James II, was educated at Eton and Cambridge, and became a leading light of the high-betting Macaroni Club – New York's deliberate imitation of White's – and the 'Father of the New York Turf'. He sold his stock by auction in March and November 1775, returned to England, and died in 1801 in Bath, Somerset.

Two other English thoroughbred mares arrived in the colony before the Revolution: Mayrant's Dutches or Duchess, and Bee's Regulus Mare. John Mayrant also imported Skim in 1760, said to be by the Cullen Arabian. Skim 'the Invincible' was champion racehorse from 1762–7, before the sons of Brutus defeated everything; all those years he was also covering. There were many other English stallions, but apparently no other mares. The stallions must have covered Chickasaw mares. Some of the get doubtless raced.

In 1769 a horse called Noble was distanced by a horse he should have beaten. It emerged that Fenwick Bull Esquire (Justice of the Peace, Notary Public) had bribed Noble's rider. 'After receiving the usual and proper discipline of the horsewhip, his worship was carried into a room by the gentlemen of the turf to protect him from the mob.'[27]

## Racing and Breeding in New York

The New York Subscription Plate continued to be run for annually. 1751 was its 25th renewal; the bowl is engraved: 'The Plate was won by a Horse cal'd OLD TENOR Belonging to Lewis Moris Jun'r. Octob'r ye 11, 1751.'[28] Morris was a signatory of the Declaration of Independence; he founded the Morrisiana Stud. The race was by this time limited to American-bred horses; this is evidence not of Indian ponies racing in New York, but of an 85-year-old bloodstock industry. The 1753 Plate was won by John Leary's Smoaker. Leary was an Irish immigrant, the first professional jockey and trainer in America; he had stables on Cortlandt Street.

More important than either Morris or Leary was James DeLancey, English educated, of Huguenot descent, member, like Morris, of a leading family (with quite different politics; he retired to England at the Revolution and stayed there). He was given to 'horse-racing, cock-fighting, and women.'[29] His Bouwerie Farm was an immense breeding and training establishment with its own gallops. He imported Wildair, by Cade out of a Steady mare descended from Place's White Turk; Lath (Protector in England) by Crab out of Crazy by Lath; and a mare by Cub out of Amaranthus' Dam by Second.

When DeLancey went home, he sold Wildair. A certificate accompanied the horse which impressively listed his winning sons and daughters, the best of the former being Simms' Wildair, the most important of the latter being Slamerkin. The certificate concludes: 'Everything of his get that have started have won except two, and them out of very bad mares.'[30]

Slamerkin was out of the Cub Mare. She has been called 'the grandmother of the American turf',[31] and reckoned more important even than Selima, Kitty Fisher, Duchess, or the Squirt Mare. For this reason the American Stud Book calls her dam 'one of the most valuable mares ever imported into this country, nearly all the best horses in America tracing to her either on the dam's or the sire's side'.

## Pennsylvania and New Jersey

Philadelphia graduated from its Central Square improvisations, and its anti-racing laws, to regular racing on a full-sized course in about 1750. There was a Jockey Club in 1760. Its racing was the first recorded in the English Calendar, in which Pennsylvania is called 'New England'. The Jockey Club failed. The 2nd Philadelphia Jockey Club was attempted in 1766; Richard Penn, the last Royal Governor, was President. A list of registered colours includes those of DeLancey and Morris from New York and certain Maryland owners.

Tifter (Young Tifter in England) by Tifter, descended from the Toulouse Barb, came to Philadelphia almost immediately after regular racing started. A few years later the colony bought Juniper, by Babraham by the Godolphin Arabian, imported in 1761 to Virginia. In England he had scored 14 wins and four seconds in 18 starts.

The New Jersey course was reached by ferry from Church Farm, Manhattan, which is why it was sited there, and why it was gobbled by Jersey City. In 1748 racing for gain was outlawed in New Jersey (except at fairs or on official holidays); it was permitted again in 1761, but not within two miles of any church.

## Stud Management in the Colonies

Horses having the eminent breeding of those discussed, and such high prices, must have been expected to repay the investment on the turf, in the paddock, or in the sale-ring. But as in England the breed as a whole benefited. Dabster, the first thoroughbred stallion in Virginia after Bulle Rock, was a good sire of racehorses but a pre-eminent sire of hunters (fox-hunting, which started about 1730, was as characteristic of tobacco-rich Virginia as racing). Aristotle (Cullen Arabian – Crab Mare), imported in 1763, was advertised in Virginia as 'remarkable for getting the best carriage and riding nags.'[32] Even Janus, maker of sprinters, got untold numbers of saddle and harness horses.

Stud management was simple. A typical stallion advertisement runs: 'The noted horse Ranter, stands the ensuing season at the Falls Plantation, in Chesterfield, and will cover mares at 20 shillings the leap, and 40 shillings the season. Very fine pasturage gratis, and good care will be taken of the mares, but I will not be answerable for any escapes. William Black.'[33] Escapes were frequent, thefts more so. Owners of stallions usually declined responsibility, in terms like those on a hat-rack in a barber-shop. But a word was often put in about the trustworthiness of the groom or slave.

In one respect stud management was tragically casual. They kept no records. There is no American equivalent to the earlier Yorkshire stud-books. The last pre-Revolution importation was 20 years before the first volume of the GSB. Horses arrived with certificates of breeding, but very few survive. History relies on newspaper snippets and above all stallion advertisements, which are reliable, and on tradition and the early American Stud Books, which are not. This is why it is impossible to say how much Choctaw and quarter-horse blood survived in Virginia pedigrees, how much 'Barb' in Maryland, how much Chickasaw and Narragansett in South Carolina.

## Quarter Racing: the New Breed of Sprinter

Quarter racing was strong in Virginia and North Carolina. The countryside had opened up. Long races were possible and popular. But necessity had become a virtue. A lot of men loved the brief, blazing excitement of the quarter-mile dash after the tense 'turn and lock' start. Shortly before the Revolution, the English officer in Virginia, already quoted, wrote: 'In the Southern part of the Colony, and in North Carolina, they are much addicted to quarter-racing, which is always a match between two horses to run over one quarter of a mile straight out, being merely an expression of speed; and they have a breed which perform it with astonishing velocity, beating every other for that distance with great ease, but they have no bottom. However, I am confident that there is no horse in England, nor perhaps in the whole world, that can excel them in rapid speed.'[34]

By this time a new breed had been created. Before about 1760 the quarter-horse was a cross of pre-thoroughbred English with Indian-Andalusian: its speed was the result of selective breeding, over a century and a half, with these ingredients. But in the last years before the Revolution, thoroughbred and quarter-horse met and mixed. The importance to the latter is illustrated by the career of a horse called Trickem.

A family called Sharrard moved from Virginia to Dobbs County, North Carolina, bringing with them their champion quarter-horse Blue Boar, Roanoke-bred by Janus. A young Scottish storekeeper had a little scrubby saddle-horse which in 1770 he rashly matched against the great Blue Boar, at a feather to 160 lb. He staked everything on his pony – store, stock, oxen, Negroes. The pony, ridden by a slave who weighed 50 lb., won easily. In fact it was Trickem, also by Janus, owned by an Old Etonian called Willie Jones, of Halifax County. Store, stock, and character had all been acquired for the purpose of this single *coup*.

Two years later Jones, in some other guise, matched a horse restricted in size by the terms. His horse had to have its feet pared so far down to qualify that it could not run. At the last moment he substituted, to the general derision, a little shaggy pony out of the shafts of his cart. This was Trickem, which won again at ridiculous odds.[35]

Certain thoroughbreds – Janus above all – imparted inexplicable brilliance to the quarter-horse. But the influence was mutual. The quarter-horse is one of the ingredients which gives the American thoroughbred an ancestry unlike any other in the world.

## Other Importations; Spanish and Indian Racing

The Swedes brought horses to Delaware in 1629, the Flemish to New York in 1660, the French to Canada in 1665. None of these colonists had any racing tradition.

But while Newmarket was being transplanted onto the Eastern seaboard, Andalusia was settling North of the Rio Grande: and racing came too. The Spaniards had crossed into *Tejas* under Azcué in 1665, and lost their horses to the Indians 10 years later. In 1687 Alonzo de Léon met mounted Indians, and early in the 18th century the French in Louisiana were buying horses from the tribes.

The Indians of those parts learned horsemanship in three ways. They watched the Spaniards, stole their horses, and imitated them. They were taught by the missions, who needed *vaqueros*. And they learned from the half-breed *Comancheros*, whose trade was illicit horse-dealing. All the great hunting and fighting tribes of Texas became superb horsemen – the Comanche, Apache, Cheyenne, and Arapaho. The very best were the Comanche, who had a passion for racing.

In Northern Mexico, racing took the form of a game called *correr el gallo*: a rider had to gallop down a long straight, hampered by a live rooster, while the others tried to intercept him.[36] The *vaqueros* of Texas had a variant in which a goose was hung upside down in a tree with its neck greased; the contestant had to pull off the goose's head as he galloped under the tree.

The Spanish got to California just before the Revolution, under Fernando de Rivera y Moncada in 1768. The horses and cattle they brought thrived in that generous climate. Horses went wild and were a pest by 1800. The Californians' horse-sports were those of the rest of Latin America, and they invented a variant of the bull-fight which anticipates the modern rodeo. Their racing was *juego de gallo*, another misuse of poultry. The chickens were buried in the sand up to their necks. The riders had to pick them up at the gallop and finish holding them by the head.

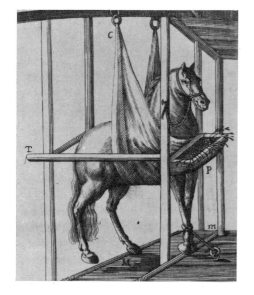

TRANSPORTING HORSES TO AMERICA. There was a shortage of horses in Spain at the beginning of the 16th century, owing to a general preference for riding mules; the good Andalusians needed by the colonists were therefore at a greater premium than ever before. Exporters, who needed a royal licence, went to much trouble and expense to get their precious freight safely across the Atlantic. This horse is slung, hobbled, haltered, and penned in; but his ears are pricked and he seems content.

NO HORSES &c. DELIVERED WITHOUT BEING PAID FOR

## 12 Nineteenth-Century Britain:

## Bentinck and Before

### Transformation of Racing in the 19th Century

In the first half of the 19th century British racing doubled in numbers of racecourses and of races run, and trebled in numbers of horses. The swing continued of younger horses running over shorter distances; by 1859 more two-year-olds ran than horses of any other age. Rules continued to develop, and the Jockey Club's authority to grow. Villains and defaulters were pursued relentlessly, and with occasional success. The legs formed themselves into the Ring, and became bookmakers. Betting was prodigious. And racing reached, in the early years of Queen Victoria, the lowest moral ebb of its history.

In the second half of the century the number of courses steadied and then dropped. But there were ever more races and ever more racehorses. There were fewer of the most grotesquely unsuitable owners, and frauds were perpetrated with more tact. The Jockey Club's authority became theoretically absolute. The rules of racing and the conditions of races assumed a modern look. The horse himself became taller, faster, sounder in the wind but less sound in the legs, and was better looked after.

### Regency, George IV, William IV

After the Escape affair the Prince of Wales left the turf in dudgeon. The Jockey Club made overtures of peace in 1805 in a letter signed by Sir Charles Bunbury and Lord Darlington: 'We humbly request that Your Royal Highness will bury in oblivion any past unfortunate Occurrences at Newmarket.'[1] The result was uneasy truce.

In 1828 the prince, now George IV, gave a dinner to the Jockey Club at St James's at which the old wounds were finally healed. He twice gave the toast of 'The Turf'; he 'said that there was no man who had the interests of the turf more at heart than himself.'

His favourite courses were Brighton, Lewes, and Ascot. In the year of his accession he raced every day at Ascot, except when his mistress Lady Conyngham 'said she was bored and would not go; he accordingly would not go either.' At meetings of the Privy Council he greatly preferred whispering with Greville about racing to transacting business. In 1829 he accepted the title of Patron of the Jockey Club at his racing dinner in June. He said then that 'in withdrawing himself as he had done from the Jockey Club he was not influenced by any unkindness to any member of it, or any indifference to the interests of the turf.' Ascot was two weeks later. 'The King has bought seven horses successively, for which he has given 11,300 guineas, principally to win the Cup at Ascot, which he has

SETTLING DAY AT TATTERSALLS. The yard behind the 'Corner' was the scene twice a week of auctions. A separate activity was conducted in the Subscription Room, the demure door of which is visible. This was the home of the Ring, who took over the yard each Monday to settle. Some of the leading legs have their own tables under the arcade. The plump man being paid is 'Crutch' Robinson. The date is about 1838.

never accomplished.' The winner that year was Zinganee, offered to the king by the Chifney brothers and refused, and bought two hours before the race by Charles Greville for Lord Chesterfield. The king was very chagrined.

His younger brother the Duke of York was equally keen. His stable was managed by Charles Greville until his death in 1827. The previous year he had managed to race at Ascot in spite of gangrenous legs. He was as extravagant and improvident as his brother: when he died he left appalling debts, including one of £300 to his jockey Tom Goodison (son of Old Q's trainer, Hell Fire Dick).[2] He was as festive as the 'First Gentleman', but in a more laborious way; it was his custom after dinner to 'drink to Cardinal Puff', a toast which involved an elaborate and tedious comic ritual.[3]

William IV was prepared to do his duty by racing, but he was quite ignorant and not very interested. 'He keeps the stud (which is to be diminished) because he thinks he ought to support the turf.'[4] Yearlings from Hampton Court were sold annually at Tattersalls. In the first year of his reign he was asked which of his horses he wanted sent to Goodwood. 'Send the whole fleet,' he said, 'some of them I suppose will win.' He was first, second, and third in the Goodwood Cup.[5] In 1831 he was 'bored to death at the races, and his own horse broke down.'

In May 1832, the middle of the Reform Bill crisis, he was hit in the eye at Ascot by a ginger-nut thrown by a 'miserable-looking ragamuffin'.[6] This quite turned him against racing.[7] Only affection for the 5th Duke of Richmond kept him on the turf at all.[8]

The young Princess Victoria had been seen at Ascot and York, but this augury was misleading. One of the first acts of the new reign was the dispersal of the Hampton Court Stud. The queen came to the Derby with Prince Albert in 1840. There were no scenes of public enthusiasm; she never came to Epsom again. She did go annually to Ascot until Albert died. As at the accession of George I, royalty ceased to be a factor on the turf.

## The Problems and Scandals of the Turf

About 1804 the 'legs' appeared: the blacklegs, the fielders. They invented the principle of laying bets at varying prices about every horse in a race. This was called 'betting-round', and later 'making a book'. The leg became known as a penciller, metallist, or bookmaker. If a leg laid heavily against a fancied horse he climbed out of his risk by hedging, but this reduced the margin of profit. It was better to allow a clear favourite to be established by weight of public money, and then stop the horse winning.

The first notorious examples of this were in 1809–11. A trough at Doncaster was poisoned, then one at Newmarket belonging to the 'stable keeper Stevens'. Two horses died, others were damaged, and 'the stable cat ran about like a maniac.' In 1811 Richard Prince's trough on Newmarket Heath was poisoned with arsenic. Four horses died, belonging to Lord Foley and Colonel Mellish. Cecil Bishop, once a dispenser at Guy's Hospital, turned king's evidence. He implicated a 'low touter', Daniel Dawson, a 'quiet, red-faced little chum . . . always so sociable over his pipe and pot in an evening'.[9] Behind Dawson were legs, the sinister Bland brothers – Joe, once a postboy, and 'Facetious Jemmy', an ex-coachman. Dawson was tried at Cambridge Assizes and hanged on August 8 1812; no-one bothered the Blands.

The first appearance of the legs in numbers was at Brighton: 'The "legs" and bettors, who had arrived in shoals, used all to assemble on the Steyne, at an early hour, to commence their operations on the first day, and the buzz was tremendous, till Lord Foley and Mellish, the two great confederates of that day, would approach the ring, and then a sudden silence ensued, to await the opening of their books.'[10] Mellish lost £20,000 on the Sancho-Pavilion match at Lewes in 1804, but 'such trifles did not weigh very long on a philosophic mind like the Colonel's. . . Mellish never opened his mouth under £500 in the Ring.'[11]

ASCOT: GOLD CUP DAY. The field for the 1839 race. Nearest is Lord Suffield's Caravan (1834, by Camel out of Wings), the winner, about to be saddled by Jem Robinson. Left is the favourite St Francis, Ion beyond, and Bey of Algiers right, respectively second, third and last. The small building nearest is the royal stand; Queen Victoria is in the royal box on her second visit as Queen. The foundation of the grandstand beyond had been laid by Lord Errol, Master of the Buckhounds, on 16 January the same year. The austerer building beyond was called the betting stand.

In 1818 Tattersall opened his New Subscription Room and, although 'Druid' uses the word of an earlier period, this was the real beginning of the Ring.[12] In the Room bets were struck all week and, each Monday, with luck, settled.

The Ring was also mobile: it followed the races. 'The town of Newmarket, containing then half the British peerage, was infested by hordes of scoundrels of the most daring, villainous looks and characters, and for 24 hours was entirely at their mercy.' At Epsom the Ring opened opposite the grandstand, and moved to the crest of the Down, where it formed round a gibbet. It was bedlam, a mixture of dukes and dregs, exactly like a cockpit.[13]

Besides the Blands, the most notable legs were 'Crutch' Robinson, 'Ludlow' Bond ('Death on the Pale Horse' because he rode a grey on Newmarket Heath),[14] Harry Hill, John Gully, Robert Ridsdale, and Crockford.

Harry Hill started as a boots in a public house. He became extremely rich. He was dirty, hard-featured, foul-mouthed, and a womanizer.[15] He ultimately lost all his money on the Stock Exchange. He was a commissioner as well as a layer of bets, and was used by Lord George Bentinck both in this capacity and as a source of underworld information.

Gully was the son of a failed Bristol butcher. He was put into the Fleet, the debtors' prison, by his creditors. He was there visited by Henry Pearce, the 'Game Chicken', champion of England. They sparred. Pearce offered him a fight, Gully to be sponsored by Colonel Mellish and his debts paid. Pearce won a punishing battle at Hailsham – 64 rounds, an hour and 17 minutes – and then retired. Gully was champion. He twice defended successfully against the uncouth giant Gregson from Lancashire. He became landlord of the Plough Inn, Carey Street; he then became a commissioner and leg in alliance with the glib little Yorkshireman Robert Ridsdale. He made a fortune. He became M.P. for Pontefract in 1832, Squire of Ackworth, Master of the Badsworth Hunt. He won the Derby with St Giles, Pyrrhus The First, and Andover. After his first victory he had a dispute with Ridsdale which ended with an assault with a whip in the hunting-field. Gully then allied himself with Harry Hill, and they and their friends formed the 'Danebury Confederacy' with the egregious Day family. 'Sylvanus' liked and admired him.[16] Charles Greville said he had good sense, good taste, and good manners.[17] William Day described his 'tyrannical and overbearing disposition'; he was 'extremely avaricious'.[18] This was after the Derby of 1845, in which Gully's horse Old England was got at by Day (whose own father trained it) and men called Bloodworth and Stebbings. All three were warned off.

The methods of Gully, Ridsdale and Hill were as crooked as they could be, their principal technique being to bribe jockeys. As late as 1853 Hill bribed Frank Butler (nephew of the Chifney brothers) to lose the St Leger on Mr Bowes's West Australian, which had already won the 2000 Guineas and the Derby. The owner and Colonel Anson had a word with Butler. West Australian won, and Hill lost £20,000.[19]

Gully had learned the hard way. In 1827 he bought Lord Jersey's Derby winner Mameluke and ran it in the St Leger. He backed it to win a great deal of money, principally with Crockford, ex-fishmonger and the biggest layer of the day. There was an appalling series of false starts, which destroyed Mameluke's chance. Several bad horses were put into the race, specifically to bring this about: and the starter himself was bribed by Crockford. With his winnings Crockford opened his gaming-house.

Crockford was the second most evil man on the 19th-century turf: 'Old Crocky, the father of hell and hazard – ye fiends! what a title! yet truly his own by infernal right . . . We well remember the old gentleman. His cheeks appeared whitened and flabby through constant night-work. His hands were entirely *without knuckles*, soft as raw veal, and as white as paper, whilst his large, flexible mouth, was stuffed with "dead men's bones," – his teeth being all false, and visibly socketed in his darling metal, as was foully developed when indulging himself with a hideous laugh with his friend Gully, or other "congenial", over the delicious flavour or odour of some little "plant", or lucky *coup*.'[20]

Crockford himself had his own come-uppance more than once. His King Richard was fancied for the Derby; according to Dick Christian (who later hunted the horse in Leicestershire) 'the lad lamed his leg the night before the race, he was, no doubt, hired to it.'[21] In 1844 his Ratan was not only got at the night before, but also pulled by the jockey Sam Rogers. The shock killed Crockford, who died on the morning of the Oaks two days later. His friends propped him in an armchair in the window of his club until after the Oaks, so that their bets were still on. Having looked like a corpse in life, he looked alive when he was dead.

A bare 30 years after the first appearance of the legs: 'No honourable man,' said 'Nimrod', 'can be successful, for any length of time, against such a horde of determined depredators as have lately been seen on our racecourses; the most princely fortune cannot sustain itself against the deep-laid stratagems of such villainous combinations.'[22] According to 'Sylvanus' on almost every page, doping, bought jockeys, bribed officials, false starts were habitual throughout the 1830s and 1840s: and almost all because of the legs and their creatures. When John Kent took Surplice to Epsom in 1848 he was eaten with anxiety because he knew how heavily some of the Ring had laid against the horse;

writing 44 years later he said: 'it was more common to poison or lame horses than is now the case;' and there were several attempts to bribe the lads at Goodwood.[23]

What created the problem was the scale of betting. As early as 1806, two full months before the St Leger, 'There is little doubt that upwards of one million guineas has already been laid.'[24] Laming a favourite could make a fortune for a leg overnight.

The volume of money involved increased when the public began betting off the course. The units were small but the numbers immense. In 1840 'there were, in my day, many retail shops in York, wherein you might purchase half an ounce of cayenne and "get pepper" to a "pony" on any great race pending, from the sedate, tranquil old gentleman who served you . . . There was a sporting, smellfungi old character, habited in drab integuments and a flaxen wig, who dealt in chemicals, and seemed a very "deacon of the craft;" ' if you wanted a bet, 'wouldn't he *then* make a rush at you over the counter, and book you before you could say "done!" . . . Even the old Quaker tea-dealer in the square would take a point more than the betting on John Scott's Ledger [*sic*] horse . . . "Old Smelt" the unctuous publican of the Shambles, did the city "business"; he making a "thoosand poond" book, and having a five pound lottery to boot.'[25]

Legs at all levels could win in another way which became a major problem. They did not pay their losses. Horses backed with no hope of settlement were 'bagged', and there was no redress against defaulters. In 1819 welshers left more than £10,000 unpaid. The figure was far larger in later years.

A great deal needed to be done.

## The Battles of Lord George Bentinck

Sir Charles Bunbury died in 1821, and although there were honourable men on the turf there was no individual with his authority. What the turf got in the 1840s was an autocrat of immense energy but questionable morals.

In his obituary of his cousin Lord George Bentinck, Charles Greville wrote: 'Oh for the inconsistency of human nature, the strange compound and medley of human motives and impulses, when the same man who crusaded against the tricks and villainies of others did not scruple to do things quite as bad as the worst of the misdeeds which he so vigorously and unrelentingly attacked!'[26]

He started riding races at Goodwood in about 1825. He started betting at the same time. In 1830 his father, the Duke of Portland, paid his Doncaster losses of £11,000, forbidding him to bet thereafter. He promised not to, and broke his promise on a gigantic scale. Less than a year later a bet landed him in a duel. He was racing at the private meeting at Heaton Park, 'an immense party, excellent house and living, and very good sport for the sort of thing in a park, with gentlemen riders.'[27] George Osbaldeston, the 'Squire of England', rode his own horse in a race and was down the field. The next day he brought it out again, and Bentinck laid him £400 to £100 against it. He won. A few days later at Newmarket Osbaldeston asked for his money. Bentinck paid, at the same time accusing the Squire of cheating. Osbaldeston challenged. After some further name-calling Bentinck had to accept. Osbaldeston was the best pistol-shot in England; Bentinck had never fired one. In the event Bentinck missed and Osbaldeston fired in the air.

At the same period Bentinck became an owner. To deceive his father he raced in other men's names, especially those of Greville and Mr Bowe, landlord of the Turf Tavern, Doncaster.

His first good horse was the filly Preserve (in Greville's name) which was favourite for the Oaks in 1835. 'To assist as much as possible in driving her back in the betting, some one hit on the following novel and well-devised stratagem. Her nostrils were painted inside and out with a mixture of starch, flour, and colouring matter to resemble mucus, before going to exercise.' She was seen by the touts appearing to be suffering from 'flu,

LORD GEORGE BENTINCK. 'Sylvanus' described Bentinck (1802–1848) as 'a tall, high-bred man of the true Anglo-Saxon tint and countenance. . . who seemed to still the Ring when the quiet, rather womanish tones of his voice were heard, offering some mighty sum against a horse in the Derby. He had the genuine cut of an English gentleman – so countrified, yet refined – so quiet, yet determined in his air.' 'Sylvanus's' friend O'Fay called him 'a lion of the turf, and a very dangerous customer! . . . He goes in for the *great coups ;* and with an innate love of sporting, and proficiency in wood and turf-craft, brings the acuteness of a superior mind, and consummate coolness, to his aid in carrying out his racing schemes.'

and her price duly went out. In the event she was beaten, and Lord George lost a lot of money.[28]

In August he and Greville differed about Preserve's future: 'on this occasion I opposed and thwarted him, and his resentment broke out against me with a vehemence and ferocity that perfectly astounded me, and displayed in perfection the domineering insolence of his character.'[29] Bentinck's horses thereupon moved from Newmarket to the Days of Danebury.

The great three-year-old of 1836 was Bay Middleton, but in his absence Bentinck's Elis was fancied for the St Leger. To the owner's fury he could not get the odds he demanded from the Ring. He threatened to scratch; he also left the horse at Goodwood, where he had been running, until it became obvious that he would not have time to walk to Doncaster. The price went out; Bentinck had his bets. It happened that a groom called Doe had been trainer to a Mr Territt, who in 1816 sent his horse Sovereign from Worcestershire to Newmarket in a bullock-cart. To Bentinck's design, the London coachbuilder Herring constructed an enormous wagon drawn by six horses. It was backed up to a high bank and Elis and The Drummer were led in. This amazing vehicle covered 80 miles a day; it got Elis well-rested to Doncaster, where he won the big race. The principle was copied and much improved by Mr Hunnybun of Newmarket. 'The introduction and universal employment of vans inaugurated a revolution in the management and engagement of race horses.'[30]

ELIS AND HIS VAN. This is Doncaster, just before the St Leger of 1836. John Day rides in Lord Lichfield's colours. Elis's travelling-companion The Drummer is being led out of Herring's enormous vehicle. Right, with the pony, is John Doe, to whom credit is given for the idea of the van.

Danebury, in those days of the 'Confederacy', was the biggest betting stable in England; and while there Bentinck began his own heavy plunging. Not, however, purely from financial greed. His admirer Disraeli said (in words later plagiarized by Greville): 'He valued the acquisition of money on the turf, because there it was the test of success. He counted his thousands after a great race as a victorious general counts his cannon and his prisoners.'[31] He despised men who raced on different lines. In 1838 Lord Chesterfield's Don John won the St Leger. Chesterfield only backed it modestly. 'Had Don John been mine,' said Bentinck, 'I would not have left a single card-seller in Doncaster with a coat to his back.'[32]

Soon afterwards Chesterfield's dispersal sale was held. Bentinck bought an old mare called Octaviana, with her filly-foal by the Chifneys' Priam, for 54 guineas. She was called Crucifix. She won all her nine starts as a two-year-old in 1839, and in 1840 the 2000 Guineas, 1000 Guineas, and Oaks (on three legs). Bentinck won £60,000.[33] 'He seriously crippled the ring, which . . . he sincerely hoped and tried to break.'[34] He kept quiet about the filly breaking down, and laid against her for the St Leger, for which she obviously did not start. According to William Day this deceit caused Bentinck's rupture with Danebury, after which he had to be sued for the training bill.[35] According to everybody else, it was because Old John Day wrote a letter to his commissioner telling him to lay against a horse of Bentinck's which was 'dead', and one to Bentinck telling him to back the horse because it would win: and he put the letters in the wrong envelopes.

Bentinck had invested a lot of his own money in the Danebury stables and gallops; he now moved his string to Goodwood. He spent much more money. His improvements were a major reason for the stable's success: 'Every day the gallops were bush-harrowed and carefully rolled, and a band of women were employed to repair the tracks, remove stones, and fill in the footprints with forks specially made for the purpose.'[36] His stud and stable outlay was at least £40,000 a year, which he could not hope to recover in stakes. He had to bet. He was easily the heaviest bettor in Britain. For years his biggest source of income was Lord Kelburne (later the eccentric, habitually unsuccessful, well-liked Earl of Glasgow), who loved matching his horses for huge sums, and never won. In the Derby of 1843 'George Bentinck backed a horse of his called Gaper (and not a good one), to win about £120,000.'[37] Gaper was nowhere, but Bentinck won £7000 from Kelburne and £30,000 altogether.

Bentinck also took on the management of Goodwood racecourse. He was a reformer of the utmost merit. Much of what he did related to public comfort and enjoyment, and will be considered later; two of his reforms were part of the war on fraud.

The first concerned starts. Bad starts were habitual and a scandal. The starter stood at the side of the horses and said 'Go,' as in Charles II's time. He was often incompetent, sometimes frightened, and occasionally bribed. Races took an hour and more to get off. At Goodwood, Bentinck was in a position to insist on punctual starts, and to fine both starters and jockeys who delayed them. More important, he invented the flag start: the starter stood in front of the horses, who started on the visual signal of the flag dropping. Bentinck himself first used this method to get off the Great Yorkshire Handicap at Doncaster; he made it invariable at Goodwood; it was at once imitated.

Bentinck also attacked defaulters. Because Goodwood was the Duke of Richmond's private property, he was able to eject them, and in 1843 he began doing so. Among those harassed were two brothers called Russell, one a lawyer; they hit back. In November 'A rascally attorney has brought actions against a parcel of people.'[38] The actions derived from the forgotten but unrepealed *Qui Tam* statute (9 Anne XIV), which limited gambling winnings to a derisory figure. The Russells stood to make half a million out of their roles as informers; they were also motivated by pique. The persons sued included Bentinck and Gully. They were acquitted the following spring on a technicality. A Select Committee of the House of Lords on Betting followed, and then the Duke of

Richmond's 'Manly Sports' bill, which Bentinck drafted and which allowed sportsmen to bet as much as they liked.

This episode increased Bentinck's popularity and power, but not as much as the Derby of 1844.

In 1843 a horse called Maccabaeus, owned by Goodman Levi ('Mr Goodman') and trained by Sadler at Stockbridge, was marked as dead in the Calendar. In October, at

Newmarket, a horse called Running Rein, also trained by Sadler, ran in a two-year-old event. The Duke of Rutland objected to it as a three-year-old, but the charge was impossible to prove. It was Maccabaeus.

'Running Rein' was entered in the Derby of 1844, and objected to before the start. For reasons which are still obscure it was allowed to run; naturally it won. Colonel Peel (later General, brother of Sir Robert, one of the best-liked men on the turf) owned Orlando, which finished second. Egged on by Bentinck, Peel objected to the winner. Weatherbys withheld the stake from Wood, an Epsom corn-chandler who was the figurehead owner; they paid it into court. Wood consequently sued Peel. 'Our case was admirably got up, owing in great measure to the indefatigable activity and the intelligence and penetration of George Bentinck, who played the part both of attorney and policeman in hunting out and getting up the evidence.'[39] 'Running Rein' was never produced, which was of itself damning. Peel won and got his stake. The racing community was so

RUNNING REIN'S DERBY. The most extraordinary race in the two centuries of the Derby's history: won by a four-year-old, who in running broke the leg of a six-year-old; the favourite the victim of foul riding, the second favourite of both doping and pulling; the whole followed by litigation, acrimony, and malefactors fleeing the country.

grateful to Bentinck that a large sum was raised by subscription and given to him. He handed it to the Jockey Club as a fund for the distressed dependants of jockeys and grooms.

The 1844 Derby also had in the field a horse called Leander. In 1840–1 the Lichtwald brothers were accused of starting horses under false pedigrees, and were forbidden to race in Mecklenburg and Prussia by the Committee of Racing of each place. 'The conduct of the German sportsmen is deserving of much praise in sifting this matter to the bottom at no small trouble, and it is hoped that the example will not be lost on English sportsmen.'[40] But they ran Leander at Epsom three years later. Like Running Rein, it was objected to before the start but allowed to race. It was struck into by Running Rein during the race, brought down, and killed. It was buried. When it was dug up its lower jaw was missing. Its upper jaw established it as at least a four-year-old; it may have been six.

In the same race the favourite, the Danebury Confederacy's The Ugly Buck, was the victim of foul riding; and Crockford's Ratan, the second favourite, was nobbled, and the owner died of his losses.

For Bentinck success followed success. In 1845 he netted £100,000. His example at Goodwood was being imitated all over Britain. He was the dominant figure of the turf as owner, bettor, administrator, and reformer.

Then suddenly, during the Goodwood meeting of 1846, he sold his 130 horses for the ridiculous sum of £10,000. He wanted (or felt obliged) to be a full-time politician, leader of the Protectionists. 'The world,' says Disraeli, 'has hardly done justice to the great sacrifice which he made on this occasion to a high sense of duty.'[41] (Day has a different explanation: 'Ill-success in racing drove him from the turf.' That Goodwood meeting a horse of his was beaten by Old John's Mathematician: 'This latter event drove him broken-hearted from the turf, and hastened his death, if it were not the absolute cause of it.')[42] A young man called Edward Lloyd Mostyn bought the horses. He sold many at Tattersalls; he refused £12,000 for only four of the 130. These four included Surplice, the yearling son by Touchstone of the great Crucifix.

Bentinck immersed himself in politics. In parliament 'his indiscretion and arrogance have excited a bitterness against him not to be described.'[43]

In 1848 Surplice won the Derby, running in Lord Clifden's name and managed by the awful Francis Villiers. Disraeli saw Bentinck the day after, 25 May, in the library of the House of Commons.

'He gave a sort of superb groan:

"All my life I have been trying for this, and for what have I sacrificed it!" he murmured.

It was in vain to offer solace.

"You do not know what the Derby is," he moaned out.

"Yes, I do; it is the blue ribbon of the turf."

"It is the blue ribbon of the turf," he slowly repeated to himself, and sitting down at the table, he buried himself in a folio of statistics.'[44]

Surplice went on to win the St Leger. Two weeks afterwards Bentinck died of a heart-attack (a 'visitation of God' in the Coroner's verdict) in his father's park at Welbeck.

# 13 Nineteenth-Century Britain:

## Rous and After

### Mid-Century Problems

The 1842 Racing Calendar announced that 'the Jockey Club, and the stewards thereof, will henceforth take no cognizance of any disputes or claims with respect to bets'. But the Jockey Club had to take cognizance of the methods by which bets were won, even by its own members. These concerned matches, handicaps, *noms de course*, and touts.

Matches at Newmarket purported to be genuine contests between the horses of gentlemen, and were bet on heavily. But they were often 'partnership concerns'; 'This stratagem has yet been too often practised indefensibly.'[1] There was another sort of unreal match: 'The uninitiated in these matters are not perhaps aware that horses are often matched at Newmarket for large sums, though with the certainty of losing, merely for the advantage of a trial with a good horse.'[2]

Handicapping suffered from horses being run fat or full of water, or pulled in the running. It is difficult to pin down many cases, but William Day says it was habitual; so does Rous.

Of *noms de course* 'Druid' says: 'out of the 800 men . . . who declare their colours, not more than 220 run them in their own names.'[3] 'Many gross frauds,' says Rous, 'have been practised by running horses attached to the nomination of a fictitious owner.'[4]

Trials were held as a prelude to betting, and watching them was therefore a heinous offence. In spite of warning-off, 'touters' were a scourge in 1835; owners often used secret weights: 'a good load of shot being frequently concealed in the stuffing of saddles.'[5] In the 1850s there were 40 or 50 regular touts at Newmarket; 'many of the principal owners employ a private tout of their own, often a young ex-jockey.'[6] In the 1870s: 'The only improvement wanted [to Newmarket] is an arbitrary power to expel forever some 50 worthless fellows who prowl about for "information", and who seek to corrupt weak and foolish lads to betray the secrets of their masters.'[7]

From 1843 the visible Ring was to an extent cleaned up, and a new phenomenon appeared: the big bookmaker who was honest. The most famous were Fred Swindell and 'Leviathan' Davies. Swindell was born a Derbyshire labourer, and became an engine-cleaner at the age of 12. He took his savings racing and preferred the life. He walked to London, and by dint of sobriety, discretion, and intelligence succeeded as a commissioner and layer. He worked for the greatest owners like James Merry, the uncouth Glasgow ironmaster, and Sir Joseph Hawley the 'lucky baronet'. He is said to have gone to live next door to Admiral Rous in order to see who called on him.[8] He died very rich.

Davies started as a builder's mate in Newmarket; his large ideas derived from working at the Jockey Club Rooms. In London he was king of the 'lists'. The lists were of runners and odds, stuck up in public-house windows. From 1850 to 1853 'the listers were in their glory; and at one period about 400 betting-houses were open in London alone, of which, perhaps, 10 were solvent.[9] Davies's lists were for £1 minimum; others accepted bets as small as sixpence. They were a social evil, encouraging clerks to embezzlement and maidservants to theft. They were closed down by the Betting House Act of 1853. By this time the 'Leviathan' had made a fortune.

At the other end of the scale there were hundreds of deplorable little men. In 1856 the Ring had 400 members; 100 were 'safe'. 'Welshers, regardless of pumps and mobbing, begin to wax rife in the land.' The Clerk of the Course at Catterick provided, specially for captured welshers, 'some stout labourers and a tar-barrel'. After the St Leger, frenzied levanters could be seen on Doncaster station scrambling onto trains heedless of their destination.[10]

Besides the frauds of the great and the groundlings, there were other urgent problems. Someone had to be found to frame handicaps both honestly and competently. The rules of racing were an outdated muddle. In spite of Bentinck's fining of jockeys, starts were still bad because owners paid the fines. The Jockey Club's prestige was low not only because of the activities of some of its members, but also because it was almost bankrupt. To cope with all this, the turf was supremely lucky to find itself being ruled by Admiral Rous.

## The Dictatorship of Admiral Rous

Like Bentinck, the Hon. Henry Rous was born to the turf. His father was Lord Rous, made 1st Earl of Stradbroke, who had a stud in Suffolk. His brother had the Newmarket racecards sent out to him when he was serving under Wellington in the Peninsula.[11] He himself went into the navy. In 1825 he commanded the frigate Rainbow in the East India Station; he there made a contribution to Australian racing. In 1836 he performed a celebrated feat of seamanship, bringing the Pique back from Newfoundland leaking and rudderless. There was an enquiry; he was exonerated; he received a perfunctory letter from the Admiralty; he went on the retired list, and devoted his life to the turf. He was first a Steward of the Jockey Club in 1838, and he was the Duke of Bedford's racing manager at Newmarket from 1840.

In the years when Bentinck was 'Lord Paramount', Rous was quietly matching horses and making a steady addition to his income. He was acquiring his handicapping skills, and becoming expert in the rules of racing. In 1850 he published his small, classic book. By this time he was beginning to be asked to handicap the horses for other men's matches. His mastery of this tricky art became nationally known when he was invited to handicap Voltigeur and the Flying Dutchman in 1851.

Handicapping had hardly advanced beyond the methods of the Restoration. At the Newmarket Craven meeting of 1825: 'In the evening the Jockey Club dinner was well attended. . . . At the dinner, the weights of the horses for the handicap were fixed, the stake itself having been made up before dinner, to enable the trainers to put their horses on muzzle.'[12] Four years later: 'the uncertainty of handy capping, which I have observed, does not always give general satisfaction.'[13]

The fault lay with owners as much as with handicappers. Rous said in 1850: 'Every great handicap offers a premium to fraud: in vain may the Jockey Club protest and express their extreme disapprobation of horses being started for races without the intention on the part of the owners of trying to win with them; horses are started out of condition; or they run for selling stakes without the remotest intention of winning.' And later: 'There is nothing so fallacious as the public running of some horses.'

By 1850 a solution was being proposed: a public handicapper, appointed by the Jockey Club, who signed his handicaps. Rous would have none of this. The requirements – of skill, knowledge, and honesty – were too great: 'Such a man is not to be found.'

Even if he were found, he would hardly accept the job: 'On the subject of handicapping, there is nothing so easy as to find fault; it is a capacious field for the scribblers on racing topics . . . the most honourable gentleman may object to be set up as a popinjay for the mark of every scribbler.'[14]

Nevertheless, in 1855 Rous took the risk. He accepted the post of honorary public handicapper, which he held until he died. He brought to it a professionalism which was quite new. He spent hours on his hack on Newmarket Heath, looking at trainers' strings. He scrutinized every race to note horses which were improving, horses which ran unfit, horses which were not trying. His notebook was always open. As a result of the experience he thus gained, he worked out a new weight-for-age scale. The rules of the day allowed him to bet on handicaps he had made, and – modestly – he often did so; although he made a few mistakes, he was never accused of sharp practice.

At the same time he took on the treasurership of the Jockey Club, and turned a loss into a profit.

His personal prestige grew gradually through the 1850s, although his career had none of the heroic drama of Bentinck's. In 1855 Francis Villiers, younger brother of Lord Jersey, fled the country leaving £100,000 in racing debts; he was a Steward of the Jockey Club at the time. The era of Rous's moral authority had not begun. In 1857 a man called Adkins, who ran a gaming-hell, was convicted of using loaded dice. Lord Derby constituted himself the conscience of the Jockey Club; he called for Adkins to be warned off. A few years later he would have left this to Rous.

When Rous emerged as 'Dictator' in the early 1860s, it was seen that his attitude to racing was at once high-minded and practical. He recognized betting as an integral part of the turf, necessary both to the interest of the public and the breeding and training bills of the great men. He respected honest bookmakers like Swindell and the 'Leviathan'. But he deplored heavy betting. This had declined in the 1850s; it came back with a rush. Sir Joseph Hawley won £75,000 when his Musjid won the 1859 Derby; Henry Chaplin £115,000 on Hermit in 1867. Both these men ran their horses with complete honesty, but Rous bitterly disapproved. The inducement to fraud was too great. Racing should be conducted to earn the trust of men 'in the 10 pound way of business'.

His knowledge of the rules made him an arbiter in the tradition of Bernard Howard and Charles Greville. He was asked to rule on disputes of every kind. The decisions which emanated from his house in Berkeley Street were no more than a personal view, but they were invested with an official, almost a divine, authority.

He was a voluminous correspondent to *Bell's Life* (the leading sporting paper, a committed friend of racing) and to *The Times* (consistently and puritanically hostile). Some of his letters were on fine points of administrative detail, some on broad issues of racing morality, some libellously personal. A few got him into trouble. In 1868 the pathetic young Marquis of Hastings, already virtually ruined, had a horse called The Earl in the Derby, trained by John Day at Danebury. It had been well backed by the public; on the eve of the race it was scratched. Rous wrote in fury to *The Times* accusing the Days of defrauding Hastings, but imputing no blame to the latter, who was a fly in the web of a spider.[15] The spider was the usurer Henry Padwick, to whom Hastings was deep in debt. Hastings rather gallantly defended the Days, who sued Rous. Rous had to make a public apology. William Day later wrote of the 'imbecile officiousness of the late Admiral Rous', and his 'fondness for censuring some one, and zeal for reforming turf abuses, or what he considered such, without waiting for proof of any kind'.[16] There is a grain of justice in the last charge.

The following year saw the beginning of Rous's feud with Sir Joseph Hawley.

This odd, solitary man was 20 years younger than Rous. He had spent some years in Florence, where he imported a few thoroughbreds. He came back to England in 1844 and had horses at Newmarket. He then bought Fyfield, Wiltshire, from the extraordinary

ADMIRAL ROUS AND GEORGE PAYNE. Lifelong friends, though in sharp contrast. Rous was frugal and careful; his whole attitude to the turf was based on the inevitability of betting but the necessity for moderate betting. Payne was extravagant, munificently generous, and an heroic plunger. Both were respected; Rous was much the more important; Payne was much the better loved.

trainer Thomas Parr, a one-time tea-peddlar who spent much of his time hiding in a hay-loft from his creditors. Hawley installed Alec Taylor ('Old Alec', father of the 'wizard of Manton') as private trainer. He went for a time to the Days, and then to John Porter of Kingsclere. He won four Derbies between 1851 and 1868, betting and winning extremely heavily. He was an intellectual; he betted coldly and successfully, like Old Q. His colours were popular because his horses ran to win, but he was not personally likeable.

In 1861–3 he supported Rous's reform of starting. Bentinck had mitigated the scandal of deliberately-delayed or otherwise foul starts, but he had not cured it. Fines did not deter. In 1863 the powers of the stewards of a meeting were significantly extended: they were able to suspend jockeys – to expel them from the turf for periods at their discretion.

In 1869 Hawley went from this practical and feasible reform to a large attempt to change the whole character of racing. He tried to convince the Jockey Club that all betting was bad; that two-year-old racing was bad; and that the Jockey Club's exclusiveness was bad. Rous wrote letters to *The Times* opposing all these propositions. *The Times*, in awesome editorials, supported Hawley. Bookmakers and racecourses violently opposed him. The turf Establishment was divided. Hawley's condemnation of betting was not thought to lie in the mouth of the biggest plunger in England, but there was serious agreement with some of his views. After much public debate[17] and private lobbying, the result was a slightly shortened flat-racing season (which Rous had himself recommended) and a prohibition on two-year-old racing before 1 May. The latter rule lasted less than two years.

Rous went on pontificating, mediating, and handicapping until just before his death, at 82, in 1877. It has often, and justly, been said of him that his dictatorship so enhanced the prestige and strengthened the arm of the Jockey Club that it made any subsequent one-man rule both improbable and unnecessary.

## Voltigeur and The Flying Dutchman

Rous's first celebrated handicap was for the great match of 1851, which aroused a greater frenzy of partisanship than any since Hambletonian-Diamond in 1799.

Lord Jersey's Bay Middleton was the third and greatest of the owner's Derby winners. He was almost too savage to train or ride, but was tamed by Jem Robinson.[18] (After his victory in 1836, the Hon. Berkeley Craven shot himself because of his losses; he had probably backed John Day's Venison.) Bay Middleton was bought as a stallion by Lord George Bentinck, but was only a moderate success at stud, though a good sire of broodmares. In the year of his owner's retirement he had a colt-foal out of Colonel Vansittart's Barbelle, bought by Lord Eglinton, and called The Flying Dutchman.

Eglinton was said to be the most popular man in three kingdoms. His career of munificence started farcically in the bottomless mud and misery of the Eglinton Tournament of 1839, in which he tried to recreate the gaudy splendour of medieval tilting.[19] He was a popular Lord Lieutenant of Ireland. He was a man of great charm and kindness, a latter-day Egremont. His horses were trained at Middleham, Yorkshire, by Tom Dawson, one of the great Lowland Scots family of trainers, and then by Fobert. In the latter's hands The Flying Dutchman won all his five starts as a two-year-old. He won the Derby, co-favourite at 2 to 1, narrowly from Hotspur. He won the St Leger easily at 9 to 4 on.

In 1847 Martha Lynn threw a colt-foal by Voltaire, which was first refused and then bought by Lord Zetland. It was called Voltigeur, and trained by Robert Hill at Richmond, Yorkshire. It ran once as a two-year-old, winning, and then not again until the Derby. Zetland would have scratched him, but for the bets of his Yorkshire tenants. He was also backed by a lot of Freemasons, Zetland being Grand Master. He was not seriously fancied, but he won quite easily. For the St Leger he started at 13 to 8 on and

STANDARD WEIGHTS FOR AGE.

HALF A MILE.

| Age. Years. | April 1. st. lb. | May 1. st. lb. | June 1. st. lb. | July 1. st. lb. | Aug. 1. st. lb. | Sept. 1. st. lb. | Oct. 1. st. lb. | Nov. 1. st. lb. |
|---|---|---|---|---|---|---|---|---|
| 2 | .. 5 2 | .. 5 7 | .. 5 12 | .. 6 1 | .. 6 3 | .. 6 5 | .. 6 7 | .. 6 8 |
| 3 | .. 7 5 | .. 7 7½ | .. 7 10 | .. 7 13 | .. 8 0 | .. 8 1 | .. 8 1½ | .. 8 2 |
| 4 | .. 8 7 | .. 8 7 | .. 8 7 | .. 8 7 | .. 8 7 | .. 8 7 | .. 8 7 | .. 8 7 |
| 5, 6, & a. | .. 9 0 | .. 9 0 | .. 9 0 | .. 8 7½ | .. 8 7 | .. 8 7 | .. 8 7 | .. 8 7 |

T. Y. C., OR SIX FURLONGS.

| 2 | .. 4 9 | .. 4 13 | .. 5 3 | .. 5 6 | .. 5 8 | .. 5 10 | .. 5 12 | .. 6 0 |
|---|---|---|---|---|---|---|---|---|
| 3 | .. 7 2 | .. 7 4 | .. 7 6 | .. 7 7½ | .. 7 9 | .. 7 10 | .. 7 11 | .. 7 12 |
| 4 | .. 8 7 | .. 8 7 | .. 8 7 | .. 8 7 | .. 8 7 | .. 8 7 | .. 8 7 | .. 8 7 |
| 5, 6, & a. | .. 8 13 | .. 8 12 | .. 8 11½ | .. 8 11 | .. 8 10½ | .. 8 10 | .. 8 9 | .. 8 8 |

ONE MILE.

| 2 | .. 4 2 | .. 4 7 | .. 4 12 | .. 5 0 | .. 5 2 | .. 5 3 | .. 5 4 | .. 5 5 |
|---|---|---|---|---|---|---|---|---|
| 3 | .. 6 12 | .. 6 13 | .. 7 1 | .. 7 4 | .. 7 6 | .. 7 7 | .. 7 8 | .. 7 9 |
| 4 | .. 8 7 | .. 8 7 | .. 8 7 | .. 8 7 | .. 8 7 | .. 8 7 | .. 8 7 | .. 8 7 |
| 5 | .. 9 0 | .. 8 13½ | .. 8 13 | .. 8 12½ | .. 8 12 | .. 8 11½ | .. 8 11 | .. 8 10 |
| 6 & aged | .. 9 1 | .. 9 0 | .. 9 0 | .. 8 13½ | .. 8 13 | .. 8 12 | .. 8 11½ | .. 8 11 .. 8 10 |

WEIGHT FOR AGE SCALE. This is part of the revolutionary scale, based on a dozen years of study, which Henry Rous published in his *Laws and Practice of Horse Racing* in 1850.

should have won easily, but he was unlucky in the running and dead-heated with Russborough. Bobby Hill was quite unnerved; he would have kept Voltigeur standing in a stable during the two hours before the run-off. Luckily John Scott of Whitewall, a St Leger specialist, advised them to walk the horse gently round all the time to stop him getting stiff. Voltigeur won the run-off after a hard race, ridden as always by Job Marson.

The Flying Dutchman had that summer won the Emperor's Plate (as the Ascot Gold Cup was called until the Crimean War), and had come back North for the Doncaster Cup.

The day after the St Leger, Voltigeur had a walk-over; The Flying Dutchman, who was short of work, was given a strong gallop. The day after that the two champions met at weight-for-age in the Cup. Voltigeur was the local hope, but The Flying Dutchman was favourite.

Job Marson could not do the weight on Voltigeur – 8 stone (112 lb.); Nat Flatman rode him. Charles Marlow as usual had the mount on The Flying Dutchman. He was drunk. There is not much doubt of this.[20] Disobeying orders, he went off in front at a tremendous gallop. Flatman tracked him and pounced at the distance. The Flying Dutchman had nothing left. Eglinton was stunned. The favourite's backers 'wandered about pale and silent as marble statues.'[21]

A match was irresistible: two miles, at York, the following spring. Rous set The Flying Dutchman to give $8\frac{1}{2}$ lb. to Voltigeur; he thus judged the horses equal in merit, because this was his weight-for-age scale between five and four, in May, over two miles. Public interest was immense. There was nothing in the betting. The jockeys were the same as in the race for the Cup, which does credit to Eglinton's loyalty. Charles Marlow did credit to himself; this time he rode a brilliantly-judged waiting race, and The Flying Dutchman won by a 'short length'.

There is a sequel. The Flying Dutchman's daughter Flying Duchess was probably covered by Voltigeur's son Vedette,[22] and foaled Prince Batthyany's Galopin. Galopin was very fast; but he just stayed the Derby distance and won by a length in 1875. Batthyany had a weak heart; when Galopin's son, Lord Falmouth's Galliard, was about to run for the 2000 Guineas of 1883, he died of over-excitement while going in to luncheon.

Galopin had another son, belonging to Batthyany, whose engagements were rendered void by the rule of the time. This was St Simon, bought by the Duke of Portland: never extended on the racecourse: a very Eclipse in pre-eminence.

## Lord Durham in the Mantle of Rous

The achievements of Rous could not be proof against the fraud of a man who should have been above suspicion.

In the middle 1880s Sir George Chetwynd, an ex-Steward of the Jockey Club, had his horses trained at Newmarket by Sherrard and ridden by Charles Wood. Chetwynd was a dashing and glamorous figure, who lived high on a small income. His stable was run entirely for betting. Sherrard was an honest man who loved his horses dearly and was good at getting them fit.[23] Wood was a clever rogue who really ran the stable.

In November 1887 an article in the *Licenced Victuallers Gazette* accused Wood of pulling a horse in a race at Lewes. Wood sued, and was awarded a farthing damages.

At the Gimcrack dinner shortly afterwards Lord Durham waded into the situation as honestly, but also as impetuously, as Rous would have done. He accused Chetwynd – not quite naming him – of racing fraud. This, from one ex-Steward to another, and at a time when the turf was supposed to have been cleaned up, caused a sensation.

In an atmosphere of extraordinary bitterness the matter was submitted to arbitration. It emerged that Sherrard was a cardboard trainer; that Charles Wood owned many of the horses in the stable; and that Chetwynd had connived over a period at this breach of

VOLTIGEUR AND THE FLYING DUTCHMAN. This was the most celebrated match in Britain in the 19th century. Voltigeur is ridden by Nat Flatman in Lord Zetland's spotted colours; The Flying Dutchman by Charles Marlow in Lord Eglington's tartan jacket.

the rules. Chetwynd was disgraced. Durham's brother concluded that this result, however unpleasant, was good for the turf.[24]

Wood was warned off for life, but in the event allowed back on the turf after a few years. His first ride in public was for Lord Durham. Rous might have been capable of this generosity: Bentinck never.

## Great Men of the Turf

Some of the notable men of the turf of the first three-quarters of the century have been mentioned, in various connections. Others can be categorized as the losers, the winners, the eccentrics, the statesmen, and the beasts.

The first of the great losers was Colonel Henry Mellish, the archetypal Regency Buck, handsome, popular, a dashing horseman, an obsessive gambler. He trained a pig to win a match for him 'by feeding it at a certain trough, which he chose for the goal'.[25] He was clever and successful on the turf: cards, dice, and extravagance removed his fortune. When it had gone he devoted himself in perfect content to farming.

Contemporary was Captain Jack Mytton, who was famous for his extraordinary physical daring when hunting, driving, or boxing. He must have been mad all his life. In his youth he drank eight bottles of wine a day; later he turned to brandy. He died in the King's Bench Prison impoverished, demented, and paralysed; he might have based his life on Hogarth's Rake.[26]

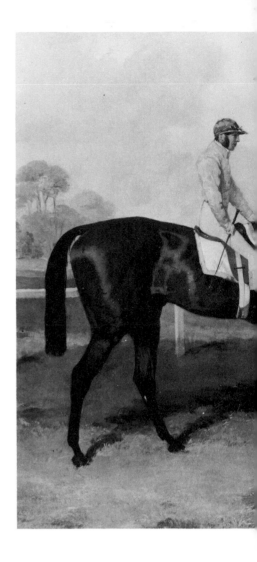

The most attractive of the great losers was George Payne. He got through not one fortune but three. When he took over the Pytchley from the indolent, munificent Lord Chesterfield, the scale of spending increased rather than diminished. He gambled on any issue. In spite of habitual behaviour of which Rous violently disapproved, the two men were devoted and lifelong friends. He died at a great age, poor but perfectly happy.

The most pathetic loser was the Marquis of Hastings. He started racing in 1862 at the age of 20. By 1864 he was having a lot of success. In that year he eloped with Lady Florence Paget, just before her wedding to Henry Chaplin. In 1865 he had 50 racehorses. He was attractive, brave, and far from stupid; there was a streak of weakness and folly in his character which destroyed him. He made five serious mistakes. He was ludicrously extravagant. He had his horses trained at Danebury. He laid heavily against Chaplin's Hermit for the Derby of 1867. He backed other men's horses as well as his own. And he got into the clutches of Henry Padwick.

Hermit's Derby, he said on his deathbed, broke his heart – 'But I didn't show it, did I?' Hermit was managed for Chaplin by the formidable Captain Machell at Newmarket. He had a good season as a two-year-old and was well backed for the Derby. A week before the race, ridden by Harry Custance, he broke a blood-vessel in a training-gallop. It is due to Machell that he ran and that he was fit enough to win. The race started in a snow-storm (according to legend; it may have been hail); news about the blood-vessel had got out. Many people laid against the horse. Many people besides Hastings had a bad day. Chaplin and Machell both made a lot of money (they both come into the category of winners). Hastings lost a fortune.

The next year he was involved in the scandal of the scratching of The Earl. He died later the same year, aged 26, exhausted and ruined.

The first of the great winners was John Bowes, a recluse with a first-class brain. He was the son of Lord and Lady Strathmore, but was born some years before their marriage. He inherited a great estate, the value of which he greatly increased. He won his first Derby with Mündig in 1835, while still an undergraduate at Cambridge. His trustees had backed it heavily in his name, expecting to collect as he was still a minor. But by the day of the race he was *mündig*, of age, and he had all the bets transferred to himself. This was the first of a lifetime of successes. He won three more Derbys. His West Australian was a very great horse, the first triple-crown winner, perhaps the best since Bay Middleton and the best until St Simon. Bowes worked hard and intelligently for his success, but he was also (much as he always denied this) lucky. He never saw his horses in the stable, and latterly never on the racecourse either. He was a figure of mystery. Though remote, he was not cold. He was happily married to a French actress, backing whom in the Paris theatre he made his only serious financial misjudgments.

James Merry was 10 years older than Bowes but his success came later. His father was a rich Glasgow merchant; he was himself an ironmaster. Though born to wealth he appeared self-made, being loud and uncouth, speaking with a broad accent, and committing absurd malapropisms in political speeches. He won the Derby with Thormanby and Doncaster. He backed his horses heavily and successfully. He was also the last great

SIR TATTON SYKES AND SIR TATTON SYKES. The horse (by Melbourne out of an unnamed mare) was bred in Yorkshire in 1843 by a Mr Hudson, and named Tibthorpe. Bill Scott bought him for £100, renamed him in honour of the master of Sledmere, and sent him to be trained by William Oates. He won the 2000 Guineas, ridden by his owner, and was fancied for the Derby. Alas, Bill Scott had been drinking hard all morning on Derby day. He became nettled with the starter, with whom he continued to argue after the others were running. When he did get off he was too drunk to keep the horse straight. Even so he got to within a neck of John Gully's Pyrrhus The First. Horse and jockey went on to win the St Leger easily, and were led in by the horse's namesake. Sir Tatton Sykes (1782–1863) was the most popular man in Yorkshire and doyen of its turf. He saw 76 runnings of the St Leger.

cocker: he had thousands of gamecocks, all of which fought until cock-fighting was made illegal in 1840, and afterwards too. Like Tregonwell Frampton he made as much money in the mains as on the turf.

The eccentric to dwarf all others was the Earl of Glasgow. He bred and raced on an immense scale, with unprecedented lack of success. He was reckoned unlucky, but he courted ill-luck as though he loved it. He constantly made matches for big stakes. If his opponent's horse was bad, his was worse; if his own horse was good, his opponent's was better. To shrewder men like Bentinck he was a gold-mine. He changed trainers and jockeys as other people change hats. But his furies and dismissals contained no vindictiveness; he often went back to men he had dismissed. His enormous stud was run on whimsical lines. He was obstinately loyal to certain blood-lines of proved uselessness. Like Sir Tatton Sykes of Sledmere, he refused to give his horses names, which caused confusion. When he was dissatisfied with a horse (as he often had cause to be) he had it shot. The slaughter over the years was appalling. With all this, he inspired great personal affection and loyalty.

It was part of an aristocratic (or oligarchic) system that the magnates of the turf accepted political responsibility, or loved political power. The brusque, dapper Lord Palmerston devotedly continued this tradition. He loved racing all his life. He first had horses with 'Honest John' Day in 1817. In 1841 he won the third running of the Cesarewitch with Iliona, the pronunciation of whose name rent the sporting and academic worlds. He was an amusing mixture – personally ascetic and hard-working, emerging from the House of Commons with red-dyed whiskers to ogle the ladies and then ride like a demon to see his racehorses.

The 14th Earl of Derby learned his racing from his grandfather. Like Bowes, he trained with John Scott of Whitewall. His relationship with that greatest of trainers was intimate and lifelong. Disraeli liked his aristocrats aristocratic, but he was aghast at Derby's involvement in racing when the two were in power together: Derby was 'a confederate always at Newmarket and Doncaster when Europe – nay the world – is in the throes of immense changes.'[27] He tried all his life to win the race named for his grandfather. The nearest he came was in 1858 with Toxopholite, grandsire of Carbine.

The 5th Earl of Rosebery – many years younger, and on the other side of the House of Lords – was the first Prime Minister to win a Derby while in office. He was sent down from Oxford for running a very bad horse called Ladas in the Derby, in which it finished last. In 1878 he married Hannah de Rothschild, whose late father, Baron Meyer de Rothschild, had won four of the five classics, with Favonius and Hannah, in 1871. Marriage gave Rosebery the Mentmore stud. For a decade he was involved in politics; the Mentmore yearlings were sold. In 1890 he began serious racing, sending some horses to Mat Dawson at Newmarket, who thereupon postponed his retirement. In 1894 he won the Derby with another Ladas, only months after becoming Prime Minister. This win aroused a frenzy of popular approval. The only dissentient voices (but they were many and bitter) came from the Nonconformist wing of his own party. He won the Derby again the next year with Sir Visto.

From a large field, principally of legs, the title of most evil man of the 19th-century turf goes to Henry Padwick. His father was a butcher in Horsham. He trained as a lawyer, but became a money-lender. He borrowed from banks at 10 per cent, and lent at rates varying between 50 per cent and 200 per cent. He thus acquired a great fortune, estates, and racehorses. He began racing in 1849, with the Days, using the *nom de course* of 'Mr Howard'. He was a great gourmet, ludicrously vain, a lady-killer. His financial power enabled him to blackmail men into running their horses fraudulently, and women to dishonouring themselves. He helped Hastings and the Duke of Newcastle to ruin. He destroyed John Baynton Starkey, 'one of the most unfortunate of those who have ever had to do with racing.'[28] Starkey was very rich. Padwick got hold of all his money and

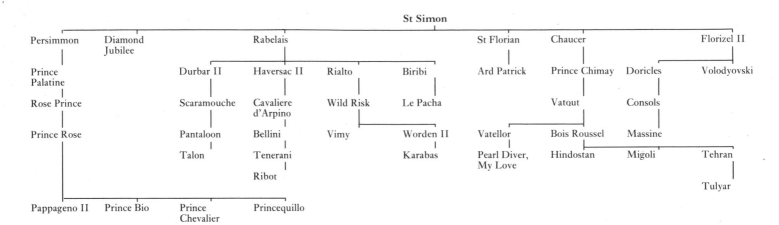

all his estates. Starkey ran away to New South Wales in 1870, leaving a wife and young children in poverty; he died there two years later. In his later years Padwick took Old John Day from Danebury to be his private trainer at Findon: a curiously just end to the latter's career.

## The Period of the Patricians

The last quarter of the 19th century was dominated, more than any period since the mid-18th, by certain patrician owners.

The first of these was Lord Falmouth. He was a parson's son, inheriting title and fortune from a cousin. He married another fortune, and with it Mereworth Castle, Kent, where he had his stud. He never bet. He once lost a jovial sixpence to the wife of his first trainer, John Scott; he gave her the sixpence set in diamonds. For several seasons between 1870 and 1882 he was the dominant owner, with home-bred horses. One reason was that after John Scott's death his horses were trained by **Mat Dawson** and ridden by Fred Archer, the giants of their respective trades. The other was his breeding policy. All his mares were subjected to a rigorous racecourse test before he would breed from them. In 1880 he had 24 mares at Mereworth; all had run as two-year-olds, nearly all at three and four; all except one were winners, and that one (by Blair Athol) had had 'flu. This policy was in sharp contrast to that of a much bigger breeder, Sir Tatton Sykes of Sledmere, the most popular man in Yorkshire. Sir Tatton sold all his colts, and sent the fillies untrained straight to the paddocks. The result was an empire of third-rate bloodstock comparable to Lord Glasgow's.[29]

Falmouth retired from racing, suddenly and completely, in 1883. This was supposed to have been due to his disgust at Fred Archer's riding of Galliard in the Derby: but such suspicion of a trusted servant, and such a dramatically petulant reaction, are quite foreign to Falmouth's generosity and good sense.

The Dukes of Westminster and Portland owned the two supreme horses of the second half of the century, Ormonde and St Simon.

Hugh Lupus, 1st Duke of Westminster, was the richest man in England. In the 1870s he spent unprecedented money building up his stud at Eaton Hall, Cheshire. He bought the Derby winner Doncaster, and Rouge Rose by the Derby winner Thormanby. These bred Bend Or. Fred Archer was to ride him in the Derby of 1880. Shortly before the race he was attacked and badly bitten by a savage animal called Muley Edris. Not only did this make his left arm useless, but his enforced rest sent his weight soaring. Bend Or narrowly beat the very good horse Robert the Devil; Archer, one-armed and weakened by wasting, rode one of the greatest races of his career. Bend Or went to stud, and in 1883 produced a colt-foal out of Lily Agnes called Ormonde. Ormonde was doubtful

DERBY DAY. This is the foot of the Downs, between Tattenham Corner and the winning-post. The booth on the left is grandly called the 'Royal REFORM CLUB'; its sign announces hazard and *rouge et noir*. The game being played on the nearest little table is thimblerig; the sharper behind the Scotsman is a three-card-trick man. These people constitute what a contemporary calls 'the degraded mob, the blasphemous, greedy, obscene Bohemianism that riots on Epsom Downs.' The 1856 Derby was won by Admiral Harcourt's Ellington at 20 to 1, a good horse by The Flying Dutchman. Prince Albert was present, but not the queen.

*Overleaf*
JOCKEYS OF THE SOUTH OF ENGLAND. *c.* 1800–1850

in the wind, a 'roarer', but he won the 2000 Guineas and the Derby easily in a good year. His only stud success was Orme, who should have won the Derby but for illness, and who sired two Derby winners; Ormonde went to the Argentine and thence to California, where he was not important. But half the contemporaries who saw him said he was the racehorse of the century.

The other half said this was St Simon. He was bought cheaply by the Duke of Portland from Prince Batthyany's executors, on Mat Dawson's advice: cheaply because his leg had been bandaged by Dawson's brother. When Dawson got him out on the gallops he said he was 'the best two-year-old I have ever seen in my life.'[30] He was not tested as Ormonde was, but judges as formidable as George Lambton said he was the better horse.[31] At stud he was magnificent.

One of the dominant personalities on Newmarket Heath was the widowed Duchess of Montrose, who raced as 'Mr Manton' but was widely known as 'Old Six Mile Bottom'. She married Stirling Crawfurd in 1876, and took over the management of his large string. She was highly individual in both dress and speech. It was widely supposed that she conceived a passionate attachment to Fred Archer.

A personage higher even than these registered his colours in 1875: Albert Edward, Prince of Wales. His early years on the turf were in great contrast to 'Prinny's' a century before – he bought cheaply and raced unambitiously. He started the Sandringham stud in 1885, and then had a few horses with John Porter of Kingsclere. In 1893 he went to Richard Marsh at Newmarket; by this time his horses were managed by the ebullient Lord Marcus Beresford. His Persimmon, by St Simon out of Perdita II, won the Derby of 1896; when the Prince led him in it was probably the high point of the popularity of the British royal family. Persimmon went on to win the St Leger, and became a very important sire. His full brother Diamond Jubilee won the triple crown in 1900: another great horse, though an evil-tempered one, and a successful stallion in the Argentine.

The owner's third Derby winner – as king, in 1909 – falls into an epoch different by far more than the turn of a century or the change of sovereign.

## Foreigners on the English Turf

The first foreign-bred horse to astonish the English was the American Prioress, which won the Cesarewitch in 1857. She came over with Richard ten Broeck, owner of Lexington, who brought a trainer, stable-lads and horses in 1856.

The French had picked up occasional prizes at Goodwood; but the first important campaign was mounted by comte Frédéric de Lagrange in the 1860s. He won the Oaks with Fille de l'Aire in 1864, trained by Tom Jennings at Phantom House, Newmarket. In 1865 his Gladiateur was easily the outstanding three-year-old in Britain, and the second triple-crown winner. (The local reaction was embarrassingly unsporting.) Gladiateur went on to win the Ascot Gold Cup and the Grand Prix de Paris; a marvellous career. He always had doubtful legs; it must have been very difficult to give him enough work without breaking him down; Jennings deserves infinite credit.

Other French winners in England during the following years caused an ill-feeling which was better founded. French horses were allowed to race in England on equal terms. Some were thrown most leniently into handicaps. But English horses were either debarred from French races, or ruinously penalized. By 1876 'Reciprocity' was demanded and appeals made to French sportsmanship. They fell on well-muffled ears.

In 1873 the Hungarian Imperial Stud bred a horse of pure English blood (by Buccaneer out of Mineral by Rataplan), which was named Kisber, after the stud. He was bought by the young Baltazzi brothers, cheerful Levantines brought up in England, and taken to Newmarket to be trained by the Rothschilds' trainer, Hayhoe. He won the Derby easily. It is a pity more Hungarian-breds did not run in England, as they had some top-class English bloodstock and their studs, royal and private, were excellently managed.

Three other notable foreigners racing in this decade were Prince Batthyany, Prince Soltykoff, and Baron Meyer de Rothschild, respectively the first Hungarian, the first Russian, and the first Jew to be elected to the Jockey Club.

In 1879 began an invasion as powerful as Lagrange's. Mr Pierre Lorillard brought over his trainer Jacob Pincus and some yearlings. One of these was Iroquois, bred in Pennsylvania by imported Leamington. Pincus's training methods were thought most odd at Newmarket, especially his reliance on the clock. Iroquois was a good two-year-old, and ran an encouraging second, when unfit, in the 2000 Guineas. Fred Archer asked to ride him in the Derby, and did so brilliantly. This victory was a great deal more popular in England than Gladiateur's, and in New York it aroused delirium.

Iroquois was a very good horse but there was an even better American in England at the same time. This was James Keene's marvellous Foxhall. He won the Grand Prix (invading France as well as England) and the Cesarewitch and Cambridgeshire in 1881, and the Ascot Gold Cup in 1882. With the possible exception of Bend Or he was the best horse in Europe in those years. His owner, like Lorillard, could be nothing but good for the turf of any country where he raced.

The same could be (and often was) said of Baron de Hirsch, who owned one of the greatest race-mares of all time, La Flèche. He raced in England, according to 'Thormanby',[32] in memory of his adored son, who had loved English racing but died young. La Flèche was bred at Hampton Court, bought by Hirsch at auction, and trained by John Porter. She won the Oaks and the St Leger of 1892, and 16 races altogether. No successes could have been more popular; none more deserved.

THE PRINCE OF WALES AND PERSIMMON. According to contemporary descriptions, the enthusiasm of the crowd after the 1896 Derby is understated here. Even Jack Watts, a jockey rendered morose by wasting, allowed himself to smile. Persimmon went on to win the St Leger, and the Ascot Gold Cup and Eclipse Stakes of 1897.

# 14 Nineteenth-Century Britain:
## Courses, Jockeys, Trainers, Marginalia

*New Courses: Goodwood and Aintree*

Racing began at Goodwood in 1801. The 3rd Duke of Richmond laid out a course, built a little stand, and held hunters' races. The participants were officers of the local militia and members of the duke's hunt. The racing 'was of a very lowly kind . . . five or six roving tents, and plenty of ice and pick-pockets.'[1]

By 1811 the meeting had grown to two days, with six races, two matches, and a total of 12 starters. In 1812 the Earl of March, heir of the 4th duke (who died of the bite of a rabid fox in Canada in 1819) instituted the Goodwood Cup. The earl was badly wounded in Spain, and was compelled to give up hunting. He became a racing man. From 1817 he began improvements to his racecourse. By 1825 the earl, now 5th duke, had his own string of horses at home, trained by the Kents, father and son. (That was the year Lord George Bentinck started riding races.)

The place had tremendous advantages: Greville noted 'an elasticity in the air and turf which communicates itself to the spirits'.[2] There were three days in 1826, four in 1833. In the 1840s it became of first-class importance because of Bentinck's management. 'All the great things were going into Sussex, while all the Turf reforms and improvements were traceable to the same quarter. Defaulters were to be banished, mere gambling was to be abolished, time was to be kept, and good conduct to be enforced by all kinds of fines and penalties – and all on the system they had adopted at Goodwood.'[3]

Bentinck considered the public as it had never been considered before. He invented the 'Telegraph Board', on which the numbers of the runners were displayed; the official race-card, which bore the same numbers; the parade in the paddock and the preliminary canter in front of the stands. He insisted that jockeys were properly dressed in the correct colours, that horses were saddled up in a recognized place, and that starts were punctual. Public understanding replaced an irritated bewilderment, and seemly order replaced chaos. In mid-century, 'to see racing divested of all its coarse and disgusting accessories – the degraded mob, the blasphemous, greedy, obscene Bohemianism that riots on Epsom Downs – a visit must be paid to Goodwood Park.'[4]

The one other important new racecourse was at Aintree, a suburb of Liverpool.

For a long time there had been races on the sands of the north shore of the Mersey, as well as at Wallasey on the Cheshire side. They were very popular. From 1807 there was racing at Ormskirk, 15 miles away, to which the whole of Liverpool flocked. These races were killed in 1816 by the enclosure of the common. On 30 August 1825 a match was held at Maghull, 10 miles from Liverpool on the Ormskirk road: 'Equestrians thronged to the scene of action; and for more than a mile, the road from Liverpool to Maghull might be seen crowded with horse and foot.'[5]

When Aintree opened in July 1827 it therefore filled a powerfully-felt need. Like York a century earlier, it was an immediate success.

## *Major Existing Courses*

The most important courses were Newmarket, Ascot, Epsom, York, Doncaster, and Chester.

After the Escape affair the light of the Prince of Wales's countenance was withdrawn from Newmarket, but under Sir Charles Bunbury's benevolent dictatorship it managed very nicely without him. With its interlocking network of courses and its great nearby stables, it continued to have far more racing than any other course.

In 1809 it followed Doncaster and Epsom with an important three-year-old sweep-stakes. This was run over the Rowley Mile (straight and extremely testing) at the Second Spring Meeting. For the first running there were 23 subscribers at 100 guineas; the race was consequently, if inaccurately, called the 2000 Guineas. Since horses' official birthdays were still 1 May, the starters were described as two-year-olds. In 1814 a fillies' equivalent attracted 10 subscribers at 100 guineas: the 1000 Guineas. This race was run on the less severe Ditch Mile until 1873. The first handicaps of national importance were inaugurated at Newmarket in 1839, the $2\frac{1}{4}$-mile Cesarewitch and the nine-furlong Cambridgeshire.

Newmarket remained unique not only in the quantity but also the discomfort of its racing. Women began to go to other courses – to boxes at Epsom, the Royal Enclosure at Ascot, the shaded lawns of Goodwood – but not Newmarket. As late as 1875 'to spend a day at Newmarket with any profit you require a good hack.'[6] Riding in with the finishing horses was forbidden by the Jockey Club in 1838, but it was normal among young owners and Gentleman Riders in the 1880s.[7]

Newmarket had become a training centre because it was a racing centre. At the end of Charles II's reign it nearly stopped being a racing centre, and in the 1850s and early 1860s it nearly stopped being a training centre. Hayhoe and Godding were the only important trainers left there. The early summer of 1863 was exceptionally dry. The gallops were brick-hard. Nearly all such good horses as remained at Newmarket were taken away to be worked on tan-gallops, or beaches, or in the soggier North. But Godding refused to move his Derby candidate Macaroni, on the basis that if it was going to race on hard ground it had better be trained on it. When Macaroni won the Derby, the New-market church-bells were rung: he had saved Newmarket as a training-centre.[8]

Ascot had 50 E.O. tables in 1800;[9] a Gold Cup in 1807; the Wokingham Stakes in 1810. In 1813 the Enclosure Act had the effect of putting a fence round the course and admit-ting the public through turnstiles. In 1814 Tsar Alexander of Russia, the King of Prussia, Blücher, and Hetman Platov came to the sports. Racing was almost ignored in public enthusiasm for these heroes. In 1818 the hunters' races were at last dead; in that year 16 thoroughbreds ran a normal programme.

In 1825 George IV instituted the Royal Procession; the modern character of Royal Ascot was established. An eye-witness described it in the late 1820s: 'The crowd was intense, like the heat; splendid, genteel, grotesque; many in masquerade but all in good humour – dandies of men, dandies of women; lords with white trousers and black whiskers; ladies with small faces, but very large hats; Oxford scholars with tandems and randoms; some on stage-coaches, transmogrified into drags – 15 on the top, and six thin ones within; a two-foot horn; an ice-house with cases of champagne; 16 of cigars; all neckcloths, but white; all hats, but black; small talk with oaths, and broad talk with great ones, cooled with ice and made red hot with brandy and smokes; all four-in-handers; all trying to tool 'em; none able to drive, but all able to go with the tongue. An Oxford slap-bang loaded in London; Windsor blues freighted at Reading; Reading coaches chockful at Dorking; a Mile End coach-wagon; German coaches; Hanoverian cars; Petersburg sledges and Phaetonees; St James's cabs; Bull-and-Mouth barouches, waggoned by Exeter coachmen. No place, no amusement, no holiday-making is so enchanting to the softer sex. Gentle and simple, grave and gay, all are on tiptoe of joy, and

GOODWOOD. This is the view from Trundle Hill in 1886, looking east. Goodwood racecourse was the creation of the 3rd and 5th Dukes of Richmond, on that part of their estates known as Charlton Downs. The turf was all lifted during the winter of 1844–45, on Bentinck's orders and under John Kent's supervision: first three, then six, inches of mould were laid on the chalk, and the turf replaced. Beyond the grand-stand is the famous lawn, and behind that the Luncheon Grove.

out jumps nature from both ends – eyes and feet. Lords' ladies tastefully costumed with roses, and lilacs untainted, or rather unpainted by Bond Street; farmers' daughters and farmers' wives sparkling in silks, rosy in cheek, tinted by soft breezes and bottled ale.'[10]

Of the two great Yorkshire racecourses, York had more flowers and smarter clothes; Doncaster bigger crowds and heavier betting. 'The Doncaster St Leger is run in the presence of a crowd of critical experts, amongst whom the race horse is the object of as serious worship as the cat, the ox, or the crocodile, was to the ancient Egyptians.'[11] Racing headquarters was the Turf Tavern, run by Lord George Bentinck's ally, Mr Bowe. York, apart from Gold Cup and King's Plate, had no race of great status until the Ebor Handicap in 1843 and the two-year-old Gimcrack Stakes in 1846.

At Epsom, the Derby and Oaks grew to supreme status in the first quarter of the 19th century. For a time facilities lagged behind sport. In 1828 the Epsom Grandstand Association was founded; this 'had its origin in an artful speculation devised by a small horde of questionable characters; and it was not before great trouble and expense had been incurred, that they were excluded from its management.'[12] Charles Dickens inspected the grandstand in 1851: 'Here we are! let us go into the basement. First into the weighing-house, where the jockeys "come to scale" after each race. We then inspect the offices of the Clerk of the Course himself; wine-cellars, beer-cellars, larders, sculleries, and kitchens, all as gigantically appointed, and as copiously furnished, as if they formed part of an ogre's castle. . . . The gallons of "dressing" that will have to be poured out and converted into salads for the insatiable Derby Day, will best be understood by a memorandum from the chief of that department to the *chef-de-cuisine*, which happened, accidentally, to fall under our notice: "Pray don't forget a large tub and a birch-broom for mixing the salad!" '[13]

Disraeli described the other side of the course in Phosphorus's year, 1837: 'It was full of eager groups; round the betting post a swarming cluster, while the magic circle itself was surrounded by a host of horsemen shouting from their saddles the odds they were prepared to receive or give.'[14] Beyond again were to be seen 'a quarter of a million, including all the ruffianism that London and every race course in the kingdom can produce . . . the disgusting scenes and language of the "hill".'[15]

'Chester, however,' said 'Nimrod' in 1824, 'as a convivial meeting, is not what Chester was. The chilling stream of refinement has passed over every corner of the empire, and neither a Welch nor a Cheshire Squire can now be so vulgar as to be seen on a racecourse after he has had his dinner. The 2-o'clock ordinaries, formerly so well-attended, and where so much mirth and good fellowship prevailed, are all knocked in the head, and private parties substituted in their room. The office of steward appears almost a sinecure, and, for my part, I never knew who they were, till the races were almost over – instead of, as in former days, having drunk their health every day in the week, with three times three. As a place of sport, however, Chester is greatly improved; and as a country meeting may rank next in the list of Epsom, Ascot, York, and Doncaster.'[16]

'Sylvanus' took the opposite view a few years later: 'The course is a vile libel upon the term hippodrome, being neither more nor less than similar to running round a plate, so circumscribed is the ground, and dangerous to a large field. But for fun, frolic, and jollification, I know no place like Chester.'[17]

The business of catering for, and controlling, the public was not easy even at the leading courses. In 1829: 'As to Epsom and Ascot, the chosen few only could see the races; the majority journeyed only to behold enormous assemblies of population. . . . In country courses populously attended, and where so many Johnny Raws, flushed with the sports, exhibit their freedom from all thought and all cares, it would not even be too much to rail in the course for a mile.'[18] A typical 'country course popularly attended' was the old Town Moor at Newcastle. It was unrailed except for the run-in, and the course was marked only by a ditch, with posts at the corners. All the big public houses in Newcastle had tents. The stone grandstand doubled as an hotel, but as a grandstand it served only a tiny minority of the racegoers, the rest of whom either wandered about dangerously, or saw nothing. All these problems were solved when the new course at Gosforth Park was opened in 1881; it was enclosed; the public paid entrance money and were controllable. But a new problem was created: the public came in far smaller numbers.[19]

## The Birth and Death of Minor Courses

Hundreds of racecourses were born in the 19th century. Nearly all died. Many died which had been born earlier. In 1832 'Newcastle, Durham and Carlisle are miserably supported, and Richmond is entirely maintained by the horses trained in the immediate neighbourhood. . . . Beverley is by great exertions kept from going down altogether, as has been the case at Hull and several other considerable places.'[20]

New courses were nevertheless hopefully founded all over the kingdom, either by corporations for the benefit of tradesmen, or by innkeepers for their own benefit. Surtees, no friend of racing, describes the one in *Plain or Ringlets*,[21] the other in *Sponge*.[22] In the latter case he seems to have in mind a combination of St Albans and Aintree; in the former there are dozens of possible originals.

The course of events was usually thus: the Mayor and Corporation sought to attract money by establishing races. They used corporation land or common. They subscribed a little money for prizes, and badgered the local gentry. The races were well attended while they were a novelty, and were greatly helped if a regiment was quartered nearby. At any country meeting there was naturally 'an infusion of gamblers, blacklegs, and pickpockets. . . . Yet races they have, and announcements are made with great sport anticipated, and stewards are victimized, and money screwed out of everybody and from every available source. And for what? To encourage our noble breed of horses? To promote the pastime of the people? Not a bit of it! They would be quite as much amused with a donkey-race.'[23]

After a few years of this, advertised races failed to fill. Tradesmen and gentry became reluctant to subscribe and owners to run: in 1850, 'there is a frequent complaint that the £100 cup is not worth £50, owing to a peculiar understanding between the clerk of the course and the silversmith.'[24] The course itself was so bad that no good horse was ventured on it. The public grew bored with the poor sport offered it. The Corporation decided to make the operation economic by enclosing the course and charging the public for entry; and the public stayed away. The posts rotted, the grandstand crumbled; the town cut its losses and the racecourse died.

Two abortive racecourses are of special interest.

The army was usually a good friend to racing. It provided the riders in amateur races, and officers were the life-blood of steeplechasing. But in 1817 it killed a promising project.

The inhabitants of Fulham and Hammersmith, weary of the journey to Epsom, tried to start racing at Wormwood Scrubs. Everything was prepared, and the first of the annual meetings was to be held on 20 August. On 14 August an official letter came to the committee from the Deputy-Assistant Quarter-Master General, threatening them with an action at law for wilful trespass.[25] No race was ever run at Wormwood Scrubs.

In 1837 a courageous attempt was made to revive, in Bayswater, the Stuart glories of Hyde Park. Mr John Whyte promoted his Bayswater Hippodrome. He put a barrier round his circuit and proposed charging admission. The inaugural meeting was fixed for Saturday 3 June. But there was bitter opposition, on moral grounds, from the parochial authorities of St Mary Abbots, Kensington. At the same time the rate-payers demanded free entry. A right of way was discovered across the racecourse, and Whyte was summonsed for obstructing it. Obedient to the summons, he removed part of his barrier,

VICTORIAN PONY RACING. 'Pony Race for One Hundred Guineas. Mr J. W. Wise's DANDY beat at Epsom by Mr W. Theobald's MAT.O. the MINT. Novr 3 1849. Dandy 6 yrs Old 12 Hands 3 Inch high was bred by Mr. T. Falkner & Got by Doubtful has run Ten Times this Season out of which he has won eight vis Hartley-Row Marlow Edgware Eton Thames-ditton Croydon & Barnet at which place he won the same day the Ponys Cup and

but navvies recruited by the rate-payers battered down more of it.[26]

Unenclosed, the meeting was duly held. The *Sunday Times* reported it with enthusiasm: Whyte was 'bringing Epsom nearer town, transferring Doncaster to Bayswater.' The course was good – both flat and steeplechase, each a full two miles round, with fine turf. The spectators stood on a hill in the middle. Plenty of mounted policemen were on duty. Dukes and noblemen were among the 20,000 spectators. Thousands of rate-payers and others had knocked down still more of the fence, and got in free. There was a £100 plate, given by Whyte, and a £50 steeplechase won by Lottery, winner of the first Grand National.[27]

On Monday 19 June there was a second meeting. Things went less well. There was again trouble with gate-crashers, who had been bribed by those parochial authorities: 'A more filthy or disgusting crew . . . we have seldom had the misfortune to encounter . . . they spread all over the whole of the ground, defiling the atmosphere as they go, and carrying into the neighbourhood of the stands and carriages, where the ladies are most

the Galloways Cup Running for both five Two Mile heats. Mat. O. the Mint has Won Three 50 Gs at Barnet one 50 Gs at Egham & 50 Gs at Ascot two 50 Gs at Epsom also 100 Gs at Epsom beating Dandy and many Other Matches he never was beat but once when Running at Epsom he ran on the wrong side of the Post.' Victorian pony-racing is almost entirely unrecorded, but the record of these two shows that it was a vigorous and well-financed sport.

assembled, a coarseness and obscenity of language as repulsive to every feeling of manhood as to every sense of common delicacy.'[28]

Two years later Whyte remodelled the course to exclude the disputed right of way, and built a high wire fence to keep out the riff-raff. He put on an excellent two-day meeting in May 1841, with seven races, two plates, and a total of £450 added to the stakes. This was thinking in big terms, and Whyte deserved success. But he was beaten by the local blue-noses and forced to close down.

## New Courses of the Late 19th Century: Sandown

Three new courses of enduring importance were founded in the last quarter of the century: Sandown, Kempton, and Lingfield Parks. There were also the excellent but now defunct Hurst Park and Gatwick in the last decade of the century. All these were undertaken in a more professional spirit. Companies were formed which bought land, put a fence round it, laid out a course and built a grandstand, devised excellent programmes which attracted high-class fields, and charged the public money to come and see them. Sandown (1875) also invented the 'club' system; this limited a Members' Enclosure to properly proposed and seconded members, thus creating a demure environment suitable for lady racegoers. In the 11th year of its life Sandown inaugurated the Eclipse Stakes (1¼ miles at weight-for-age and sex) which was the first £10,000 race in Britain and has ever since had virtually classic status.

The whole policy worked. It was imitated by every course which could afford it. It was a long-delayed continuation of Bentinck's policy of suiting the management of racing to the public which supported it.

The standard of these good courses was so high that the bad ones became intolerable. In 1883 the Jockey Club announced that further new racecourses were not welcome. They would not be recognized unless they had a straight mile (which remained, however, most exceptional) and met other stringent standards. The country was cured of its rash of bad little courses, and there has been ever since a steady decline in their number.

## Types of Races

There were more sweepstakes at the expense of matches, more two-year-old races, and more handicaps. There was a continued swing away from the extreme distances of earlier racing; there was also a swing away from very short races. (Both these opposing tendencies reflected the standardization of the thoroughbred by selective breeding.) Four-mile heat-racing was dying at the beginning of the century. 'Nimrod' said: 'This is an improvement, not only on the score of humanity, but as far as regards sport, for horses seldom come in near to each other, after having run that course. Indeed, so much is the system of a four-mile heat disliked, that when it does occur, the horses often walk the first two.'[29] By 1856 the only surviving four-mile races were the Royal Whip and two Queen's Plates at the Curragh, the Queen's Plate at the Caledonian Hunt, and the Whip.

At the other extreme: 'In the old time, however, we had (at least during several years) half and quarter mile races at Newmarket, at which a great three part bred gelding, Rocket by Rocket, the property of Lord March, was the winner, whatever weight he gave. . . . We used to enjoy seeing Hell Fire Dick start this gelding for a short race. The horse held sideways, curvetting and rearing, Dick with his eagle and hawk's eyes, holding him fast in that position, watching the word – at the start, off flew Rocket, with a velocity which demonstrated that he had not his name for nothing.'[30]

These tiny-distance races survived into the 1840s. The Duke of Bedford's Taurus (managed by Rous) won five matches at half-a-mile but could not stay a yard further.[31]

The give-and-take principle was revived in Scotland in 1839. The technique of

WILLIAM SCOTT. Bill Scott (1793–1848) had neither the intelligence nor the sobriety of his brother John, but he was a great jockey. He won the first of his nine St Legers in 1821, the first of his four Derbys in 1832. He was, said 'Sylvanus', 'wealthy, sound in head, and as hospitable, kind-hearted a fellow as ever trotted through the streets of York. . . When in his best form, no man ever excelled Bill Scott as a horseman over the flat.' His last ride was on his own St Christopher in the Derby of 1847. He died the following year at Malton.

measuring, and the arithmetic which followed, had been quite forgotten; 'Druid' records terrible confusion.[32]

Selling and claiming races were ancient, if exceptional. The first on record is the Basingstoke Plate of 1689. The winner was sold to 'him that throwes most at three throwes with two dice, for 40 guinnies'.[33] This is in modern terms a claiming race. There are a few other examples in the next century and a half. In 1850 claiming races (called 'selling races') became part of official programmes. In 1866 the first selling race by the modern definition was held: the winner was auctioned.

## Unofficial Racing

In 1829 'Racing of cocktails is something of a novelty.'[34] Cocktails – half-breds – had races as part of normal programmes, or, increasingly, their own meetings. Thoroughbreds were not allowed to compete. But they did. A rueful fellow told Henry Corbet about his local Farmers' Race, run in heats about 1850: 'somehow or other this farmers' race never seemed to be fairly won by a farmer. Lots of them tried for it at first, but a thoroughbred screw of some sort or other was generally smuggled into it.'[35]

Racing ponies or Galloways were sometimes very well bred, but since the death of give-and-take articles they were unable to compete with full-sized racehorses. Like half-breds they had their own races and increasingly their own meetings. 'Druid' again and again mentions pony racing; he speaks with particular respect of a champion owned by the Days of Danebury, which won a lot of pony-races in Hampshire.[36] In Yorkshire, racing ponies were trained on Langton Wold with the horses.

Prizes for these events were small. They broke the letter of the previous century's legislation which fixed minimum prizes at £50. In 1824 the *Stockport Advertiser* printed advertisements for Cheadle and Bullocksmithy Races. An informer brought an action under 13 George II c. 19.[37] The editor was dismayed and indignant; he used his columns to point out that 'rustics, whose one holiday is this fair, will now go to bull-baits, bear-baits, and cockfights, instead of harmless and respectable pony-races.'[38]

Cheadle and Bullocksmithy races may have been harmless and respectable; if so they were unique. 'Flapping' meetings – unrecognized by the Jockey Club – attracted the dregs because there were no rules. Dunniker Park, near Kirkcaldy, which combined flapping races with Highland games, was 'a bonanza for the bookie'[39] about 1880. Elsewhere a pony-race which was meant to be three circuits was run, by the entire field, round four circuits. The wrong pony had been in front at the end of the third lap, the rider unable to hold it; they had to run another circuit to let the right one win. Every jockey, the judge, and all the stewards must have been in on the arrangement.[40]

Military races were held to be just as bad. The officers of garrisons fixed their races the evening before, in mess, and betted accordingly. In the 1850s, a public trainer who lent a horse to an officer for a military race was appalled at the morals of the gallant riders.[41]

Certain entirely 18th-century kinds of racing survived. Heaton Park had country house racing like that enjoyed by Lady Sarah Lennox. The ancient meeting of Burgh Barony was revived for the succession of each Earl of Lonsdale: a one-day festival of great animation. Matches arranged between gentlemen over the port and walnuts were still normal at the Bibury Club meetings of the 1880s.[42]

## Jockeys

Frank Buckle imitated Sam Chifney's riding; Sam Chifney junior imitated also his morals. He won a lot of races with his last-second 'Chifney Rush'; a lot of races were lost by other riders imitating it. He and his trainer brother William made a lot of money, and

FREDERICK JAMES ARCHER. 'The Tinman' (1857–1886) was the supreme jockey of the 19th century, champion 1874–1886. This pastel was done in 1883, the year of his marriage but a bad time for him in other ways. Lord Falmouth was on the verge of giving up racing, and the Duke of Portland had taken some sort of dislike to Archer; they were the two most important patrons of Mat Dawson's stable. Suffering, self-doubt, and iron determination all show in this likeness.

lost it. Their peak was 1830, when their Priam won the Derby. 'It was then,' said a contemporary, 'that the Chifneys were omnipotent, with the finest houses in Newmarket, and the profuse style of living that caused their establishments to vie with those of the nobles of the land.'[43] They were undone when 'Plenipo' beat Shillelagh (1834) and Athenian was unplaced behind Bay Middleton (1836). William relapsed into destitution, Sam into lethargy.

Jem (or Jim) Robinson modelled his mode of life on Buckle's, his riding style on Chifney's. The speed and power of his left-handed whipping was amazing. In 1824 he won £1000 by bringing off an unusual treble: he won the Derby on Cedric, he won the Oaks on Cobweb, and he married Miss Powell, all in the same week.

Elnathan 'Nat' Flatman was 'one of the most honourable and meritorious men of his class . . . one of the most respected and honourable "knights of the pig-skin" that ever performed upon an English race-course.'[44] But 'Druid' says 'At no point of his career had he ever been quite a first-class man . . . rather a good jockey by profession, than a great horseman by intuition.'[45] He had a passion for ratting, which he shared with General Peel. They used to put their terriers into the Duke of Rutland's ricks at Cheveley, one of which, to make sure of good sport, Nat stocked with rats.[46]

Bill Scott was brother of the trainer John. He was a dashing and forceful rider, with the ability (rare in any age) of assessing all the horses in a race.[47] In 1846 he owned Sir Tatton Sykes, on which he won both the 2000 Guineas and the St Leger. He should have won the Derby too: but he was drunk. He was often drunk: it killed him two years later.

John Scott's other principal jockey was Harry Edwards. 'Druid' admired the 'unvarying brilliancy and power of his set-to and finishes'.[48] But 'Sylvanus' says: 'He would rather "nobble" for a "pony" than get a hundred by other means . . . yet he was truly a magnificent horseman.' He went eventually to Nantes 'where he trained, rode, and "nobbled" à la Française, in a small way.'[49]

The method of riding the 'set-to', as 'Nimrod' instructed the French, was to sit right down in the saddle, drop the hands, and use both spurs and whip. Spurs were the more important.[50] Jem Robinson and Harry Edwards spurred in front of the girth.[51] John Lawrence, alone of contemporaries, deplored this severity, which was not only cruel but ineffective. It was not always the jockeys' fault. He records 'the deplorable case of a game little horse, called Hussar, by Snap, the property of that sleek, smooth-tongued, fat-witted humbug Hull, the horse-dealer. I met the horse on the road, coming to town from Epsom, where he had run. He was lacerated and cut up alive, from shoulder to flank, his sheath torn to ribbons, and his *testes* sorely and dangerously wounded.' Billy Barnes, the jockey, was appalled at what he had done. But these had been Hull's orders: ' "Make him win or cut his bloody entrails out – mark – if you don't give him his bellyful of whip, you'll never ride again for me. I'll find horse if you'll find whip and spur." '[52]

Most of the outstanding jockeys who began riding between 1850 and the end of the century were honest. Most engaging of these was Harry Custance, an amusing, well-educated man. He was made an official Jockey Club starter when he hung up his boots. Custance's great friend was John 'Tiny' Wells, another honest man, who rode for Sir Joseph Hawley. He outgrew his nickname, becoming big and heavy. He was notable for whimsical garments, especially hats. He greatly admired himself in some of his strange hats.

George Fordham, 'the demon', was a marvellous judge of pace. Like Jem Robinson in his day, he was a master at concealing his intentions and the condition of his horse. Again and again he foxed Fred Archer in matches, who became nettled. 'In one race', said Archer, 'George comes up and taps me in the last stride on the post. I am determined not to have this happen again, and then in the next race he just gets home and I beat him a stride past the post; with his clucking and fiddling you never know what the old chap is up to.'[53]

SAM CHIFNEY JUNIOR. 'Sylvanus' said: 'As for Sam, he was out-and-out the *beau ideal* of a jockey when in his prime; and for elegance of seat, perfection of hand, judgement of pace, and power in his saddle, was excelled by no man who ever sat in one.' Chifney (1786–1855) is here shown at 21, returning to scale. Five years later he blatantly stopped the favourite Manuella in the Derby of 1812. He won the Derbys of 1818 and 1820 for 'Squire' Thornhill, who gave enough money to outweigh the bribes of the legs. He became so lazy that his last years were spent in a kind of stupor.

Tom Cannon, who was John Day's son-in-law, was said to have the best hands of any jockey, very light, sensitive, and strong, communicating to the horse's mouth, it seemed, by electricity. His sons Kempton and Mornington Cannon were top jockeys and as incorruptible as their father.

Towering in reputation above all these, then and since, stands Fred Archer. He was brought up to racing. His first win was in a Galloway steeplechase at Bangor. In a good day for them both, he joined Mat Dawson at Newmarket, and began to ride for Lords Falmouth and Hastings (who is not to be confused with the marquis). The Dawsons more or less adopted him, making better parents than his own. He rode with extraordinary power and determination. He was severe on his mounts even by the standards of the time. He was exceptionally tall, and, though practically illiterate, unusually intelligent. He had an immediate understanding of horses he rode which seemed intuitive. He more nearly dominated the turf in the 1870s and 1880s than any other jockey in history.

He was a fascinating and tragic mixture. Mat Dawson called him that 'damned long-legged tin-scraping young devil',[54] meaning he was too fond of money. (This may be the origin of his nickname 'the tinman'.) But he poured money at his insatiable family. He was easily hurt, and almost unhinged by his wife's death. Two things destroyed him. One, sympathetically analysed by his biographer,[55] was the mixture in his personality of sensitivity and intelligence on the one hand, and a furious will to win on the other. The other was his battle against weight. His normal riding weight, in the winter when he went hunting, was 11 stone (154 lb.). To get it down he used a dreadful mixture in a black bottle, which those who tried it said was dynamite. Misery induced by wasting, personal unhappiness, a few snubs from men he thought trusted him, and the unresolved conflict in his personality combined to make him shoot himself in 1886, at the age of 29.

Archer was the unspoiled darling of the public. Some other jockeys were the spoiled darlings of their employers. Again and again this complaint is to be heard. As early as 1858 'Druid' spoke hardly of the conceited and incompetent young jockeys of the day.[56] The two causes of this new arrogance were over-rewarding and listening to their advice. Early in the century £10 had been a good present to a winning jockey. The rate did not greatly increase for 50 years. Then in the 1860s Richard ten Broeck, with American ideas, and Sir Joseph Hawley, with ideas all his own, began the practice of munificent awards – sometimes the whole stake. Rous thought this was terrible.

As to accepting jockeys' opinions, Rous said in 1844 that this was folly. In 1847 Francis Villiers took the word of both Frank Butler and Jem Robinson that Loadstone was better than Surplice, and therefore laid heavily against the latter for the next year's Derby. 'In this case,' says the trainer of both horses, Rous's 'warning words were prophetically correct.'[57] William Day makes the same point with more spleen, bitterly mocking the conceit which latter-day jockeys were acquiring as a result of being constantly asked for their advice.[58]

In 1875 Sir John Astley – 'The Mate', impoverished, cheerful, honest, universally liked – became a Steward of the Jockey Club and Chairman of its Rules Committee. The result was a set of rules, in 1879, controlling jockeys. They were not allowed to own a racehorse or to bet. Most important, they had to be licenced by the Jockey Club.

At the end of the century there was widely supposed to be a 'jockey ring' – a sinister confederation of jockeys, bookmakers, and professional backers, which fixed races. There is doubt about this. There were jockeys who rode dishonestly at the orders of bookies. There may have been a few races fixed by the jockeys beforehand. But responsible opinion at the time was inclined to disbelieve in a 'ring' which involved many of the leading jockeys.[59]

## Trainers and Training Methods

The greatest trainers at the beginning of the century were Robson and Prince, both at Newmarket. Robson was 'the veritable Emperor of Newmarket trainers'; 'Druid' says he deeply influenced Newmarket training practice, following, himself, Sir Charles Bunbury's system. But when John Day, his jockey, became a trainer, he was remarkable in his generation for the old-fashioned severity of his sweats.[60] Prince's was the big betting stable (with Foley, Fox and Mellish); he taught Sam Chifney senior, who taught William Chifney, who was also a believer in severe sweats. Later Prince adopted the elder John Kent, who went to Goodwood with his son; they trained on more modern lines, and the younger John Kent admits his debt to Robson.[61]

The first great public trainer was John Scott of Whitewall, who trained the winners of 16 St Legers, nine Oaks, and six Derbys. He was the first Yorkshire trainer to win the Derby (Mündig, 1835). He had the best horses and the richest owners. He rode his first winner for his father, a trainer and jockey in the south, at the age of 13. He went to Croft's Middleham stable, with his brother William; then became Mr Houldsworth's private trainer at Rockhill, and afterwards Mr Petre's at Whitewall. Petre went bankrupt, but not before he had won four St Legers, including three in a row (1827–9). Scott bought Whitewall, and trained his horses on Langton Wold. This has been marvellously described by 'Sylvanus'.[62] The Wold swarmed with touts hoping for a look at John Scott's classic candidates; he hunted them with an American dog trained to hunt runaway slaves.[63] His moral record is not unblemished, but he had close and enduring relationships with honourable men like Derby and Falmouth. When he died in 1871 he was 'universally regarded as the chief of English trainers, and indisputably first in his profession'.[64]

Another great Yorkshire trainer was William I'Anson. He bred, owned and trained Blink Bonny, who in 1857 was the first filly since Bunbury's Eleanor to win both Derby and Oaks. I'Anson was remarkable for what he asked of his horses: Caller Ou (St Leger 1861) ran a total of 101 races, winning 51. But when Blink Bonny's son Blair Athol won the Derby (1864) it was his first time on a racecourse, because of tooth-trouble and a bribed stable-lad: a remarkable training feat.

I'Anson was a Scotsman; so were the Dawsons, from Gullane. George Dawson trained Van Tromp for Lord Eglinton. His son Matthew, of Heath House, Newmarket, trained for Merry, Falmouth, Portland, Hastings, and Rosebery. From the early 1870s his was the most consistently successful stable in England. Mat's brother John trained for Prince Batthyany, his nephew George for the Duke of Rutland. Between them, these Dawsons trained nearly 50 classic winners. Not one of them lost his broad Lowland accent.

Captain Machell was not a trainer but a racing manager. He had been a penniless officer in a line regiment, supplementing his pay by backing himself in various athletic contests. The turning point in his life was serving in Kildare, after which he gravitated to Newmarket. His speciality was looking after the racing affairs of rich young men, to whom he was completely loyal, and for whom he made a lot of money. He also made a lot for himself. The victory of Hermit and the breeding of Isinglass were among his achievements.

The greatest trainer in the last quarter of the century was John Porter of Kingsclere. He was given his start by Sir Joseph Hawley, for whom he won the Derby with Blue Gown in 1868. Porter went on to train Ormonde and Flying Fox for the Duke of Westminster, Isonomy for the greedy brewer Mr Gretton, and the triple crown winner, Common, for Lord Alington and Sir Frederick Johnstone. Porter won over 1000 races, including seven Derbys and six St Legers. After he retired (in 1905) he was the prime mover in starting Newbury Racecourse.

JOHN SCOTT. 'Sylvanus' saw 'the wizard of the North' (1794–1871) working his string on Langton Wold about 1842: 'Some were walking in single file; others were undergoing the operation of rubbing after a sweat; all of which the intelligent chief of the establishment – seated on his hack – was superintending with eye and voice, ordering his forces about the field in the "preparation" they were undergoing, and personally prescribing the needful, discriminating treatment applied to each animal entrusted to his charge.'

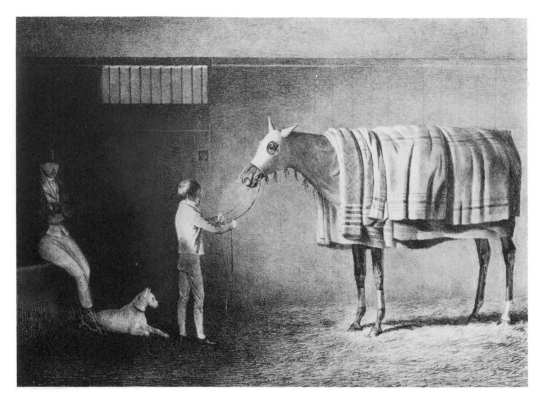

TRAINING METHODS. Horses were allowed to become gross before they went into training. Training-grooms got the weight off by purges, given as often as twice a week; by four-mile 'spins' in heavy clothes; and by sweats in the stable. Each box had a stove, and the horse, laden with rugs, was given a 'sauna'. As soon as the sweat was removed by scraping, whisping, and rubbing, the horse was rugged and hooded again. This régime, illustrated 1823, was still normal in 1840; it gave way to more moderate methods rather suddenly about 1845.

Trainers changed profoundly during the century. 'Nimrod' thought it ridiculous that 'John Watson, a training-groom' should be called 'Mister'.[65] Later in the century William Day mocked their gentlemanly pretensions.[66] But such airs were a symptom of a change greatly for the better. In 1864: 'As a rule, a trainer is now a well-conducted, comparatively well-educated man. . . . The ignorant cunning sot, once too true a type of his order, is dying out.'[67] And in 1879: 'There can be no question that trainers and jockeys are far more honest in the present day than in the past, and that they are certainly quite as honest as employers.'[68]

Training methods changed more gradually, in spite of Robson. 'Nimrod', as 'Nemrod', instructed the French that horses should be worked in head, body and breast sweaters, which should be light but very hot;[69] but he elsewhere notes that purging and sweating should be used more carefully than they were.[70] John Scott in 1842 gave his horses 'a bursting four-mile spin in their clothes'.[71] But not long afterwards 'Druid' says 'Heavy-clothed sweats are fast going out of fashion.'[72] Speaking of The Flying Dutchman's preparation by Fobert in 1848–49, Corbet says: 'Horses are no longer loaded with clothes and fagged and scraped, but they get the same amount of work without the unnecessary severity at once so general and so fatal. Common sense has of late years driven out much of the conventional practice of the training-stable, and a horse is now treated in accordance with his peculiar temper and constitution.'[73] A fairly dramatic change seems therefore to have occurred during the 1840s.

Stable-lads were on the whole contented and well looked after. Most were taken to church every Sunday, and John Day's were given extended Bible readings too. At James Merry's private stables at Russley in 1862, 'Jack gets 10 pounds a year and a suit of clothes, with three good meals a day, and in spite of his weight, a fair share of beef and beer.' He looked after one horse, which he adored. In a public stable it was the same, except for the suit of clothes.[74] In 1875 John Snowy worked as a lad for Robert Binns, at Rosegill Lodge, Middleham. The lads were hard-worked, but well-treated and happy. It was the same at the nearby stables of John Osborne and Tom Dawson. The lads were kept on a wasting diet to keep their weight down; they had huge meals when they took their horses to race-meetings, and always came home overweight. 'Taking it all round, it was a jolly life at Middleham.'[75] But Snowy was sacked for selling a stable tip.

### Tipsters, Card-Sellers, and Freaks

In the second quarter of the 19th century the public began to bet, in small sums, on a few big races. It had no information. In the 1840s tipsters began to provide it.

The first was a man called Wingrave. As 'A Retired Club Steward' he gave Voltigeur for the Derby. He then turned into 'Harry Buckstone, late valet to a sporting nobleman, who, being in possession of several important racing secrets, will send the winners of the Two Thousand Guineas and Chester Cup to a select number of gentlemen on receiving a remittance of five shillings.'[76]

The 'lists' of the early 1850s turned tipping into a major industry. 'The journals read by the sporting world were filled with advertisements promising any number of certain winners for an incredibly small number of postage-stamps.'[77] James Desborough 'although hating self-praise and idle puff, so prevalent in the present day, boldly defies the world to find his equal.'[78] One of his equals was a lady who called herself, at various times, 'Mr Adelaide Merryweather', 'John Screwman', 'Arthur Lancefield', and 'a disabled jockey's wife'. She tipped a winning double to a prosperous grain-merchant who, in gratitude, married her.

The 'lists' were abolished by the Act of 1853, but the tipsters were by now entrenched. Surtees called them in 1860: 'a growing and dangerous evil, and one that completely baffles the efforts of the legislature to suppress them.'[79]

The first tipster to operate publicly on a racecourse was 'Liverpool Charlie', who stood outside the Sefton Arms at Aintree selling sealed envelopes for threepence. He was always drunk but did very well. The idea spread fast, and prices went up. One illiterate man could always make £5 before a race. A big black tipster used to dress up in a silk hat, and break 'large swede turnips' with his head. Another started selling tips with pieces of butterscotch, for a penny, at Thirsk; he ended with several racehorses in training. Epsom was easy: 'Any fool can make money on a Derby day. In fact, they throw it at you.' Newmarket was unique in having no public tipsters at all.[80]

The card-sellers were first noticed in numbers in about 1835, and during the next 20 years became a big new industry. There were 400 in the North; 200 or 300 were peripatetic, racing everywhere, like the Ring. Half were women. 'Sally Birch', 'Big Ann', and 'Fair Helen' were their successive queens. Ascot was their great carnival, at which the clowning of 'Donkey Jemmy' was specially profitable. The card-sellers walked between meetings, averaging 25 miles a day.[81]

In the late 1870s they had come to be called spivés (origin, no doubt, of the mysterious word 'spiv'). Many travelled hundreds of miles by train without tickets; but hundreds, perhaps thousands, still walked between every racecourse in Britain. With any money they made they immediately betted.[82]

Tipsters despised card-sellers, but not as much as card-sellers despised acrobats and freaks like 'the fat acrobat, who has passed the best years of his life in lifting a needle from the ground with his eyelid.'[83] Surtees at a country meeting saw 'acrobats, Ethiopians, organ-grinders, monkey-masters, and . . . the two fattest boys under the sun'.[84]

## Communications

Racing results and betting odds travelled slowly. It was remarkable that, in 1836, the result of the St Leger got from Doncaster to Manchester – 58 miles – in two hours and 20 minutes. The same year a Birmingham innkeeper was able to give his customers the result six hours and 21 minutes after the race. A messenger called Mr Bendrey brought a certificate, signed by the judge, the 94 miles, using five horses.[85]

The first result carried by a pigeon was that of the St Leger of 1825. A bird took the news of Memnon's victory to London; specially trained dogs took it to Manchester. By the 1840s this had become normal. An eyewitness described the biggest-ever flock of pigeons released after Nutwith's St Leger in 1843; they went all over Yorkshire and Lancashire.[86] When the Duke of Richmond's Red Deer won the Chester Cup in 1844, John Kent sent the news to Goodwood by pigeon.[87] The biggest user of pigeons was *Bell's Life*, which had its lofts on the roof of the office. The paper's pigeons usually took an hour and a quarter from Goodwood to London, but could do it in under an hour in good conditions.[88] In 1852, Daniel O'Rourke's year, 'the news of "What won the Derby?" was disseminated by means of the carrier pigeons. The flight of hundreds of these birds directly the winner had passed the post being quite a novel sight.'[89] (This writer is using the word 'novel' loosely.)

By 1860 progress had destroyed this pretty necessity: 'Eclipse himself would cut a poor figure alongside the electric telegraph.'[90]

# 15 British Steeplechasing

## Ancestry; Early Matches

The ancestors of steeplechasing are various and obscure. They include wild-goose-chases and hunting-matches.

The wild-goose-chase was apparently a Tudor invention; a match across country, with no particular objective. 'Whichever horse obtained the lead at 12-score yards from the starting-post, the other was compelled to follow him wherever he went, and to keep within a certain distance of him, as twice or thrice his length, or else to be "beaten up", whipped up to the mark by the judges who rode to see fair play.' If the leader got a distance clear, he had won: or if the following horse 'refused some break-neck leap which the other had taken.'[1] In the mid 17th century: 'the wild-goose chase is such an unmerciful and unreasonable toil, as the name itself doth import, without any mediocrity or order, I will pass over it as an exercise not worthy of the time, because it is the hazard of the spoil and ruin of such excellent creatures; for if two good horses be met, the match cannot be tried, till one of them be half spoiled, if not both: nay, sometimes they are both brought so weak, that they are neither of them able to go, and then when they are, so Turkishly tormented, the match is fair to be drawn.'[2] To distance the second horse was to 'pound' it; hence the other name for these matches, which was current in Ireland. 'Pound' kept this meaning in the hunting-field into the second half of the 19th century.[3]

Hunting-matches were races behind hounds, these chasing a stag or buck. The first recorded are James I's. In Charles II's reign: 'This day, for a wager before the king, my lords of Castlehaven, and Arran. . . . did run down and kill a stoute Bucke in St James's Parke.' There was also a mysterious 'Hunting Match' at Mossfields on the third day of Bartholemew Fair in August 1663. It was much resented by the people of the fair, but was an old custom revived.[4]

The earliest steeplechase matches were between hunters, owners up, crossing country from a start-point to some distant but visible objective. The first recorded was in Ireland in 1752, between Mr O'Callaghan and Mr Edmund Blake, from Buttevant church to St Mary's, Doneraile, known as St Leger church.[5]

Such matches were run slowly, because hunting was done slowly. Hounds were a hybrid predominantly bloodhound, heavy and leisurely, and 'The old ENGLISH HUNTER was a strong half-bred horse . . . being bred between the racer and the lighter kind of cart mare.'[6]

But in the 1750s and 1760s hunting was transformed. In 1763 there was a match at Newmarket between the Cheshire hounds, bred on a new principle, of Mr Smith Barry, and the Quorn hounds, bred on the old principle, of the great Hugo Meynell. Smith Barry's hounds, following a drag, won by a great distance.[7] All foxhounds thereafter

'THE MOONLIGHT STEEPLECHASE'.
This event was allegedly run by the
officers of a regiment stationed at
Ipswich in 1803: 'The First Steeple-
Chase on Record. Cannon-Ball, on his
"Gunpowder" horse, challenging the
champion to a struggle for the lead.
They charged the last fence together:
and while the "Great Gun" jumped
smash through the middle of the gate,
the grey, still hand in hand, stepped
neatly over the strong hurdle fence and
bank, by a jump on and off. Subden
came third: the Lounger's horse,
kicking his heels up at his master, and
careless of his "woe ful" cries. Simpson
was making a good line of his own
across a field: and two, dismounted in
the distance, were exercising alike their
patience, ingenuity, and powers of
persuasion, in the subjection of their
refractory steeds.'

became lighter, quieter, and far faster because of a greyhound cross.[8]

To follow them, hunting men got fast horses. By about 1770 'no eminent hunt was at that period without its share of thorough bred, seven eighths, and three parts bred horses.'[9] The Irish were importing English thoroughbred stallions and with them covering seven-eighths-bred mares; a great many horses thus produced came to the English shires, where they hunted and ran matches. The Irish also bred thoroughbred hunters: 'In some of the rich grazing counties, as Meath and Roscommon, a large, long blood-horse is reared, of considerable value. He seldom has the elegance of the English horse; he is larger-headed, more leggy, ragged-hipped, angular, yet with greater power in the quarters, much depth behind the knees, stout and hardy, full of fire and courage, and an excellent leaper. It is not, however, the leaping of the English horse, striding as it were over a low fence, and stretched at his full length over a higher one; it is the proper *jump* of the deer, beautiful to look at, difficult to sit, and, both in height and extent, unequalled by the English horse.'[10] Dick Christian said; 'Thorough-bred horses make the best hunters. I never heard of a great thing yet but it was done by a thorough-bred horse.'[11]

Riders treated this transformed hunting-field as a race. 'I've seen the gentlemen single themselves out and ride jealous.'[12] This led to challenges. In 1790 there was a 9-mile match, Melton Mowbray to Dalby Wood, 1000 guineas, between Mr Lorraine Hardy and Mr Willoughby. The same year was the first recorded cross-country race, as distinct from two-horse match: 8 miles, Barkby Holt to Billesdon Coplow and back, 100 guineas a side, won by Charles Meynell (son of Hugo) from Lord Forester and Sir Gilbert Heathcote: 'no rules as to gates or roads; each to come as he could'.[13]

The riders usually followed a lead. In 1803 a Sporting Dictionary defined a 'hunting match (generally termed a steeplechase)' as 'made by parties, to ride their own horses across country to some point agreed on, encountering all difficulties, and taking the leaps in stroke. This kind of match is, upon most occasions, run with a few couple of hounds; a person going forward with a drag to the spot appointed where the match is to be decided.'[14] But the presence of hounds had in fact become exceptional. By 1800 the riders followed a pilot, a hunt servant who knew the country. The pilot started 60 yards ahead and waved a handkerchief to show where fences could be jumped.

In November 1804 a three-horse steeplechase was the first ridden in colours. The same year the first military 'chase was run – a match between two officers of the 5th Light

GRAND LEICESTERSHIRE STEEPLE-
CHASE. This, in 1829, was one
of the last of the old cross-country
steeplechases run in a straight line (or
as near as might be) from one landmark
to another: before Coleman had the
idea of a finish near the start. The
horses were thoroughbred hunters,
Leicestershire-bred or Irish. Dick
Christian rides the dapple-grey Magic;
he finished second after two falls.

Dragoons, near Newcastle. (This is on the assumption that the Moonlight Steeplechase of 1803 was Henry Alken's fantasy.)

Typically matches and races were owner-ridden. But professionals rode in the 1790s. They were hunt-servants – grooms, whippers-in, second horsemen, huntsmen. The most celebrated were Dick Christian, Bill Bean, and Jem Hills.

Christian started in Sir Horace Mann's Kent stables, aged 12, and rode on the flat. He went back to the shires, became a groom and second-horseman, married, and had 21 children. He continued to ride races on the flat. He became a farmer for a time, but rode and trained horses also. He returned to hunting, as whipper-in and huntsman. 'Dick Christian had practically sounded the depth of every ditch and brook in Leicestershire, for more than half a century.'[15] He was pilot in nearly all the Leicestershire steeple-chases, except when riding himself. Until the mid-1820s, he was the leading professional steeplechase jockey. He wasted with hot gin-and-water and frequent sweats.[16] Captain Becher, one of the greatest of the next generation, said in the weighing-tent after a race at Dunchurch: 'Gentlemen, if I had Christian's nerve, I'd give all I have in the world.'[17]

Bill Bean was 'the Arch-trespasser of England' when drag-hunting and stag-hunting from 1790.[18] He rode steeplechases well into late middle-age. Jem Hills won the first steeplechase ever run in Wiltshire. He was whipper-in for the Beaufort hounds, and rode a horse belonging to the Master, Lord Ducie.

Osbaldeston, who won a great many cross-country matches, followed Thomas Assheton-Smith as Master of the Quorn in 1817. 'No man that ever came into Leicestershire could beat Mr Smith.' But he disapproved of steeplechasing. With the Quorn and then the Pytchley Osbaldeston hunted hounds himself six days a week, and sometimes took out two different packs in one day.[19] 'He was a rare match-rider across country; I never saw a better at that game.'[20]

## The Revolution at St Albans

The idea of a steeplechase course consisting of fences built on a racecourse was old, but a long time catching on. In 1794 at the Newmarket Craven Meeting there was a match over a mile, with five-foot bars every quarter-mile. At Bedford in 1810 there was a three-mile sweepstakes, eight artificial fences, each 4 ft 6 in., run in heats. This course continued in use until the middle 1820s, but the principal was not general for another 30 years.

Other important attributes of modern steeplechasing date from 1830, when Thomas Coleman started his races at St Albans.

As a young man, Coleman's job had been riding the hunters to hounds in Windsor Great Park to qualify them for races at Ascot. In 1820 he bought the Chequers Inn on the edge of St Albans. He rebuilt it on a generous scale and renamed it the Turf Hotel; it was famous for its cellar and its billiard-tables (George Osbaldeston once lost £3000 in a week). He trained horses for Lord George Bentinck and others. (Much later, Coleman's information was valuable to Bentinck when he exposed Running Rein.)[21]

In 1830 Coleman put on the first St Albans Steeplechase. 'Other managers liked four mile straight . . . they left the riders to hunt the country for their line.'[22] But Coleman picked an out-and-back course, starting and finishing near the Turf. The course was marked with flags; the line was kept secret until the start by the flag-holders hiding under hedges. Lord Ranlegh's Wonder, ridden by Captain Macdowell, won from Lord Clanricarde's Nailer, owner up.

(Clanricarde was important to this phase of steeplechasing's history. He was George Canning's son-in-law and, for a time, secretary. He had learned his racing in Ireland. He was dashing and attractive. His participation made this new sport glamorous and talked-about.)

The next year the race was bigger and better-organized. Moonraker won; Captain Becher rode Wildboar, which was unplaced and died after the race.

By 1832 St Albans was a major and established event. George Osbaldeston was umpire and chose the line. On 8 March the 20 starters were saddled in front of the Turf Hotel. They were mounted at the command of a bugle-call. The fences were big but not very dangerous. Becher fell on the flat when in the lead on Corinthian Kate; he remounted and finished third. Moonraker won, from Grimaldi. Osbaldeston thought Grimaldi had been badly ridden, and should have won. A match therefore followed, on the Elmores' land near Harrow, for £1000, Osbaldeston riding Grimaldi. It was a course of big fences and good grass, more 'of the character of a race course than a laborious hunting country'. There were vast crowds, jammed roads, and long delays caused by disputes; ladies in open carriages were lashed by a cruel wind. In the race, Moonraker went the wrong way and Osbaldeston on Grimaldi won easily: but there was an objection because of a bump after they had gone two miles. This was referred to the Jockey Club, which upheld the result.[23]

St Albans also had a hurdle race, which Coleman 'got up specially to please the ladies.'[24] The idea of racing over hurdles was, according to legend, invented by the Prince Regent; he was riding with friends on the downs above Brighton, and they amused themselves by popping in and out of sheep-pens. The first hurdle-race was held at Bristol in 1821. This was three one-mile heats, five flights per heat. Like all hurdle-races until 1867 it was run under flat-racing rules.

## The Revolution Develops: Cheltenham and Aylesbury

Steeplechasing was transformed by the sweepstakes principle; by a course marked with flags; by concern for the spectators; and by the profits made by innkeepers.

The effect was that the three meetings of 1832 grew to 66 in 1842. The most important were Cheltenham, the Vale of Aylesbury, and Aintree.

Flat racing started at Cheltenham in about 1815. It was successful and popular, except with the Rev. F. C. Close (later Dean of Carlisle, and better known as Dean Close) who preached a sermon which was printed as a pamphlet in 1827: *The Evil Consequences of attending the Race Courses Exposed.* In Cheltenham race-week 'It is scarcely possible to turn our steps in any direction without hearing the voice of the blasphemous, or meeting the reeling drunkard, or witnessing scenes of the lowest profligacy.'[25] Nevertheless the Cheltenham Grand Annual Steeplechase was inaugurated in 1834 and run in the Vale of Prestbury. In 1837 it was won by Becher on Vivian, and in 1839 and '40 by Jem Mason on Lottery. In 1841 a new course was used, at Andoversford, but in 1847 the Grand Annual came back to Prestbury. The course had natural obstacles, but it was well-planned and well-flagged.

The Vale of Aylesbury Steeplechase started in 1835. The course was four miles, between Waddington Windmill and Aylesbury church. Brooks were the principal hazard; the Vale was laced with them. Becher and Vivian won the first running.

Immediately after this St Albans collapsed, owing to the hostility of local farmers to the destructive crowds who came to see the sports. Coleman's success was his undoing. 'Although the tap root was dead at last, the sport blossomed everywhere in the Midlands.'[26] There was hunt racing in Yorkshire, initiated by the Badsworth in 1833, and Lord Eglinton got it going in Scotland. In a country town in about 1840, 'in accordance with the especial spirit of the times, a steeple-chase fever broke out amongst the inhabitants.'[27]

## Aintree and the Grand National

A Mr Lynn had been licensee of the grandstand of the defunct Maghull racecourse. He owned the Waterloo Hotel in the Liverpool suburb of Aintree. In July 1829 he opened a flat-racing course. In 1836, 'in accordance with the especial spirit of the times', he inaugurated the 'Grand Liverpool Steeplechase': a sweepstake, gentlemen riders at 12

LIVERPOOL GRAND STEEPLECHASE. This, in 1839, was the fourth Grand Steeplechase on the Aintree Course, but it is considered the first Grand National. They ran twice round a two-mile circuit, jumping 29 obstacles. Part of the course was plough. There were two brooks, each taken twice. The favourite was The Nun, Allen McDonough (stripes), the winner Lottery, Jem Mason (white blaze, behind him), and the second Seventy Four, Tom Oliver (extreme left, jumping). Captain Becher on Conrad had already fallen into the other brook for the second time

stone (168 lb.), 20 fences in each of two circuits, and two flights of hurdles in the straight. Captain Becher won on The Duke. In 1837 the City of Liverpool gave £100 added money. The Duke won again, but Becher was ill and another jockey rode.

Mr Lynn lacked either luck or skill. He wrote to the artist Ferneley in 1838 that the venture had lost him all his money.[28] A syndicate then took over Aintree racing, with a distinguished Race Committee including Lord George Bentinck and Lords Eglinton, Derby, Sefton, and Wilton. The first race under the new dispensation was on 26 February 1839: four miles, 29 jumps. There were 53 entries, wide public interest, and heavy ante-post betting at the Talbot Hotel. 17 started. Becher, on Conrad, fell into a brook on the first circuit, remounted and carried on, fell into it again on the second circuit, and this time stayed there while the field jumped over him. Elmore's Lottery won, ridden as always by Jem Mason.

This race is regarded, illogically but invariably, as the first Grand National. It was still called the Grand Liverpool. It became the Liverpool and National in 1843, and in that year a handicap. In 1847 it was called the Grand National.

Part of the course was plough-land. The obstacles were both natural and artificial. The two brooks were widened. In 1840 a stone wall was added for the benefit of the Irish, and an oxer for the Leicestershire men.


## The First Great Riders

The oldest of the first generation of leading professional jockeys was Becher. He was a clerk in the Army Store-Keeping Department. He may have served in the Peninsula; he was certainly with Wellington's army in Brussels. He came back to Norfolk as a horse-breeder and coper after the war. From about 1820 he worked for Thomas Coleman at the Turf, a job of which he said he 'never had such a lark in his life.'[29] By 1829 he was riding cross-country matches all over England. The horse he is most associated with is Captain Lamb's Vivian. His later life was cushioned by a sinecure appointment: Inspector of Sacks for the Great Northern Railway at Boston, Lincolnshire.

Duels between Vivian and Lottery were a recurrent sensation of the late 1830s: Vivian usually the winner, but aging.

Lottery's rider was Jem Mason. Mason's father was a breeder and coper of hunters who lost his money in a stage at Pinner. Near the stage was the Dove House yard of a Mr Tilbury, one of the biggest horse-dealers in the country. He had a full-sized race-course, with jumps. Jem Mason, still a boy, began schooling horses for Tilbury. He also hunted with Bean (de Burgh Staghounds) and Sebright (Hertfordshire hounds). In the hunting field he was noticed by the Rev. Lord Henry Beauclerc, and given the ride on The Poet at St Albans in 1834. He won with 4 stone dead weight – 56 lb. of lead.

From Tilbury, Mason went to John Elmore's stables near Harrow. Elmore's stable jockey and rough-rider was Dan Seffert, who was nearing retirement. It all worked out well. Elmore and the Marquis of Waterford were 'the two original props, professional and amateur, of the steeple-chase.'[30] Mason became Elmore's jockey, married his daughter, and rode his Lottery.

Lottery was a half-bred by Lottery out of Parthenia by Welbeck. Called Chance, he won once on the flat in 1834. He ran at various London courses, including Whyte's Hippodrome; in 1837 he was third behind Vivian at St Albans. In 1838 he went to the Epsom trainer George Dockeray. He was also hunted: 'Jem never did no good with Lottery till he rode him with Josh Anderson's stag-hounds.'[31] He won at Aintree in 1839, and for two years dominated steeplechasing. He was debarred from races, or given impossible penalties; he was the reason for the growth of handicap steeplechases.[32]

Jem Mason was a tremendous dandy. He always rode in white kid gloves, and his boots were the combined achievement of two different London bootmakers. He was in great contrast to his close friend Tom Oliver, the third nationally-known jockey of the time.

Oliver (or Olliver; he was almost illiterate as a young man, which may explain the doubt) was a rough, tough Sussex boy, often in scrapes, always in debt. He was brought up in an Epsom training stable by Page, his uncle. He won the 1842, '43, and '53 Grand Nationals and was four times placed. He became a successful trainer and a great tutor of jockeys: his pupils included Adam Lindsay Gordon (author of *How we Beat the Favourite*) who venerated him.

Dick Christian said of Becher: 'he was stronger, I think, than Oliver; Jem Mason's not so hard as them two.'[33] Oliver himself said of Mason: 'I can say without fear of contradiction that he was the finest horseman in England – I have never ridden with him without envying the perfection of his style.'[34]

## Hostility to Steeplechasing

Steeplechasing had violent opponents throughout the first half of the 19th century. There were three lobbies: the humanitarian, the hunting, and the moral.

John Lawrence in 1829 preferred the 'modern STEEPLE HUNT' to the 'old WILD GOOSE CHASE' but still said it was 'sufficiently oppressive and ruinous to the horse.' Of both forms: 'I do regret the cruelty of driving brave, and generous, and useful animals into useless and unprofitable dangers and hardships, from which they can scarcely escape with impunity and soundness, and through which, so many have been rendered miserable cripples ever after.' It was this indignation, rather than any suspicion of blasphemy, which led him to deplore 'the rising favourite, but not very defensible amusement of hunting the steeples of holy mother church.'[35] On the day after Lottery's Grand National, the *Liverpool Mercury* said: 'It was no doubt a very exciting spectacle, but we can no more be reconciled to it on that account than we are to cockfighting, bull-baiting, or any other popular pastime which is attended with the infliction of wanton torture to any living being.'[36]

'Nimrod', uniquely influential as a spokesman for hunting, said about the same time: 'A new system of racing has lately sprung up in England which we do not know how to commend. . . . What are called hurdle races are still more absurd.'[37] In 1840: 'Steeplechasing, the worst description of sporting   having all the false excitement of gambling without its fair chances; and all the show of hunting without its beautiful spirit – is raging through the land.'[38] 'Nimrod's' implacable hostility was neither moral nor humanitarian. His position is made clear when he reports himself urging the German sporting aristocracy to have nothing to do with steeplechasing: hunting depends on the goodwill of farmers, and steeplechasing crowds – ignorant townsmen and insolent legs – forfeit this goodwill.[39]

The Savonarola – a sporting Dean Close – was Surtees. Steeplechasing inundated a respectable country town with 'its swell-mob, sham captains, and all the paraphernalia of odd laying, "secret tips", and market rigging. Who will deny the benefit that must accrue to any locality by the infusion of all the loose fish of the Kingdom?'[40]

## The Period of Decadence

Until about 1850 steeplechasing grew in esteem as well as in size. In 1845 Henry Wright, of the Haymarket, London, published his Steeplechase Calender. He listed races and matches from 1826, and the registered colours of 89 owners. He was unable to print generally-applicable rules because there were none.

In the 1850s the sport proliferated minor meetings rather than started major ones. It was the sort of growth which contained the seeds of immediate decay. New courses were started by the wrong people for the wrong reasons, and run on the wrong lines. 'Nine-tenths of the steeple-chases and coursing-matches are got up by innkeepers, for the good of their houses.' It was made possible by the railways: 'but for the Granddiddle Junction, ———shire would never have had a "Grand Aristocratic Steeple-Chase". A few friends or farmers might have got up a quiet thing among themselves, but it would never have been a regular trade transaction.'[41]

The war against defaulters and touts made the legitimate turf too hot for some of them; they took to the lawless 'illegitimate' side. 'No fair bet,' said the *Sporting Review*, 'can be made on a steeplechase owing to the number of accidents which take place, but it offers ample employment for the sharper.' As the sport was 'got up', echoed *Bell's Life*, 'for the most part as an instrument of fraud and barefaced swindling, it gradually but surely sunk into the lowest depths of degradation.'[42]

Fraud and scandal discredited steeplechasing; so did incompetence and ill-directed policy. 'Steeplechases are generally crude, ill-arranged things. . . . There is always something wanting or forgotten. Either they forget the ropes, or they forget the scales, or they forget the weights, or they forget the bell.'[43]

Fences had been too dangerous, but Clerks of Courses began to err in the opposite direction. In order to attract big fields, they made fences too easy and weights too low. The *Sporting Review* of January and March 1857 said that bad racehorses were beating proper steeplechasers, and untrained boys riding instead of strong and experienced horsemen. In the 1860s the obstacles became contemptible even at Aintree: 'It almost requires a microscope to discover the fences.'[44]

Another reason for decadence was the absence of so many young officers. The names of captains – real ones, not the 'sham captains' of Surtees – crop up in dozens of races and matches until the 1840s. They also had their own races. The principal military steeplechase was started in the early 1830s by a retiring officer of the 5th Dragoon Guards, who gave a cup. This was first run for in 1834. In 1841 the first Grand Military meeting lasted three days at Northampton. It was parochial, but it set a standard. Then Britain's ever-growing military commitment in India removed some of the officers, and in the 1850s the Crimea removed most of the rest. What British steeplechasing was missing is shown by the races on 3 December 1855 in the Crimea: big jumps, big fields, perfect going. The Sultan afterwards gave three gold cups.

These were bad years, but there were still great horses and celebrated riders.

About 1840 the father of the sporting writer Joseph Osborne saw a mare working as near leader in the Shrewsbury Hirondelle, the fast coach to Holyhead. He liked her, bought her, named her English Lass, and sent her to stud. She bred a number of indifferent animals, and then Abd-el-Kader, by the good sire of jumpers Ishmael. 'Little Ab' was small for a 'chaser – 15.2 hands – and vicious as a young horse; but after an apprenticeship in Ireland it won the Nationals of 1850 and '51.

The greatest jockey of the period was George Stevens. He was a Cheltenham specialist, but he also achieved a unique feat in winning five Nationals, the first in 1855. He died after a fall from his hack, aged 38.

Horses like 'Ab' and jockeys like Stevens were rare gleams in a drab period; the re-making of steeplechasing was urgent and it had to be fundamental.

## The Period of Renaissance

Fothergill Rowlands – 'Fogo' or 'Fog' – was the son of a Monmouthshire doctor and himself a doctor. He preferred horses. His own were trained by Tom Oliver, who taught him to ride races. He became a leading G.R., and won the Grand Steeplechase at Baden Baden on his own Medora. He then trained his own horses, and later became a public trainer at Epsom. Surveying steeplechasing, he deplored what he saw. In 1857 he began a deliberate attempt to recapture the glories of the 1830s; he organized a Grand National

VALE OF AYLESBURY. 'Second Day Thursday 11th Feby. 1836. Carrying 11 Sto. 15 Sovs. each with 100 Sovs. added. 15 Started. Fleet Maisten Brook with the Chapel in the distance; here the chase became very interesting, Horses and Riders doing their best, VIVIAN keeping the lead, THE PONY, LAURESTINA & GRIMALDI, lying at this point well placed, CANNON BALL struggling at the brook, ROCHILLE clearing in good style followed by YELLOW DWARF, RED DEER, BUTTERFLY &c.'

Hunt Steeplechase, to be supported by four leading hunts, at Market Harborough. The horses were to be hunters, the riders amateurs. The first race in 1859 was ill-supported and a failure. But it was important in more than its idea: it had a set of rules, known as the 'Harborough Act'.

The next year Rowlands got 12 hunts to subscribe, and 31 hunters started. In 1861 Rowlands moved his race to Cheltenham. The winner was George Ede ('Mr Edwards'), the leading amateur, who was killed at Aintree in 1870. A similar race was also run at Market Harborough. Both were successful. They were races between big horses jumping big fences with heavy weights, the whole conducted efficiently and honestly – the opposite of what was going on elsewhere. The public loved it and betting was heavy.

At the same time there was a sudden demand for rules. In November 1862 *Bell's Life* called for them editorially. A letter presumed to be from B. J. 'Cherry' Angell and W. G. Craven (a member of the Jockey Club) suggested rules. Admiral Rous suggested certain amendments. In 1863 Angell and Craven recruited Lord Grey de Wilton, and the three formed themselves into the 'Grand National Hunt Steeplechase Committee', deriving its name from Rowlands's race and associating itself with his philosophy. The committee was joined by a number of other members of the Jockey Club. In 1864 it adjudicated on a case referred to it from Melton Mowbray, which related to the vexed and constant problem of a rider's amateur status. In 1865 a more difficult case came up, involving a leading personality: was a horse (Henry Chaplin's Emperor) eligible for the Grand National Hunt Steeplechase when it was boarded at the yard of – though not trained by – a public trainer? There was also a case about the validity of an entry when the Secretary had lost the owner's letter. In each case the Committee came to a decision (aided by Rous) which common sense and equity support. This created confidence.

In 1866 the Grand National Hunt Steeplechase Committee was reconstituted: mostly members of the Jockey Club, and especially those who were Gentleman Riders such as Lord Poulett and George Payne. In 1867 the Jockey Club widened the Committee's frame of reference by ruling that hurdle-races were to be run under its rules: the next year the first official Steeplechase Calendar was published.

By 1870 there were clear rules and a recognized authority. It was a long time before either was obeyed.

## The Rise and Fall of the Amateurs

These and the next years of steeplechasing were dominated by amateurs.

There was a great gulf between the best and the ordinary. Surtees said in 1852: 'we know of no more humiliating sight than misshapen gentlemen playing at jockeys. . . . What a farce to see the great hulking fellows go to scale with their saddles strapped to their backs, as if to illustrate the impossibility of putting a round of beef upon a pudding-plate.'[45] Four years later 'Druid' said: 'For the comedy of errors in crossing a country, amateur steeplechases are worth watching.' The riders were either overdone or under-done, never just right: just right was 'three parts of a bottle of port wine, two glasses of brandy-and-water, and a pipe.'[46]

But a few years later certain amateurs were competing on equal terms with the leading professionals. Arthur Yates rode all over Britain and Europe, and later trained both horses and amateur riders. George Ede rode Lord Poulett's The Lamb (a small grey, Limerick-bred) to his first Grand National win in 1868. Three years later Poulett dreamed his horse would win again; it did, ridden by another amateur Tommy Pickernell, who had been leading rider in Tasmania. Ede had been killed the year before. The Lamb was killed the year after, breaking his leg in a patch of bog in a race in Germany. Maunsell Richardson was called 'Cat' because of his athletic and gymnastic prowess: he shared this with his confederate Captain Machell, who was as important in

MCDONOUGH, OLIVER AND MASON ON BRUNETTE, DISCOUNT AND LOTTERY. Jem Mason (right) and Tom Oliver (centre) were the outstanding professionals of the late 1830s and 1840s. Oliver was the stronger, Mason the more elegant. Allen McDonough (left) was the leading Irish amateur. He last rode at Punchestown aged 64. Mason died in 1866, Oliver in 1874, McDonough in 1888. Lottery won the Grand National in 1839, Discount in 1844. He was previously called Magnum Bonum, and his name changed as a result of his price getting smaller and smaller when he was up for sale. Brunette won the Grand National Steeple Chase at Ashbourne, Co. Meath, in 1843; she ran disappointingly at Aintree in 1847.

steeplechasing as on the flat. Machell won three of the four Nationals of 1873–6; Richardson trained and rode the first two. He was said to be the best steeplechase rider in Britain, amateur or professional.

It was not easy for these men. According to one of them, the professionals habitually fouled them. This rider once saw, on a bend, a professional tip an amateur out of his saddle and over the rail. The professionals particularly resented Captain Roddy Owen. Owen was second in the National on Arthur Yates's Cloister in 1891; he won it on Father O'Flynn in 1892, in spite of the attentions of the professionals, which were vigorous in that race.[47]

(Cloister was one of the very best Grand National winners; second in 1891 and '92, he won in 1893 with the huge burden of 12.7 stone (175 lb.). Owen died of cholera, serving under Kitchener in South Africa in 1895.)

The most graceful of the amateurs, according to a writer who knew them all,[48] was the Hon. George Lambton, who later became an outstanding trainer. Lambton ascribed his own skill to his apprenticeship in hunters' flat races. In the 1870s and 1880s these were popular and attracted heavy betting. They were killed by imitation gentlemen who fixed the races and brought them into disrepute. This was one reason for the eclipse of amateur riders.[49]

Another was the decadence of the National Hunt Steeplechase, which had started the period of amateur dominance. The race was glorious in the 1860s and 1870s. But its committee grew weak and venal, and important owners withdrew their support.

A third reason was the Boer War, which had the same effect as the Crimea. Blew wrote in December 1899: 'The loss of so many valuable lives must for an indefinite period affect sport in general' and steeplechasing in particular.[50] Arthur Yates said that the best men died or were killed; the ones who never went out to the war were not fit to ride over fences.[51]

The greatest horse of the last years of the century was Manifesto. He was bred in Navan in 1888 by Harry Dyas, who loved his horses, gave them plenty of time, and backed them when the moment came heavily and successfully.

Manifesto ran in England unsuccessfully as a four-year-old, then won the Champion Steeplechase at Leopardstown. In 1893 and '94 he had only four races in all. Then he was ready for his serious career. He ran in six Grand Nationals from 1895 to 1901, winning twice. In his last attempt he was third to the Prince of Wales's Ambush II. That time he was ridden by Ernie Piggott, father of Keith (a leading rider in his day and then a trainer) and grandfather of Lester. Piggott was one of a generation of professionals who put the amateurs quite into the shade.

## The Struggle towards Authority

Although steeplechasing had a government, it was largely ungovernable.

In 1870 the Jockey Club announced anti-flapping rules: any horse that ran at a non-recognized meeting was disqualified for life. Many courses could not meet the Jockey Club's requirements; many individuals lost their opportunities for wholesale minor fraud on the legitimate turf. Some went on to steeplechasing. Rules had never been so clearly stated, or so habitually broken. There were foul riding and non-triers in every race; hunters' certificates were forged; ringers were often run.

In 1875 the Grand National Hunt Steeplechase Committee ordered that every jumping meeting must be advertised in the Calendar, the advertisement to state that racing would be under National Hunt Rules, and to name the officials. This gave the Committee all the theoretic powers it needed. But full enforcement was slow and laborious. Racecourse managements were inept and often crooked; from several it was impossible to extract prize-money even months after a race. Stewards were idle, ignorant, and dishonest. All

GEORGE EDE AND TOMMY PICKERNELL. 'Mr Edwards' was one of the greatest Gentleman Riders of all time. Immediately after leaving Eton he apprenticed himself to a great jockey and tutor of jockeys, Ben Land; he rode 20 winners in 1858 and more each subsequent year. He won the National in 1868. He died after a terrible fall at Aintree the day after the National of 1870. Pickernell came back from Tasmania to ride as 'Mr Thomas'. He rode in 17 Nationals, winning in 1860, 1871, and 1875. He retired from riding after a bad fall at Sandown in 1877. In 1884 he was made the first Inspector of National Hunt Courses.

this was tackled slowly, piecemeal, course by course and scandal by scandal: but it was a long time before stewards could be trusted to stay sober, or adjudicate on disputes without reference to their own bets.

The problem was complicated by a sharp new growth in steeplechase meetings in the last quarter of the century. As in flat racing a few years earlier, there were far too many courses, and the bad ones were terrible. There was also the problem of little, easy fences. In 1882 the Committee laid down rules for the minimum size and number of fences, and stipulated water-jumps and open ditches. Enforcement began with the appointment, in 1884, of Tommy Pickernell as Inspector of National Hunt Courses: he had won The Lamb's second National (1871) and two other Nationals; he knew what was wanted.

A schism divided steeplechasing here which could not be concealed. On the one hand was the heroic Fogo Rowlands philosophy – steeplechases should be testing, and won by big, safe jumpers of the hunter type. On the other hand, thoroughbreds flipping over 'park' fences were safer bets and the small fences less cruel to horses and less dangerous to men. No syncretism was possible between these philosophies: only compromise.

## Hunt Racing and Point-to-Points

Hunt meetings were in origin simply race-meetings put on by members of a hunt. Some, like those at Perth in Scotland, had a connection with hunting which was purely nominal. Early in the 19th century a hunt meeting was likely to be steeplechasing: but often normal professional steeplechasing when this began in the 1830s. At the Worcestershire Hunt meeting of 1836 Captain Becher rode Vivian as at St Albans or the Vale of Aylesbury.

Fogo Rowland's races at Market Harborough and Cheltenham were for hunting men riding hunters: but the first hunt which organized races for its members was the Atherstone in the early 1870s.[52] By 1883 the Pytchley was doing the same thing, and the Worcestershire had a 'Red Coat Race' – hunting men, dressed as such. ('Pink' is the name not of a colour but of a tailor; it is curious that a shibboleth should be based on ignorance.) The introduction of a turning-flag, and a finish near the start, followed at the hunt level Coleman's precedent at St Albans.

There was fraud from the beginning – horses which were not hunters, and riders who were not amateurs. The National Hunt Committee intervened in 1882 and again in 1889. In order to keep the races authentic, the courses were obliged to be long and the prizes small. This did not of itself deter cheats: there were still bets to be made: so the National Hunt Committee's rules against fraud (already applied to professional steeplechasing) were brought to apply to hunt races.

In 1888 five hunts – the Warwickshire, North Warwickshire, Pytchley, Bicester and Heythrop – combined to mount the Midland Sportsmen's Races at Kineton, Warwickshire. The rules were of an antique type: the course was kept secret, and riders were forbidden to open gates or go more than 100 yards along a road.[53] The House of Commons Point-to-Point was held on this course until, in 1892, two riders were killed. The Stock Exchange Point-to-Point started in 1892, the Pegasus Club (confined to members of the Bar) in 1895; the former is dead, the latter lives.

At the turn of the century nearly 50 hunts held races. The biggest field was always the Members' – the 'Red Coat Race'. Farmers wore bowler hats. Ponies were also raced, and for them the give-and-take principle was reintroduced; the norm was taken as 14.3 hands.[54]

BAILY'S MAGAZINE
OF
Sports and Pastimes

Th<sup>os.</sup> Pickernell J<sup>r.</sup>

VOL. XXI.

1871.

# 16 Ireland

## 18th Century

The rebellion which ended at the Boyne in 1690 set Irish racing back for a quarter of a century. Revival began about 1725. In 1731 'Horse racing is become a great diversion in the country. The Commons of Ardmagh were threatened to be taken up for some public use, but the people of the town contrived to apply them to a greater advantage by making a horse-course round about them. . . . The company that comes to these races help to keep up the people's spirits by consuming their liquors – the chief manufacture of the place. The Collector of Excise affirms that His Majesty's duty is visibly increased thereby.'[1]

During the 1730s racing grew, as in England, to an unknown but excessive extent. 13 George II of 1739, which stipulated a £50 minimum prize in England, made it £20 in Ireland.

In 1741 Cheny's Calendar listed Irish meetings for the first time. The biggest race was a £60 prize at the Curragh. There were 12 other courses, but the prizes at Mallow, Mullingar, and Limerick were not run for as the races did not fill.

In the 1750s Goldsmith complained that 'there has been more money spent in the encouragement of the Paddereen mare in Ireland in one season, than given to learned men since the times of Usher.'[2] The Paddereen mare was really Irish Lass, and belonged to Mr Archbold of County Kildare. She won the Royal Plate at the Curragh in 1745 and '47. Paddereen means rosary (Irish *paidirin*); she wore one in her match with Black and All Black. 'We hear,' said Goldsmith, 'there is a benevolent subscription on foot amongst the nobility and gentry of this kingdom, who are great patrons of merit, in order to assist Black and All Black in his contest with the Paddereen mare.'[3]

Black and All Black was really Othello by Crab. He was imported by Sir Ralph Gore. In 1750 he won the 100 Guinea prize given by 'The Society of Sportsmen at the Curragh'. He was matched in September 1751 against Lord March's Bajazet, at the Curragh, for 1000 guineas (this is Heber's figure; an Irish report says 10,000). Side-betting was heavy. Black and All Black won. 'Bonfires were lit in many of the streets of Dublin and beer distributed.'[4] During the race Bajazet's jockey adroitly got rid of his weights, which were quietly picked up and handed back to him before he weighed in. 'Nevertheless, the quick visual organs of the Celtic duellist and sportsman caught sight of this act of racing legerdemain, and with typical impetuousity he seized Lord March's representative by the shoulder and threatened to thrash him on the spot if he did not at once acknowledge his guilt, as well as at whose instigation he had acted.' The jockey, terrified, implicated March. Gore challenged March. They met at five o'clock the following morning. 'Great was his lordship's surprise to see his opponent appear on the ground with . . . a polished oak coffin, which, *sans cérémonie*, he deposited on the ground, end up, with its lid facing Lord March and his party! Surprise, however, gave place to terror when his lordship read the inscription plate engraved with his own name and title, and the date and year of his demise, which was the actual day, as yet scarcely warm!' March made 'a full and complete apology to his opponent, which was graciously accepted.'[5]

In 1757 another dispute at the Curragh was referred to the Jockey Club at Newmarket: the first time that such reference was ever made.

In 1771 Tuting and Fawconer listed 10 meetings. The list overlaps only slightly that of 30 years earlier. At Kilcoole, County Wicklow, Ordinaries, Balls and Assemblies were advertised with particular enthusiasm. At Kilcock, County Kildare, only sworn inhabitants of the town were permitted to profit from tents and booths on the racecourse.[6]

The Irish Turf Club existed by 1789, being referred to in the first edition of Pat Sharkey's Irish Racing Calendar, which was published 'by Order of the Noblemen, Gentlemen, and Stewards' of the Club. It determined disputes from 1790 onwards.

Sharkey names 18 courses in 1790: a list different again from earlier ones. Each course had one meeting a year, except the Curragh, which had a programme like Newmarket's: two April meetings, and one each in June, September, and October.

The headquarters of Ulster racing remained the Maze course of the Down Royal Corporation of Horse Breeders. Besides the marked apathy of Ulstermen towards racing, it had troubles of a special kind: from the English Calendar of 1792 it appears that the starter had to have a Bible among his equipment, in order to swear that he had not said 'go' if there was a false start.

In 1798 the Irish invited the French to land in County Mayo and liberate them. There was no racing in Ireland that year.

## 19th Century

Recovery was immediate. The Irish Calendar lists eight active meetings in 1800: many had disappeared; Dundalk and Waterford had appeared. There was certainly racing not recognized by the Turf Club or reported in the Calendar.

At Tralee the prizes included a £50 plate given by 'the Gentlemen of the Profession of the Law of the County of Kerry'. For a horse to qualify, its owner must have spent not less than £200 in litigation, and lost. Horse of owners who had spent £1000 in the courts, and lost, were allowed 3 lb. The first running (1805) ended in a prolonged and bitter dispute on which the Stewards of the Turf Club had to adjudicate.

In 1821 George IV visited Ireland. A special meeting was arranged for him at the Curragh on 1 September. New stands were built; the servants had new liveries; a great deal of money was spent. The weather was bad, and it became known that the king was suffering from a severe loosening of the bowels. A special privy was accordingly built on the course, the seat made exceptionally large to accommodate the royal person. The king had to use this facility during the running of the principal race; it worked.[7] He gave to the Turf Club a whip, like Newmarket's, to be run for under Newmarket Rules.

Irish racing grew steadily. It was not much affected by famine or emigration, because the peasantry and humbler townspeople had not much patronized it. The public's money was wagered more heavily on, and the crowds were larger at, regattas and foot-races.

At this period a few big owners had their horses trained at home; this was the practice of Lord Waterford in the middle of the century and Lord Drogheda towards its end. But most Irish horses were trained on the Curragh, by private training-grooms. The public trainer came later to Ireland than England: but the big ones – McDonough from the 1850s and Linde from the 1860s – trained large strings with great success.

From 1841 Lord Waterford, who had been prominent on the English turf, brought his racing interests home. Racing benefited, especially in the South. He was killed in a hunting accident in 1859.

By this time Irish prizes were large enough to attract raiders from England. John Day, and later John Osborne and William I'Anson, sent horses. The specialist was a Mr Cockin, who won a number of Queen's Plates at the Curragh from 1860. The rules were consequently changed in 1868: Queen's Plates were thereafter limited to horses which had been trained in Ireland for six months.

Courses continued to die and others to be born. It was, said an owner, publisher, and racing manager, very difficult to start a racecourse in Ireland because of public apathy and lack of capital.[8] Baldoyle was the first financially sound new course: it was built by a company formed for the purpose, on land it bought. In 1888 Captain Quinn specifically imitated Sandown Park: he collected shareholders, bought land, and laid out Leopardstown on the fringe of Dublin. It was inaugurated on 27 August; an eyewitness records big crowds, good prizes, and miserable discomfort.[9] Still following Sandown, Quinn put on the Leopardstown Grand Prize, the first race in Ireland worth £1000; it always attracted English runners.

By a dreadful mischance, the Leopardstown five furlongs was in fact just under $4\frac{1}{2}$. Colonel MacCabe's Sabine Queen was beaten on this course by Mr Gilpin's Medina. MacCabe had been an athlete, and unlike other Irish racing men was used to clocking; he found the winner's time incredible, measured the course, discovered the mistake, and lodged an objection. The Leopardstown and Turf Club Stewards overruled it, breaking, as MacCabe furiously pointed out, their own rule that 'no race shall be under five furlongs'. In a subsequent match, Sabine Queen easily beat Medina over a proper five furlongs at Baldoyle. There was intense public interest and heavy betting. According to MacCabe this episode was the turning-point: the Irish as a nation thereafter transferred their interest from regattas to the racecourse.[10]

Phoenix Park, also Dublin, followed Leopardstown, modelling itself on Hurst Park. It was the only Irish racecourse besides the Curragh which had flat-racing only. Galway in the West and Limerick Junction in the South became the racing centres of those parts of Ireland. Down Royal's Maze remained the one important Ulster meeting.

Snowy tried being a bookmaker in Ireland in 1894. The local bookies froze him out or terrorized him. He turned tipster, at Baldoyle; the Irish were enchanted, never before having been promised the names of winners. He reports a fraud habitual on the Irish turf: starting-prices were always false. Winners were always returned at unexpectedly short prices; beaten horses were at wonderfully generous odds.[11]

## Irish Breeding

The draft of horses sent to Ireland from the royal stud at Tutbury came somehow into the possession of Lord Thomond (Barnabas O'Brien, 6th Earl) of Bunratty Castle, who died in England before the Restoration. It is impossible to say what happened to the horses, but they were extremely good ones, and it is likely that they had an influence disproportionate to their number.

The Duke of Ormond, in County Kilkenny, was the first breeder who went at the business of improving the Irish horse on a scale, and on lines, comparable to contemporary Englishmen. He imported Spanish, Arabian, and English 'Eastern' stallions, to which he sent his best and biggest Irish mares and imported Galloway mares. He bought English mares of Eastern blood from Fairfax and others, and begged Eastern stallions from the king for the sake of his country's breed.[12]

Breeding horses and other livestock grew steadily throughout the 18th century. This meant arable land being turned into pasture, causing hardship and agrarian crime on the part, said Horace Walpole, of 'a sort of riotous levellers',[13] the Whiteboy Movement. Irish horses were still half-bred; the best were already known for their power and natural jumping.

In the early 19th century thoroughbred breeding increased, but on a limited scale. Good Irish thoroughbreds were few. The best was Harkaway (1834), by Economist out of Fanny Dawson, bred in County Down by the piratical Ulsterman Tom Ferguson. Having won nearly every big race in Ireland, Harkaway had a string of successes in England, including two Goodwood Cups. Among the good horses he beat was Lord George Bentinck's Grey Momus. Such defeats as he suffered were of Ferguson's devising.

This record prompted 'Nimrod' to say of Irish breeding: 'the improvement has gone progressively on since the days of Mr Bowes Daly and his contemporaries. The fame and name of Harkaway will never be forgotten in England.'[14] Harkaway retired to stud in Berwickshire. His most important son was King Tom; he also got good broodmares.

In the same period the full brothers Birdcatcher and Faugh-a-Ballagh were bred on the Curragh. They were by Sir Hercules out of a mare called Guiccioli, who had failed at auction to reach her reserve of £30. Birdcatcher sired The Baron (1842), also bred on the Curragh, out of another unsold mare, whose asking price was only £20, called Echidna. The Baron won three races out of four at the Curragh in 1845, went to England to be trained by John Scott of Whitewall, and won the St Leger and Cesarewitch. He was sire of Stockwell and Rataplan.

Horses of this class were exceptional in Ireland in the first three-quarters of the century. In its last years there were a few such as Barcaldine (by Solon, by West Australian, out of Darling's Dam), one of the very best horses of his time, a most important sire, and the reason for the survival of the Matchem male line in Britain.

England had for a century gone to Ireland for half-bred 'chasers and hunters, as in previous centuries for hacks: in the 1890s she was beginning to buy Irish thoroughbreds. The reason was that by now the leading Irish breeders were aiming deliberately at the level of the English classics.

The most successful was John Gubbins of County Limerick. He bred Galtee More (by Kendal out of Morganette), who came to England to be trained by Sam Darling at Beckhampton, won the triple crown of 1897, and was sold to Russia under farcical circumstances. In 1902 Galtee More's half brother Ard Patrick (by St Florian) won the Derby; he was a good horse, but he was lucky to beat Sceptre.

## Irish Steeplechasing

The origins of Irish steeplechasing are the same as English. It was immediately bred by flat-racing out of fox-hunting. A remoter ancestor was the pounding-match (the English wild-goose chase). As in England, this was replaced by the cross-country match, to an agreed mark instead of follow-my-leader, early in the 18th century. The first recorded match is Irish, that in County Cork in 1752.

Hunters' flat races were throughout the 18th century a part of the English, and a larger part of the Irish, racing programme. At Kilcock in 1748 there was a £15 prize for Irish-bred hunters which had been in at the death of fox or hare. In the 1770s there were hunters' races at Londonderry and Ennis in which the horses qualified for their flat races by jumping various obstacles.

Cross-country races were a regular thing a few years earlier than in England. At Roscommon in 1790 there was, reports the Calendar, 'a drag chase of five miles across country over many high leaps'. They were running after hounds; it is conceivable they were not racing. In January 1793 the infant Turf Club was asked to decide a case referred to it from Ballyshannon: the winner of a four-horse race, carrying a feather, dismounted in order to take a big jump. In 1807 a 'steeple-chace' was run at Ballybrophy. In 1813 the first weight-for-age steeplechase was run at Racroghan; there were six starters; the weights were as for flat-racing.

On 22 January 1819 there were six starters for a four-mile steeplechase at Lismore, Gentlemen Riders, £50 added: 'It was a complete tumble-down race. The winner got four falls; Doctor six; Dandy one; and Thrasher one – in all twelve falls, but nobody killed. Even betting at starting that there would be six falls.' This was already 'a sort of racing for which the Paddies are particularly famous.'[15]

In England 1830 was the year of St Albans. In Ireland the same thing happened at about the same time. Pierce Egan watched the Shamrock Challenge Steeplechase on 14 March 1832, on the Ashbourne course in County Meath; 'we thought all Ireland and the County Meath had left Dublin on a string of jaunting-cars, sociables, tax carts, Stanhopes, dennets, tilburies, buggies, and shandera-dans, not to talk of the horse-men.' There was a false start, but it was impossible to recall the field until they had run a full circuit.[16] This race was run in heats, which were frequent until late in the century.

As in England, the upsurge of public interest had a great deal to do with certain glamorous personalities; as in England, none was more valuable to the sport than the attractive Lord Clanricarde.

To English visitors in the 1830s, Irish 'chasing seemed a good deal more perilous than their own. The spectators presented a particular hazard: when a horse from a different country, or one the crowd had not backed, was running prominently, the rider was stoned: 'here a man has to run the gauntlett at the risk of martyrdom – to put himself in the way of becoming a second St Stephen, or, in plain language, being stoned to death.'[17]

In this and the following decades Irish steeplechasers became a power on English

THE PRINCE OF WALES AT PUNCHESTOWN. 'In the rere of the Royal Standhouse,' said the *Irish Times*, 'have been provided a most chastely constructed refreshment saloon, and a suite of accompanying appartments for their Royal Highnesses and party. Cooking houses, lavatory and other necessary appurtenances are attached, all of which are draped and upholstered in the most exquisite manner.' Travellers from Dublin by train clung to each other or to the roofs of carriages, so great was the crowd; those who came by road appeared prematurely aged, owning to the white dust. On the second day (17 April 1868) the Prince followed one race on horseback; he is riding the grey on the left.

racecourses. The first to win an Aintree Grand National was Mathew (usually spelled Matthew) in 1847, ridden by the Irish jockey Denny Wynne. (His son, J. Wynne, was killed in the National of 1862.) Sixth in Mathew's year was the most popular horse in Ireland, ridden by the most popular amateur: Brunette and Allen (usually spelled Alan) McDonough. Brunette was bred in County Meath, by Sir Hercules out of a half-bred mare. She was heavily backed by the Irish (and by McDonough) in Mathew's race, but she ran with an infected throat and a temperature. McDonough was born in County Galway in about 1808. He was riding races at the age of 16, and winning on his own horses before he was 20. He won the 1838 proto-National on his own Sir William, and was second in 1840 and '41. He betted heavily, and had some appalling falls. English jockeys were jealous of him, and some of his smashes were not accidents. From 1850 he trained on the Curragh.

The second Irish-bred winner, and the first two-timer, was Abd-el-Kader in 1850 and 1851; also bred in County Meath. Like many Irish half-breds, he was intended for flat-racing; but he was so savage that he was gelded, suffered a set-back, was retired to hunting, and there revealed his brilliance as a fencer.

Like flat-racing, Irish steeplechasing continued to grow in size and popularity, in spite of famine and emigration. Punchestown started in 1850 and Fairyhouse in 1851. A great help was the Lord Lieutenancy of the sporting Earl of Eglinton in 1852 and again in 1858–9. Another great help was the army, both Irish officers and Englishmen stationed in Ireland.

The Turf Club continued to control the sport. In spite of the stone-throwers of the 1830s, it seems to have been cleaner than English steeplechasing of the same period, probably because there was little heavy betting. In 1864 the Irish Calendar printed Grand National Steeplechase Rules, virtually identical to the English rules of the year before.

Punchestown grew from the Kildare Hunt's one-day meeting to the recognised head-headquarters of Irish steeplechasing. Its races were described in 1868, by the Prince of Wales to Queen Victoria, as 'a kind of annual national festival'.[18] This was his excuse for going there, quite against the Queen's wishes, on 16 and 17 April. There was a crowd of 150,000.

In 1869 the Irish Turf Club followed the Jockey Club's 1866 precedent, and the Irish National Hunt Steeplechase Committee was formed. It first met in 1870 in Dublin. The sport it controlled was extremely buoyant: in 1874 'no-one who has paid any attention to steeplechasing in Ireland can have failed to observe that a very large proportion of the horses we have seen during the last season have displayed merit of a very high order.

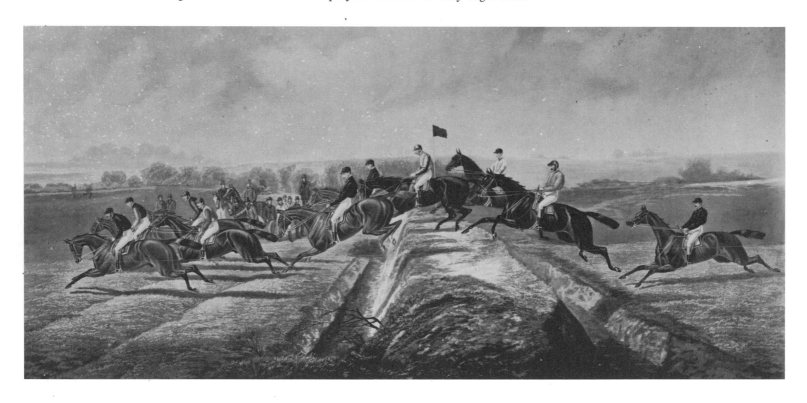

Moreover, such is the popularity of the sport that the number of steeplechase horses in Ireland amounts to about three times the number of performers on the flat.'[19]

In the last quarter of the century the most remarkable people in Irish steeplechasing were the trainer Henry Eyre Linde, of Eyrefield Lodge on the Curragh, who raided with extraordinary success at Aintree and Auteuil; and the family of amateurs who so often rode for him: the brothers Tommy, Johnny, Harry and Willy Beasley. All four rode in the National of 1879. Tommy won three Nationals and one Grand Steeplechase de Paris. Harry won the latter race twice, and the Prince of Wales's Plate and the Conyngham Cup (the big races at Punchestown) seven and six times respectively. Willy was killed at Punchestown in 1892.

Irish jumpers were better than ever. From 1889 to 1899, every National except one was won by an Irish-bred. (The one, ironically, was the Shropshire horse Father O'Flynn.) It was inevitable that the owners and trainers of such horses should go for the big prizes at Aintree and Auteuil; Irish steeplechasing suffered a drop in quality as a result. But it was neither serious nor permanent.

CONYNGHAM CUP, PUNCHESTOWN. Punchestown was started by the Kildare Hunt in 1850, and in the next 10 years became the headquarters of Irish steeplechasing. The first ditch or 'grip' of this famous double-bank was 6 ft. 6 in. wide and 3 ft. deep; the top 6 ft. 6 in. wide; the second ditch 4 ft. wide. The take-off was banked up. The whole 17 ft. was 'flown', but rarely.

# 17 Nineteenth-Century France

## Official Racing and the Haras

By a decree of 13 Fructidor XII (31 August 1805) Napoleon established racing. This decree ordered that racing should be held from the year XIV (1807) in the seven principal horse-breeding *départements* of the Empire; prizes should be given to the winners, and the whole should be controlled by the Ministry of the Interior.[1]

Louis XVIII, restored after Waterloo, carried on this policy on a moderate scale; *l'Arrêté du Ministre de l'Intérieur* of 27 March 1820 and a *Règlement* of April reaffirmed Napoleon's measures. In 1823 racing at le Pin was started by the comte de la Genevraye, *Directeur*, on a course known as la Bergerie.[2] There was also a little racing in Paris, in the Champ de Mars. M. Rieussec got up a few races in August 1819. In September 1823 there was a 'royal prize'; jostling in the race caused a dispute on which the king adjudicated.[3]

Four *arrêtés* of Charles X between 1825-8 expanded the *Haras* and ordered some racing to test the products. His son, the Dauphin, started a thoroughbred stud at Meudon in 1827; he imported Rowlston and an English trainer called Corringham. In that year Lord Henry Seymour had several matches against Colonel Charittie, who was well known on the English turf.[4]

Louis Philippe passed more laws in 1832 and '34. Such races as resulted were held in or near the studs, especially Le Pin. The law of 3 March 1833 established a *Régistre Matriculé* – a stud-book. The *Haras* concentrated on the Percheron and two types of *demi-sang*: the Anglo-Norman in Normandy and the West, and the Anglo-Arab in Limousin and the Midi. The former was an ancestor of the French trotter. A few private breeders were also re-establishing some of the pre-Revolution studs; one of these at least had its own racing, that of the comte de Tocqueville at Dieppe.[5]

The Anglo-Norman was substantially improved by a number of English thoroughbred stallions imported between 1815 and 1830. One notable half-bred was also imported: Young Rattler, by Rattler out of a half-bred mare called Snap, who has been called the 'Messenger of France' because of his influence on the trotting breed.[6]

The official breeding operation was on an immense scale, and was subjected to meticulous, even stifling, ministerial control. The importation of English stallions, and the provision of statutory prizes at the *Haras* race-meetings, were terribly expensive. Yet the whole thing was largely a failure. This was because of the apathy of the French countryside to the saddle horse. Peasants were interested only in heavy draught-horses which earned their keep on the farm. Consequently John Elmore supplied 2500 horses under contract to the French government; and he was only the biggest supplier of many.[7] It was clear to sympathetic observers like 'Nimrod' that France badly needed thoroughbred racing on the English pattern.[8]

## *The Société d'Encouragement and Chantilly*

In the Rue Blanche in Paris there had been from about 1825 an 'English Jockey Club and Pigeon-shooting Club', run by Mr Thomas Bryon. In 1830 it had 18 members; four were English; one was the eccentric *déraciné* Lord Henry Seymour. In 1833 this group (substantially) formed two new but coterminous bodies: the Jockey Club and the *Société d'Encouragement pour l'Amélioration des Races de Chevaux en France*. Seymour was first president. There were 12 members, with two honorary royal members additionally, the duc d'Orléans and the duc de Nemours.

These men had since the beginning of the July monarchy (1830) matched imported thoroughbreds in the Bois de Boulogne, and called themselves 'gentlemen-riders'. In 1833 these matches became the *Société d'Encouragement's* races.

In the Autumn of 1833 Prince Labanoff was staying at the Chateau de Chantilly to hunt. He noticed the superb resilience of the turf, and proposed an impromptu race. This was won by M. de Normandie, well known to the Leicestershire hunts, who was Anglomane to the point of speaking French with an 'insular' accent. The idea of a racecourse there was born. There was plenty of room for racing, training, stabling, and breeding. The duc d'Orléans arranged for races to be held and his own horses to be stabled there. Later the park and much surrounding forest became the property of the *Société d'Encouragement*.

The first races were held on 15 May 1834. They were uncomfortable but successful. The members of the Jockey Club wore their new uniform – an olive-green coat with gold buttons. Stewards, officials, and rules were copied from England. For some reason Lord Henry Seymour boycotted the races. But the town of Chantilly was delighted, cooperated fully, and provided some prize-money.[9] Small grandstands were built after the first meeting, which was repeated in May 1835. The *Société d'Encouragement* gave a prize, the king gave one, the town gave one. Seymour was still absent.

A race called the Grand Prix on the Champ de Mars was also run in 1834. It was won by Félix (by imported Rainbow) for M. Rieussec. But this was eclipsed by a race at Chantilly in 1836, the Prix du Jockey Club, the French Derby: three-year-olds, $1\frac{1}{4}$ laps – 2500 metres, slightly over the English Derby distance. Lord Henry changed his mind about Chantilly; three of the 10 entries were his. He won with Franck (by imported Rainbow) from four others. The weather was bad and the stands not waterproof: several pretty ladies got wet. *Les dandys* were there by the hundred on horseback, carrying *le little-stick* in the English fashion.[10]

Except among Anglomane racing men and the tradesmen of Chantilly this event aroused no interest. The only race noticed by the press was a *course des Haies*, a hurdle-race. 'Nimrod', aghast, asked a French nobleman: ' "Will the French ever take to racing, and come to understand the principles of it?" "*Never*," said he in reply; "they know nothing about it, and are too conceited to learn." '[11] The *Journal des Haras* (which had been founded in 1828 by M. de Pochau) did notice the event, with disapprobation.[12]

The first handicap in France was run at Chantilly in 1837 on Prix du Jockey Club day. The big race was again won by Seymour, with Lydia (also by Rainbow). In 1838 *le Two Year Old Stakes* was run over half a mile. In 1841 two-year-old racing became regular at Chantilly; 'Nimrod' notes that French racing and breeding needed this, both to test bloodstock young, and to encourage breeders by providing an earlier return on their investment.[13]

Another important event of 1834 was the publication of the *Calendrier de Courses de Chevaux ou 'Racing Calendar' Français*, by Thomas Bryon, now agent of the *Société d'Encouragement*. The *Société* itself had grown from 14 to about 100, with seven English.[14] The *Calendrier* became the *Bulletin Officiel* in 1841. The *Code de Courses* – rules of racing – was published in 1840.

LORD HENRY SEYMOUR. Seymour (1805–1859) was the second son of the 2nd Marquis of Hertford. He was born in Paris, his mother being the French adopted daughter of the celebrated wit George Selwyn; he lived there all his life. He never married, which in view of his love of crude practical jokes was fortunate. His will included substantial bequests to four favourite horses, which were never to be ridden again; the rest of his enormous fortune went to various Paris hospitals.

CHANTILLY. This engraving was published in 1843, but the dark clouds and umbrellas suggest the 1836 meeting. The course was two years old, the elegant little grandstand one. The Prix du Jockey Club was inaugurated; a large and fashionable crowd got very wet. The gentlemen on the right are members of the Jockey Club; they wear their olive-green coats with gold buttons.

Racing in the 1830s was extremely limited. In 1840 the year's programme consisted of the Paris (Champ de Mars) and Chantilly May meetings; the Versailles Summer meeting on two consecutive Sundays; and the Paris and Chantilly Autumn meetings. The *Calendrier* shows an average until 1840 of less than 60 different horses starting per year, belonging to two dozen owners. A letter of 1840 says: 'The races on Sunday were favoured with superb weather, and the extraordinary sight was seen of nine horses running together – nine live horses, nine rivals – a rare spectacle in the Champ de Mars. Generally one horse runs all alone, contending against no opponent, and always coming in first.'[15]

## Lord Henry Seymour and his Friends

The first few years of French thoroughbred racing were dominated by Lord Henry Seymour and the duc d'Orléans; the year's programme was a duel between the two.

Seymour was thought odd, even for an Englishman. He was very rich; he travelled in a fantastic carriage; he was fond of giving his friends powerful purges and exploding cigars. He imported Ibrahim (2000 Guineas) and Royal Oak, sire of Poetess and ancestor of Gladiateur; he also imported Thomas Carter as trainer and Thomas Robinson (brother of Jem) as jockey. His establishments were at Chatigny, where Royal Oak stood, and Sablonville. He won the Prix du Jockey Club four times, the Grand Prix at Paris, and the Prix du Cadran ($2\frac{1}{2}$ miles, Champ de Mars, from 1838), as well as hundreds of lesser races and matches.

The duc d'Orléans built splendid stables at Chantilly. His horses were trained by George Edwards, who brought English stable-lads with him. He won the Grand Prix three times, the Prix du Cadran three times, the Poule d'Essai (French 2000 Guineas, Paris, from 1840) and the Prix du Jockey Club. In 1840 his Beggarman, English-bred, won the Goodwood Cup, beating Pocahontas.

The prince de Moscowa, son of Maréchal Ney, was best known as a musician. 'Nimrod' bought him Lord Jersey's Mendicant, which won him 11 races in 13 starts.[16] No wonder he was affable and Anglophile.

Rieussec, who started those little races in the Champ de Mars, was a horse-breeder all his life, at Versailles and then Viroflay. He imported Rainbow, the most influential sire in the first decade of French racing. He was murdered in 1835 during an attempted assassination of Louis Philippe. His English racing manager, Palmer, then became the first public trainer at Chantilly.

Lupin followed Rieussec at Viroflay; Dollar stood there. He was on the turf for 60 years, and won the Prix du Jockey Club eight times.

An Anglomane as devoted as Normandie (but with a normal accent) was the banker Charles Laffitte. He was treasurer of the Jockey Club, and from 1838 director of Chantilly. He had some fierce brushes with the local trainers about their use of the racecourse for training; he considerably improved the course. In the year of his appointment: 'Chantilly is almost a *fête-champètre*;' it was the final event of the Paris season to which it was mandatory to go.[17] In the event the weather was bad and the attendance miserable. Lord Henry Seymour won every major race.

In 1840 Chantilly had a scandal like Epsom's four years later. Seymour's Jenny (by Royal Oak out of imported Kermesse) was considered a certainty for the Prix du Jockey Club, but she was second to Eugène Aumont's Tontine (allegedly by Teetotum out of Odette). Seymour objected on the grounds that Tontine was not French-bred but an English filly called Herodia. The case was investigated by the Jockey Club and by the courts, but was ultimately left unproven.

In 1842 its two most important men left the French turf. Lord Henry Seymour suddenly gave up racing, like Lord George Bentinck four years later but with less obvious reason. And the duc d'Orléans died after a coaching accident. Chantilly was never the same again. The racing remained far the best in France until the days of Longchamp, but no longer a *fête champètre*.

## The English Professionals

The horses of the early 1830s were all trained on the public roads in the Bois de Boulogne, which (like the racecourse at Versailles) were either brick-hard or awash.[18] The movement to Chantilly began with the duc d'Orléans in 1834. By 1840 virtually every French thoroughbred was trained there, except those which belonged to the *Haras*. The numbers of horses (and owners) trebled in the decade 1835–45. Somebody had to train and ride them. No Frenchman was qualified; so there was a great wave of Englishmen. In 1842 there were 200 horses at Chantilly, in the care of 12 English trainers. By 1845 there were more than 20 trainers.

These men formed a curious colony, intermarrying, English-speaking, taking over not only the industry but also the area. The methods they brought with them were those of Newmarket: sweats, purges, and four-mile gallops.

There were French jockeys from about 1850. The first big race won by one was the Prix de Diane (French Oaks, at Chantilly from 1843); the winner was Z. Caillotin on Honesty. The comte de Lagrange said that they could be quite as good as the English if they could attain the necessary *sang-froid*.[19] But as late as the middle 1890s the jockeys were 'all, or almost all English; the Frenchmen who have tried this trade having rapidly recoiled from its continual fatigues and privations.'[20] 'Nimrod' admitted that French 'exercise boys . . . answer the purpose well.'[21]

Maisons-Laffitte became a training-centre, as well as a racecourse. It was invaded but never inundated by the English. Trainers from the south west redressed the balance.

## Longchamp and the Grand Prix de Paris

In the middle of the century the number of French racecourses varied between 20 and 90, according to the shifts of ministerial policy; almost none attracted either popular support or good horses.

In certain areas, such as Brittany and the south west, there was a lively local tradition. At Tarbes (Hautes Pyrénées) the people were devoted to racing; at their racecourse at Loubière there were so many starters that each prize had to be run for in two or three divisions. The farmers bought Arab and English stallions, and their horses were – at a level immediately below the thoroughbreds of Normandy – the best in France.[22] 'Nimrod' urged on the French a pattern of provincial racing based on good prizes limited to locally-bred horses. As it was, there was no inducement to breed outside the Paris area.[23] Tarbes was almost unique. Successive governments tried to do substantially what 'Nimrod' suggested: to paltry effect. The elaborate and expensive machinery of government-run racing continued to show a dismal return throughout the 1850s. Even Chantilly was thinly attended. In 1844: 'All that the races at Chantilly need to be popular is a railway. Until there is an economical train for the *demi-sportsmen* the races will be the exclusive property of the Jockey Club.'[24] There was a service in 1846, but it was a laborious journey, and the public still stayed away.

Owner-breeders therefore had inadequate opportunities for their horses, and raced them for inadequate rewards. They attacked the problem in two ways. They got themselves a magnificent new racecourse on the doorstep of Paris; and they found another profitable arena, the English turf.

GRAND PRIX DE PARIS. This was 1864, the eighth year of Longchamp, the second of the Grand Prix. The first running had confirmed France's worst fears about internationalizing a classic race. But in the second Henry Delamare's Vermout, by The Nabob (third from left, ridden by Kitchener) beat Lagrange's Oaks winner Fille de l'Aire, French-bred by Faugh-a-Ballagh (far left, ridden by Edwards) with William I'Anson's Derby winner Blair Athol by Stockwell (Challoner) only third. Tom Challoner is said to have been unnerved by the Anglophobe French crowd, but all the other jockeys were English too. The official on the left is baron de la Rochette, who 22 years later first suggested the *pari-mutuel* monopoly.

From 1853 the *Société d'Encouragement* was in negotiation with the Ville de Paris; the negotiations were at last successful in December 1856, and the Longchamp course was born in the Bois de Boulogne. The first races were held on the last Sunday in April, 1857. In spite of bad weather, every rosy prediction came true. There were big crowds and good racing. The *Société d'Encouragement* agreed with the city on an Autumn as well as a Spring meeting.

In 1863 the Grand Prix de Paris was inaugurated: three-year-olds, over one mile seven furlongs. It was planned as an international race, and had been fully discussed with Admiral Rous. This idea has been credited to Napoleon III; he successfully influenced the Jockey Club by way of his intimate the duc de Morny, creator of Deauville races. The prize was an *objet d'art*, gift of the emperor, and a substantial sum of money – half from the municipality, half from the five chief railway companies of France – added to stakes already substantial.

There was strenuous opposition to this forward-looking idea in both England and France. The race was to be run on Sunday 31 May; Henry Chaplin, Sir Joseph Hawley, Lord Falmouth and the Duke of Westminster were among the leading English owners who, on sabbatarian grounds, refused to have anything to do with it. The French objected on the ground that the English were bound to win. They were right: the first running was won by Mr Savile's The Ranger, by Voltigeur.

The comfort and proximity of Longchamp made racing what it had never before been in France, except at a very few places like Tarbes: a day's outing for the public. They dressed up; they drank; above all they betted.

## The Invasion of England: Lagrange and Gladiateur

A few French-bred horses ran in England in the 1840s, all unsuccessfully. Beggarman (Goodwood Cup 1840) was English-bred, English-trained in France, and English-ridden. But by the early 1850s French owner-breeders had developed enough confidence in their product to want to test it against the best; they also wanted more prizes than France offered. The epoch of raids began.

Alexandre Aumont had taken over his brother Eugène's stable – started under Thomas Carter at Chantilly about 1836 – after the Tontine scandal of 1840; he founded the Victot stud, near Caen in Calvados. His trainer from 1850 was Tom Jennings. In 1851–2 Aumont's Hervine (by the French-bred Mr Wags out of Lord Henry Seymour's great

LAGRANGE AND GLADIATEUR. Comte Frédéric de Lagrange (1816–1883) was the son of one of Napoleon's generals, and himself a successful businessman. He was an early (though not a founder) member of the *Société d'Encouragement*, but took small part in racing until 1856, when he bought Alexandre Aumont's stud and stable. Thereafter, until his death, he was the greatest owner-breeder in France; his personal internationalizing of racing has no 19th-century parallel. Gladiateur was bred at Chantilly, trained by Tom Jennings at Newmarket, and always ridden by the excellent but myopic Harry Grimshaw. He was far the best three-year-old in Europe in 1865; in 1866 he won the Ascot Gold Cup by 40 lengths.

mare Poetess by Royal Oak) was the best racehorse on the continent. She won the Prix de Diane and the Prix du Cadran, and many major races in France and Belgium. She tried for the Goodwood Cup in 1852. Tiny Wells (still tiny) rode her; she had travelled badly and was unplaced. In 1853 she went for the Goodwood Cup again, and was second to another French horse, Lupin's Jouvence, who had won the Prix du Jockey Club and Prix de Diane. It was now possible for the French to believe that they could take on the English on their own ground.

In 1854 they tried often but unsuccessfully. In 1855 Aumont's Monarque (Hervine's half-brother, probably by The Emperor) won the Poule d'Essai and the Poule des Produits (Paris), the Prix du Jockey Club (Chantilly), the Grand St Léger (Moulins) and the 'Continental Derby' (Ghent); he failed in the Stewards Cup (Goodwood) and the Cesarewitch (Newmarket), In 1856 he was third in the Stewards and Goodwood Cups. In October of that year Aumont was ill; he sold out to comte Frédéric de Lagrange.

Meanwhile prince Marc de Beauvan had been head of a syndicate – the first 'Big Stable' – whose horses were trained by Tom Jenning's brother Henry at la Morlaye. He sold out to baron Nivière. Nivière and Lagrange formed a new confederacy, the second *Grand Ecurie.* Their combined empire included la Morlaye under Henry Jennings, Victot, Lagrange's stud at Dangu (Chantilly), and Phantom House, Newmarket. The last was under Tom Jennings, who went with Monarque to Newmarket in 1857. The 'Big Stable' did very well in France, not well in England, although Monarque won the Goodwood Cup. In 1858 he won the Newmarket Handicap under a big weight, and Mlle de Chantilly (Prix de Diane 1857) won the City and Suburban (Epsom).

In 1861 Langrange and Nivière won 118 races in both countries, and were fifth in the owners' list in England; this represented a very large number of runners and a very big investment.

Monarque broke down in the Great Metropolitan in 1858 and retired to stud at Dangu. He was extremely important. He got Gladiateur, bred at Dangu in 1862, out of Miss Gladiator by imported Gladiator.

Gladiateur, trained by Tom Jennings at Newmarket, was the second English triple crown winner. He was also the easiest-ever winner of the Grand Prix de Paris. An English contemporary called him 'a phenomenon, an Eclipse, a Bay Middleton, a horse that marks an era'.[25] A Frenchman said: 'The 31st of May, 1865, will remain for ever memorable in the Turf annals of the two countries. For the first time their undisputed sceptre had been wrested from our neighbours' hands; for the first time a foreign horse had beaten the pick of the produce of the United Kingdom. The fact made a great noise; it was the culmination of the work undertaken by the *Société d'Encouragement*; it was the reward of the audacious efforts made by the comte de Lagrange. After the first moment of stupefaction the English themselves could not restrain their admiration for this wonderful animal. "When Gladiateur gallops", wrote the English papers, "the other horses seem to stand still". The French thoroughbred still had a rival, but no longer a master.'[26]

The Franco-Prussian war destroyed the Second Empire and put a stop to the major French races. Lagrange sold nearly all his bloodstock (but not Monarque) to M. Lefèvre. By the end of 1871, when the French turf was making a rapid recovery, Lefèvre was one of its magnates. In 1874 Lagrange embarked on a new 'Big Stable' with Lefèvre, so successfully that by 1876 the confederacy were the leading English owners. In that year over 100 French horses ran in England.

Even Gladiateur had not prepared the English for this invasion, and there was great bitterness on two counts. On the one hand, the English could not believe they could be beaten fairly; they were convinced that the French horses were older, or doped, or had false pedigrees. Tom Jennings was a particular focus of this feeling, and was once physically set upon by so dignified a man as Mat Dawson.[27] On the other hand, there was a howl for reciprocity. Lord Falmouth pressed on Rous the unfairness of English racing being wide open to the French, while all but a handful of races in France were closed to the English. This lobby wanted the classic and other major races closed to foreigners until the French were more sporting. The French position was that English owners wanted not to race in France, but to keep French horses out of England.[28]

Lagrange split with Lefèvre in 1878. Lagrange kept Dangu and Phantom House, Lefèvre Chamant and Lowther House. Rivalry succeeded amity. Lagrange died in 1883.

Lagrange was the outstanding figure on the French turf from the late 1850s until his death. He was generally venerated for his courtliness and honesty;[29] but a close friend said he was '*capricieux et indéchiffrable*', and admired more than liked.[30] In England he won a Derby, two 1000 and two 2000 Guineas, two St Legers, and four Ascot Gold Cups. In France he won eight Prix du Jockey Club, six Prix de Diane, and two Grands Prix de Paris.

Tom Jennings moved from Phantom House to Lagrange House, built from bricks he made himself and named for his patron. His son, also Thomas, moved into Phantom House and was a successful trainer. Old Tom was known at Newmarket as 'Waterworks Tom', because he reorganized the water-supply.[31] At Chantilly he was known as 'Old Hat' Jennings, and was chief of those who 'surrounded their craft with priestlike mystery.'[32]

## Paris and the Provinces

Early thoroughbred racing was virtually confined to Chantilly, the Champ de Mars, Longchamp and Deauville, which was the summer resort of Paris racing. Other northern courses, convenient for breeders, were Caen, Cabourg, and Dieppe.

The appetite of Parisians for racing – and that of the authorities for clean racing – was fed by a new organization, the *Société Sportive d'Encouragement*, which started demurely in 1887 and grew to a major role by the turn of the century. It was a racecourse company, non-profit-making, licenced by the Ministry of Agriculture, putting on racing on its own tracks according to the rules of the *Société d'Encouragement* or those of the steeple-chasing or trotting societies. Its courses were Maisons-Laffitte, Enghien, la Marche, St Ouen at the end of the century, and later St Cloud. The *Société de Sport en France* was formed by a group of amateurs in 1883. It raced at Achères and Vincennes, then Fontaine-bleau and Colombes, and later le Tremblay.

In certain traditional horse-breeding areas *sociétés* were formed which placed themselves under the rules of the *Société d'Encouragement*. Brittany was one such. The Nantes *Société* was founded in 1837; Breton *sociétés* multiplied: small, decentralized, patronized by local horses and local people, after the fashion of that province.

In the south west, the *Société d'Encouragement du Club Bordelais* served an area with a greater sense of centralization and far more money. They raced at Bouscat, where from May 1851 the Derby du Midi was run. There was also a course at Mont-de-Marsan, in the Landes, from 1847; and later at Pau (Basses-Pyrénées), considered the best provincial course in France, with a Poule d'Essai from 1860. This area produced the only horses, and horsemen, which in the 19th century impinged on Paris.

The south east had the *Société Sportive de Marseille* from 1860, with a good racecourse. The Grand Prix de Marseille was the richest provincial race. Avignon, Aix, Nice and Cannes had later courses, and there were many smaller ones. Lyon was the centre of Eastern racing, with a course called the Grand Camp from 1866. Moulins and Vichy also became important. Racing in the North East was always on a small scale because it was not a breeding area; seaside courses like le Touquet became minor versions of Deauville. Amiens and Strasbourg had once been breeding centres, and might have become racing centres if successive wars had left them alone.

In 1866, after 33 years of ceaseless battle, the *Administration des Haras* and the *Société d'Encouragement* reached a truce. Thereafter the *Société*, subject to the Ministry of Agriculture, was solely responsible for its rules. All the *sociétés* which ran racecourses were autonomous except in the matter of these rules and of the dates of their meetings.

In 1886 there were, throughout France, 133 racecourses, of which under a dozen were not recognized by the *Société d'Encouragement*. The role of the *Société* was therefore enormous; this was admitted by its separation, that year, from the Jockey Club: racing administration was one thing, a fashionable club another. This made possible the inclusion into the *Société* of influential racing men whose trade, or background, would at any period have kept them out of *le Jockey*.

AUTEUIL. An 'Irish bank' was at this period one of the obstacles in the Grand Steeple-Chase. Its design was unlike the double at Punchestown (see p. 174), and more resembled an obstacle in a modern 'event' course than anything to be galloped over. It was said to be one of the reasons for the success of Henry Linde and his Irish horses at Auteuil; he won the Grand Steeple-Chase in 1882 and 1883, both times with four-year-olds, about the date of this engraving.

## Steeplechasing

French steeplechasing started at about the same time as thoroughbred flat racing. Even more specifically than the English, it was born in Leicestershire. M. de Normandie hunted there for a dozen seasons. He certainly saw and almost certainly took part in cross-country matches. He probably inspired the first English-type steeplechase in France, in 1829 or '30, near St Germain. Normandie beat six others, who included the prince de Moscowa and two Englishmen. His trustworthiness and knowledge of England made him the most frequently chosen official – steward, starter, or judge – in the early days at Chantilly. Though never a major owner or breeder, he has an important place in French racing history. The duc d'Orléans and the duc de Nemours both rode in steeplechases in this earliest period, until forbidden by their father because of the danger.[33]

Most French gentlemen still used the *manège* seat, which did not lend itself to jumping fences. But the ones who had been to Melton learned the English seat, such as comte Peltier, who once 'leaped over a gate, two lords, and a baronet'. The result was that they took to jumping fences and brooks in their own hunting-fields, an exercise which had previously formed no part of the ritual of the French chase.[34]

From 1830 some of the matches in the Bois de Boulogne included obstacles. By 1834 there were *courses au clocher* – races to the steeple – at Croix de Berny. In 1835 there were the beginnings of regular steeplechases at la Marche. In 1845 there was a cross-country race called la Croix de Berny, though not held there.

LONGCHAMP. There were three grades of enclosure: *au pesage*, the restricted paddock area, where the public was most chic, the pickpockets most numerous, the bets heaviest, and the bookmakers paid the highest rent for their pitches; *aux tribunes*, in the stands, where the typical racegoer (according to a contemporary) alternated between envy of the rich and contempt of the poor,

At about this time M. de Thannebourg was *Inspecteur Général des Haras*; on a visit to England (during which he bought The Baron, conceivably sire of Monarque) he saw a steeplechase at Worcester. This so excited him that he got a dozen English horses, potential stallions, to contest a steeplechase at le Pin. The course was terrifying; only two finished. But the locals who saw it were as excited as the Inspector General. Three horses were claimed out of the race and a great many mares sent to them. The winning jockey was given his prize entirely in five-franc pieces, which he was hardly able to carry.[35]

These events were for gentlemen-riders, Melton-trained aristocrats. But the best French steeplechaser of the 1850s was always professionally ridden. This was a thoroughbred colt by Royal Oak (or Nautilus) out of the French-bred Niobé, foaled in 1846, and named Babonino. In 1849 it ran on the flat, and was useless. Its owner wanted to sell it for whatever he could get. There were no takers. In 1851 baron de la Motte, a Gentleman Rider and supporter of steeplechasing, bought the horse (now five), called him Franc Picard, and got the English Lamplugh to train and ride him. He was small and said to be a roarer. In 1852 he began his steeplechasing career. He won races at la Marche, le Pin, Craon and Saumur. To the fury of the *Administration des Haras* he beat their half-bred champion Emilius, a larger and more powerful animal. In 1853–5 he won at all the major French and Belgian steeplechase courses – Caen, Spa, Dieppe, Bordeaux. In these campaigns he beat a lot of English steeplechasers who made frequent raids on what should have been the easy pickings of the continent.

In 1856 Franc Picard ran at Aintree, together with his stable companion Jean du Quesne. Franc Picard had top weight; he was unplaced, carrying 12 lb. more than the highest-weighted placed horse. Jean du Quesne ran prominently but failed to stay. Franc Picard then ran badly at Coventry, and won at Birmingham. He afterwards broke down in a race at Dieppe (which he won) whose Grand Steeplechase had been his private property for years.

Other notable French-bred steeplechasers to run in the Grand National were Alcibiade and l'Africain. Alcibiade was bred by Lagrange at Dangu and ran in England on the flat; Lagrange let him go out of a selling-race at Epsom in 1863 to 'Cherry' Angell. Ridden by Captain 'Bee' Coventry, in his first and last National, he won in 1865. L'Africain belonged to M. Vailland. He was cast in his box on the way to Aintree in Alcibiade's year, but he ran in 1866. 'They pulled him, watered him when he was not thirsty, tempted him with beans when he was not hungry, pulled at him and raced him in the wrong places.' His last owner was a sausage-maker; it is assumed he was ultimately eaten.[36]

French steeplechasing was developing like English, though far more slowly. It was known, as in England, as '*le sport illégitime*'. It shared the problem of controls. To provide them, the *Société Générale des Steeple-Chases* was founded in 1863, with 18 members under prince Murat. It raced at Vincennes and its writ ran over about 10 other meetings. In 1873, after the war, it was reconstituted under the prince de Sagan, great-nephew of Talleyrand, whose own nephew said of him: 'supremely elegant, very ignorant; wonderful clothes, no taste; brilliant with women, to whom he was lawless and faithless.'[37]

Headquarters moved from Vincennes to Auteuil, a course quite different from the English in character: a mixture of soft natural hedges, bullfinches, oxers, a stone wall, and a formidable rail-ditch-and-fence. In 1874 the Grand Steeple-Chase Internationale de Paris and the Grande Course des Haies d'Auteuil were inaugurated. During the next 20 years each of these races was won 12 times by French horses, eight by English and Irish.

The number of meetings continued to grow, the most important being Pau and the suburban Enghien course of the *Société Sportive*.

Trainers were until the end of the century overwhelmingly English, jockeys sometimes French. A French writer said in 1896 that the French jockeys were better over the sticks;[38] but most winning riders had Anglo-Saxon names.

and the usual maximum bet was 100 francs; and *sur la pelouse*, the 'course' or 'heath' and by extension the cheapest enclosures, patronized by 'butchers, printers, wine-sellers, cab-drivers, housewives, clerks, students, workingmen, hairdressers, and doorkeepers,' betting an average of 20 sous. This last group were the most careful and often the most expert bettors.

The dominant owner of the early period of the *Société des Steeple-Chases* was baron Finot. He used to drive from Maisons-Laffitte, where Harper trained for him, to the races at Auteuil, in an English trap drawn by a horse he was running the same afternoon.[39]

## Trotting

In 1832 an officer of the *Haras* called Ephrem Houël planned a trotting-meeting, and after protracted manoeuvring the first one took place at Cherbourg in 1836. Trotting-races – always ridden, never driven – became part of the routine of the *Administration des Haras*.[40]

In 1847, at Chantilly on Prix du Jockey Club day, there was a *course au trot* ridden by amateurs. There are occasional mentions of similar events in the next decade.

In 1861 an Imperial Decree included trotting-racing among the major state-sponsored activities. In 1864 the *Société d'Encouragement pour l'Amélioration du Cheval de Demi-sang* was formed under the Ministry of Agriculture. A decree of 1866 made it the parent of all trotting societies, with a standing comparable to its thoroughbred and steeplechasing equivalents. Its first president was the marquis de Croix, a big private breeder.

Part of the Third Republic's programme of reconstruction after the war was an international trotting meeting at Maisons-Laffitte. After the success of this, the *Société du Demi-sang* got the use of Vincennes.

In the next year trotting received the set-back of some odious publicity. On 5 July 1879 two trotters, Verny and Mauvais-Tête, were matched for 15,000 francs over 120 kilometres. They started at the Arc de Triomphe, trotted out into the country, and were to finish on the racecourse at Longchamp. Mauvais-Tête died on the way back. Verny finished, hobbled into his stable, fell, and never got up. The press was disgusted.

In 1895 trotting headquarters moved to Neuilly-Levallois, then to St Cloud, and finally back to Vincennes. Meanwhile the Enghien course of the *Société Sportive*, on the other side of Paris, added trotting to its mixed programme. Trotting became popular all over France. Ridden races were still more important than harness at this stage.

During the 19th century the Anglo-Norman became *le trotteur français*, a cross of imported English thoroughbred, half-bred, and Norfolk trotter stallions with native half-bred mares, with a later injection of American standardbred.

One of the most important tap-roots derives from the two favourite horses of Marie-Antoinette, l'Aleyrion and le Parfait. During the Revolution a dealer got hold of them and hid them in the remote farm of a M. Marchand. Out of one of Marchand's mares le Parfait bred La Parfaite, who was covered by l'Aleyrion. Théodore Lallouet's many winners between 1885 and 1895 descend from this mating.

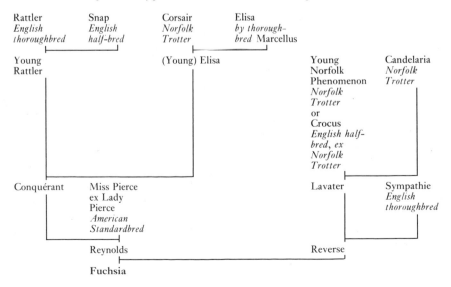

The most important tap-root of all is Elisa. Her dam, also Elisa, was by the thorough-bred Marcellus out of imported Jenny. Her sire was the Norfolk trotter Corsair. Young Elisa won four races as a three-year-old, when in foal, at Falaise, le Pin, Saint-Lô, and Avranches. She had 19 foals; all, of both sexes, went to stud. The most celebrated, on the track and at stud, were Conquérant and la Crocus. All modern French trotters have Elisa's blood.

In tail-male, nearly all French trotters descend from five stallions: Conquérant and Normand, both by Young Rattler; Phaëton; and Lavater and Niger, both by Norfolk trotters. The ingredients of the *trotteur français* are perfectly illustrated by the pedigree of Fuschia, the greatest of all French trotting stallions, foaled in 1883. He was prepotent and prolific; he was champion sire of trotters from 1893–1906. He sired 389 trotters; he had 115 sons who were sires of trotters, every one of which got a winner.

The pattern of breeding was more like that of the English or Irish hunter than of anything in the thoroughbred world. Thousands of small men had one or two mares each, which they sent to be covered by the stallions of the *Haras*. The industry, though so decentralized, was substantial; a lot of French trotters were exported to Italy, Belgium, and Holland, all of which developed trotting successfully during the 19th century.

## Betting

Mr Palmer opened his 'New Betting Rooms' in Paris in 1833; but if he intended a second Tattersalls he was disappointed. 'Nimrod' noted with surprise that there were no legs in France; the racing grandees betted in the old English fashion, and equally heavily. £12,000 was wagered on one race at Chantilly. Even among the gentlemen of the Jockey Club betting on this scale gave rise to anxiety about the impartiality of officials; 'Nimrod' himself was asked by the Stewards to be judge, because they needed, and could not otherwise get, a 'perfectly disinterested person'.[41]

PARIS BETTING-SHOP. This drawing was published in *L'Illustration* of 22 March 1890, at a time when the French had not determined on a policy about betting. Bookmakers were still operating, under growing threat of extinction, on the racecourses; the rue Hanovre betting-shops had been closed down; the *pari-mutuel* had not been given official recognition or its monopoly of on-course betting. Certain tobacconists acted as agents, neither legalized nor quite illegal, for M. Oller's company. They continued to do so illegally after 1891, and legally from 1930.

In 1853 the English Betting Act, and the strong line against defaulters taken by the Jockey Club, sent some undesirables into flapping-racing, some into steeplechasing, and many to France. Consequently the vicomte Daru founded the *Salon des Courses*, the purpose of which was to provide a headquarters for, and to regularize, big and professional betting, on the analogy of Tattersalls Committee. Reputable English bookmakers were thereupon attracted to Paris; they formed *le Ring* or *le Betting*.

It was a surprise to many Frenchmen that the *Société d'Encouragement* admitted bookmakers to Longchamp. Contemporary opinion accounted for this breach with tradition and seemliness on two grounds: the magnates liked taking money from the Ring better than taking it from each other; and racing had become so vulgar that bookmakers completed the decor.[42]

The earliest bookmakers had been peripatetic; in this period they were stationed on *le piquet*, a bench which raised them above the crowd. They had blackboards, lecterns, and huge blue cotton umbrellas. After each race a man called *l'All-Right*, a 'rubicund servitor', ran to the *piquet* to tell them that the winner had weighed in. The bookmakers were English, Belgian, and French. The English were the richest, the most numerous, and least honest. 'They leagued with the Belgians to despoil the French, and with the French to despoil the Belgians.'[43]

For the first time interest was taken by thousands of people off the course. There were shirt-sleeved men in bars, illegal but unconcealed, taking bets. In the 1870s and 1880s there were the *betting-shops* of the strange *quartier des books* off the rue Hanovre: *boutiques louches*, sombre and silent, with whispering groups of obsessed gamblers in the street outside.[44] In the middle 1890s all this was abolished.

*Le tout*, also called *l'espion*, became 'a sort of special mushroom at the great training-centres'; he was detested and hunted as at Newmarket. He was often the intermediary by whom a bookmaker bribed a jockey, this practice becoming common by 1880.[45]

In April 1886 M. de la Rochette ('the Admiral Rous of France')[46] proposed the abolition of betting. There was a loud outcry, both from those who believed that this would kill racing, and those who liked betting. In February 1887 the *Conseil Municipal* decided to charge bookmakers a crippling rent for their pitches: but as bookmaking was already theoretically illegal, and immoral, this was deemed unethical. On 15 March 1887 the *Président du Conseil* of the Ministry of the Interior, at last outraged by *la passion du public pour le jeu*, instructed the Prefect of Police that bookmakers were to be removed,[47] and letters were sent to Longchamp, Auteuil, and Vincennes.

By fortunate chance, a M. Oller had meanwhile invented the *pari-mutuel*, a device for the distribution of a pool. The three societies applied for authorization to use it. But as the law stood (articles 1965 and 1966 of the Penal Code) the *pari-mutuel* was also technically illegal. The bookmakers had been standing on an ambiguity in the law: a bet made in the paddock, *enciente du pesage*, was skilful and thus legal, while a bet made in the cheap enclosures, *la pelouse*, was chance and thus criminal.

Early in 1891 there were in the Senate and the *Chambre des Députés* 'long and fastidious debates which proved the absolute ignorance of the parliamentarians in everything which concerned the question of horses'.[48] The debates resulted in the Act of 2 June 1891, of which Article 4 banned all betting, and Article 5 lifted this ban in respect only of the *pari-mutuel* run by the racecourse. The Ministry of Agriculture was able to say: 'The Pari-Mutuel is betting organized in an absolutely disinterested manner by Racing Societies which have no interest in attracting or instigating bets, and which act only as agents of the public in a passive and mechanical way, collecting bets and distributing dividends to the winners.'[49]

Everything was thus solved, except that five years later there were between 500 and 1000 secret agencies of the *pari-mutuel* in Paris alone, attracting, like the 'lists' and the *boutiques louches*, the bets of clerks and milliners.[50]

*Right*
SOUVENIR D'AUTEUIL 1881. The *Société des Steeple-Chases en France* opened Auteuil in 1873, in the part of the Bois de Boulogne between the fortifications and the Butte Mortemart. The *Grand Steeple-Chase International* and the *Grande Course des Haies* were inaugurated in 1874. The winners the year of this painting, 1881, were the marquis de Saint-Sauveur's Maubourguet and Henry Linde's Seaman. The patriarch on the left may be the comte de Montgomery, a founder member of the *Société*.

*Overleaf*
LONGCHAMP. Laffon describes Grand Prix day in this period. Dawn brought waterers, who drenched course, paddock, and lawns. Then came gardeners, who raked all the paths, and sweepers who hunted paper and cigar-butts. At nine arrived the secretary of the *Société* with a battalion of inspectors and controllers. At 10 a 'black and cheerful mob' advanced on the gates, the 1700 employees of the *pari-mutuel*. At 11 arrived another black mob, less cheerful, the brigade of police reserves; and on the *pelouse* a squadron of Republican Guards deployed. At noon the telegraphists reached their offices, followed by sellers of chocolate, pencils, cigars, and racing tips. At last, in time for lunch, came the public, on whose behalf 'a feminine army corps of dressmakers, milliners, florists and glovers has been mobilised.'

## Racing in Belgium

Belgian racing started at about the same time as French, and was always closely linked to it.

'Nimrod' found the Belgian aristocracy much heartier, easier-mannered, and more sporting than the French – in fact, more like the English:[51] although, according to 'Druid', 'The Belgians have but little taste for blood horses,'[52] preferring their gross draught animals.

In 1840 there were two meetings at Brussels; Prince Albert was there with the Belgian royal family. There were meetings that year also at Ghent, Liège, and Aachen. There were in addition trotting-matches 'after the peculiar custom of the country.'[53]

The most important man in Belgian racing was comte Duval de Beaulieu, 'the Sir Charles Bunbury of his country'; under his leadership the Belgian *Société d'Encouragement* was formed, which shared its Calendar with the French.

In 1840 the King's Cup at Brussels was won by Waverly, Belgian-trained and ridden by Olivier, from Lord Henry Seymour's Morotto, trained by Thomas Carter and ridden by Thomas Robinson. Olivier was one of the only two continentals 'who deserve the appellation of jockey'; the other was also Belgian.[54] But on another occasion, also at Brussels, Olivier came in for 'Nimrod's' most bitter scorn for taking on Seymour's second string instead of his first, going fast when he should have waited, and (worst) whipping a beaten horse.[55]

Belgian racing developed steadily, alongside French. Its rapid growth was from 1880. The *Société d'Encouragement* was energetic and well-run, under M. Vanderton, and English thoroughbreds were imported in large numbers. Many Belgian races were open internationally, and attracted English and German as well as French horses.

By 1890 the principal meetings were at Brussels, Ostend, Ghent, Antwerp, Spa, and Waregem. Brussels had three courses. The Belgian Derby and the Grand Prix de Bruxelles were run at Boitsfort, as well as the Prix du Roi.

The Belgians invented the idea of relegating a peccant winner to second place instead of disqualifying it altogether; this was later adopted generally.

Until the end of the 19th century most of the trainers and jockeys were English.

## The Language of French Racing

In 1896 every horse on *le turf* went, with *le pedigree* in *le Stud-Book*, from *le stud-groom* to *le head-lad* and *le stable-boy*; it travelled in *le box* to be ridden by *le jockey* or *le gentleman-rider* in *le handicap* (made by *le handicapeur*), *le steeple-chase*, or some other event in *le Racing-Calendar*. If *le crack*, and seen by *le tout*, it was unlikely to be made *l'outsider* by *le bookmaker*. It was backed by *le sportsman* for *le pony* (25 louis) or *le fifty*, unless it had *le walk-over* or *le pickpocket* had been busy. When *le starter* dropped his flag, the horse ran to *le winning-post*, if a victim neither of *le doping* or *être broken-down*. After winning it was *all-right*, and the successful punter celebrated with *l'oueské* or *le clarett*.

FOUR JOCKEYS. Sympathy between racing and the theatre is traditional. In England Lily Langtry, George Edwardes of the Gaiety, Toms Walls and Edgar Wallace were typical of theatre people who loved their racing; in France Léon Volterra is the supreme example. Art also bridges the gap between boards and turf. Degas and Toulouse-Lautrec drew inspiration, the one from ballet, the other from the music-hall, and both from racehorses and their jockeys.

# 18 Nineteenth-Century Europe and Russia

## Italy: The Survival of Ancient Racing

Nineteenth century Italy inherited two degraded traditions: the *palio* and the races of riderless barbs.

The *palio* survived in Siena, and still celebrated the Feast of the Assumption in August. On the 12th of the month, cartloads of sand were emptied over the circumference of the piazza, and mattresses were tied to corners. Early on the 13th was the first of the *prove*, the trials; 15 or 20 deplorable horses ran in batches round the piazza. Every year a few ran out down the via San Martino. The purpose of the *prove* was to eliminate any good horses which had accidentally been entered; 10 were left, whose numbers were painted on their quarters. They were drawn for publicly, in the door of the palazzo, in an atmosphere of suffocating suspense. There were further trials until the final *prova generale*, on the evening of the 15th.

On the 16th High Mass was celebrated in the *Duomo*. There was a banquet.

On the 17th the city was up at dawn, and crowds began to pour in from the countryside. Drums were beaten and bells rung, and everyone wore fancy dress. The horses were taken to the churches of their wards, and they and the jockeys blessed. Immediately after the sprinkling of holy water on the runners, the *contrade* met to make deals. Large bribes were given, a practice made respectable by antiquity.

A cannon was discharged in the piazza del Campo and the course was cleared. Each *contrada* paraded.

As seven in the evening struck the runners appeared. They were no longer caparisoned, nor their riders in emblazoned tabards. The jockeys wore canvas doublets and solid metal helmets, and carried not whips but clubs.

The rope barrier was dropped. The horses did not, however, start at once to gallop, but stood still while the riders clubbed each other. They continued to do this whenever possible during the race. The winner was chaired, cheered, embraced, and lavishly entertained by his *contrada*.[1]

The riderless barb races had spread from Rome to Pisa, Lucca, Bologna, Florence, and other cities; but in the 19th century they were restricted to Rome and Florence. They were as cruel and humiliating as ever. In the middle of the century many of the runners were bad English thoroughbreds, imported cheaply for the purpose.[2]

The races were abolished in 1872, on grounds of humanity.

Piemonte had no tradition of *palio* races like that of the cities of Tuscany, but early in the 19th century there was racing in the streets of Turin. A race in 1809 began on the Rivoli road and went by the Via della Dora to the Piazza Imperiale. The riders wore tunics and white pantaloons: uniform of a type unfamiliar in Turin, so a model was provided for imitation.[3]

RIDERLESS BARBS IN FLORENCE. As in Rome, the races for the hapless *barberi* survived boisterously into the 19th century. In Florence the horses were goaded with ivory balls carved into spikes; these animals seem also to be wrapped in barbed wire.

### Birth and Growth of Modern Italian Racing

Naples, Rome, Florence, Turin and Milan were centres of completely separate societies. In the first half of the 19th century they all embarked on racing.

As might be expected from classical history, Naples was first.

In 1808 the principe di Butera imported English thoroughbreds to his Sicilian stud. Not long afterwards he and his friends established a racecourse on the Campo di Marte. The English colony participated. On 21 January 1829 there was an English winner, almost certainly a thoroughbred.[4] In 1830 Charles Greville, touring, 'rode to the racecourse and round the hills'.[5] In 1840 the rules included a provision that the riders wear such colours as the owners found agreeable. Uniform breeches and boots were stipulated.[6] English thoroughbreds continued to be imported, and races restricted to them gradually supplanted other events.

Florentine racing began a little later. Its first well-known figure was the duca di Lucca. Its early years, like those of Naples, depended largely on the English colony. By 1827 there was an annual meeting, and soon afterwards a *Società* with a regular course and rules. The course was a mile from the town, on a farm belonging to the Grand Duke; it was inconveniently narrow. At the three-day Spring meeting of 1840 there were so many entries that the races had to be divided. English thoroughbreds were set to give 30 lb. to Tuscan and 14 lb. to other Italian horses. There was also a hurdle race with English riders: 'As is generally the case in these silly exhibitions, two of the horses fell.'[7] At the October meeting of that year the young Sir Joseph Hawley's Capriolo won the big race, his Chateau Lafitte another. His confederates were John Massey Stanley and Count Anatole Demidov.

In Lombardy, Milan had racing of a kind early in the century. In 1830 the Milanese aristocracy formed a society to organize Spring and Autumn races for the next 10 years. The first race was 18 May in the Piazza d'Armi.[8]

In the same year King Carlo Alberto of Piemonte began importing English thoroughbreds. In the early 1840s a French patron of Tom Jennings recommended him to the King. In 1844 Jennings bought Julia (fourth in the Oaks) and smuggled her to Turin by painting her legs white. She was housed in the royal stables and trained in the royal park; she won all the new races in Piemonte. Jennings's son later wrote (loyally if inaccurately): 'Beyond the annual race at Siena and the race for riderless horses in the Corse in Rome there was no horse racing in Italy at that time. . . . The efforts of Prince Carignan and my father, Tom Jennings, to provide a new sport entitled them to be regarded as its principal founders in that country.'[9]

Meanwhile Jennings's future father-in-law Henry Carter (brother of Lord Henry Seymour's trainer) was doing the same thing in Milan for the duca di Litta. They imported the English thoroughbred Mainstay, which was as pre-eminent in Lombardy as Julia in Piemonte. The two were naturally matched, the contest taking place on the frontier. Julia won, ridden by Jennings.

Political disturbances killed racing in Milan in the 1840s, but it started in Rome. 'The establishment of a pack of fox-hounds by the Earl of Chesterfield was followed by races and steeplechases, and these produced an immediate change in the quality of the horses bred on the Roman Campagna. The first races at Rome, under English auspices, were held about 1842. In that year several of the Roman princes clubbed together to buy an English thoroughbred stallion. Soon afterwards one of the large *mercante di campagna* (graziers), Signor Polverosi, called familiarly by the English "Dusty Bob", imported several English stallions, and began to breed thoroughbred horses. His example was imitated.'[10] An official document of 1844 lists seven races: five for English thoroughbreds, one for Roman horses, and one for the horses of Roman owners, ridden by grooms.[11]

There was considerable growth all over Italy in the 1850s. Naples moved its racing from the Campo di Marte to Agnano, and dropped English weights and measures in favour of Italian. In Tuscany, a new racecourse was opened on the royal estate of San Rossore, Pisa, in 1852. Milan had a new *Società per le Corse* and a new racecourse at Senago in 1857, with new and comprehensive rules. On the other side of the Apennines there was racing at Bologna, and in Piemonte at Asti as well as Turin.

Peace and unity had two effects. King Victor Emanuel II began importing English thoroughbreds, and was at once followed by private individuals. And the racing societies of Milan, Turin and Bologna drew up joint rules.

An English observer wrote in 1879: 'some attempts have been made by the young Italian nobles, aided by English committees, to get up races in the English style. An Italian Derby, however, is a matter for the far-off future.'[12] In fact a race called the 'Derby' had been run at Milan on 13 May 1864. In 1879 a Stud Book was started by government order. In 1880 The Jockey Club Italiano was founded; its original members represented Rome, Turin, Milan and Varese, Bologna, Florence, and Naples.

In 1881 the new Roman racecourse, Capannelle, was laid out by principe Marcantonio Colonna, who had studied the tracks of France and England. The official Italian Derby was first run there in 1884.

At this point there were 40 racecourses in Italy, from Palermo in Sicily to Merano in the Dolomites. The best was San Siro, Milan, opened in May 1888; it was planned on the best English and French models. Its Premio del Commercio, from 1889, was the most valuable race in Italy.

A lot of good thoroughbreds were imported in the 1870s and 1880s. In 1877 the Ministry of Agriculture decided that French precedent was to be followed, and a top stallion bought and used to improve the breed. The Ministry decided on a steeplechaser who would hand on his strength and toughness, and got Austerlitz (by Rataplan) who had won the Grand National of 1876. He was a complete failure.

One Italian horse (and its owner) took England completely by surprise. The Cavaliere Ginistrelli moved all his thoroughbred stock from Portici, near Naples, to Newmarket in about 1880. He there bred, of Italian blood, a mare called Signorina. In 1904 he sent her to be covered by Isinglass, but on the way, in Newmarket High Street, she was met and incontinently covered by the unfashionable stallion Chaleureux. The result was Signorinetta, who won the Derby and Oaks. Ginistrelli was convinced that she owed her brilliance to being the child of a love-match. So eminent an authority as Frederico Tesio, who knew both horse and owner, shared this belief.[13]

Italian trotting started earlier but grew more slowly.

In 1808, in the Prati delle Valle at Padua, trotting-horses pulled heavy, four-wheeled *padovanelle*, Paduan carts. The single recorded winner was Giovanni Rossi; his son Giuseppe founded the Crespano Veneto stud and was an outstanding driver of harness horses.

Trotting-races spread slowly, and to a few places, during the next 60 years. Unlike the French, the Italian trotters were harnessed. One of the few horses celebrated enough for his name to survive was Giuseppe Rossi's Rondello, flourishing about 1860, by a Hungarian sire out of an Italian dam. A few thoroughbred stallions covered Italian mares, but there was no breeding specifically for the trotting-track before 1880.

In 1881 Vincenzo Stefano Breda pioneered specialized breeding of the Russian, Norman, and American type, at his Carmignano di Brenta stud. He imported the Orlov stallion Nagrad, and in 1882 the American trotter Elwood Medium and two American mares. Breda's trotters were a cross of English thoroughbred, standardbred, Orlov, and native. By 1900 there were many studs breeding on Breda's lines.

The most important track was San Siro, Milan. Rome followed. The great growth of the sport belongs to the 20th century.

## Germany

'Perhaps the most horse-loving country in Europe is Germany,' said 'Nimrod'.[14] There had been royal and noble studs for centuries. Breeds like the Mecklenburger were wonderful horses, powerful, courageous, all-purpose. Breeders successfully used crosses of Friesland, Arab, and English blood. It was amazing to English travellers that none of the German states started racing before they did.

Thoroughbreds, and thoroughbred racing, were introduced by Baron Biel of Zieron, near Wismar on the Baltic, who had an English wife and many English friends. By way of Richard Tattersall ('Old Dick', grandson of the founder) he imported broodmares and three stallions of good class; he shortly had a large stud of German-breds of pure English blood, as well as some excellent half-breds. Biel's trainer was Webb, whose father was a Newmarket farrier; the horses were trained on the seashore.

The English thoroughbreds flourished, in spite of a climate which made it impossible to get horses in training early, and which insisted on late foals. When they were raced against German horses, they beat them so easily that Biel had no-one to race against. Consequently he distributed thoroughbred foals among his neighbours by means of a sporting and eccentric auction. Early in the year, before foaling, all the mares were given numbers, and the numbers put in a hat. Biel and his brother drew six of the numbers for themselves; the rest were auctioned. The foals were handed over after weaning. This procedure was witnessed by Tattersall and 'Nimrod', who visited Biel in 1829.[15] By this time Holstein and West Prussia were beginning to be well stocked with thoroughbreds.

The earliest organized racing was at the spa of Doberan, 25 miles from Wismar. Its principal patrons were the Duke of Holstein Augustenburg and his brother Prinz Friedrich, who hunted with the Atherstone. By 1830 there was thoroughbred racing also at Gustrow (25 miles from Doberan) and Brandenburg.

In the next decade racing was started by the King of Hanover at Celle; at Brunswick nearby; and at Hamburg, a course of 'first-rate excellence',[16] which by July 1840 had 14 races in its two days, 50 different owners, and a crowd of 10,000 people. With thoroughbred racing not 15 years old, this success is remarkable. Brunswick's Jockey Club used the Newmarket Rules. Berlin racing began hardly later.

These new courses were in different states, but they had the wisdom to be in league. When the Lichtwald brothers – the biggest horse-dealers in Germany – were found guilty of running horses with false pedigrees in 1840–1, they were warned off all the courses. (They accordingly shifted their operations to Britain.)

The rapid growth of racing encouraged thoroughbred breeding on a large scale, and Biel's example was followed throughout North Germany. The most important stud was Count Hahn's at Basedow. Hahn made a heavy investment in England; his most distinguished importation was Lord George Bentinck's Grey Momus, (2000 Guineas 1838). It was to Hahn that Tattersall and 'Nimrod' entrusted Frank Buckle's whip, which was run for on the leading courses. Hahn was the first successful German invader of England, his German-bred Turnus winning the Stewards' and Chesterfield Cups in 1850.

The first racing in the south was at Baden-Baden in the Black Forest. This was started in 1858 by a Frenchman, M. Benazet, licensee of the casino. Its position made it convenient for French raids and most inconvenient for the North German studs; its Grand Prix (or Grosser Preis) was consequently won every year from 1858 to '69 by French horses. In 1870–1 war kept the French away. In the latter year the Duke of Hamilton made a raid; he won every major race with, ironically, his French-bred horses.

Germany was at this moment being united under the leadership of Prussia, and the attitude of the national government was as favourable as that of kings and dukes 40 years earlier. During the Congress of Berlin Bismarck asked Disraeli 'whether racing was still much encouraged in England. I replied never more so . . .

' "Then," cried the Prince eagerly, "there never will be Socialism in England. You are a happy country. . . . So long as the English are devoted to racing, Socialism has no chance with you." '[17]

Accordingly racing continued to grow, with Frankfurt, Breslau, Leipzig and Dresden added to the list of major courses. Breeding also continued to grow. Blenkiron's 'monster' Middle Park Stud was dispersed by Tattersalls in 1872; to take advantage of the prodigious number of blood-horses placed on the market the *Norddeutscher Zuchtverein* (North German Breeders' Union) was formed to import and pass on English bloodstock.

In 1887 it turned over its functions to the Import Society, run by Count Lehndorff, financed by the pari-mutuel; it bought mares, carefully selected, and resold them to private breeders at low prices. It also subsidized the purchase of foreign stallions (including the Hungarian-bred Kisber) with the proviso that a certain number of nominations were given free to approved thoroughbred mares.[18]

At the same time the government added a thoroughbred stud at Graditz, run by Lehndorff, to its half-bred studs. In 1899 Graditz had 60 broodmares and five stallions, all of top-class English blood. Everything that Lehndorff did, both at Graditz and for the Import Society, was directed towards breeding for soundness. He believed profoundly in the most searching racecourse tests, of fillies as well as colts, and deliberately followed the example of Lord Falmouth at Mereworth.[19]

The German government was not motivated by that love of sport which, in an earlier generation, had started German racing. Bismarck wanted to divert the people from brooding and disaffection. Lehndorff was after fast, stout cavalry. In spite of these unsporting philosophies, the whole thing worked.

This is demonstrated in three ways. First, Volume XI of Hermann Goos's Stud Book (1897) lists 900 broodmares, all private except those at Graditz: a substantial industry. Second, there were at this date dozens of valuable prestige races. Berlin and Hamburg

BERLIN. Racing at Berlin was only a decade old but already extremely successful. In noble patronage and popular support, North German racing resembled that of Britain and Hungary rather than France, Italy, Austria or Ireland. At this date most of the trainers and jockeys were English, but German-bred horses were already good enough to win in England. The race on the occasion illustrated was apparently run for charity, to benefit the indigent of East and West Prussia.

(where the German Derby was held from 1869) had most. The other important race-courses at the turn of the century were Hanover, Leipzig, Baden-Baden, Frankfurt, Doberan, Dresden, and Breslau. At all these places big fields of high-class horses ran for good prizes. Thirdly, German racing was undoubtedly the cleanest and best-run in the world.

## Austria-Hungary

'Nimrod' did not penetrate into the South-East; if he had, he would never have said that the Germans were the most horse-loving people of Europe. This title, from time immemorial, belongs to the Hungarians. They kept alive, in the 19th century, their ancient Magyar tradition of daring and accomplished horsemanship. They hunted and raced, and the aristocracy bred on a vast scale. They imported Arabs and Orlovs.

Austria and its other provinces had little of this tradition, but in 1823 Robert Ridsdale sent a horse to Prinz von Liechtenstein. A 15-year-old stable lad called Tom Ward travelled with the horse. Racing of a tentative kind had just started in Austria, and Ward, probably the first English jockey in the Empire, rode for the prince; he was lionized. He later worked for the Duca di Lucca, who was important in the early history of Austrian as of Italian racing. Ward became his Master of Horse, then confidential secretary; he imported a number of Yorkshire thoroughbreds into Austria. He eventually became head of the Austrian Finance Department, and a baron of the Empire: the only Yorkshire stable-lad to achieve such distinctions.

By 1831 'Races have been established in various parts of the Austrian dominions, and particularly at Buda and at Pest [sic], in Hungary.'[20] The other 'parts' were Vienna and Milan. The Austrians had some participation in Italian sport, none in Hungarian. Hungary's racing and breeding were entirely distinct from Austria's. The greatest point of difference was the scale of private breeding and importing in Hungary, to which there was no Austrian parallel.

The Hungarian government also made an important contribution. In 1854 the government stud of Kisbér was established. English thoroughbreds were imported: by 1860 Kisbér had 33 thoroughbred mares and 10 stallions. In 1863 five stallions and 35 mares were bought from Sir Tatton Sykes of Sledmere. In 1864 came Buccaneer from England, who sired the English Derby winner Kisber. All this made Kisbér the most important thoroughbred stud in the Empire; with the efforts and successes of individuals it made the Hungarian horse as good as any in Europe.

The Emperor Franz Josef made peace with his Hungarian subjects, but the breeding and racing activities of the countries remained separate. The Austrian Jockey Club was founded in 1867, under Count Nicholas Esterhazy; the Hungarian Jockey Club – originally the Pester – in 1869. Hungary still had many more thoroughbreds and its racing was still quite different: 'Races in Hungary are attended, unlike those of France, by enthusiastic crowds of peasantry. Gentlemen riders of the first class are numerous.'[21] As in England and Ireland, this was the result of a tradition not only of horsemanship, but also, specifically, of foxhunting.

By contrast, in the last years of the century, the Austrian government had 2199 stallions at 37 studs and stallion depots; of these horses only 96 were thoroughbred, and of these only four top class. They were hardly used to breed thoroughbreds. Besides Lipizza itself, several of the studs bred Lipizzaners; the others were mounting the cavalry. The one government stud limited to thoroughbreds produced nothing outstanding. There were only four major private studs. The pari-mutuel subsidized breeding, but only the government half-breds. Neither private breeder nor thoroughbred benefited from it. An Austrian horse-lover described his own government in 1899 as lazy, incompetent, and uninterested in racing: a number of valuable imported horses were, for

KISBER. The 1876 Epsom Derby Winner was Hungarian-bred of imported English parents. He was by Buccaneer, by the Derby winner Wild Dayrell, who descended from Sir Peter Teazle, out of a Rataplan mare whose dam was by Birdcatcher. His owners in England were the jovial young Baltazzi brothers, Rugby educated Levantines. He appeared at Epsom on Derby day thanks to a moneylender who got the Baltazzis out of trouble with another moneylender. He was greatly fancied and won with great ease. He was nobbled before the St Leger. At stud he was disappointing.

example, allowed to die of cold on railway journeys.[22] Vienna remained the only important racecourse.

In Hungary the government helped constantly and largely, hindered only by the fact that it was bankrupt. It put up the prize-money for races, made government stallions available, and subsidized the importation of good horses. Budapest had 30 days racing in 1899; Spring, Summer and Autumn meetings of 10 days each. Fifteen minutes by train from the city was the training headquarters of Alag. Alag had its own racecourse, belonging to the Jockey Club and leased to the Association of Gentlemen Riders. This had flat, hurdle and steeplechase meetings: a sort of Hungarian le Tremblay. There were seven principal provincial racecourses.

Hungary had four government studs, of which Kisbér was still for thoroughbreds and still of immense importance. It had 16 stallions, of the highest quality, but only 13 mares of its own. Its sons of Bend Or, St Simon, Isonomy, Hermit, Doncaster and Galopin were for the mares of private men. Immediatcly aftcr producing Kisber, this policy bred Kincsem, one of the greatest race-mares of all time. She won all her 54 starts: all the Hungarian classics, and big races in Austria, Germany and France. She also won the Goodwood Cup in 1878.

A royal commission controlled all this, consisting of nine members of the Jockey Club. Their British agent was Prince Esterhazy, who was also military attaché at the Austrian embassy in London. The get of his imports won every important race in the Empire.

The greatest private owner-breeder was Count Elemer Batthyany, president of the Jockey Club; like Esterhazy he continually imported English broodmares. He raced all over Europe. The second biggest was Count Festetics Tasziló, who won races as far away as England. The Englishman Charles Planner traincd for both.

## Russia

Peace came to Russia in 1815, and with it two English horse-dealers called Stuckey and Luke Nott. They presented themselves at the imperial court, and sold Tsar Alexander some deplorable horses. Thc Tsar and his advisers were well-intentioned but ignorant. As in the 18th century, breeding, both government and private, was haphazard; there were by now a lot of English thoroughbreds in Russia, but with few exceptions they were wasted.

Two important things happened in 1825. A racecourse was opened at Lebedjan (Lebodan). And on 4 August there was an official experiment to determine the merits of the English and Cossack brccds. This took the form of a 47-mile race, on public roads near St Petersburg. There were two English horses, Sharper and Mina, well-bred but second class. Oné of the two Cossacks was from Hetman Platov's stud, and both were champions. The English gave the Cossacks more than 3 stone (42 lb.). Sharper broke a stirrup-leather and bolted. Mina went lame. One Cossack was 'completely knocked up'. The other was almost falling with fatigue; its jockey dismounted and a tiny child was put up; horsemen each side held it up. Sharper was now giving about 5 stone, and had exhausted himself by bolting. He still won by eight minutes. 'It was a cruel affair; yet nothing short of such a contcst would have settled the question.'[23]

There were two immediate consequences: more importations, and more racing.

The government contracted with English agents for 30 stallions a year. Several class horses were imported by the Imperial Horse-Breeding Board, which had been founded by Alexander in 1819. In 1836 it produced the first Russian Stud Book. Meanwhilc English dealers had strings of thoroughbred stallions in Russia, which they led round the country. They ran them in races and then sold them, or covered Russian mares for a fee.

In 1833 the Moscow racecourse was founded, principally by Miasnov, a large breeder and prolific writer on bloodstock. In 1841 the St Petersburg course at Tsarskoe Zelo was opened. Cossacks, Circassians, Arabs, and thoroughbreds ran at these courses and at Lebedjan. At the last place there was a 20-mile race in a single heat for 2225 guineas. The English always won, even over extreme distances.[24] The purpose of racing was to test blood-lines and breeding theories; it was not undertaken for fun.

In 1843 the Tsar imported the 17-year-old William Archer to ride, train, and manage his stud. He stayed for two years, training at Tsarskoe Zelo. (He went home to win the Grand National on Little Charlie in 1858, and sire Fred.) The Tsar also imported more thoroughbreds. His most important purchase in this period was Van Tromp (St Leger 1847). The Tsar disliked his picture but grew to love the horse. Unfortunately Van

Tromp's fertility was low. Nicholas was much more sophisticated about bloodstock than Alexander, but he was superstitious: no trace of white was countenanced anywhere on any horse.[25]

The Grand Duke Alexander had as trainer and jockey George Taylor, from Newmarket, and four Newmarket 'exercise boys'. Count Branetsky had 700 broodmares, English foxhounds, and an English huntsman. He went from Arab to thoroughbred stallions because they got better half-bred hunters. This was typical of the Russian attitude to the thoroughbred. Many of the Tsar's thoroughbreds were bought as parade horses; the enormous remount stations in South Russia had 1000–1500 mares each, all as near thoroughbred as possible, purely for cavalry. They were not really keen on racing.

As in Miasnov's day, there were exceptions: such as baron Petrovsky, who venerated Sir Joseph Hawley and John Scott of Whitewall, loved English dogs, and had fighting geese, which entered the mains like Mr Merry's gamecocks. In winter his horses galloped, shoeless, on harrowed snow. All his foals were encouraged to swim.[26]

Serious training in the 1860s began in April. The first meeting was Moscow, in June; it lasted a month, with three days racing a week, four or five races a day. All details were controlled by the Jockey Club. There was little betting, and that mostly by the English jockeys. There was a July meeting at the new course at Toola, August at Tsarskoe Zelo, and September at Lebedjan. These were the four principal meetings. Owners travelled their strings, walking them great distances.

There was further expansion of racing and breeding in the 1870s and 1880s. Under its Director, Count Woronzov-Dashkov, the Imperial Horse-Breeding Board imported many more English and French thoroughbreds. The pari-mutuel increased prize-money and subsidized breeding after the German and Hungarian fashion.

By 1890, therefore, Russian breeding was on a numerically enormous scale, and rationally run. But it was not really successful. Foreign horses were given massive penalties, as they would otherwise have won easily. Almost no Russian horses raced abroad. One, Perkun, a champion at home, was trained at Newmarket in 1884–5 by Edwin Martin for Count Krasinsky; it won one low-class five-furlong handicap in 16 starts.

The racing failed to impress Captain Hayes: 'Flat racing in Russia is carried on in very poor style. Several waifs and strays of our turf hang on to it, because they cannot get a job anywhere else; and a few good English jockeys, having been lured by false hopes or deceptive representations, find themselves riding in that country – but not for long.'[27] English jockeys were treated with contempt and unfairness by officials and club-members;

TROTTING AT ST PETERSBURG. The Semenovsky Platz trotting track was on the river Neva, opposite the palace and racecourse of Tsarskoe Zelo. Trotting was a winter sport, and trots were also held on the frozen river (compare trotting to skeleton sleighs on the Chicago River in 1855, described p. 241). These events were far more popular in Tsarist Russia than galloping races.

they were not allowed to wear uniform, and were treated like *muzhiks*, freed serfs. Five young English jockeys and three trainers died shortly before Hayes wrote. The racing season had lengthened, from mid-May to mid-October, still three days a week. Four races a day were for professional (English) jockeys, the others for gentlemen riders and Russian boys.

In 1897 the Grand Duke Dimitri (uncle of Nicholas II) succeeded Dashkov at the head of the Horse-Breeding Board; he rightly decided that a new top stallion was needed, and began to negotiate for John Gubbins's Galtee More (triple crown 1897). The horse was bought by General Arapov, by way of the International Agency and Exchange Limited, whose director was William Allison. A detailed record of this curious transaction therefore exists.[28] The Russians paid 20,000 guineas, then a record for a horse in training; the deal was gravely jeopardised by General Arapov becoming over-excited in a London restaurant, and thinking that the ladies dining there were courtesans.

In 1899 there were 32 racecourses altogether, and 220 days racing: 1209 flat races and 265 steeplechases. The average prize was good – 1000 roubles, over £100. There were 1500 thoroughbred mares in the Russian Stud Book.

## Russian Trotting

Orlov's stud was bought by the government from his widow after his death, and his stock became widely dispersed. All Russian trotters of the 19th century descended from it, though there were further infusions of thoroughbred blood, and, late in the century, of standardbred. Training was generally on Orlov's lines – timed dashes over a straight quarter-mile. As in France, trotting was primarily a winter sport; it was a good deal more popular than thoroughbred racing.

George Wilkes wrote in 1867: 'We find that there are but two nations of the earth which possess a race of animals known as the trotting-horse. One of the nations is Russia; the other, the United States. In the first-named country, we find an animal proceeding from the Arabian foundation, graft, it is said, upon the Flanders stock, which is called the Orlov trotter; but this breed, though bending the knee when striding, and though having in other respects the trotting action, is considered by good judges as being only half-developed.'[29]

'Half-developed' seems a fair judgment, of training and driving as of horses. All were horribly shown up by the Americans. The Russians sent some horses to the Chicago Exposition of 1893; the hospitable Americans gave them some prizes, but according to

TROTTING TO DROSHKY. The droshky is a light four-wheeler, comparable to the American match-wagon but with smaller wheels and these curiously-angled shafts like those of sleighs. This magnificent horse, called Beauty, justifies Captain Hayes's description of the long, strong Orlov trotters and their impressive action. Neither horses nor drivers, however, came out well in competition with the Americans.

Frank Starr, an American trainer in Russia, this was only out of kindness: the horses were not admired.[30] They did suit Russia, however. Similarly-bred carriage-horses were extraordinarily tough: they could be kept standing in the street in extreme cold the whole length of a dinner-party without ill-effect.[31]

As well as Russian horses being shown to America, American were shown to Russia. C. K. G. Billings took his champion Harvester to the Moscow Exhibition, and the government offered him $75,000 for the horse. Billings declined.

The biggest establishment towards the end of the century was the Grand Duke Dimitri's, between Kiev and Kharkov: 'a few houses and a large number of stables, riding schools and a straight covered drive a quarter of a mile long.' The trainers were Starr and Murphy. The covered training-track was floored with sawdust; in dry weather it was coated with rock-salt, which kept the going good by attracting water.[32]

Of the many trotting-tracks the most important was the Semenovsky Platz at St Petersburg, across the river from the Tsarskoe Zelo racecourse. There were trotting-races every Sunday during the winter, on hard-packed snow. The Trotting Club was run by a German, Herr Wachter; it was extremely successful. Big crowds came every week, and the pari-mutuel turnover was much greater than that of the racecourse.

Trotting would have been dominated by American horses and American professionals if the Russians had permitted it. Foreign horses were allowed into very few events, and there heavily penalized. American trainers and drivers were much resented because of their success. The stewards showed dreadful favouritism. They had to. Will Caton and his brother Frank ('the best trainer and driver that has ever been in Russia')[33] and George Fuller, besides Starr and Murphy, were far more skilful than the Russians.

Many matches were against the clock, a practice dating from Orlov's time: 'owners as a rule like this time arrangement, because it obviates the disagreeable possibility of their being put alongside animals being driven by Americans.'[34]

At the end of the century the bottom dropped out of the American horse-breeding market: 50,000 horses were exported in the one year 1897. As thoroughbreds and their handlers went to England and France, trotters went in great numbers to Russia. The Orlov was pretty well eclipsed.

## Switzerland; Holland; Scandinavia

Early in the 19th century Switzerland had two kinds of racing: *l'épreuve de force*, a contest of heavy draught-horses, and trotting in harness. The latter amazed 'Nimrod', who had seen Belgian and French saddle-trotting, but not Italian or Russian harness-races.[35] Thoroughbred racing was tentatively introduced into Switzerland by capitaine Rossier, who saw the English Derby of 1822 (won by the Duke of York's Moses) and began importing thoroughbreds. A Jockey Club was founded, and racing begun at Payerne.

One would expect the home of the Friesland trotter to have ancient racing; in fact there was none in Holland, except among English officers in the early 17th century, until the early 19th, when annual trotting-races began.

The Scandinavian countries developed thoroughbred racing and trotting in the second half of the century. A large number of thoroughbred horses were imported, few of high class.

Racing did not become a major part of the life of any of these countries; nor did it catch on in Spain or Portugal.

# 19 America:

## Revolution to Civil War

### The Revolution and its Effects

Anti-English feeling grew throughout the colonies in the late 1760s. In 1770 the wave of imported thoroughbreds stopped. Congress instructed the states to 'discountenance and discourage every species of extravagance and dissipation, especially all horse-races and all kinds of gambling'. In 1776 war was on.

Owners rode some of their thoroughbreds into battle. George Washington, when serving with Light Horse Harry Lee, saw a group of Connecticut Rangers all on greys. These were all by imported Ranger, which had been rescued from a shipwreck. In 1779 Ranger was bought by Captain Lindsay of Virginia for 125 hogsheads of tobacco, and became known as Lindsay's Arabian. He sired George Washington's Magnolia and his cousin William's Ranger.

Many horses were stolen by British troops. The cavalry commander Tarleton seized 'sixty famous ones' in a single raid.[1] Others were smuggled away and hidden, and their identities and breeding lost.

A few country meetings were held in South Carolina, in defiance of the law; and the occupying British held races at Flatlands Plain, Brooklyn, which they renamed Ascot Heath. With these exceptions racing stopped.

The peace of 1783 produced two contradictory results.

On the one hand, there was a desire for gaiety after rigour, of which, where it was traditional, racing formed an obvious part. On 1 March 1783 the Maryland Jockey Club met, months before peace was signed. The dispersal of studs and the shortage of horses caused importing to begin again at once: among racing men at least there was no abiding resentment of England. Everything seemed back to normal.

But the tolerant Church of England was no longer established. Austerer sects took over the consciences of the states. To their disapproval was added a resentful egalitarianism: racing was the sport of the gentry. Religious and political lobbies combined to abolish North Carolina racing (largely quarter-horse) immediately after the Constitution was ratified.

One other process was a major part of those years: the expansion of the nation westwards.

### Virginia

Virginia had four main racecourses in the early years of peace, all in the Southside: Fairfield, Broad Rock and Tree Hill, all near Richmond, and Newmarket at Petersburg. Each had its own Jockey Club. Prizes were initially smaller but interest as great as ever.

The shortage of horses began to be made good at once. In 1784 Malcomb Hart of

Louisa, Hanover County, imported Medley from Richard Tattersall. Medley (1776) was by Gimcrack out of Arminda by Snap; owned by the wild Sir John Lade he won 11 plates and many matches in the early 1780s. He stood for eight seasons in Virginia, dying of colic in 1792. John Tayloe III said: 'his stock is decidedly the best we have had. His colts were the best racers of their day, although they were generally small; but their limbs were remarkably fine, and they were distinguished for their ability to carry weight.'[2] Tayloe's Calypso was an outstanding filly and broodmare, perhaps the most important of all Medley's get.

This John Tayloe, second of Mount Airy, went to Eton immediately after the Revolution, and then to Cambridge. He was the leading owner and the leading breeder in Virginia until his death in 1828. But he was not an owner-breeder. His stud became a commercial enterprise. The horses he raced were mostly bought.

This attitude to thoroughbred breeding was not new to Virginia, but it was stronger. Another exponent, 20 years older than Tayloe, was Colonel John Hoomes of Bowling Green, Caroline County. He had a good stud, not large, just before the Revolution, and raced his home-breds successfully in the 1780s. Via Tayloe he made contact with Tattersall, and from 1792 began importing high-class horses speculatively: 19 stallions and 13 mares by 1802, nearly all of which he sold.[3]

His most important purchase – and the most important horse ever to go to America – was Diomed.

Diomed's life is extraordinary. He made much more history than anyone realized at the time by winning a new three-year-old sweepstakes at Epsom in 1780; he was a good horse but not a great champion; he hardly ran thereafter and never won. He was a failure at stud, his fee by 1798 having dropped to two guineas and his fertility (he was 21) having become low. He was bought by Messrs Lamb and Younger for 50 guineas, bought from them by Hoomes as a speculation, and sold by him to Colonel Selden; he first stood at Chesterfield in 1800.

American air, feed, treatment, or broodmares worked an amazing magic in the old horse. His fertility returned. He was champion sire in 1803, the first season his get ran in Virginia. The list of his important progeny – winners of big races and influential stallions

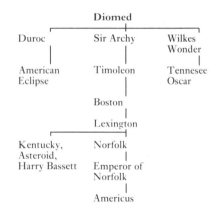

                    Diomed
Duroc          Sir Archy          Wilkes
                                   Wonder
American       Timoleon           Tennesse
Eclipse                           Oscar
               Boston
               Lexington
Kentucky,      Norfolk
Asteroid,
Harry Bassett  Emperor of
               Norfolk
               Americus

DIOMED. After a racing career spectacular only in retrospect, Diomed went to stud at Up Park, Hampshire and then Barton, Suffolk. He got Grey Diomed, who went to Russia, and Young Giantess, dam of Eleanor. Otherwise he was largely a failure. It is impossible to say how, at the great age of 23, he suddenly became a prolific and prepotent sire of extraordinary merit.

*Right*
JOHN RANDOLPH OF ROANOKE. Randolph's long career, as statesman and turfite, spanned quarter-racing, early thoroughbred racing, and nearly two generations of independent America. It is not clear by what genetic oddity his beloved Janus produced sprinters even from the stoutest mares.

*Above*

JOHN TAYLOE III OF MOUNT AIRY.
The heir to Mount Airy (*c.* 1768–1828)
was a successful owner and breeder in his
family's tradition. The best filly he bred
was Tayloe's Calypso (by Medley out of
a Childers mare); the best colt Sir
Archy (by Diomed out of his imported
Castianira by Rockingham).

– is incredibly long for a horse of his age and record. 'Without Diomed, the most brilliant pages of our turf story could never have been written. Taking him all in all, Diomed, as a progenitor of the American race-horse, stands alone, towering magnificently in accomplishment above all others. . . . He is Diomed, one and kingly.' He died in 1808. 'There was almost as much mourning in the old colony land over his demise as there was at the death of George Washington. . . . The Virginians regarded the death of Diomed, though truly, counted by years and accomplishments, he had run his race, as a great national catastrophe.'[4]

Diomed nicked with Medley. Tayloe said: 'It is a fact well known, that the best racers begotten by Old Diomed were from Medley mares.'[5] He nicked even better with Rockingham (by Highflyer out of Purity by Matchem). Tayloe imported Rockingham's daughter, Castianira, in 1799. She ran once, winning, in 1800. She was sent to Diomed in 1804, and threw Sir Archy (sometimes rendered Archie), inbred $3 \times 4$ to Herod.

Sir Archy first ran in 1808 at Fairfield, Richmond. He was twice second. Colonel William Ransom Johnson bought him at the end of the season; next year he was undisputed champion. He was bought at the end of that season by Allen J. Davie and announced as a stallion, prematurely retired because there were no opponents for him. He died in 1833. His blood was dispersed from New York to the Gulf of Mexico: 'He filled a hemisphere with his get.'[6] He was one of the grandsires of Boston, the other, Florizel, being also by Diomed. Florizel was out of a mare by Shark (by Eclipse's sire Marske), the third important arrival. Shark was a great racehorse in England, with record winnings. He was imported in 1786 by Benjamin Hyde; he was principally a sire of broodmares, and as such of first-class importance.

Tayloe and Hoomes sought and achieved the best. This was becoming less and less typical of Virginia breeding. A lot of bad stallions were imported cheaply from 1790 to 1805, which commanded high fees because of the glamour of their English birth. Then anti-English feeling grew again; few imports were made after 1806, and none from 1812 to 1830. Virginia breeders assembled studs of any material they could get, and went in for quantity, confident of a market in an expanding country which was not importing thoroughbreds. It was lucky that Medley, Diomed and Shark were fertile and prepotent.

One man, as owner-breeder, swam furiously against this stream: John Randolph of Roanoke. He bought mares of good class; he imported even better ones, such as Duchess (by Grouse by Highflyer) in 1803 and Lady Bunbury (by Trumpator, a grandson of Matchem) in 1804. His favourite male line was Janus. Randolph bred on a large and expensive scale, and raced all that he bred; consistently, until his death in 1833, he failed. This was partly bad luck; also bad judgment. The descendants of Janus were sprinters without bottom. Randolph therefore amassed larger and larger numbers of losing and unsaleable horses; there were 160 at his dispersal in 1834.

At the opposite extreme was William R. Johnson, a North Carolinan who went to Virginia after the Revolution. He had a private two-mile training track, dead straight, at his Oaklands stable; one season he started horses in 63 races and won 61 of them. From 1807, when he was only 35, he was the 'Napoleon of the Southern Turf'. Unlike some men with such titles, he was trusted and respected.

Meanwhile the puritans were getting control. In 1792 a state law fixed $7 as the maximum bet; the law was widened and strengthened in acts of 1798 and 1819. There was some swing of public opinion away from austerity in the 1840s (ascribed to the success of the romantic Waverley novels)[7] and the betting laws were repealed in 1849. Virginia then had 13 recognized racecourses.

Unfortunately all but a few Virginian racing men seemed as determined to degrade their own sport as puritans to destroy it. In the 20 years before the Civil War it became dishonest and unseemly. By 1850 no lady went racing in Virginia.

## Washington and Maryland

Washington City had a Jockey Club by 1798. Its racecourse was inaugurated that year by a match between General Ridgely's Cincinnatus (by Lindsay's Arabian) from Maryland, and John Tayloe's Lamplighter (by Medley) from Virginia. Lamplighter won.

In 1800 Washington became capital of the Union; from 1802 racing was at the new National Course. Many presidents raced there, especially Jefferson, Adams, and Van Buren. There were dinners, balls, ambassadors, and the best horses from Maryland and Virginia.

A decline set in about 1844. Senators and officials, sensitive to the climate of the time, did not care to be seen on the turf. Perhaps even in Washington racing became dubious and ruffianly. The National Course was dead in 1846.

In spite of Maryland's early start in 1783, its racing glory had passed. Its land was impoverished by tobacco and it was too far north for cotton. It became a poor state. Racing headquarters moved from Annapolis to Baltimore, but there were only two courses in the state in 1800 and only three in 1840.

## The Carolinas

In 1783 Charles Town became Charleston, home of the second South Carolina Jockey Club. Racing was as merry and fashionable as ever. Dr Irving, for 40 years secretary of the Jockey Club, said of New Market in 1786: 'everything combined to render race-week in Charleston emphatically the *carnival* of the state, when it was *unpopular*, if not *impossible*, to be out of spirits, and not to mingle with the gay throng.'[8]

In 1788 the second South Carolina Jockey Club broke up and the third was formed. This had money trouble, and in 1791 General Pinckney formed the fourth. In 1792 racing moved from New Market to the new Washington course, which was bought by subscription of Jockey Club members. Racing started the first Wednesday in February and lasted a week.

All the important owner-breeders in South Carolina bore high military rank. Colonel William Alston of Waccamaw had Betsey Baker, the Brilliant Mare (bred by Fenwick at John's Island) and the Tartar Mare by Flimnap. Colonel William Washington had, besides Ranger, the champion Shark by imported Shark. General M'Pherson imported a Highflyer, a Buzzard, a Trumpator, and three Sir Peters. General Hampton in 1800 won every prize at Charleston. Colonel Singleton in the next generation imported Whalebone and Orville blood. Colonel James B. Richardson and his son-in-law Colonel Spann had Bertrand, champion of the state about 1830. In the late 1830s and 1840s Colonel (later General) Wade Hampton was the leading importer and breeder. His many white jockeys included the great Gil Patrick; he also had half a dozen Virginia Negro riders.

In 1837 Richard Tattersall, who had sold so many horses to all these men, followed his own German precedent of 1829: he gave a whip to the South Carolina Jockey Club to be run for under Newmarket Rules. It was first won by Hampton's Monarch (by Priam).

Throughout this period, and in contrast to Virginia, South Carolina racing remained honest and elegant. 'Charleston, South Carolina, is, we believe, the only place where ladies habitually grace the course with their likeness.'[9]

Colonels, cotton-fortunes, ladies, and magnificent horses did not impress the puritans. In 1837 an anonymous tract was published in Charleston: 'HORSE-RACING and Christian Principles and Duty Incompatible . . . horse-racing, as a public amusement, is absurd, cruel, vicious, demoralizing, adverse to the principles of Christianity and hostile to the best interests of society.'[10]

At this date South Carolina had ten racecourses, of which only Charleston was important beyond the state. North Carolina recovered from puritanism, and had six courses.

## Kentucky

Kentucky was first colonized from Virginia and the Carolinas a little before the Revolution. The settlers brought horses with them: mostly quarter-horses, perhaps a few thoroughbreds. Immediately after the peace there were certainly thoroughbreds in the District, and both racing and breeding grew at remarkable speed.

Parts of Kentucky were densely wooded. As in Virginia nearly two centuries earlier, paths were cut through the trees and quarter-horses raced. As early as 1788 the first stallion advertisement appeared in the *Kentucky Gazette* for Pilgarlick (by Janus), a half-bred considered less speedy only than Darius. Darius was also by Janus, out of one of his own daughters, she being also out of one of his daughters.

The unwooded part of Kentucky was limestone, like Ireland; on it grew the blue-grass, which was immediately revealed as the best natural grazing in the world for horses. The first thoroughbred was imported to the District about the same time as Pilgarlick and Darius: Mogul, by DeLancey's imported Lath out of Poll Flaxen by imported Jolly Roger.

In 1789 there was racing at Lexington – three-mile heats at weight for age – undoubtedly of thoroughbreds.[11] In 1793 Kentucky was a state. Lexington already had a Jockey Club, and there were three-day meetings at Georgetown, Bardstown, and Shelbyville when they were still villages. By 1800 there were eight racecourses in Kentucky.

Breeding grew even faster. Stallions were imported in the 1790s, predominantly from Virginia but from every other racing state too, including New York. There were at least three large studs by 1795 and very many smaller ones. They got the stock of Fearnought, Wildair and Medley, and, as soon as it became available, that of Diomed and Sir Archy. The first imported English stallion was Blaze, advertised in 1797. Others followed rapidly and in large numbers.

Kentucky was pastoral and poor, without the old wealth of tobacco or the newer one of cotton. By 1840 it had 17 racecourses – more than any other state, four more than Virginia – but prizes were small even at the major new course at Louisville. Kentucky therefore bred primarily for sale to other states. It had 36 advertised stallions, far more than Virginia, less only than Tennessee.

The most famous episode on the early Kentucky turf was the meeting between Wagner and Grey Eagle at Louisville in September 1839, put on by Yelverton N. Oliver. Wagner

WAGNER AND GREY EAGLE. Wagner (1834) was by Sir Charles (by Sir Archy) out of Maria West (by Marion, by Sir Archy, and tracing to Janus); his reputation grew and grew in 1837 and 1838, and by 1839 he was considered supreme. He was rashly challenged by Grey Eagle (1835), who was by Woodpecker (by Bertrand, by Sir Archy) out of Ophelia (by Wild Medley, a stallion of obscure breeding but also representing Sir Archy). Grey Eagle was 'romantically beautiful', and the first Kentucky-bred to be talked of as a national champion. Wagner beat him twice, and went on to become much the more important sire.

(by Sir Charles, and inbred $2 \times 3$ to Sir Archy) was Virginia-bred and champion of the Deep South; it was ridden by a slave called Cato. Grey Eagle (by Woodpecker, and inbred $3 \times 3$ to Sir Archy) was the star of Kentucky; it was ridden by Stephen Welch, who was good but much too light. 'The crowd was immense and the excitement at fever point.'[12] Wagner just won two four-mile heats. This was Monday. They met again on Saturday. Grey Eagle won the first heat; Wagner, with Cato the stronger jockey, the second; in the third Grey Eagle broke down. This was a terrible blow to Kentucky. Cato was given his freedom.

## Tennessee

Tennessee was settled about the same time as Kentucky, and began racing as soon or even sooner. There were allegedly seven thoroughbred stallions standing in Sullivan County as early as 1790,[13] and nine were advertised in the *Knoxville Register* in 1795, all the sons or grandsons of imported horses. In the early 19th century there were no less than eight grandsons of (O'Kelly's) Eclipse. Covering fees were payable in cotton, pork, beef, or cattle on the hoof.

The most important early stallion was Barry's Grey Medley (by Medley) who stood in 1800 near Nashville. On the turf he was always ridden by a slave called Altamont, who had belonged to George Washington in Virginia. Diomeds and Sir Archys arrived soon afterwards, and stallions were imported from England.

Tennessee racing probably began in the 1790s. By 1807 (four years after Tennessee became a state) there were three Jockey Clubs: at Clover Bottom, Nashville, and Gallatin. In 1839 there were 10. The first champion was Haynie's Maria, bred in Virginia (1808), one of Diomed's last get, out of a daughter of Tayloe's Bellair by Medley. She was sold to Captain Jesse Haynie of Summer County; she won over all distances from a quarter to four miles.

Maria was trained by Green Berry Williams, and always ridden by a 4ft 6 in. Negro hunchback called Monkey Simon, who was born in Africa and believed a prince. Williams's parents were Virginians who had settled in Georgia. They came of a famous quarter-racing family, and Green Berry was a successful jockey as a boy. He settled in Tennessee in 1806, taking three thoroughbreds to Summer County. After Maria, the most celebrated horse he trained was Walk-in-the-Water (1813), a half-bred son of Sir Archy. He ran four-mile heat races until he was 15 (by one account 18); he won more of them than any other horse. Williams later went back to Virginia, and there trained for 'Napoleon' Johnson and John Randolph of Roanoke. He trained for 70 years.

The victories of Haynie's Maria aroused the jealous fury of Andrew Jackson, 'Old Hickory'. He was born in Carolina, rode as a mounted orderly, aged 13, in the Revolution, and settled in Tennessee before he was 21. He was a founding father of Nashville race-course, and owned and betted with consistent success. With his Truxton (by Diomed) he won a series of matches against Charles Dickinson's Ploughboy. They later fought a duel, in which Jackson was wounded and Dickinson killed. In 1812 and thereafter he tried with horse after horse to beat Haynie's Maria: with Pacolet, Stump-the-Dealer, DeWett's Mare, and Western Light. In the end he threw in his hand and went into partnership with Haynie. When he was President he raced under a pseudonym, but supervised his stable as closely as ever. His racing manager was the Rev. Hardy M. Cryer, who owned the great broodmare Madame Touson, by Grey Medley. Her sons, the 'four Tennessee Tousons', were all by Jackson's Pacolet and all trained by Green Berry Williams.

Another notable Tennessee cleric was the Rev. Hubbard Saunders of Summer County. He bred Tennessee Oscar (1814) by Wilkes Wonder (by Diomed) out of a daughter of imported Saltram (though there is a persistent doubt about Saltram). Oscar was 'owned and run by that high-toned gentleman, Dr Roger B. Sappington, of Nashville;'[14] like Highflyer, Oscar was never beaten and never paid forfeit.

Summer County, in the west of the state, was where by now all Tennessee horses were bred: 'This is, I suppose, the acknowledged centre of the "race-horse region". Blood stock here is all the go. To be without it is to be out of fashion, and destitute of taste.'[15]

In 1830 Colonel George Elliott and an Irish immigrant called James Jackson (no relation to Andrew, and later his enemy) imported Leviathan, by Muley out of a Windle mare. Leviathan had been a very good racehorse, and as a four-year-old owned by George IV. In Tennessee he had made a spectacular mark by 1834, and was five times champion sire. In 1835 Thomas A. Pankey and Hardy Cryer got imported Luzborough (by Ditto, Derby 1803, by Sir Peter Teazle), a stallion they considered superior. An altercation in the columns of the *Nashville Whig* was followed by a match: any Leviathan against any Luzborough, at Nashville, in March 1837. Sarah Bladen was the Leviathan, Leila the Luzborough; betting was unprecedented. Sarah Bladen distanced Leila in the first heat. Thomas Barry of Gallatin (who had a share in Luzborough) renewed the challenge: but Jackson's Exotic (Leviathan) beat Barry's Luzborough filly easily.

In 1836 Jackson had made a more important purchase still: Lord Jersey's Glencoe (by Sultan) who won the 2000 Guineas of 1834, but weakened inside the distance when third to 'Plenipo' in the Derby. Before leaving England Glencoe sired Pocahontas. In America he was prodigiously influential, especially because of his fillies. He was eight times champion sire and founded an enduring male line.

Balie Peyton was at this period becoming a leading owner and breeder at Station Camp, Summer County. He had the idea of a Produce Stakes (unnamed offspring of named stallions) for the whole Union, entries to be made in 1839 and the race to be run at Nashville in 1843. There were 30 entries, from every racing state south of the Potomac: nine by Priam, four by Glencoe, three by Skylark, two by Leviathan. At $5000 a side, a stake of $150,000 was possible.

Four actually started, on 10 October: a Skylark colt (out of Lilac by Leviathan); Balie Peyton's Great Western by Luzborough; Thomas Kirkman's filly Glumdalclitch (by Glencoe out of Giantess by Leviathan); and Wade Hampton's Herald, got in England by Plenipotentiary, foaled in South Carolina out of imported Delphine by Whisker. Glumdalclitch won; and at the party after the race was renamed Peytona. She went on to meet Fashion at the Union Course.

## New York and the North; the North-South Matches

Racing in the North was slow to get going after the Revolution. By the end of the century there was a little racing at Hempstead and Bath, on Long Island, at Poughkeepsie, and at Trenton, New Jersey.

In 1802 racing was forbidden in New York by the state legislature on moral grounds; with some reason: it was apparently very dishonest. Dealers managed to evade the law by matching horses at country fairs: 'bootleg' racing, because of the footwear of the riders.

Massachusetts had a course at Medford from 1811. Legislation constantly threatened or reprieved it; under these unstable conditions it only lasted six years.

Racing was allowed back into New York to a modest extent in 1818–19; abolished in 1820; allowed again in 1821 for a five-year probationary period, in Queen's County, supervised by the sheriff. This permitted the opening of the Union Course. Its 'skinned' track, much faster than grass, became a model. But it only really drew the public two years later, with the first of the North-South matches in New York: American Eclipse against Sir Henry.

Eclipse was bred in 1814 in Queen's County, Long Island, by General Coles. He was by

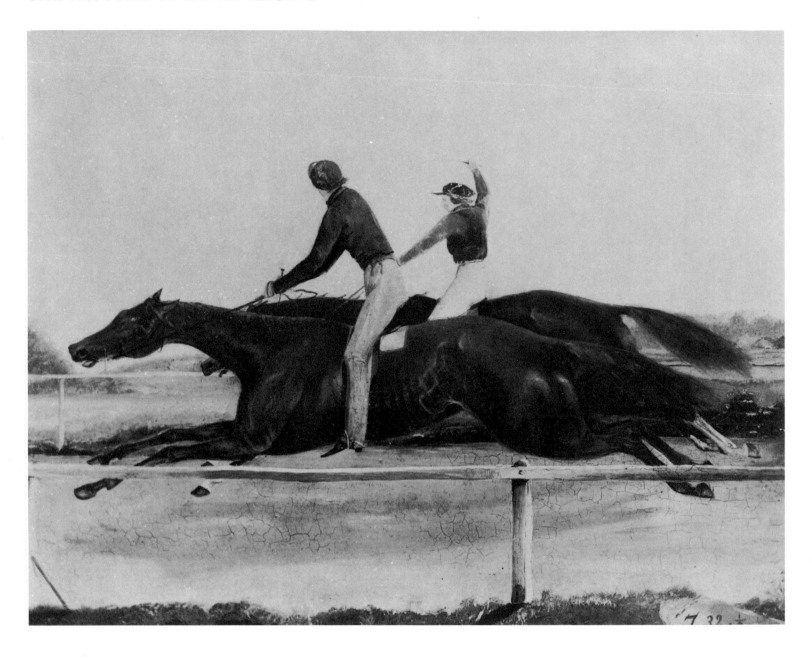

Diomed's son Duroc out of Messenger's daughter Miller's Damsel. His second dam was by Pot-8-os, his third by Gimcrack. Owned by Cornelius W. van Ranst, he won what races there were in 1818–19, was retired to stud (by force of law) in 1820–1, returned, when the law allowed it, to distance Sir Archy's daughter Lady Lightfoot in 1821, and in 1822 again beat everything.

James J. Harrison of Virginia made the first North-South challenge with his Sir Charles (by Sir Archy): four-mile heats, at Washington D.C. Eclipse represented the North and won; Sir Charles broke down. Hubristically, the North – van Ranst and John C. Stevens – issued a general challenge, the world against Eclipse, four mile heats for $20,000.

The challenge was taken up by a Virginia group including William R. Johnson and John Randolph. They assembled a string of the best Southerners and tried them together. They came North in 1823 with five – four Sir Archys and a Timoleon. They short-listed to Sir Henry and Betsey Richards. Sir Henry was picked – a four-year-old by Sir Archy and inbred 2 × 2 to Diomed, his bottom line tracing to Janus. 60,000 people watched the race at the Union Course; they did not include Johnson, who was disabled by his dinner of the night before. Eclipse, at nine, gave the four-year-old 18 lb. Sir Henry was ridden by the Virginian boy John Walden, Eclipse by the experienced William

FASHION AND BOSTON. Boston (1833; pedigree p. 215) was the best horse in Virginia from 1836 to 1840, nearly all his races being in four-mile heats. Fashion (1837) was by imported Trustee. Trustee was third to Sir Giles in the Derby of 1832, both being owned by the confederacy of Ridsdale and Gully, and both being sold to America. (Sir Giles was a failure.) Fashion was the best horse in the North in 1840–42. When the two met at Camden in 1841, Boston was exhausted by racing and covering; no wonder Fashion won.

Crafts. The race is described by a contemporary, 'An Old Turfite':[16] in the first heat Walden sat still; Crafts rode a bad race, whipping and spurring madly, and giving his horse a deep cut on a testicle. Sir Henry won. Purdy took over from Crafts in the second heat, and Eclipse won. In the third Arthur Taylor took over from Walden, and Eclipse just won again. They went 12 miles, going hard all the way.

The challenge was renewed by the South, but van Ranst mercifully retired his horse.

Before Eclipse returned to the turf in 1821 he got the filly Ariel (dam by Financier) who won 42 races in 57 starts. The Southern champion was Flirtilla, by Sir Archy out of a Robin Redbreast mare. They met in four-mile heats for $20,000 at the Union Course in October 1825. The crowd was the biggest since the Eclipse-Sir Henry match. Ariel won the first heat, Flirtilla the next two.

Another sequel to the earlier match was an Eclipse-Sir Archy cross: Black Maria, bred by Henry Hall at Harlem in 1826, by American Eclipse out of Lady Lightfoot by Sir Archy, and owned by John C. Stevens. She beat the Southern champion Trifle, also by American Eclipse, at the Union Course in October 1832. She retired to Balie Peyton's stud where, unlike Ariel, she was an excellent broodmare. One of the few horses ever to beat Black Maria was William R. Johnson's Bonnets O'Blue (by Sir Charles). She was sent to the North and became dam of Fashion.

Fashion was foaled in 1837, by imported Trustee who stood in New Jersey. She was owned by William Gibbons, trained by Samuel Laird at Colt's Neck, New Jersey, and ridden by his son Joseph, the 'Northern Gil Patrick'. Except when recovering from a cough, Fashion was unbeaten and unapproached from 1840–2: 'one of the sweetest, fleetest, gamest misses of the turf that had been seen since the time of Black Maria.'[17]

The South also had a new champion: Boston, son of Sir Archy's mysteriously-bred son Timoleon. He was bred in Virginia in 1833. He was named after not the city but the game, having been won at the card-table, according to legend, by Nathaniel Rives from the breeder John Wickham. He won as a three-year-old, and was then bought by William R. Johnson and trained by Captain John Belcher. Thereafter, known as 'Old Whitenose', he conquered the South. As a six-year-old he won eight races running, seven being four-mile heats. He had to campaign as far south as Augusta to find opponents. In 1841 he retired to stud and covered 42 mares; came back into training; and in September and October won four races in four starts, all four-mile heats.

On 28 October he met Fashion at Camden, New Jersey. Not surprisingly he was over the top and could hardly gallop. Fashion beat him. They met again next year, Joe Laird on Fashion, Gil Patrick on Boston. Patrick rode one of his few bad races, making too much use of his horse; Fashion won again.

Next year Glumdalclitch emerged from the Peyton Stakes champion of the South and renamed Peytona. A new North-South match was suggested by Balie Peyton: 13 May 1845, at the Union Course. Fashion v. Peytona drew what was said to be the biggest crowd ever assembled in America for any occasion,[18] estimated between 70,000 and 120,000. Very few people saw any racing. Peytona won for Tennessee. The mares met again on 27 May at Camden; Fashion won.

These celebrated matches, more than anything else, made the Union Course a success: but it was the only racecourse in New York state. Pennsylvania had one course, New Jersey four. There were no others north of Maryland. A visiting Englishman said: 'although the Southern gentlemen did their utmost to cleanse away the stain [of dishonest racing and decadent racehorses], the fanatical puritanical spirit of many Northern states, tabooed the institution for years; thus it only had a partial existence, and but few horses were imported, and those always to the South.'[19]

The galloping racehorse was sinful; the trotting-horse (for obscure theological reasons) was not. This is the reason for the enormous growth of trotting in New York and the North.

### Expansion South and West

Like Carolina, Georgia became rich on cotton (Eli Witney's gin was invented in 1792). The state had thoroughbred studs by 1820. Racing grew steadily; by 1840 there were five courses in Georgia, the leading one being Augusta.

Settlers went south from Tennessee into Alabama early in the century, and took their horses with them. The principal early racecourses were at Mobile and Florence; by 1840 there were 10. Of the Tennessee turfites who settled in Alabama the most important was James Jackson, whose Glencoe stood in Alabama until 1844.

Mississippi raced mainly Tennessee and Alabama horses. It had eight racecourses by 1840, of which the principal was the Pharsalia track at Natchez.

Louisiana had a rich and civilized society of great antiquity, but its racing began late. It was the creation of American newcomers; the French aristocracy of New Orleans were never interested. One of these newcomers, Yelverton N. Oliver, opened the Eclipse course at New Orleans and founded the New Orleans Jockey Club. Shortly afterwards the Metairie course was opened by a rival Jockey Club, and there were several others near the city. In 1839 Louisiana had eight racecourses.

In 1840 Richard ten Broeck appeared on the New Orleans turf. He was a knickerbocker, who left West Point, for unknown reasons, in 1830; he seems to have been a professional gambler on the Mississippi river-boats for 10 years. He became a friend of William R. Johnson; in 1847 he managed both the Mobile and Metairie courses, and in 1851 he bought Metairie outright. It became the best racecourse in America.

From Louisiana racing went west into Texas; from Tennessee south-west into Arkansas; from Kentucky west into Missouri, north-west into Illinois. Ohio and Indiana were racing (one course each) by 1840. In Chicago it started that year, and in 1844 the Chicago Jockey Club was formed; it had a four-mile track with a one-mile track inside it. It failed. A new course was opened by the lake in 1845 for both thoroughbred racing and trotting.

### California

The Spanish horse-games, which included racing of a kind, were established in California before the Revolution. Racing of a more familiar kind became frequent in the 1830s: Dana, having rounded the Horn, says the beach at Santa Barbara was 'a favourite place for running horses'.[20] There was a little state legislation regulating the sport, and there were court actions of the kind frequent in Virginia two centuries earlier. The horses were Spanish.

The gold rush, beginning in 1848, brought a wave of population and a wave of horses, which included Eastern thoroughbreds. In 1851 the Pioneer Course at San Francisco was opened, on the Eastern model and using the Union Course rules. There were many others over the next few years: no less than eight racecourses are said to be buried under modern San Francisco. Thoroughbreds arrived from Australia as well as from the East, and there were enough good ones for heat-racing in 1853.

In 1854 an unraced thoroughbred called Belmont arrived in California, sired in Ohio by a New Jersey stallion. Belmont was the foundation sire of the Coast, of both thoroughbreds and trotters. His best son was Langford, sire of Thad Stevens.

### Lexington

One of the leading breeders in Kentucky from the middle 1820s was the Marylander Dr Elisha Warfield Jr, who retired from medical practice and took instead to the paddock. In 1836 he bred the filly Alice Carneal, by imported Sarpedon out of Rowena, a grand-

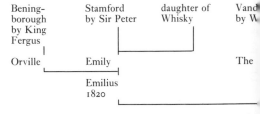

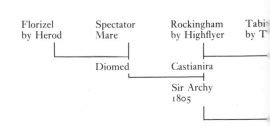

daughter of Sir Archy and tracing on the bottom line to Gimcrack and Highflyer. War-field sent Alice Carneal to Boston, and in 1850 she bred Lexington.

Lexington was first trained by a freed slave called Burbridge's Harry; he was seen, liked and bought by Richard ten Broeck, and went to A. L. Bingham's stable at Natchez. On 1 August 1854 he met Lecomte, also by Boston out of Reel by Glencoe (thus in America, but not Britain, his half-brother) on the Metairie course. The race was the Great State Post Stakes, designed for the champions of every racing state, the identities of the runners being declared only at the start. Lexington won easily from Lecomte and two others.

A week later the two sons of Boston met again for the Jockey Club Purse. For some reason Lecomte, who must have been a great horse, won both heats – Lexington's only defeat in seven races. Ten Broeck was greatly put out, and in the *Spirit of the Times* issued a general challenge: Lexington against any horse over four miles, or against Lecomte's winning time of seven minutes 26 seconds.

Lexington took on the clock at Metaire on 2 April, 1855, watched by people from everywhere in the Union. He was ridden by Gil Patrick – probably his last ride in public – who put up 3 lb. overweight at 103 lb. He was allowed a running start and pacemakers. The ground was fast. The official time was $7.19\frac{3}{4}$, but most watch-holders made it half a second less. The local newspaper said: 'The most brilliant event in the sporting annals of the American turf, giving, as it has, the palm to the renowned Lexington, came off yesterday over the Metairie course, and its result greatly surpassed the most ardent hopes and enthusiastic expectations of the friends of the winner and the lovers of the turf sports.'[21]

Lecomte's connections challenged; on the 14 April they met in a match. Lexington won easily.

The next year ten Broeck took horses, trainer and stable-lads to England, and would have taken Lexington too. But he was going blind (as Boston also did) and retired to stud before ten Broeck sailed.

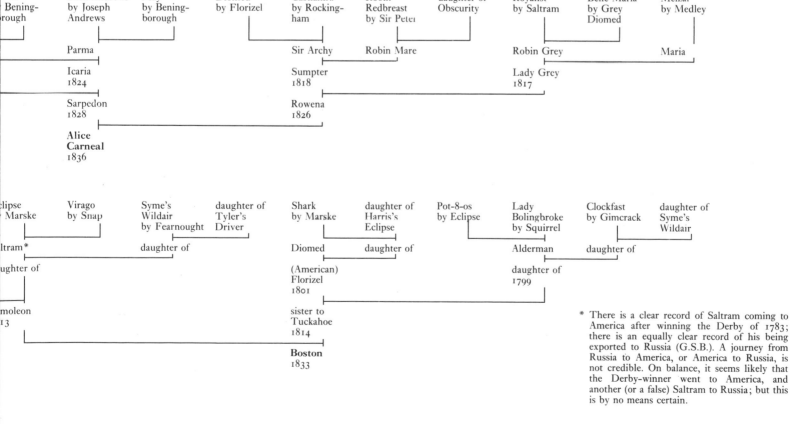

\* There is a clear record of Saltram coming to America after winning the Derby of 1783; there is an equally clear record of his being exported to Russia (G.S.B.). A journey from Russia to America, or America to Russia, is not credible. On balance, it seems likely that the Derby-winner went to America, and another (or a false) Saltram to Russia; but this is by no means certain.

While he was in England ten Broeck met Robert A. Alexander of Woodburn Farm, Kentucky, and sold him Lexington. Alexander was a Scotsman whose parents emigrated after the Revolution; his father was a friend of Ben Franklin. He was born in Kentucky but educated at Cambridge. He was extremely rich. He was a scientific farmer and stock-breeder, and took to racing and horse-breeding the year he bought Lexington. Woodburn became the biggest stud in the world, and Lexington its 'blind hero', 16 times champion sire, sire of 231 winners.

## The 'Heroic Distance'

In England, four-mile races were rare by 1800, and dead, apart from a few eccentric exceptions, by 1850. Heat-racing was dying in 1800, dead soon afterwards. The classic races were middle-distance 'dashes'.

America observed this with disdain. There was a strongly voiced opinion that American racehorses should be bred from the old stock – the blood of Morton's Traveller, Fearnought, and Jolly Roger, imported when the English still ran proper races – and not the decadent sprinters of the new century. Nevertheless, 45 out of the 160 advertised stallions in 1839 were imported.

'Nimrod' took an English view of the Black Maria-Trifle match on the Union Course in 1832, of which he knew from the young *Spirit of the Times*. The horses ran a punishing 20 miles. No English thoroughbred could have done it. The Americans were wonderfully stout, but the contest was cruel.[22]

The difference showed when Richard ten Broeck was racing his Prioress in England. She was Lecomte's half-sister (in English terminology), and trained as well as bred to stay. She was one of three dead-heaters in the Cesarewitch of 1857, and won the run-off because it was the kind of racing she was used to.

An English visitor in America, who 'not only visited the majority of the American races, but obtained the *entrée* to many of the training and breeding establishments,' was clear that the horses had more bottom than the English. He noted that three and four-mile races, and heats, were still frequent; he concluded: 'I believe that the introduction of a good American stallion would be beneficial to those who want to breed weight-carrying, fast, lasting horses.'[23]

But American racing was changing as English had changed. In the 1840s and 1850s there was a swing away from four-mile heats towards mile heats and 'dashes'. Horses normally ran as three-year-olds, often as two-year-olds. One reason that has been suggested is the Anglomania of American racing men; boys were educated in England, and learned to appreciate longer programmes of shorter races, and to deplore the cruelty (or tedium) of four-mile heats. Another probable reason is the need of owners and breeders to get an earlier return on their investment. A third is a change in the American as in the English thoroughbred, gradual but unmistakable, the result of selective breeding and of new importations.

As late as 1905 this was regretted: 'the English dash system of racing has become too popular on this side of the Atlantic for the good of our stock.'[24]

## The American Stud Book

There were more than 30 important studs in 1770, most in Virginia and Maryland; all but a handful of their mares are as much of a puzzle as the Royal Mares of Restoration England.

After the war two things happened to make this state of things unsatisfactory. One was Weatherby's General Stud Book; this may not have impressed Virginians, who relied on memory and oral tradition: but it did impress New Yorkers and Marylanders. The other

LEXINGTON. Lexington (1850; pedigree previous page) was the best horse bred in America in the 19th century. Like Man o' War 67 years later, he represented an exceptionally long-established American male line, although there was much recently-imported blood close up in his pedigree. He had limitless stamina and courage, and also the pulverizing speed which enabled him to distance his opponents in many heat-races. He became one of the greatest sires of winners in racing history.

thing was the increasing importance to Virginia, and then to Kentucky and Tennessee, of selling their thoroughbreds.

In 1815, therefore, an American Stud Book was proposed; a lot of material was collected by the Philadelphia bookseller John Bioren. It was all destroyed in a fire in his shop.

In 1822 J. J. Harrison, owner of Sir Charles and the sort of Virginia breeder who needed pedigrees to market his stock, recruited Theophilus Field and started collecting material. So a few years later did John Randolph of Roanoke. A new factor making the project urgent was the stud importance of Timoleon, whose dam's side breeding was dubious.

In 1828 Cottom published a Virginia Stud Book as an appendix to Dr Mason's *Gentleman's New Pocket Farrier*; much of the research, done by George W. Jeffreys, was in *Virginia Gazette* stallion advertisements, which was sound but not comprehensive, and no help with the mares.

In September 1829 John Stuart Skinner of Baltimore brought out the first issue of his monthly *American Turf Register and Sporting Magazine*, which collected and printed a great deal of breeding information. In December 1831 William F. Porter started the weekly *Spirit of the Times*, in New York, which also had pieces about breeding, contemporary and historical, and was another forum for discussion of the subject.

J. J. Harrison recruited Patrick Nisbet Edgar, an eager young man who rode all over Virginia collecting pedigrees from the memories or fancies of breeders. In 1833 Edgar published the '*American Race Turf Register, Sportsman's Herald, and General Stud Book*, containing the pedigrees of the most celebrated horses, mares, and geldings, that have distinguished themselves as Racers on the American Turf, from one quarter of a mile race up to four miles and repeat; also, such as have been kept in the stud – as stallions and mares for breeding, from the earliest period to the present times: and from which have descended the most valuable blooded stock at present in the United States. The whole calculated for the use and information of amateurs, breeders, and trainers of that most noble and useful animal, the Horse.'[25]

Because of his sources, Edgar is neither comprehensive nor reliable. He has one feature of great interest: many horses are characterized as 'C.A.Q.R.H.' or 'F.A.Q.R.H.' – Celebrated or Famous American Quarter Running Horses. These horses reappear in Bruce's (ultimately) official A.S.B.: but without Edgar's qualifying initials. This demonstrates the importance of the quarter-horse in Virginia's foundation stock.[26]

Benjamin Ogle Tayloe (son of John Tayloe III of Mount Airy) published his *History of the American Turf* in 1834. In the same year J. S. Skinner published the American edition of Weatherby. Presumably aware of Edgar's inadequacy, and wanting Maryland and the Carolinas covered, Skinner persuaded Tayloe to do a proper A.S.B. Tayloe in turn enlisted an experienced racing man, Wiley J. Stratton. But Tayloe and Stratton, like Randolph and Skinner himself, seem to have been daunted by the size and complexity of the job, and the book never happened.

In the same period, Dr John Irving was producing the papers which, collected, were published as *The History of the Turf in South Carolina* in 1857; unfortunately this does not constitute a South Carolina Stud Book. In Kentucky the *Franklin Farmer* was trying to collect and publish a Kentucky Stud Book. It failed.

In 1857 'Frank Forester' published *Horses and Horsemanship of the United States*, based partly on Tayloe, contemptuous of Edgar. The author was actually Henry William Herbert, son of a Dean of the Church of England and grandson of an earl, educated at Eton and Cambridge. He came to New York in 1831, and became a successful writer of stirring adventure stories for boys. He was knowledgeable about trotting, but not about the thoroughbred.

When Fort Sumter was fired upon, there was still nothing approaching an American

RICHARD TEN BROECK. Ten Broeck was born about 1810. He left West Point owing to dissipation, insubordination, or both. He became, by some accounts, a professional gambler, by others, a *chevalier d'industrie*: perhaps also both. In the 1840s he emerged as an imaginative racecourse manager. In 1853 he bought a three-year-old colt called Darley after a race at Lexington, and renamed it Lexington. Though he thus owned the best horse in America, he was too aggressive to be popular. In England from 1856 he became J. R. Keene's racing manager, with more personal but less financial success. He returned to America to die in poverty and obscurity.

Stud Book, and the issues had been thoroughly clouded by the mistakes of Edgar and 'Frank Forester'.

## Racing in Canada

Both French and English brought horses to Canada: but the population was thinly spread over a vast area, the climate was severe, and no-one raced. More horses were imported from America, before and after the Revolution: but not thoroughbreds. This was a two-way traffic: Lower Canada was breeding tough trotters and pacers from the beginning of the 19th century, and many of these went south.

ONTARIO STEEPLECHASING. On 9 May 1843 the army in 'Canada West' put on a Grand Military Steeplechase at London, 100 miles west of Toronto. This was only the second year of racing in Ontario, which in the next 15 years became more successful than that of Quebec because of an English rather than a French population. Canadian steeplechasing, beginning thus early and vigorously, was the principal parent of American.

The first racing was probably started by the 4th Duke of Richmond, who died in Canada in 1819. 'Nimrod' says it began in New Brunswick and among the Scottish settlers in Nova Scotia.[27]

The first racing recorded was at Montreal, which had a racecourse and Jockey Club by 1828. In that year the Jockey Club Purse was won by the Long Island bred 11-year-old Sir Walter from the Pennsylvania-bred 14-year-old Cock of the Rock. Sir Walter was by Hickory (by imported Whip) out of a Diomed mare; Cock of the Rock was by Duroc, out of a Messenger mare who was full sister to Miller's Damsel. As their breeding suggests, these were both successful racehorses in America before export.

Montreal had a new course at St Pierre in 1830. The prizes were small, and all the winners American.

In about 1830 at Trois Rivières, on the north bank of the St Laurence between Montreal and Quebec, racing was started by Lord Aylmer, Governor of Quebec Province. He persuaded William IV to give a King's Plate of 50 guineas, which was first run for, in two-mile heats, in 1836. It was limited to horses bred in Lower Canada; it succeeded, said a Canadian contemporary, in 'completely establishing the manly and interesting sport of racing in these hyperborean backwoods.'[28] Quebec ran for it, as the Queen's Plate, in September 1838; thereafter it was run for on various Lower Canada courses.

Montreal had meanwhile developed fox-hunting of the English type, which led to steeplechasing also of the English type: gentlemen on hunters, often their own, over a 'big and severe' course.[29] This was well established in 1840. By this date Halifax, Nova Scotia, had a Jockey Club and two annual meetings.

Ontario had garrison steeplechases in 1842 and a Grand Military Steeplechase in May 1843. The Toronto Turf Club was formed that year, racing on a course called Newmarket. It opened the Carlton Course in 1859.

Horses continued to come from America. The first major Canadian breeder was Benajah Gibb of Montreal; he imported a mare from England about 1825. It was expected that this precedent would be widely followed, and the government provided large sums to import English thoroughbreds.[30] But there were only two dozen each of imported stallions and mares as late as 1875, of doubtful breeding and no great importance. Canadian bloodstock derived almost entirely from America, and mainly from Virginia and Kentucky, whose breeders found a new market.

## Quarter Racing in the West

The quarter-horse went westward further and faster than the thoroughbred. It was the kind of horse owned by the simpler of the families who settled the new territories, and its handiness, speed, and hardiness made it an excellent cow-pony.

The settlers brought with them a love of quarter-mile racing. They ran their horses immediately, constantly, and everywhere, though the physical limitations which had given birth to quarter-racing were remote from the huge spaces of the prairies. Both tradition and the horses they had made quarter-racing far more a part of life in the South-West than thoroughbred racing ever became.

By perhaps 1850 the quarter-mile racehorse and the cow-pony, though similar, were distinct, as men had enough money for the luxury of a specialized sporting horse. The quarter-horse was thereafter of the Virginia type, invariably part thoroughbred. Many were descended in tail-male from Janus, many others from Sir Archy.

'Quarter' became a misnomer: races varied from $\frac{1}{8}$ to half a mile. There were hundreds of meetings at county seats and rail-heads; hundreds more, especially in Texas, unofficial and unrecorded, at cow-towns and behind ranch-houses.

# 20 *America:*
## *Civil War to 1914*

### *The Civil War and its Consequences*

Virginia, South Carolina and Louisiana were ruined by the war. There was a little defiant racing in South Carolina early in the conflict; towards its end there were neither horses to race nor spirit for racing. In 1865 there was hardly a thoroughbred or a dollar in the racing states of the South.

Kentucky and Tennessee were neutral, but they were constantly fought over. Many of the studs were devasted, and much of the bloodstock dispersed for safety or raided for remounts. Kentucky nevertheless continued racing: Lexington only missed one season, when an army was camped on the racecourse. Breeding was damaged but neither destroyed nor impoverished. Kentucky benefited greatly from the destruction of the old South. It had as material, above all, the first get of Lexington.

In the North, there was intermittent racing during the war at Paterson, New Jersey, and Philadelphia. Chicago raced occasionally. In 1863 Idlewild (by Lexington out of Florine by Glencoe – breeding which anticipates a whole era of racing) was brought North from Kentucky by his owner Captain Thomas G. Moore. Moore hired the old racecourse at Centreville, Long Island; in June Idlewild beat the best local horses in a four-mile dash.

In New York State, Saratoga racing started in 1863. In New York City Leonard Jerome was planning a new racing dispensation.

The most important phenomena of the decade of reconstruction were the almost total removal of the racing world from South to North; a firm attempt to put New York racing on a sound social, legal, and financial basis; and the domination of the racetrack by the sons of Lexington.

### *Jerome Park and the American Jockey Club*

In 1854 a number of New Yorkers saw the need for a central authority like the English Jockey Club. They founded the National Jockey Club, and proposed a national headquarters like Newmarket. Every racing area wanted this Mecca; agreement was unattainable. The National Jockey Club therefore built its own plant at Newton, Long Island; it failed, and became the Fashion Course, more important for harness than thoroughbred racing. The idea nevertheless persisted.

In 1863, in the middle of the war, the Saratoga Association was formed to add another attraction to a popular watering-place and gambling resort. Distinguished New York names were on the prospectus, but the money came from John Morrissey, boxer, gambler, boss of Irish immigrants, and leader of the Dead Rabbits gang on the Bowery. An experimental four-day meeting was held on the Horse Haven track in the pinewoods,

LEONARD W. JEROME AND AUGUST BELMONT. These two successful and much-travelled men were responsible not so much for the rebirth of American racing after the Civil War as for the form it took when reborn: well-managed, fashionable, and honest. Jerome was the architect of the new dispensation, Belmont its king.

where trotting was already established. It was very successful. In 1864 Horse Haven became a training-ground and a new track was opened. It was immediately a major meeting.

In the same year Paterson, New Jersey, mounted the first 'American Derby'. As a prestige race, this was a revolution in America, being a 1½-mile dash. The winner was Norfolk, another son of Lexington out of a Glencoe mare. The war had a year to run, but the fighting was far away.

In 1865 there was both need and opportunity for a major new effort in the North. The South was destroyed. The North was full of raped or refugee thoroughbreds. Kentucky and Tennessee needed new markets for their bloodstock. Saratoga and Paterson showed that a public existed. Moreover, the experiment of 1854 had to be repeated on a sounder basis: American racing needed a governing body with prestige so great that it could fight off both puritans and gangsters. Such existing New York tracks which had survived the one had been taken over by the other.

Need and opportunity were met thanks to Leonard W. Jerome. He was born and brought up in western New York State, son of a prosperous farmer. He became successively lawyer, newspaper publisher, crusading liberal politician, and Wall Street financier. He was a horseman and a lover of trotting-races. His taste for opera and horses was sharpened when he was consul in Trieste in 1852, and his enthusiasm for thoroughbred racing fanned in Paris in 1858–9. He bought Kentucky (by Lexington out of Magnolia by Glencoe) from R. A. Alexander and won the Saratoga Springs Inauguration Stakes in 1865.

That year Jerome bought an estate at Fordham, Long Island. He began to build a course: a circle with a hill in the middle. He had enthusiastic support from his friend August Belmont.

Belmont was the same age as Jerome, and a man of equal energy, culture, and love of racing. His father was the biggest farmer in the Rhenish Palatinate; he came to America as a young man in 1837 as Rothschilds' first American agent. He was an important owner and breeder before the Civil War.

Jerome and Belmont looked to Saratoga for their racecourse; they looked to England for its administration. In April 1866 the American Jockey Club first met in Jerome's office in Exchange Place; it declared these aims: 'To promote the improvement of horses, to elevate the public taste in sports of the turf, and to become an authority on racing matters in the country.'[1] Support was immediate, membership exclusive.

As soon as the Jockey Club existed and the track was built, Jerome leased the latter to the former. The first meeting was in September 1866. The whole fashionable world came, ladies as well as gentlemen, General Grant as well as John Morrissey. A contemporary said: 'Racing was a social function. Jerome Park was in its glory, and the race-horses all belonged to one's friends.' The *New York Times* said: 'Nothing goes on at Jerome Park which the purest-minded person could object to. There is no bribing of jockeys, no "dosing" of horses with laudanum. Never did the history of racing in any country begin with so fair a page.'[2]

An Englishman visited it in about 1870. On 15 October, he reported, two and four-wheeled vehicles poured from New York, having 'brushing' matches all the way. 'Soon the piazza around the club-house is filled by one of the gayest throngs of beauty a racing-man ever gazed upon. . . . If Jerome Park is unlike a park, it is certainly as much unlike an English racecourse as anything I ever saw. Still, it is a racecourse, if an invention; races take place there; it is the temple of the American Jockey Club; and is one of the pleasantest resorts for a few hours' diversion a traveller could visit. . . . The racecourse consists of circuitous roads formed on a plateau beneath the club-house. These roads, or tracks, wind round in a way something like a figure 8, and their surface is like Rotten Row, though a little harder. One instantly asks why turf is not preferred to a hard road;

and the answer readily given is that the loose earth road, hard as it is, is the more suitable for American horses.'

The Englishman was startled by the silence: no bookies were calling. But 'an elderly gentleman leaning out of the window of an elevated box is selling pools.'

The race starts and is run at a furious pace; towards its end: 'On they come, the two leaders leaving the other three concealed in a thick wall of dust, and everybody is wrong as to what is winning; a black boy, his two eyes looking like white rosettes in his ebony face, is "coming"; he has got his saddle forward on his horse's withers, and his feet are apparently kicking at his horse's mouth; but no matter, his horse is a good one, has plenty left in him to finish with, and wins by half a dozen lengths. . . . The extraordinary part of the business is, that such great speed should be attained with such wretched jockey-ship. It would be difficult to say which ride the worst, the white or black boys, so bad are both. . . . Riding is at least one thing which our Transatlantic friends do not do well, especially in the matter of jockeyship.' But the horses were good: very brave and very fast: 'The conclusion an Englishman arrives at after witnessing such a scene is, that the American horses are trained to run their races very fast, and that they all apparently, until they are beaten, pull tremendously.'[3]

## The Revival of Racing

In 1868 some gentlemen at a dinner-party at Saratoga agreed to run a Dinner Party Stakes two years later at Baltimore. Track and club both had to be created. The Maryland Jockey Club was reformed under Governor Oden Bowie, and in October 1870 it opened Pimlico. Preakness won the Dinner Party Stakes. Maryland racing expanded with the Bennings track (D.C.) in 1876 and Timonium in 1878. This brought State back to its antebellum racing strength.

Tracks near New York were hard hit by the tremendous success of Jerome Park, but in 1870 Long Branch, New Jersey, started an important new one at Monmouth Park. Long Branch was a resort attracting large crowds; it was an obvious and successful choice. The Monmouth Oaks was inaugurated in 1871. Under Pierre Lorillard's presidency ten years later, Monmouth had the longest meetings and the biggest prizes in America.

JEROME PARK. 'The American Jockey Club Races. Tom Bowling winning the Jerome Stakes for 3 year olds, value $5,500; Dash. Two miles: October 4th 1873.' Tom Bowling was one of Lexington's most successful sons, though not in the class of his greatest. He here leads from Count d'Orsay, Fellowcraft, Springbok and Merodoc. Fellowcraft and Spingbok were both by R. A. Alexander's other stallion Australian; Springbok won the Belmont Stakes that year; in 1874 he won the Saratoga Cup and in 1875 dead-heated for it with Preakness.

In the early 1870s racing began again at New Orleans and Mobile in the Deep South, and Memphis and Nashville in Tennessee. In Kentucky a new track at Louisville was opened on Churchill Downs in 1875. The first meeting introduced the Kentucky Derby and Oaks. Latonia opened in 1883.

There were many meetings in the Middle West before the end of the war, and many more soon after it. Cincinnati and Columbus were the principal of dozens of tracks in Ohio; Laclede, St Louis, the principal of dozens in Missouri; in Illinois there were new tracks every year, and soon far too many.

## Progenitors and Blood-lines

Glencoe moved from Alabama to Nashville, and R. A. Alexander collected his mares to be covered by Lexington at Woodburn. The most important products were Kentucky, Norfolk, and Asteroid. Kentucky, virtually unbeatable, went from Jerome to Belmont. Norfolk, after winning the American Derby, went west and won the inaugural race at Ocean View Park, San Francisco, in 1865. Asteroid, who raced mainly in Kentucky, was said to be the best of the three. They came at a fortunate moment of optimism and growth: they caught the public imagination and brought a new generation to the turf.

Lexington died at Woodburn in 1875; he was mourned like Diomed. His enduring importance is by way of his own and his sons' daughters. He did not depend on Glencoe (an American historian entirely discounts the nick):[4] for example one of the greatest race-horses in America immediately after the war was his son Harry Bassett (1868), bred at Woodburn out of Canary Bird by imported Albion. One of the only horses ever to beat Harry Bassett was Longfellow (1867), owned by a Kentucky racing man 'Uncle' John Harper, when, early in July 1872, he won the Monmouth Cup, a $2\frac{1}{2}$ mile dash. Harry Bassett was perhaps unfit. Later in the month he got his revenge at Saratoga, Longfellow finishing on three legs. John Harper wept unconsolably.

Longfellow was by imported Leamington, out of Nantura by Counterplot. Leamington was by Faugh-a-Ballagh. He was a good stayer in England, but, like Diomed, a failure at stud at home. He was bought cheaply by Sir Roderick Cameron and imported to his Staten Island stud in 1865. He then went to Erdenheim, Pennsylvania, owned by Aristides Welch. A contemporary said (in 1877) that he was 'in our deliberate judgment

HARRY BASSETT AND LONGFELLOW. These were two of the very best horses in America in the early 1870s, the one by Lexington, the other by his new challenger in the sire list, Leamington. They met twice in 1872. This is their first race, at Monmouth Park. Longfellow was a massive Roman-nosed brown with a white blaze; ridden by a jockey called Swim he 'smashed up' Harry Bassett (sometimes rendered Henry). In the Saratoga Cup (which he had won the year before) he broke down, but forced his rival to a new record for $2\frac{1}{2}$ miles. Longfellow was leading sire in 1891.

the horse of highest type now living';[5] in 1875 he displaced Lexington as champion sire.

With Longfellow, Leamington's best sons were Parole and Iroquois, both belonging to Pierre Lorillard. Lorillard and his brother George were the sons of a French immigrant, and multi-millionaires from tobacco and snuff. Both had enormous stables; their horses constantly met. Pierre's Rancocas Farm was smaller only than Woodburn; he was alleged to have his racing-plates made at Tiffany's. George won the Preakness five years running in 1878–82.

Parole burst into prominence in a three-horse race at Pimlico in October 1877. The favourite was John Harper's Ten Broeck (by Phaeton out of a Lexington mare, daughter of Longfellow's dam), which was the best horse in Kentucky and the Middle West. He came to Maryland because he could find no opponents at home. Second favourite was George Lorillard's Tom Ochiltree (by Lexington out of a Voucher mare), Preakness winner of 1875 and a Pimlico specialist. The outsider was Parole (out of a Lexington mare), a four-year-old gelding. To the dismay of the entire Midwest Parole beat Ten Broeck by four lengths. In 1879 Lorillard took Parole to England, where – trained by Jacob Pincus – he beat Isonomy at Newmarket, won the City and Suburban at Epsom six days later, and the Great Metropolitan the day after that.

Iroquois was bred by Welch at Erdenheim, out of Maggie B.B. by imported Australian. He did all his racing in England, trained by Pincus; He won the Derby and St Leger of 1881, and five other races out of seven as a three-year-old. Unlike Gladiateur's, these were popular victories in England, partly because in the Derby Iroquois was ridden by Fred Archer. They were even more popular in America: the New York Stock Exchange was joyful bedlam and all trading was suspended. Iroquois came back to America to stand; he was champion sire in 1892.

In 1857 Bonnie Scotland (by Iago, second in the St Leger, out of Queen Mary) was imported to New England. He covered half-bred mares in a rural area until he was sent as an old horse to Nashville. He was then immediately successful, displacing Leamington as champion sire in 1880. His best get were out of Lexington mares, a nick of enduring importance: for example Luke Blackburn (1877), out of Nevada by Lexington, won 22 of his 24 races as a three-year-old.

Luke Blackburn belonged to the brothers Phil and Mike Dwyer, owners as successful as the Lorillard brothers though of different background, their father being a Brooklyn butcher. Besides Luke Blackburn, they had Hindoo, by Virgil also out of a Lexington mare, one of the few horses ever to beat Parole. 'It is doubtful', said a man who knew the horse, 'if any horse in England could have beaten him in the great classic events.'[6] He was two-year-old champion, and then won 18 out of 20 races as a three-year-old. His son Hanover (1884) and grandson Hamburg (1895) were about the best horses of their times in America. The line descends from Glencoe.

This male line was very successful, but not as important as Bonnie Scotland's. The latter's timing was fortunate. He got sprinters and middle-distance horses, who arrived on the track as four-mile heats died and the English dash-race became invariable. The last four-mile race regarded as a national championship took place at Louisville in July 1878. Ten Broeck, still the best distance horse in the Midwest, was challenged by Mary McCarthy, champion of California. The going was heavy and the Western filly unable to act in it; Ten Broeck won. 'Such a scene of wild and extravagant excitement, I never saw before, and never expect to again, outside the impulsive state of Kentucky.'[7] The last regular event in four-mile heats was the Great Long Island Stakes at Sheepshead Bay; in 1883 this race became a four-mile dash, in 1884 two-mile heats; in 1885 it died.

Two other stallions imported in this period were similarly happy in their timing: Australian and Alarm.

Australian was one of the few significant sons of West Australian. Besides being dam's sire of Iroquois, he was great-great-grandsire of Man O' War; through the latter's get he causes the Matchem male line to flourish more lustily in America than anywhere else.

Alarm was a grandson, by a horse called Eclipse, of the Orlando who was awarded Running Rein's Derby. He was a latter-day Janus, founding a dynasty of sprinters. His grandson Domino was the first outstanding thoroughbred sprinter in America. Domino's great-great-grandson Equipoise (1928) was one of the very best horses of the 1930s. Other descendants include Colin (1905) and the prodigious money-earner Dr Fager (1964). For half a century no blood in America contributed so much to speed, except that of Lexington's great-grandson Americus: and his influence was by way of a daughter, and in Europe. It returned in the person of Nasrullah.

## New York from 1880

From the moment Jerome Park opened, the Jockey Club was fighting off puritans and racketeers. Then a greater threat appeared: urban development.

The men of the American Jockey Club therefore formed themselves into the Coney Island Jockey Club in 1879, and held racing at Prospect Park. Meanwhile they laid out a course at Sheepshead Bay, which was inaugurated in June 1880. It was dominated by Jerome, Lorillard, Belmont, and James R. Keene. Sheepshead Bay was at once the most important track in the East.

Keene was English-born, and went with his parents as a child to California. He came East, already rich, and embarked on the turf and on Wall Street. On the former he successfully challenged the dominance of the Lorillards; on the latter he was destroyed by Jay Gould. His most celebrated horse was Foxhall, bred at Woodburn, and named by Keene after his son, who became America's leading amateur steeplechase rider. Foxhall went to England where, managed by Richard ten Brocck, he was probably the best horse in Europe. Keene replaced his lost fortune with another, and he and his son bought Domino (1891), who broke the stakes record when he was still a two-year-old.

In 1894 a different group formed the Queen's County Jockey Club, and opened the Aqueduct track. The later magnificence of 'Big A' obscures its shoestring origins. But it was popular and profitable, and was shortly rebuilt on ampler lines. Jamaica was another popular track with no fashionable pretensions.

In 1905 Belmont Park, Long Island, was started by August Belmont II and James R. Keene. Also involved were J. P. Morgan and William Collins Whitney.

Whitney was a member of an old New England family, a lawyer and politician who turned a good fortune into a great one by acquiring control of the New York public transport. He took up racing in 1898, and was an ally of the younger Belmont from 1900. He won the English Derby of 1901 with Volodyovski, an English horse which had been leased to Lorillard's partner Lord William Beresford until the latter's death. Volodyovski was American trained and ridden, by John Huggins and Lester Reiff. In that year Whitney was leading owner in America with horses he had bought; two years later he was leading owner with horses he bred. The year after that he died, but like Keene and Belmont he had a son as keen as himself.

In 1890 Lorillard repeated an attempt occasionally made over the previous 40 years: he invited the managements of all the New York tracks to form the Board of Control. Four years later this body broadened the basis of its membership by including the principal racehorse owners; it became the Jockey Club, with 50 members and seven Stewards. Once again, it was intended to function like the English equivalent. It made rules and warned off misdoers. It licensed tracks, trainers, and jockeys, took over the Stud Book, and published its Calendar. Its prestige was enormous but its power qualified.

WILLIAM C. WHITNEY. Whitney, of an old family and massively successful, had one of history's most meteoric turf careers. Within three years of starting racing he won the English Derby and was leading owner in America. Within five he was also leading breeder. Within six he was dead. His family retains his tradition of racing in two continents.

## The Middle West

Racing continued to expand throughout the Middle West. There were hundreds of courses in Illinois, Ohio and Missouri. The most important centres continued to be St Louis and Chicago. The latter opened Washington Park in 1884, a large, excellent track. The Washington Park Jockey Club was modelled on Jerome's: an association of aristocrats, whose racing was fashionable and honest. It put on the American Derby in its first year.

In Missouri and Illinois there were many tracks quite unlike Washington Park. There was cut-throat competition, political graft, and control by gangsters and bookmakers. The political pendulum was swinging once again towards puritanism, and in the early 1890s the puritans had, in the Midwestern turf, a fair target. The good was attacked with the bad; racing was under growing threat of extinction.

## California

The Civil War hardly caused a ripple in the Pacific. Racing expanded rapidly in the 1860s. In 1863 Bay View Park was built, under the leadership of Senator George Hearst (father of William Randolph). In 1865 San Francisco engulfed the Union and Pioneer tracks, and threatened Bay View. A new Pacific Jockey Club built Ocean View Park on an isolated seaside site.

In 1873 California believed that it had the best horse in America in Thad Stevens, by Langford out of a Glencoe mare. He was a popular favourite because of his method of winning – running lazily until the last yards, then scrambling home. The Pacific Jockey Club offered $20,000 for a four-mile heat race at Ocean View. Thad Stevens was challenged by Eastern horses, True Blue and Joe Daniels. He beat them. Next year Ocean View increased the prize to $25,000. The seven starters included Joe Daniels and a marvellous mare called Katie Pease (by Planet out of a Glencoe mare). She won easily. In 1875 the prize went up to $30,000. Foster, by Lexington, won in an atmosphere of profound suspicion. He had retired to stud in Oregon, and came back into training to win. He was ridden by Billy Lakeland, who later trained Domino for the Keenes.

California was rich in larger-than-life characters.

Theodore Winters, known as 'Black T' because of his moustache, came west from Illinois and made a fortune in business. He bought Norfolk, and stood him at his Rancho del Rio stud. He also bought Maria (by Malcolm) who had six foals by Norfolk; between them they won an enormous number of races.

The best of these was Emperor of Norfolk, who was bought from Winters by 'Lucky' Baldwin and was one of his four American Derby winners. (He bred the other three himself.) Baldwin was a boatman on the Illinois and Michigan Canal who came west with the gold-rush. He ran a livery-stable, and took a block of shares in a Nevada mine as payment of a small debt. The mine struck gold and Baldwin was suddenly very rich. He started his Rancho Santa Anita near Los Angeles in 1873, and had a private race-track on his property. The most important horse he bred was a very fast animal he called Rey del Carreras; this was sold and renamed Americus. Through his daughter Americus Girl he is one of the most important sources of speed in modern pedigrees.

One of the best West Coast horses was Salvator (1886) by Prince Charlie out of a Lexington mare. His most celebrated victory was over Tenny at Sheepshead Bay on 25 June 1890, which inspired a poem by Ella Wheeler Wilcox:

> One more mighty plunge, and with knee, limb and hand
> I lift my horse first by a nose past the stand.
> We are under the string now — the great race is done —
> And Salvator, Salvator, Salvator won![8]

Tenny was ridden by 'Snapper' Garrison, only 22 at the time, the best jockey between

Gil Patrick and Tod Sloan. Salvator was ridden by Isaac Murphy, a Negro from Kentucky, 10 years older, retained by 'Lucky' Baldwin. He was a Fordham to Garrison's Archer, gentle and skilful. His lifetime record remains almost incredible: his wins were 44 per cent of his rides. He destroyed himself by wasting, dying before he was 40.

Salvator was owned by James Ben Ali Haggin, a lawyer from Kentucky with a Turkish grandfather, who made another of the gold-rush fortunes. His Rancho del Paso, Sacramento, had two million acres of grazing.

A different metal provided the fortune of Marcus Daly, an Irish immigrant who founded the Anaconda copper mines. His Bitter Root Stud Farm in Montana was smaller only than Haggin's; he also had studs in France and England. In 1891 he had 219 personal entries at a single track, Monmouth Park. He bred and raced trotters on a similar scale.

Another huge mixed stud and stable was that of Senator Leland Stanford at Palo Alto, started in 1873. The Bay District Course which replaced Ocean View was under his control; he also founded the Pacific Coast Blood Horse Association, intended as a western Board of Control.

A governing body of this kind was needed: in 1894 *Goodwin's Official Turf Guide* listed 40 tracks in California.

## Blackout and Recovery

In 1866 the first American bookmaker opened in Philadelphia. He made a book on cricket, rowing and racing. His precedent was followed immediately and everywhere.

Bookmakers gave the public the facility to bet, and tracks needed the public's gate-money. Consequently programmes were increasingly framed to create betting opportunities; handicaps and claiming races became more and more popular. Inevitably the quality of the racing deteriorated.

At the same time, thoroughbred racing was suffering from trotting. In 1870 the National Trotting Association was formed to clean up a dirty sport. It was sufficiently successful to drive a large criminal element from trotting to the turf. This element bribed jockeys and doped horses, behaved so uncouthly that decent people stayed away, and got control of tracks.

Jerome and Lorillard had seen the pari-mutuel in France, and saw in it an answer at once morally acceptable and financially viable; but the pari-mutuel did not catch on. Many tracks tried it. It did not suit gamblers or track managements. The last ought to have benefited from their pari-mutuel percentage; in fact they already benefited far more by controlling bookmaking.

Bookies therefore multiplied in the last 30 years of the century. Their turnover was vast. This inevitably produced dishonest racing in the absence of a central authority.

The pressure on trainers was enormous. By men like Sam Hildreth, John E. Madden and James Rowe, who trained for people like the Whitneys and the Keenes, it was resisted. By others it was not, and some of those others took their doping and venality to Europe. The pressure on jockeys was even more noticeable: and on none more so than James Forman 'Todhunter' Sloan.

As a small boy in Indiana, Sloan had such short legs that he was known as Toad; this became Tod, then grandly Todhunter. His first job was as an assistant balloonist. His build, strength, and quick-wittedness made him a good and then a brilliant jockey. In the matter of riding style he is probably the most influential single man in the history of racing. 'Snapper' Garrison rode unusually short, but Sloan amazed America by tucking his knees under his chin and lying along his horse's neck. He is said to have learned this from Indians, or from Negro boys jumping onto horses without bridles. His 'monkey on a stick' style was derided, but he won so many races that it was at once imitated, and became universal. It prevented the use of the spur, facilitated that of the whip; it kept the rider's weight over the withers, which balanced the horse; it greatly reduced wind-resistance.

Like Fred Archer, Tod Sloan was a social lion; unlike Archer he loved it. Like Sam Chifney a century earlier, celebrity and a percentage of prize-money were not enough for him. He was ostentatious and spendthrift. He betted. He rode some curious races.

Besides bookmaking, bad management, and dishonest trainers and jockeys, racing suffered from surfeit. There were too many tracks in most racing states; many had too much racing. In 1890–1 Gloucester City, New Jersey, had a continuous 176-day meeting which included Christmas and New Year's Day. In 1893 East St Louis, Illinois, had a 364-day meeting.

Gate-money, concessions, and fraudulent races made tracks very profitable; they therefore attracted the protection racket, from gangsters, police, and politicians. Only a very few tracks were rich enough, and run by men honourable and influential enough, to escape all this.

The result was inevitable: starting in Missouri and Illinois, state after state banned racing. In New York, betting was illegal from 1908. In that year the number of tracks in the United States was down from 314 (in 1897) to a bare 25. In 1910 Sheepshead Bay was killed. In 1911–12 there was no racing in New York State.

Canada benefited. Kentucky and Maryland racing also profited: but the Kentucky and Tennessee breeding industries were desperately hit. Thoroughbreds were exported in their thousands to Canada, Australia and New Zealand, Latin America, and Europe. Many trainers and jockeys had already moved to England and France; many owners also moved their strings to Europe.

The return to sanity was started by Matt Winn. He began as a poor boy in Louisville, but early in the new century he was managing Churchill Downs. In 1906 he broke away from the Western Turf Association and with nine others formed the American Turf Association. The war between the Associations was so bitter that the state of Kentucky exercised powers it already had by statute, and the Kentucky State Racing Commission became the effective authority. This precedent was eventually followed by all states whose consciences permitted racing; it made recovery possible.

In 1908, just before the Kentucky Derby, the Mayor of Louisville decided to enforce a law against bookmaking. The Court of Appeals upheld the mayor, but ruled that pool-betting was legal. Winn discovered and dusted off some old pari-mutuel machines which had been tried long before and discarded. By Derby day – 5 May – he had found 11. They did good business. Thereafter, in every racing state in America, the pari-mutuel was the only legal medium of betting.

The Belmont track reopened in 1913, inheriting the big races of the other New York tracks. The public was as delighted as the racing professionals. Saratoga opened the same season.

Chicago reopened the following year, and all over the country the racing lights began to come on again. But the numerical majority of courses were dead beyond resuscitation.

TOD SLOAN. 'Snapper' Garrison is said to have initiated two revolutions: he went flat out from start to finish, and he rode short. But an Indiana boy almost freakish when young went so much further in both regards, and was so overwhelmingly successful, that the world-wide adoption of the new technique is clearly to be credited to him. Alas, neither his morals nor his common-sense matched his ability.

## The American Stud Book

The pre-war Stud Books of Cottom and Edgar being clearly unsatisfactory, two other men entered this field of scholarship.

The first was the Iowan John H. Wallace, writer, publisher, and student of the standardbred. The first volume of *Wallace's American Stud Book* came out in 1867. In 1870 he completed Volume II, by this time miserably aware that his first volume was entirely unreliable. Wallace's Stud Book was ill-received. It was inaccurate; it used what he called the 'American system' of listing all horses alphabetically, instead of the

Weatherby system, to which everybody was accustomed, of listing foals under their dams; most fatally, Bruce had already published the first volume of his *American Stud Book*.

Sanders DeWeese Bruce was the child of Scottish immigrants to Kentucky. He had a crockery store in Lexington, then ran the famous Phoenix Hotel. He owned racehorses and collected pedigrees. He fought with distinction on the Northern side in the Civil War. In 1865 George Wilkes's *Spirit of the Times* was so Northern in bias that Southern breeders refused to look at it; Bruce consequently founded *Turf, Field and Farm*, of which the first issue appeared on 5 May 1865. The Stud Book came out in instalments in this publication.

The first volume, A–K, was published in book form in 1868, sponsored by Chicago racing men. They held a large stock of unsold copies. Bruce had a quarrel with these backers. With his Volume II he issued a revised Volume I. Volume II was not L–Z, but M–Z. The new Volume I was A–L. The old Volume I was valueless, and the backers greatly chagrined.[9] Six volumes were published, the last in 1894. Bruce was distressed financially when a fire destroyed Volume V: he was saved by Lorillard and Belmont. In 1896 the Jockey Club adopted Bruce and made his book official.

In spite of this accolade, Bruce is unhistorical. Like all his predecessors, he was primarily concerned to identify the earliest American horses with entries in G.S.B. The identification was often ingenious, usually speculative, sometimes clearly false. The most famous example is Fallow (or Follow), sire of Timoleon's fourth dam, and identified by Bruce with Vernon's Fallower.

## Steeplechasing

The first recorded jumping race in America was at Hoboken, New Jersey, in 1844. The Hoboken track, owned by C. S. Browning, had been put out of business by the Union Course, and was now used for trotting. The new race was in heats; in each four 4 ft hurdles were jumped. A Canadian won, beating Hiram Woodruff on a local horse. The experiment was repeated in 1845. Then Browning died, and with him his jumping races.

His idea was imitated, on a small and impermanent scale, at various places before the Civil War. The best documented races were at Fauquier White Sulphur Springs, a fashionable resort in Virginia. These lasted from 1846 to 1849. The course was a mile circuit with two ditches and two stiff 5 ft fences oddly described as hurdles.[10] The horses were probably half-bred hunters, the riders amateurs, and the prizes insignificant.

Steeplechasing of a more recognizable kind started at the successful Paterson, New Jersey, track in 1865. On 7 June there was a race over three circuits of the mile course. The obstacles were artificial, but imitated fair hunting country. There were four runners. The Canadian Nannie Craddock won. Dennis Ready, who rode his own Zig Zag, took the wrong course. 'Many thought it a cross. We thought him drunk,' said a reporter. 'Ready was not so much drunk as he was dishonest,' said his editor.[11]

These horses toured, giving what seem to have been exhibitions. Nannie Craddock, Zig Zag, and two others ran at Lincoln, Massachusetts, on 10 November 1865: 'Steeplechasing has hitherto been considered an exlusively English sport, but we are glad to know that through the exertions of some of our first citizens who have taken to breeding thoroughbred horses, that peculiarity of racing is being introduced into this country, and with the aid of several gentlemen from Canada the first steeplechase of any note ever witnessed in this part of the country took place at Lincoln in this State, yesterday.' Several hundred ladies and gentlemen were present, in spite of raw weather; there were no accidents; Nannie Craddock won by a length from Copeck. 'The whole affair was admirably managed and successfully carried out, and we hope that it is but the inauguration of similar meetings at another season.'[12]

In October 1869 Leonard Jerome added a steeplechase to the programme at Jerome Park: a $25 sweepstake with $1000 added. 'The novelty of the thing just struck the people, many of whom had not the remotest idea of what a steeplechase was. . . . Thus the mystification brought interest in the event, and likewise brought out the largest assemblage seen before the inauguration, or since. . . . The 'chase was a success. The people pronounced it "immense", and it was the all-absorbing topic for weeks.'[13]

Thereafter a steeplechase was a regular part of the Jerome Park programme. It added to the popularity of the meetings. In June 1875: 'the balconies of the clubhouse, terraces below, the slopes on either hand, and all the green, where till then no foot had been, swarmed with elegant ladies and their attendant gentlemen.'[14]

Pimlico held its first steeplechase on 28 October 1873, on turf. From this date there was usually one 'chase on every day of racing. There were 'chases, more or less regularly, at Saratoga, Washington D.C., and New Orleans. At Newport, Rhode Island, in September 1877: 'It would be impossible to enumerate the prominent ladies and gentlemen present. . . . The course is most picturesque in its situation, surrounded with scenery of a romantic nature. It was pronounced by prominent horsemen to be the finest in the country. The turf is thick and springy, the ascents and descents gradual, and in every detail no improvement could be suggested.'[15] There were three steeplechases and a polo-pony race in two days.

Beacon Park, Boston, held its first meeting over four days from 3 September 1878. It moved to Clyde Park in 1881. In 1882 the Myopia Hunt Club (all of whose members wore spectacles) put on a meeting at Medford, near Boston, which became the 'Country Club' meeting.

On 19 May 1883 the Meadow Brook Hunt Club mounted their Hunt Cup. On 10 May the following year the Rockaway Hunt Club put on its Great Long Island Steeplechase in direct imitation of the Aintree Grand National. This attracted 18 starters – by far the biggest steeplechase field to date. A Maryland horse won, ridden by an amateur, but there were professionals in the field. The distinction between the two branches of the sport had not been made.

At Pelham, Westchester County, the first meeting on 18 October 1884 was attended by Jerome, Lorilland, and the cream of the New York turf. The amateur element was strong. The riders in the Farmers' Race really were farmers, as their clothes insisted; one was dressed for baseball.

Hunt Club racing of a distinct point-to-point type was started in 1859 by the Rose Tree Fox Hunting Club, named for the ancient Rose Tree Inn in its country near Philadelphia. They raced over the post-and-rail fences already there, adding hurdles and a wall. In the 1870s there were flat, hurdle, and steeplechase races, all completely amateur. The Myopia meeting near Boston became, by contrast, normal open 'chasing over artificial brush fences.

The Genesee Hunt Club (Geneseo Valley, between Rochester and Buffalo, New York State) was founded in 1876 and ran its first races on 19 October 1885. They raced for a silver jug, four miles across country, go as you please. This became an annual event so amateur that no records were ever kept.

The Maryland Hunt Cup originated with the Elkridge Fox Hunting Club, who bought a cup in 1894 and challenged the Green Spring Valley Hunt. The course was $4\frac{1}{2}$ miles in the Worthington Valley, near Baltimore, had massive timber fences, and was limited to hunters and Maryland hunt members.

The only comparable obstacles were those of Meadow Brook, of which an Englishman wrote in 1892: ' "Surely you don't ride at a flight of rails like that?" I inquired, pointing to a first barricade that met my troubled gaze – to wit, a morticed erection of oaken bars, each of them as thick as a man's thigh and the lot carried considerably higher than an ordinary Leicestershire gate. "Why, yes! That's nothing much. The farmers aim at

JEROME PARK. This is the Handicap Steeplechase Purse of $600, of which $100 to the second, run on 6 November 1877. From the right the horses are Deadhead, New York and Dandy; they finished in that order. Races like this so increased the popularity of Jerome Park that the normally-empty grass slopes (see illustration p. 224) 'swarmed with elegant ladies and their attendant gentlemen.'

setting their fences at four feet eight, to keep their stock in." I asked no more, but held my peace while the horrid parallel intruded itself upon my mind, of the condemned man in the prison cart catching a first view of the gallows awaiting him. But I gazed and gazed as each successive bone trap hove in view; and, you may depend upon it, the longer I looked the less I liked them.'[16]

In Virginia and South Carolina amateur steeplechasing was all the racing there was. In Virginia, once again in Fauquier County, the Warrenton Riding Club put on races over very stiff country from 1875. Effie Deans won the first race, from a horse ridden by an Englishman: 'The air was rent with deafening cheers that seemed to reel like drunken shouts from the multitude.' The winner 'had won it by the hardest, most dashing ride ever performed in the country.'[17] South Carolina had the Aiken Chase, run over the natural fences of the Aiken Drag made bigger.

While hunting men were racing over their terrible timber, the fences in the open steeplechases at Pimlico, Saratoga, Chicago and the rest had degenerated (like those in England a few years earlier) into small brush affairs which were galloped through rather than jumped over. Thus the two branches of American steeplechasing grew more and more sharply different. The amateur prospered; the professional showed shrinkage rather than growth.

Prize-money in the professional branch remained small compared to the flat; steeple-chasing depended on a small number of sporting owners, of whom the principal were the Whitneys, Foxhall Keene, and Thomas Hitchcock. Hitchcock went to Oxford, where he rode in the Christ Church Grind in 1882. His first win in America was at Meadow Brook in 1883. He trained jumpers successfully for himself and his brothers. He was the moving spirit behind the Grand National Steeple Chase at Sheepshead Bay in 1899, and the Champion Steeplechase of America at Morris Park in the same year. (Morris Park, Westchester County, had been, like Gravesend, financed by James Morris and run for the Jockey Club by Leonard Jerome.)

Organization and authority, on the lines of the English National Hunt Committee, were attempted in 1891 with the National Steeplechase Association, founded by August Belmont II. It amalgamated with the National Hunt Association in 1897, and became the National Steeplechase and Hunt Association. Its rules were widely, but not universally, accepted.

## Canada

By the time of the American Civil War, the focus of Canadian racing had moved from Quebec to Ontario. In 1859 the Toronto Jockey Club petitioned for the Queen's Plate, on the ground that its racing was now the more important, and in 1860 got it. It moved to various Ontario courses, and was limited to Upper Canada horses.

At this point Canada got a number of good American horses, sent north for safety; these included a draft from Alexander of Woodburn, mostly by Lexington, which were at once the best in Canada.

In 1881 the Englishman T. C. Patteson founded the Ontario Jockey Club. Its first president was Sir Casimir Gzowski. Its first races were 17–18 September 1881, its new course Woodbine, Toronto. Woodbine became the permanent home of the Queen's Plate in 1884; the race shrank from two-mile heats to a $1\frac{1}{4}$ mile dash.

Gzowski was succeeded by his vice-president William Hendrie, a very successful owner-breeder, and the first Canadian to win major American races on the flat. After Hendrie the leading figure was the distiller Joseph Seagram. He won the Queen's Plate at Woodbine eight times running, 1891–8, then twice more in 1900 and 1901. When it became the King's Plate he won it five times from 1905. He was the biggest breeder in Canada, and imported from both Britain and the U.S. He was President of the Ontario

Jockey Club for 13 years, and, like Hendrie, a member of the English Jockey Club.

The best horse in Canada in this period was Advance Guard (1897), bred in Tennessee by Great Tom out of a granddaughter of Leamington. He won 48 races out of 162, running all over Canada and the United States. He went to stud at Woodburn; when the bottom dropped out of the thoroughbred market he became a fine sire of hunters.

Canadian racing grew as the St Lawrence basin became richer and fuller of people. There was constant traffic across the frontier. American horses came to Ontario and Quebec; Canadian steeplechasers raided south; and in the 1880s American speculators started tracks near the border but inside Canada. Windsor, Ontario, opposite Detroit, started as a trotting-track in 1884, but became a thoroughbred racecourse when racing was killed in Michigan. Fort Erie, opposite Buffalo, started in 1887.

Montreal formed a new Jockey Club in 1907, with the Blue Bonnets course. Edward VII endowed a King's Plate for Lower Canada horses. As at Woodbine there was regular steeplechasing.

In 1911–12, with American racing blacked out, horses and horsemen swarmed north. In some ways this was good for Canada; in some ways very bad. If the large crooks went to Europe, many of the small ones went to Ontario. There were suddenly dozens of fraudulently-run little tracks. This aroused a moral and political reaction like America's; immediately after the First World War betting was outlawed. The recovery of Canadian racing, like American, was made possible by the pari-mutuel.

## The Indians

The great fighting tribes of Texas became marvellous horsemen, and the Comanche best of all. In about 1840 they were described by a traveller as passionately addicted to racing and to heavy betting.[18]

In the 1870s this addiction had if possible increased. At Fort Chadbourne, Texas, the Comanches under Chief My-la-que-top had 'a miserable sheep of a pony, with legs like churns, three inches of rough hair all over the body, with a general expression of neglect and helplessness and patient suffering which struck pity into the hearts of all beholders.'[19] With this pathetic creature they challenged the horses of the garrison. The pony carried 170 lb. and was ridden by a young Comanche buck carrying a club. Heavily backed by the Indians, he beat the third best horse of the garrison by 400 yards. He then beat the second best. Amazed, the U.S. Cavalry produced their best horse, 'a magnificent Kentucky mare of the true Lexington blood'. The Indians chuckled and piled on more money. 'The Indian threw away his club, gave a whoop, and the sheep pony pricked his ears and went away two feet to the mare's one. The last fifty yards of the course was run with the rider sitting with his face to the tail of the pony, grimacing horribly, and beckoning the rider of the mare to come on!'

The sheeplike pony was a fast quarter-horse, camouflaged in his winter coat. The Indians' *coup* is reminiscent of Willie Jones and his Trickem in North Carolina 100 years earlier.

Another tribe of Indians, far to the north-west, gave their name to a new breed of horse which was raced. This was the Appaloosa, a variously coloured breed characterised by large spots and a white rump. In conformation the Appaloosa is a quarter-horse of pony size (14.2 to 15.2 hands: the quarter-horse is the same size as the thoroughbred). The name has been said to derive from the Appalachian Mountains, or the Spanish *pelusa* or French *pelouse*: it comes in fact from the Palouse Indians. [20] The Appaloosa was bred primarily in Oregon, and raced at country fairs in the North West.

THE FIRST FUTURITY. America lagged far behind Europe in two-year-old racing; the invention of the six-furlong Futurity at Sheepshead Bay, at $40,900 the richest race ever run until then in America, was a deliberate attempt by the Coney Island Jockey Club in 1888 to establish two-year-old racing as a major part of the programme. (Maurer's picture is dated 1889, which has confused some historians.) The inaugural race had a field of 14; it was won by Proctor Knott, a gelding by Luke Blackburn out of Tallapoosa by Great Tom, ridden by S. Barnes. Haggin's Salvator was second, beaten half a length after a titanic struggle; Galen was third. The Futurity went to Saratoga in 1910 and 1914, to Belmont 1915–1958, and then to Aqueduct.

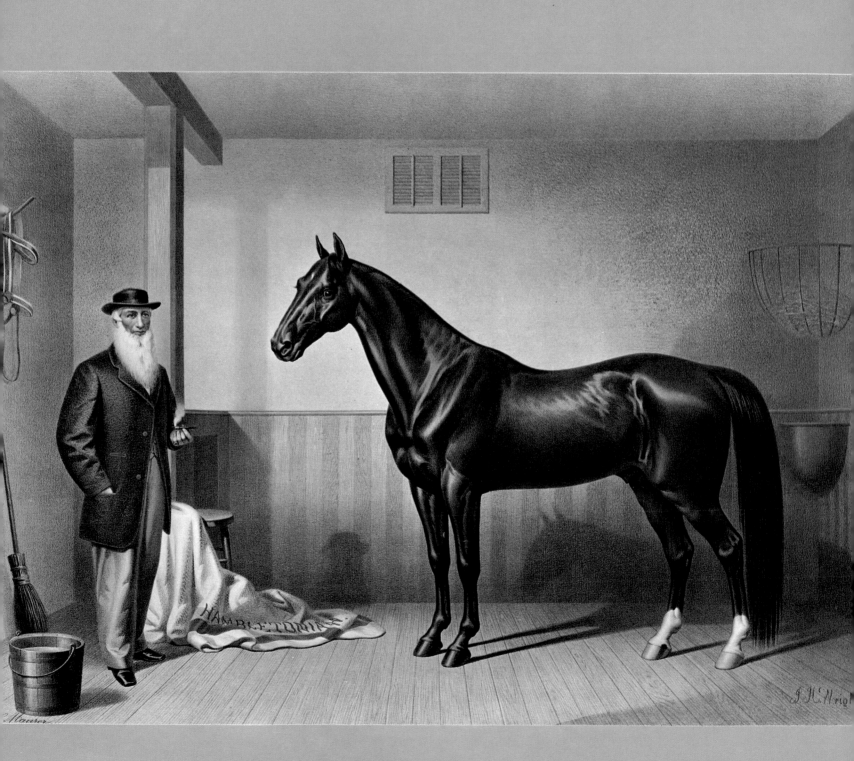

# 21  American Harness Racing

## 18th-Century Origins

In the early 18th century roads good enough for the wheel were restricted to the streets of towns. In the North, this had two results: the development of pacers for travel, and the growth of harness-racing in the streets.

The great pacer was the Narragansett. Rhode Island, more tolerant than northern New England, had a lot of pacing-races at such places as Little Neck Beach. In the puritan states, trotting in harness was a seemly mode of travel, and impromptu races were inevitable. In New York State the 'court party' were importing, breeding, and racing thoroughbreds; the 'country party' trotted. Especially in Orange County, 'brushing' matches became a tradition of great local vitality.

The Revolution meant cavalry; it also meant wheeled transport. A contemporary said: 'In the Revolutionary War trotting horses became more valuable for teaming than pacers, would sell better in the market and could be easier matched. After the war, trotters were valuable for transportation and raising of pacers consequently ceased.'[1] The roads must have been improving greatly. The trotting-horse was also improving. In about 1778 a traveller described the gaunt New England horses whose high-action, long-striding trot made them intolerable to ride for any distance, but magnificent in harness.[2] Puritan opinion was meanwhile hardening against thoroughbred racing. This combination of circumstances created American harness-racing.

## Trotting in New York

In 1802 in New York thoroughbred racing was illegal. There were no tracks. Horses could only run on the road. Trotters, saddled or harnessed, were perfectly happy on the road, and matches against the clock were morally acceptable. In 1806 Yankey, a Connecticut-bred from New Haven, trotted a mile on the public road in 2 minutes 59 seconds (hereafter written 2.59), 'a rate of speed', said a newspaper, 'it is believed has never before been excelled in this country.'[3]

There had been many matches against time in 18th-century England, but this intense preoccupation with the clock – legal, even moral, in origin – was special to America. It influenced the handling of the thoroughbred, since owners, breeders, and even trainers were often concerned equally with trotters and thoroughbreds. It has been argued that clock-watching in training (with which Jacob Pincus amazed Newmarket when he prepared Iroquois to win the Derby) derived from the trotting tradition of meticulous timing.[4]

The year after Yankey's mile record, 3rd Avenue was built in New York north from the Bowery to the Harlem River; its length, width, straightness and surface made it the

RYSDYK'S HAMBLETONIAN. Hambletonian (one of many of the name) was bred about 1850 by Aballah, a Messenger, out of a mare who was a Bellfounder-Messenger cross. Typically, the breeder was an upstate New York farmer, the owner a hired man. Hambletonian's early successes were in the show-ring, as country fairs had hardly started racing: but in the early 1860s he established himself as the outstanding sire of trotters. His best get were Dexter, who broke all records, George Wilkes, leading sire in Kentucky, and Electioneer, leading sire in California.

city's trotting-track. The Jamaica Road on Long Island, which led from the Brooklyn Ferry landing into the area of the Long Island stock farms, was a rural equivalent. Light vehicles were matched together, without moral obloquy, on both roads.

Saddle-trotting was a more serious business. 'The first trotting race of any note I ever saw came off in the Summer of 1817 on the Jamaica Turnpike, Long Island, between the halfway house and Snedicor's for $1000, two miles out, under saddle, between a large bay horse owned by John Treadwell, Esquire, Long Island, and a small chestnut road horse from Boston, called Boston Rat, about fourteen hands, two inches, high. When the time was called, the Rat was brought out of the barn close at hand, clothed in an entire suit of brown linen – not a hair visible from the tip of his nose to the coronet of his hoof, intended to prevent knowledge of his color as they had further objects in view. The horses were ordered to the scratch, the bay horse mounted by William Baxter and the Rat by Mr Samuel Purdy of Eclipse fame. The Rat took the lead from the score and won easily, no time being kept to my knowledge. This was a "ring-in" by some sharps from Boston, but the thing was soon exploded, the knowledge of the little horse having trotted in two-thirty-eight before coming to New York having spoiled further chances for speculation.'[5]

## Messenger

The Boston Rat was one of the champions who were coming out of the North-East. Others were The Boston Horse and Boston Blue, both of which broke records. This obscurely-bred tribe was eclipsed by a new male line of overwhelming importance.

G.S.B. in 1800 said of Lord Grosvenor: 'His stud of racers is unparalleled. And from a superb creature called Mambrino, formerly appertaining to his lordship, the breed of horses for the coach is brought nearly to perfection.'[6] Mambrino was a thoroughbred of the Darley Arabian male line. He sired thoroughbred racehorses as well as 'horses for the coach', which were natural trotters. His pedigree explains the former fully, the latter not at all.

In 1780 Mambrino sired Messenger, a big, ill-tempered grey out of a daughter of Turf, she out of a daughter of Regulus. Messenger was exported to Philadelphia in 1788, intended as a sire of thoroughbred racehorses. He stood in Pennsylvania, New Jersey, and New York; he died on Long Island in 1808. He sired a good many thoroughbreds, including Miller's Damsel, dam of American Eclipse. When thoroughbred racing was suppressed, Messenger was put to 'cold-blooded' mares. So were his sons. He was not imported to get trotters; his sons were not bred to do so. The greatest ancestor of trotters owes his influence to puritan legislation.

In 1822 a Mr Boot of Boston imported the Norfolk trotter Bellfounder, who arrived with a pedigree which John H. Wallace later found quite incredible. To Wallace's eye when he came to England in 1878 (his purpose being to track down Bellfounder's true pedigree), Norfolk Trotters were like Morgan horses: slower than Messengers, but useful for substance. 'Bellfounder's blood mingled kindly with old Messenger's blood, and that of the whole trotting family. The Hambletonians . . . were out of a mare by Bellfounder.'[7]

## Trotting on Tracks

In 1821 New York relented; racing was allowed back. Trotting had meanwhile become established and popular.

The effect of the new laws was to allow trotting as well as thoroughbred racing on tracks. The first track trot was on 27 May 1823, on the Union Course, the day and place of the great match between Henry and American Eclipse. It was the brainchild of Harry Costar, a young blood who trotted against his friends on 3rd Avenue. He arranged with the

Jockey Club to include a trotting race – saddled, two-mile heats, for $1000 – as an additional attraction. The field of six included Costar's Betsey Baker, a Boston horse called The Moccasin, and Topgallant, who won.

Topgallant was by Coriander by Messenger, out of a half-bred mare by (Bishop's) Hambletonian by Messenger – inbred 2 × 3. He had been a racehorse; when that career was killed he pulled a cart in Philadelphia. One day he and his team-mate bolted; he was seen to trot as fast as the other galloped; he had a new career. He was trained and ridden by George Woodruff, uncle of Hiram. Hiram was only six at the time of this race, but he was riding Topgallant at work four years later.

In 1825 the New York Trotting Club was formed, and the next year opened Centreville, Long Island, a mile beyond the Union Course on the Jamaica Turnpike. The Club put on three days' racing, saddle and harness, in two and three-mile heats. The track was ideal for training as well as racing, so training-stables blossomed all round Centreville. It was already a horse-breeding area; it became a specialized trotting-horse breeding centre.

Five years later the second New York track was opened: Harlem Park, on land belonging to the Red House Tavern. This was owned by John Woodruff, George's brother; it was inherited in 1845 by his son Hiram. The old Beacon Course at Hoboken was rebuilt for trotting by that Browning who also experimented with hurdle races.

In 1828 Philadelphia formed the Philadelphia Hunting Park Association, which built a track and put on trotting races. This event was welcomed by 'Nimrod', who had not heard of Centreville or Harlem.[8] A correspondent wrote to the *Sporting Magazine* that a horse had trotted the mile at Philadelphia in 2.35 (faster than Boston Rat by three seconds; than Yankey by 24). This was simply disbelieved in England, until events the next year showed not only that it was true, but that, already, a new breed of horses existed which trotted faster than any in the world.

## Supremacy of the American Trotter

Trotting-races, all ridden, became popular in England in the first quarter of the 19th century. John Lawrence claimed sole credit: 'It cost me upwards of twenty years' solicitation and botheration, both oral and scriptural, to induce our trotting jockeys to set up racing weights, and make use of chosen level roads;' this 'has since become the established custom in all regular trotting matches.'[9] Pierce Egan described 'the chaps in the Sporting World, denominated "*Trotters*"; their very souls, as it were, seem interested upon nothing else but "trotting-matches", – it is quite a *mania* among them, from the proprietor of the humble *donkey*, the natty kill-bull up to the *Heavy Swell*.'[10]

In 1828 news of the Philadelphia 2.35 mile prompted Lawrence to say: 'American miles must be shorter than English miles.'[11] But next year he was writing: 'In the present Spring, 1829, two American trotters have arrived, one of which, Ratler, with nine stone, trotted ten miles over a level road, in about thirty-one minutes and a half.'[12] Ratler was already a champion in America, both in harness and ridden; he was brought to England by his owner William Whelan, Hiram Woodruff's friend. After the time-trial, he was matched against a celebrated Welsh mare Miss Turner, on 25 April 1829, for £200, 10 miles between Cambridge and Godmanchester. This aroused extreme interest; all Newmarket came to watch. Ratler was ridden by his American groom William Hagerty; he gave the mare a minute and about three stone (42 lb.). English rules were used: if either horse broke (from trot to gallop) it had to stop and make a full turn. Ratler won in 30 minutes 40 seconds, 'a feat unparalleled in the history of horse-flesh in this country.'[13]

A Mr Melville had meanwhile been training his Paddington Mare to trot in harness 100 miles against the clock for a wager, but abandoned the idea. Instead he imported Tom Thumb – a 12-year-old, only 14 hands tall – and his American groom. They had

Yale University Art Gallery; the Mabel Brady Garvan Collection.

LADY SUFFOLK. 'Lady Suffolk, the celebrated trotting mare, and her rider, Albert Concklin as they appeared on the BEACON COURSE, HOBOKEN, N.J. on the 12 July 1843.' Lady Suffolk, who inherited the size and colour of her ancestor Messenger, brought the mile record down to 2.26½, trotting against the clock at Hoboken. She was then a 10-year-old. She trotted another 11 years, latterly in harness.

only 10 days to get him fit. Tom Thumb trotted from the fifth milestone on Sunbury Common into Staines, and thus back and forth for the 100 miles. He did it in an incredible 10 hours 7 minutes. (The previous record, set up by Crockett's Mare in 1793, was 11 hours 40 minutes.) Pierce Egan said Tom Thumb was 'unseemly in his aspect – rough in his coat, and, at first sight, slouching in his gait. . . . The match-cart, which was made in America, was one of the lightest we have ever seen, not more than 108 lb., and decidedly the most compact, although not the most elegant. . . . Many began to "guess" that he would vindicate the fame of the Yankee breed of trotters, which are acknowledged to be the best in the world.'[14]

The 'Yankee breed' were the best in the world because they had a much larger proportion of thoroughbred.

## Saddle to Harness

After Topgallant's day, the greatest trotter in America was Lady Suffolk, 'The Lady of Long Island', who first raced as a five-year-old in 1838. She trotted 162 races in 16 years,

Yale University Art Gallery; the Mabel Brady Garvan Collection.

FLORA TEMPLE AND PRINCESS. '. . . in their great match for $5000, over the Eclipse Course, L.I. June 23rd 1859. Two mile heats in harness.' This was the second of their three meetings in June and August. Princess (once Topsy) won both heats. Her fastest mile was 2.26. Flora in August did 2.22. Princess, here leading, is driven by Jimmie Eoff, Flora by D. Tallman. Princess was 12, Flora a little older.

her owner Dan Bryan being, though honest, thick-skinned and greedy. She had limitless courage; she broke every record.

Lady Suffolk's first 50 races were under saddle. This was still usual in the early forties: which was partly a consequence of tracks, partly of people. All tracks had bad surfaces and tight corners; none were banked. All were dominated by amateurs who were apt to be big, strong men and to prefer riding. In the 1840s these men – the generation who had invented the sport – were ageing. But they preferred driving themselves to putting up professional riders. Thus, after 50 races under saddle, Lady Suffolk trotted 112 in harness.

The survival of a jolly, amateur spirit is well illustrated by a wagon match on the Beacon Course on 16 June 1841, involving Samuel Cooper and Hiram Woodruff: 'In the fourth heat the horses were lapped every inch. Finding he could not pass, anyhow he could fix it, Hiram commenced singing his little hymns in a voice of such volume and power as would have raised Lablache or Fornasair out of their boots. Washington wouldn't break up for the reason that as soon as Hiram would begin shouting, Sam commenced giving his irresistable imitation of a crazy coffee-mill, in so loud a tone as to drown Hiram's yells so far as Washington was concerned, besides making Hiram laugh in spite of himself.'[15]

In 1804 the two-wheeled sulky had been invented, the body hanging on eliptical springs from enormous wheels. In 1829 Pierce Egan marvelled at Tom Thumb's 108 lb. 'match cart'. In 1839 there was a famous series of matches between Hiram Woodruff's Dutchman and Awful; the sulkies weighed 82 and 68 lb. In 1843 they were still considered horrible by the old school: 'In his sulky, Hiram Woodruff looked, as all riders in those ugly contrivances do, like an animal with an axletree through him and wheels to his hips, but he drove so beautifully as to abate the usual ridicule of the vehicle.'[16] There were still a lot of races to wagon, a four-wheeler usually made to weigh 250 lb. In races involving the two, sulkies gave wagons three seconds a mile.

There were a few ridden matches in the 1850s; but by the middle of the century the wheel had so far displaced the saddle that all trotting was known, generically, as harness-racing.

## Flora Temple and Topsy

In 1850 a Dutchess County man saw a little bob-tailed mare tethered to the back of a farmer's wagon. He bought her, and passed her on to one of the 3rd Avenue dashers, George Perrin, who named her Flora Temple and sent her to Hiram Woodruff. She was the darling of the New York ladies; she was compared to a cricket and to a humming-bird; she became the first trotter so pre-eminent as to be unmatchable.

In 1847 in New Hampshire a filly called Topsy was foaled, descending on the top line from Messenger. She was too wayward to ride or drive; she worked in a sawmill. She was bought as a broodmare by A. M. Billings. He only allowed her back to her foal if she kept to the trot. If she broke she had to go all the way back to his office and start again. Billings sold her in 1855 to David A. Gage, a Chicago hotel-owner. George P. Floyd long afterwards wrote: 'During the winter we used to drive our horses for speed on the ice of the Chicago River and it made a grand drive usually from November to March. In December, 1855, a race was made for a wine supper for 10 between the Tremont House bay mare Topsy and the Briggs House gelding Sorrel Charlie, to be trotted on the ice over the river. The supper was to be served at the losing hotel. The race was trotted to skeleton sleighs. Topsy was driven by Otis Dimmick and Sorrel Charlie by the writer. The supper was served at the Briggs House! This was Topsy's first race.'[17]

Otis Dimmick was the top driver in the West, and he did extremely well with Topsy. She was sold to New Orleans, and then to California, where Jimmie Eoff renamed her

Princess and raced her at Sacramento. On 2 March 1859 she met Glencoe Chief in a 10-mile match to wagons for $36,500. She won. Eoff brought her to New York (by sea, by Panama) to meet Flora Temple.

On 16 June 1859 they met: three-mile heats to wagon. Flora Temple won. On 23 June they met again: two-mile heats to sulky. Princess won. On 6 August they met a third time: mile heats to sulky. Flora Temple won, bringing the mile record down to 2.22. Clearly it took a trotter as great as Princess to extend Flora. (In 1840 a saddled horse was set to give three seconds to one in harness; but by 1859 sulkies were so light that harnessed horses were faster.)

Meanwhile several parts of America had developed a taste for trotting greater than they could satisfy with local horses. Stars from Long Island and Kentucky began to tour, running in exhibition matches for a share of the gate-money. This was known as hippo-droming, and it was the only way Flora Temple could find races. Flora and Princess toured together, trotting in front of huge crowds, from Maine to Illinois. Flora Temple brought her own record down to 2.20. She retired after 11 seasons and 103 races, of which she was beaten in 17. In 1875 she still looked 'very lusty and jolly'.[18]

## Vanderbilt and Bonner

The railroad spoiled 3rd Avenue for trotting, which moved over to 8th and Harlem Lane. There brushing was at its most expensive and exciting. Its king was Cornelius Vanderbilt, too uncouth to mix with the great, but with his railway fortune able to buy superb horses. He bet heavily and often backed himself in matches.

An even larger owner of trotters was Robert Bonner, publisher of the *New York Ledger*. He took up driving for his health; he loved strenuous competition, but refused on moral grounds ever to race or to bet.

Eighth Avenue brushing included team-racing with pairs or, occasionally, more. Both Bonner and Vanderbilt had famous teams. Typically, Vanderbilt challenged Bonner. Bonner, refusing to bet, had to refuse the challenge. Instead, he drove a celebrated time-trial on the Fashion Course, after the regular races, on 13 May 1862. His team were the 'Ledger Mares'.

> The trump of fame has told the name
> Of each delightful charmer;
> Beyond compare are Flatbush Mare
> And glorious Lady Palmer.[19]

Bonner then offered $10,000 as a gift (still not betting) to any owner-driver who could beat his time. Vanderbilt kept quiet. All this took place in the middle of the Civil War.

An English lady visited Bonner's stable a little later; she inspected an 18-month old colt just bought for £3000 (not dollars) for his pedigree: 'I should have thought five shillings nearer the value of the goose-rumped, heavy-headed little quadruped.'[20] (This English view of the American trotter was not unusual. An English officer thought Rysdyk's Hambletonian looked exactly like a mule.)[21] Bonner himself supervised all shoeing in his stable; 'he told me we knew nothing about that art in England'.[22]

Some of the best trotters in America were lost to the track because Bonner bought them. The most startling example was Dexter, trained by Woodruff, supreme champion of the late 1860s. Bonner bought him for $35,000, in order to drive him on 8th Avenue.

## Breeding

The backgrounds of Flora Temple and Topsy are typical. They were both bred by up-country farmers who owned a mare or two which they had covered by members of

TROTTING IN HARLEM. The Red House Tavern and its land, in far northern Manhattan, were owned by John Woodruff, who in 1830 opened the Harlem Park trotting track. His son Hiram inherited the property in 1845, established America's most famous trotting stables, and became by far the most influential and respected man in the sport. From the look of the vehicles and the driving in the wagon-race shown, it was early in his tenure.

well-known families. There were no records or pedigrees. All that were known were a few male lines: the Messengers, Bellfounders, Morgans, Clays, Pilots.

Messenger blood was diffused all over the Union, principally by his sons (American) Mambrino and (Bishop's) Hambletonian. The Bellfounders were not in the same class, but Bellfounder nicked with Messenger. The Morgans were not usually raced, but the Black Hawk branch in Vermont produced a champion in Ethan Allen. The Clays were nearest in class to the Messengers; they descended from Henry Clay (by Andrew Jackson). The Clay horse George M. Patchen beat Flora Temple more times than any other trotter. The Pilots were Canadian: Pacing Pilot was an Ontario horse who went to New Orleans and transmitted first-class pacing and trotting ability.

Jonas Seeley, of Sugar Loaf, Orange County, one day bought in New York a broken-down little mare which had been bred by his father. She was by a Bellfounder out of a mare by Hambletonian. Seeley covered her with a useless rogue called Aballah, himself inbred to Messenger. He sold mare and foal cheaply to his illiterate hired man Bill Rysdyk, who called the foal Hambletonian. Rysdyk's Hambletonian, and his get, began winning at local fairs.

(The fairs began early in the century when Elkanah Watson, of Berkshire County, Mass., tied two imported Merino sheep to an elm-tree in Pittsfield and charged people a few cents to look at them. A new institution was born, which spread widely and rapidly. All kinds of animals and produce were shown and judged, including harness-horses: but these were never raced until, to the scandal of the farming press, the U.S. Agricultural Society Fair at Philadelphia in 1856 included trotting races. Thereafter attendance at all fairs depended on races.)

'AT THE FAIRGROUNDS'. Trotting races became part of the attractions of the fairs in the 1860s; during the period of trotting's most rapid growth – the early 1870s – the smallest fairs at the remotest villages had races. The vigour of this rural tradition kept trotting alive during its nadir just before the First World War.

Hambletonian covered a Henry Clay filly which died. The orphan foal (which liked rum) was bought by the New York amateur Eph Simmons; he named it Robert Fillingham and beat Vanderbilt in an 8th Avenue brushing match. It then went into serious training with Horace Jones at Fashion. On 10 September 1862 it trotted a match against the great Ethan Allen. The betting was unprecedented. Robert Fillingham won. He went on winning. He was renamed George Wilkes, after the editor of the *Spirit of the Times*. In 1873, at the end of his career, he was sold to Lexington. Kentucky had been breeding good trotters for 50 years; George Wilkes made them much better.

His success made Rysdyk's Hambletonian the most fashionable trotting stallion in America, supplanting Mambrino Chief, another Messenger. His son Dexter broke records for saddle, sulky and wagon, and then, when Bonner removed him from competition, for price. Another son, Electioneer, went to Leland Stanford's Palo Alto and became the leading sire in California. Hambletonian's own covering-fee rose to a startling $500.

Hambletonian's excellence derived from his thoroughbred blood. This suggested to a new generation of commercial breeders that still more thoroughbred could only mean still greater speed. John H. Wallace violently opposed this policy. Not only, he said, would new infusions spoil the character of the American trotter by making it less hardy: it would also produce horses which it would be impossible to stop from galloping. Both views contained truth; both were overstated. Stanford, using thoroughbred stallions, bred extremely fast trotters, many of which could not be kept to the trot. The modern standardbred is a very nice balance between the theories of Stanford and Wallace.

## Growth, Decadence, and Reform

The English historian Rice wrote in 1879: 'At present most of the races – and all those of any importance – in the New World are run between horses either driven in harness or ridden by jockeys over trotting courses.'[23] Rice hardly does justice to Jerome Park and the rest: but it is true that trotting grew enormously in the years after the Civil War. The 1095 races of 1869 grew to 3304 in 1875; in the latter year 5400 trotting-horses started.

This growth had a number of consequences. It meant more tracks. Most villages had one; big cities had several. As programmes grew longer, races had to get shorter. One-mile heats to sulky became standard. Saddle and wagon races almost disappeared. More races over shorter distances met the demand of the public for more betting opportunities. They also reflected a change in the horse. The breeding industry grew prodigiously; only a small proportion of post-war trotters could stay the old distances. Races had more starters: a pre-war average of two or three became an average of eight or 10. The large numbers of inferior horses had to have races framed to give them a chance; they were divided into categories according to their best times. Inevitably horses were pulled to keep them in the lower classes.

Good horses were toured, not in the hippodroming exhibitions of Flora Temple and Princess, but in proper races. In order to co-ordinate dates and conditions, the Quadrilateral Trotting Combination was formed, in 1873, by the managements of the Cleveland, Buffalo, Utica, and Springfield tracks. This became the Central Trotting Circuit, adding Rochester and Poughkeepsie, in 1875, and the Grand Circuit the following year. It was inaugurated at Cleveland in July. Three of the best-known drivers, Doble, Green, and Mace, apparently arranged that Doble should win with his marvellous 19-year-old Goldsmith Maid. In spite of ruthless tactics by the three, a young Kansan called Marvin upset the *coup* by winning with his Smuggler.

This disreputable arrangement, by famous men at a leading track, shows what had happened to trotting in the years of growth. The old amateur spirit had gone. Owners,

drivers, track-managers, and officials were rogues. Trotting became by far the largest gambling medium in the country, thus attracting every kind of criminal. The social tone fell with the moral. In New York in 1866: 'Few women will attend the Fashion course, never the Union or the Centreville courses.'[24]

In 1870 a reforming group founded the National Association for the Promotion of the Interests of the Trotting Turf, which became the National Trotting Association. Its objects were: 'uniformity in the government of trotting, the elevation of the standing of the American Trotting Turf, and the prevention, detection, and punishment of frauds thereon.' Forty-eight tracks joined at once, then more and more, until staying out was virtually a declaration of dishonesty. 'The change from infamy to respectability', said John Wallace, 'was magical.'[25] Women reappeared on the track. Drunks, gamblers, gangsters, and pickpockets moved into thoroughbred racing.

## Times, Tracks and Sulkies

Hiram Woodruff was against early work. He said trotters must be treated quite differently from throughbreds, given plenty of time, and expected to get to their best at seven or eight.[26]

In the 1870s this philosophy was completely abandoned. At Palo Alto trotters went into training as soon as they were weaned, going very short distances meticulously timed. (In order to test his theories, Stanford sponsored Eadweard Muybridge's Zoopraxoscope, an ancestor of the ciné-camera and projector.) Two-year-olds and yearlings clocked some extremely fast times. Racing young horses was thus possible; it was also as attractive to owners and breeders as in thoroughbred racing.

The new generation of fast short-distance trotters made spectacular improvements to times. The Orange County horse St Julian trotted the mile in $2.12\frac{3}{4}$ in California in 1879. The next year Vanderbilt's Maud S. (granddaughter of Hambletonian) did $2.10\frac{3}{4}$ in Chicago. In 1884 she did $2.09\frac{3}{4}$, $2.09\frac{1}{4}$, and then (having been bought by Bonner) $2.08\frac{3}{4}$.

Breeding and training on Stanford's lines were partly responsible for faster times. So were track surfaces, which were better engineered and better kept. The turns were the limiting factor; even when they were banked the sulky skidded and slowed. In 1887 the 'kite track' was invented. It was bad for spectators but good for times, which were cut by two seconds. Two sets of records then became official: a horse would be credited with 2.11 and 2.09 K.

The ball-bearing had meanwhile been invented in England. In 1888 Dr Dunlop invented the pneumatic tyre. The two were combined in the bicycle. In 1892 Sterling Elliot put bicycle-wheels on a sulky. The veteran Doble refused to drive the ludicrous, tiny-wheeled vehicle; the crowd mocked it. A young man called Ed Geers drove it and won. Small wheel, ball-bearings, and pneumatic tyres knocked two seconds off times, made the kite-track unnecessary, and in the single season of 1892 became universal. In 1892–3 every trotting and pacing record was broken, and the mile brought down to 2.04.

The limiting factor now became wind-resistance. The driver's seat was accordingly lowered. Then in 1894 J. D. Chandler broke a record driving Online by using a pace-maker to cut his wind-resistance. This device was picked up by Geers and used in races. It became a normal tactic: a position tracking the leader was the 'golden spot'.

In August 1897 the pacer Star Pointer broke two minutes with a mile in $1.59\frac{1}{4}$. The first trotter under two minutes was Lou Dillon in 1903. She had a pacemaker. Dan Patch, the greatest pacer of his time, made a new record with three pacemakers: ahead, beside, and behind. Prince Alert broke this record: his pacemaker carried an enormous canvas windshield. A newspaper called it an 'Auto-trotto-yachtic' race.[27] Dan Patch recovered his record, finally pacing a mile in $1.55\frac{1}{4}$ at Lexington. Pacemakers were then disallowed and times became a little slower.

ROBERT J. This horse, the 'Pacing King', brought the mile record down to 2.01½ in 1896. This was made possible by the tiny, derided bicycle-wheels with ball-bearings and pneumatic tyres. The driver offers a lot of wind-resistance, and breaking the two minutes required a change of position and the use of a pacemaker. The 'sidewinder' action of the pacer is well illustrated.

## Exports, Amateurs and Twilight

In 1888 A. E. Terry took some American trotters to Paris. His Misty Morning won the international Prix de Ste Maude, beating the Russian Kozyer and the French Capucine, both champions. Terry took his string on to Hamburg, Berlin, and Vienna. The European trotters were tougher and more powerful, and could manage long distances on bad surfaces. But Terry's were much faster.

This led to a moderate export trade, mostly from Kentucky, to France, Italy, and Russia.

In 1893, just as every record was being broken, the industries of Kentucky and California had suddenly no domestic market. Foreigners could buy good American horses cheaply. Well-bred trotters were exported in enormous numbers. Trainers and drivers went to France and Russia. Trotting began to recover about the turn of the century; by this time European trotting had been irrevocably changed by American horses and American methods.

Horses, harness, and sulkies came on the domestic market very cheaply. Professionals were out of business; amateurs bought them. Brushing-matches had been driven off 8th Avenue by streetcars, so a New York Driving Club was formed, which held amateur races in Fleetwood Park. The idea spread to Philadelphia, Baltimore, Cleveland, and Chicago, and there were festive inter-club matches. These 'Matinée' meetings were fashionable and well-run; there was no betting.

There was still a sentimental attachment to the old street matches; in New York the Road Drivers' Association managed to have brushing matches on Jerome Avenue, and then on a two-mile speedway along the Harlem River. This also spread to other cities. The amateur sport, both track and road, grew lustily while the professional was in distress.

The greatest trotting-horse of the Matinées was the mare Lou Dillon, owned by C. K. G. Billings (son of the owner of Topsy); she broke two minutes in 1903. She was beaten in the race for the Memphis Gold Cup by Major Delmer, owned and driven by Elmer E. Smothers. Smothers's trainer afterwards confessed that Lou Dillon was doped. Billings brought a law-suit, which failed for lack of proof: but the purity of the amateur sport had been irreparably defiled.

Although there was general recovery in the noughts, and favourites like Dan Patch could draw the crowds, harness-racing was in an unhealthy state. The car drove brushing off its remaining roads, and tracks had more and more competition for the public's money, especially from baseball. In 1905 there were about 50,000 trotters in training; only 10,000 ever reached a track; only 5000 paid their way. Money could only be made dishonestly, and the sport sank again as it had in the 1860s.

The legislation of an earlier age had given harness-racing its chance, but the laws of this period hit trotters as hard as thoroughbreds. The Grand Circuit tracks stayed open, but with small crowds and small prizes. Most tracks shut. In 1912: 'The only hope for the trotting game now is through the fairs, state and country. They constitute about ninety-five per cent of all meetings.'[28] This was not the 'blackout' of thoroughbred racing, but it was not far off.

The wave of exports of the middle 1890s was repeated. The most spectacular example was Harvester, who was trained by Ed Geers for the Milwaukee brewer August Uhlein; he was unbeaten as a three-year-old and five-year-old, and only once beaten as a four-year-old. He was bought by Billings and taken with his other horses to Europe in 1912. Billings refused an enormous offer from the Russian government for Harvester. He contemplated crossing American trotters with Orlovs, but in the end brought Harvester back to Virginia. He was not, ironically, a good sire.

# 22　South Africa

JAN VAN RIEBEECK. The leader of the first Dutch colonists was the founding father of the Caper, the half-bred horse of Cape Colony. Like Columbus, he found a horseless country, the prehistoric African species having been destroyed by tse-tse fly and horse-sickness. The Javanese horses he imported were descendants of those sent to Java direct from Arabia from about 1300 (Ibn Batuta reports the trade). To them were added Persian and South American (Andalusian) horses. The first English thoroughbreds consequently had some good genetic material to work on.

## Origins at Capetown

The Dutch arrived in South Africa in 1652. They needed horses. Jan van Riebeeck asked for a shipment in 1654; it arrived from Java the following year. Van Riebeeck criticized the horses as too light.[1] In 1689 stallions were imported from Persia. A local breed developed, still small. In 1778 some South American stallions were brought, and in 1792 – three years before the Dutch surrendered to the British – the first English thoroughbreds.

In 1795 Mr Pringle, Agent of the British East India Company, brought a thoroughbred mare, and another Englishman a stallion called Nestler. Nestler sired The-Hen-that-Lays-the-Golden-Eggs, a broodmare of great value; and out of Pringle's mare bred South African Eclipse.

In June 1796 the 34th Regiment formed a Turf Club at Capetown, and on 18 September 1797 the first garrison races were held: four days, four military races and a match, and a Dutchman's Purse of 40 pagodas for local residents. Tom Walduk, riding Mr Vos's Aert, unused to the English saddle, fell in the first heat, but won the next two. 'The meeting was attended by all the fashion in Africa. . . . On Friday an elegant Ball and Supper given by the Club was opened with the greatest éclat by Lady Anne Dashwood and General Fraser. The Hon. Mrs Campbell, patroness of the Club, appeared in an elegant dress, with a bandeau on which was worked in gold letters "African Turf Club". . . . We are happy to say this gay scene was attended with only two accidents. Lord Macartney's groom in running had his leg broke from his horse falling. And Mr Maxwell, his lordship's secretary, had a narrow escape of his life, having tumbled into a pond, coming from the Ball.'[2]

The same year J. F. Kirsten imported Lord Grosvenor's Mambrino and three other stallions, and two thoroughbred and two half-bred mares.

In January 1800 Lady Anne Barnard wrote to Lord Macartney, now back in England, that under the new Governor Sir George Yonger 'our races are to be encouraged, for in addition to the Cup given by the Lieutenant-Governor the Governor is to give the *King's Plate*.'[3] There was a Spring meeting that year, 13 races over five days, starting 6 October. The races were on Green Point Common, which was rough, stony, and beset by dogs. All nationalities were interested, especially the Malays, who were addicted to betting. Cows, grazing on the course, often joined in the races.

In April 1801 a match was held at 10 stone; one horse bolted; the other rider lost an iron and weighed in light. The shoes and all their nails had to be taken off to make the weight.

In 1802 General Sir Francis Dundas was Governor. He started a new African Turf Club, which held a three-day meeting in March and another in October. 'Since the possession of the Cape by the English', said a contemporary, 'the breed of horses has been attended to and materially improved, and the races established by the garrison have contributed greatly to this end.'[4]

The next year the Cape was ceded back to Holland. The Turf Club died, and its clubhouse and effects were sold by auction. In 1806 the British were back again, and the Turf Club reformed with 150 members. The new Club held its first meeting on 14 April 1807: seven races in four days, limited to country-breds the property of members. There were four meetings that year, in all of which a horse called Sir Charles, of unknown ancestry, started and won. The Club then died.

It came to life again in 1810; Sir Charles was forbidden to run, and went to stud. In 1813: 'We have to announce the arrival from England of a superb elegant gold cup, the liberal donation of the late William Maude (formerly possessor of Wynberg) to this settlement, for the improvement of the breed of horses. The donor directed that His Majesty's King's Plate Articles should be observed by such horses, mares and geldings as will run for the Wynberg Gold Cup, carrying 12 stone each, the best of three heats on the Wynberg Course. Distance about one mile and three-quarters.'[5] In its early years it was won by descendants of Nestler and Mambrino.

## Lord Charles Somerset

In April 1814 Lord Charles Somerset arrived as Governor. His dictatorial personality was more acceptable to the Dutch than to the English, but his devotion to racing and breeding was genuine, and his methods successful. He reconstituted the Turf Club, and at the meeting of October 1814 himself had seven winners. He imported about 30 thoroughbreds, turned an official Experimental Farm into a stud, and encouraged others to import. Among those who did was a speculative shipper, Captain Christopher; his most notable contribution was Roderick Dhu, by Sir Peter Teazle.

Somerset's policy brought about a remarkable improvement in the Cape horse, noted by several travellers in the early 1820s.[6] Breeding became a major industry. (The Burgher Senate recognized this in 1822 by giving a Town Cup and Purse to benefit local breeders.) Its importance was not primarily on the South African racecourse, road, or farm, but in export to India. Captain Christopher was one of many exporters. Capers had been taken to India as early as 1796 and raced there from 1812; in the 1820s the trade became vital to the South African economy. The half-bred Caper by an imported thoroughbred stallion was the colony's most valuable cash crop. The biggest importers and breeders, after Somerset himself, were rich Boers such as Sebastian van Reenens, who imported the prolific sire Loyalist. Mauritius also imported and raced Capers, and the British garrison started racing on St Helena.

Racing spread rapidly east from Capetown: to Paarl in 1815, Uitenhage and Stellenbosch in 1816, and half a dozen other places by 1825. Its popularity was ascribed, by a British official from India, to there being nothing whatever else to do.[7] 'Nimrod' quotes a description of Hottentot jockeys riding races with bare feet.[8] Many races were also owner-ridden. Stellenbosch was the biggest provincial meeting; in the mid 1820s Lord Charles Somerset would arrive with a suite of servants and a string of horses. Capetown remained headquarters; the first Cape Derby was run there in 1828 – South African-breds, otherwise exactly as Epsom. P. V. van der Byl won the first three Derbies, with Eagle, Haphazard, and Blücher.

LORD CHARLES SOMERSET. Somerset was the younger son of the 5th Duke of Beaufort, who had been Master of the Horse. He inherited a love and understanding of horses, and a personality which combined arrogance of manner, hatred of opposition, and a certain ruthlessness of method. These qualities enabled him to bring about, within 10 years, a startling improvement in the half-bred Caper and its racing. The one was never again as good after his time; the other not until the 1880s.

## Decline of the Caper

In the next 30 years in Cape Province there was a certain decline. Stellenbosch, after the glories of the 1820s, closed in 1830. The Albany Turf Club at Grahamstown closed in 1837, though it managed to restart in 1842.

Breeding also deteriorated. There were grave difficulties – horse-sickness and military disturbance. The South Africans made their problems worse by underfeeding young stock, ignorant breeding, and a superstition (like that of the Russian court) against white markings. Stallions, including expensive imported ones, were looked after as casually as mares. Of four neighbouring breeders in 1845, one had three live foals from 61 mares, the next two from 30, a third six from 36, and the last eight from 43, of which six died.[9]

This was all very foolish. An English officer wrote in 1858: 'The Cape horses have been universally praised by travellers; they are particularly hardy, game, and docile. The climate in many parts of the colony is well suited to breeding. . . . At Cape Town the breed is a compound of the English thoroughbred and the Arab. Several well-known horses have found their way to the Cape, having been purchased for exportation when they were stale or broken down.' These imports have 'acted as fountains for supplying a stream of pure blood through the equine veins of Africa. Nearly a hundred horses of tolerable English fame have been landed at the Cape within the last twenty years.'[10] The South African Stud Book[11] shows about 90 thoroughbreds imported from 1845–50, more in the next two decades, and some also from South America, Australia, New Zealand, and France. Extremely few were mares: South Africa made little attempt to breed thoroughbreds. 'Druid' said in 1856 that the colony had imported good horses in Lord Charles Somerset's time, but now got very poor stuff.[12] Consequently 'a horse is frequently seen with forequarters equal to fifteen hands, and hindquarters only large enough for a pony.'[13] The result was that the Cape lost the Indian market to Australia.

There were exceptions. Miss Whipthong (by Mr Giles out of a Buzzard mare) was imported in 1815. She had a daughter Cat-o'-Nine-Tails (by imported Kutusoff) whose great-granddaughters by imported O'Connell were The Belle of Rondebosch (1841) and Sweet Lass of Rondebosch (1844). The full sisters won everything in 1843–6. In April 1845 The Belle won the big race at Green Point in a south-east wind so violent that the other horses could not gallop against it, and in dust so dense that the race was invisible. She went to Lucknow, Sweet Lass to Mirzapore; both were champions.

Horace Hayes wrote in 1900: 'The Cape horse of 40 or 50 years ago was a strong, serviceable animal that was well up to remount form, and was prized in cavalry regiments in India. At present he is as extinct as the quagga. His place is now taken by a weedy slave.'[14]

Cape breeding was not helped by the circumstances of Cape racing. Green Point was still unenclosed; cows still joined in; dogs caused accidents; the course was rough and covered with stones. In 1847 the Club undertook to clear the largest rocks off the course two months before racing, in order that the horses could be trained.[15]

Natal started racing in 1852. The first meeting was at Durban, on the Clairmont course, on 14 January. The finish was roped; the whole town turned out; a 'Stand called Grand' had been built, but most spectators preferred their carriages.[16] A South African historian says the races were from the beginning for thoroughbreds,[17] but in 1852 this is frankly incredible. An Englishman said the racing was well-contested and amusing. One race was mile heats with four flights of hurdles. Most of the riders fell and one ran out in the first heat, but one 'very powerful-looking jockey on a distanced horse, insinuating that he would break anyone's head who said he was distanced, seemed to have some influence with the judge, who decided that this man's horse was to be allowed to start in the second heat.'[18] He won the second heat, and had only to walk over for the third. But he sent his horse home. Another claimed the prize. There was a terrible altercation. All the disputants, and all the officials, were English.

## Thoroughbreds and the Rand

In 1860 the country began to make rapid progress. Racing and breeding grew likewise.

Apart from prosperity and expansion, the phenomenon of the 1860s was the racing of thoroughbreds. Some were imported, some bred. In 1861 Mr Manuel, whose stud was just outside Capetown, imported Ropedancer (by Voltigeur); she beat every half-bred Caper until 1866. Manuel, influenced by his jockey Jack Thomas – later a great trainer – then won the Cape Town Trial Stakes every year from 1866 to 1871, always with a thoroughbred. Imported Brian Boru, in April 1866, won the Queen's Plate and Governor's Plate – consecutive races – and the Visitors' Handicap at the same meeting, giving local horses up to $4\frac{1}{2}$ stone (63 lb.). The locals were 'Cape thoroughbreds', by imported stallions out of half-bred mares.

In Natal, there was racing at Pietermaritzburg as well as Durban from 1869. The Breeders' Plate was won three years running, from 1870, by sons of imported Naughty Boy. The Durban Turf Club opened a new course in 1881, and ran a Natal Derby from 1882. This was always won by thoroughbreds.

There was some racing in the Eastern Province in the early 1870s; the Jockey Club of South Africa opened the Port Elizabeth course in 1882. Capetown had a 'South African Derby' in 1882, but the race of that name which was regarded as the real one – until it moved again to Johannesburg – was Port Elizabeth's in 1885. It was won by Oxygen by Plunger, a most valuable importation by Mr Cloete. Marquis, also by Plunger, won the second running; he was bred by J. A. Faure at Eerste Rivier (once van der Byl's) and was considered by contemporaries the best horse ever bred in South Africa.[19]

Racing was established in the Transvaal by 1880. In 1887 Financier, another son of Plunger, won the Malmain Gold Cup at Mafeking. Johannesburg was still an outsize mining-camp in 1885, but it already had the City and Suburban racecourse. In 1889 there was a celebrated match there between Black Prince and Discount. Black Prince won but weighed in light. The Stewards followed the 1801 Capetown precedent and allowed his shoes. They were not enough. According to one account, when the nails were added the jockey just made the weight; according to 'Jim Crow' Black Prince's mane and tail were cut off and added as well.[20]

In 1890 Johannesburg was a city of 60,000, with a fine new racecourse. Two things made racing in the Rand an immediate success: a largely British and German population, and incalculable wealth.

In 1892 Green Point and Kimberley were moribund, and only Port Elizabeth was flourishing in the South. In Natal, Durban and Pietermaritzburg were at a low ebb.[21] In the Orange Free State, a few sportsmen at Bloemfontein and Harrismith tried to get up races, but with only moderate success; but racehorses were useful for smuggling diamonds over the frontier. It was in the 'primitive races' at Dordrecht, during the Kaffir Wars, that Robert Sievier ran his first racehorse, which won second money in a two-horse race.[22]

Johannesburg, by contrast, had prizes of £1500; there were flat and steeplechase courses, with proper starts and an enclosed paddock like Sandown's. There was also flourishing pony-racing. There were a great many bookies – a term used locally to include card-sharps – of whose skill at cheating the simple Boers the Johannesburgers talked with pride. English horses were dominant. Imported Vichy (by Hermit) had won only two selling-races in England in 15 starts. Cured by Hayes of a sprained suspensory ligament, he won the Johannesburg Handicap.[23]

The Boer War stopped English horses coming. Argentines took their place, and won nearly every big race from June 1899 to September 1905. Australians also began to arrive in 1903, the first brought by Richard Wootton. With peace came English horses again, as well as a number of Irish; those that did not win races were important to South African breeding, which still needed constant infusions of fresh blood.

# 23 Australia and New Zealand

## Origins

The first horses arrived in Australia from the Cape in 1788. They were lost by a convict herdsman. Between 1795 and 1800 about 40 came, of many more sent. Chileans also arrived from Valparaiso.

The first race-meeting was put on by officers of the 73rd Regiment in October 1810, at Parramatta, just inland from Sydney. A horse called Parramatta won, and Miss Betty won a trotting-race. This garrison racing foreshadowed all subsequent Australian turf history by being an immediate success. There were three or four day meetings in August the next three years, and then, after an inexplicable gap, May meetings from 1819. By 1821 the races were large and well-organized. The runners were largely Capers but the first thoroughbred stallions were beginning to arrive from England.

In 1825 the Governor Sir Thomas Brisbane, 'patron saint of the Australian turf',[1] founded the Sydney Turf Club; there were two days in April, three in September. Racing at Parramatta was in March. In 1826 Sydney had a new course. In 1827 Campbelltown opened, with three £50 races. In 1828 a horse called Abdulla won a £1000 match (an enormous stake for the place and time), and then won two races the next day.

In that year the Australian Racing and Jockey Club was founded, racing at Parramatta, maintaining its rivalry with Sydney. The racecourses were 14 miles apart, yet 'as remote as Epsom and Doncaster.' In the next 12 years racing started at 10 places within 100 miles of Sydney. By 1837 these courses were enclosed and charging gate-money. New South Wales was civilizing itself by means of 'race-courses, public-houses and jails'.[2]

In 1840 the Australian Race Committee started Homebush. They adopted Newmarket Rules and held a St Leger and a Gold Cup. In April 1842, at Homebush, the Australian Jockey Club was formed. The first two-year-old race in Australia was run in September.

Far to the South, in the Port Philip Settlement, the first races were held in 1838. Five hundred people came, on 6 March, to see four races round Batman's Hill. Batman himself (who founded Melbourne) won two of them with his Postboy. The next year there were two meetings and twice as many people.

Meanwhile two Ayrshire brothers, James and Alick Hunter, were riding races against each other on a piece of open ground on the Saltwater River. In 1840 this was adopted as the official racecourse and named Flemington. It was inaugurated in March by the Port Philip Turf Club. This split into the Victoria Jockey Club and the more influential Victoria Turf Club, which were in a state of constant and damaging war. They were both disbanded in 1853 and the Victoria Racing Club formed. It ran a Victorian Derby at Flemington from 1855. The Melbourne Cup was four years older.

Caulfield, near Melbourne, opened in 1858 as a course for amateurs. It was inaugurated with a 'hurdle race for bullocks' with ten starters.[3]

Adelaide started racing about the same time as Melbourne. In 1855 the South Australia Jockey Club ran a St Leger and in 1860 a Derby.

Racing in Tasmania – Van Diemen's Land – may have started earlier than Melbourne or Adelaide. 'Nimrod' in 1843 reports three days racing at Hobart, with 6000 people on the course.[4] A Colonel Mundy said: 'The running was absurdly bad, but there were some very nice horses on the course.'[5]

There were thus four totally distinct racing communities. In 1859 the first 'Champion Race' was held between the states, at Melbourne.

The following year the Australian Jockey Club moved from Homebush to the new Randwick course in Sydney. The rate of progress, rapid from the beginning, was thereafter almost vertiginous.

## Creation of the Waler

The early racehorses were Capers. The expansion of the 1820s and 1830s justified the importation of thoroughbreds from England. It has been calculated that 22 stallions arrived by 1839.[6] Some of these were good; sons of Whalebone, Emilius, and Priam. The most successful was Cap-a-Pie, imported in 1838 or 1839, by The Colonel out of Sister to Caetus; he was sire of Sir Hercules, one of the greatest stallions in Australian history, sire of The Barb and Yattendon. None of these stallions left an enduring male line, but their mares were the foundation of the Waler.

Before 1835 the mares were Caper or a Caper-Chilean cross. Between that date and 1855 thoroughbred mares came from England. They were widely dispersed, and no records were kept of their progeny. Some of the 'squatters' who had them, aware of the value of purity in the market, sent them only to thoroughbred stallions. Some were covered by half-bred stallions, and thoroughbred stallions covered half-bred mares. It follows that Australia had plenty of thoroughbreds, but they were indistinguishable from half-breds except in conformation or their owners' conviction. Thoroughbred or half-bred, by the middle of the century Walers were magnificent horses. Australia profited immensely from the deterioration of the Caper, and the Waler became the pre-eminent horse of India.

Good stallions continued to arrive. The most important after the middle of the century were The Premier (imported 1849), leading sire for many years; and, above all, Fisherman, by Heron out of Mainbrace. He ran in 119 races in England, winning 69 including

FISHERMAN. Fisherman (1853), by Heron out of Mainbrace, was bred in England by W. S. Halford, and then changed hands repeatedly. He was a horse of the utmost stoutness and quality, and the most important stallion imported to the Antipodes until Musket. He sired three Victorian Derby winners, but his enduring importance is as an ancestor of broodmares, such as his daughter Mermaid, dam of Melody, dam of Melodius, dam of Carbine's best son Wallace.

the Ascot Gold Cups of 1858 and '59. He was imported to South Australia for £3000 in 1860.

Importations of this class, the popularity of racing, and the value of the export trade made thoroughbred status important. Archibald Yuille's *Australian Stud Book* insisted on a high standard of historical certainty. Inevitably, many mares claimed as thoroughbred were excluded. Their owners were furious, since yearling values changed dramatically. Yuille stood firm.[7] The thoroughbred Waler can accordingly be accepted as a thoroughbred.

The Tasmanian horse was distinct. 'Nimrod' was told that only English thoroughbreds raced at Hobart in 1843,[8] which is hard to believe; but they certainly imported good horses from an early period. The government gave energetic assistance and the climate was favourable. But according to a Tasmanian about 1860, as the colonists spread north from Hobart they included less knowledgeable men who needed horses quickly; they imported low-class thoroughbreds and bred them injudiciously.[9]

## Growth of Racing from 1860

The Australian Jockey Club had a Derby at Randwick in 1861, then the two-mile Sydney Cup. Racing started in Queensland, and there was a Brisbane Cup in 1870. Flemington, Adelaide, and Hobart added to their prizes and their programmes. 'In 1870 the stakes run for at the races of the Australian colonies exceeded in value those of all the governments of the Continent put together; without counting the catch-weight races which are held whenever a few stockmen . . . are gathered together.'[10]

In spite of its new course and its splendid fixture-list, Sydney racing was in the 1860s far below Melbourne. 'The supporters of the turf at that time were men of small fortune and still smaller character.' Horses run at Sydney were 'owned and manipulated by the dregs of the Australian population'.[11] Things were shaken up by the Irishman Sir Hercules Robinson (later Lord Rosmead), Governor of New South Wales 1872–9; Randwick climbed to Flemington's level.

Western Australia started in a small way in the 1870s. In 1879 there was a Perth Cup. Progress was slow because until gold was discovered the country was poor and thinly populated.

In the last third of the century, Australian racing developed at several levels.

The top level was as good as the best in the world. At Flemington in the 1880s 'stand, refreshment rooms, beautiful lawns, and flower-beds, far surpass anything in England. The weighing-stand, casualty-rooms, lavatories, jockeys' dressing-rooms, down to the minutest details, have been rendered well-nigh perfect.'[12] There were large and expensive training-tracks of sand, cinder, and tan. Time-trials were widely used. (The training-tracks swarmed with touts with stop-watches.) 'Melbourne', said an English bookmaker, 'stands alone as the greatest horse-racing city in the world. The entire population seems to exist on racing.'[13] Nat Gould agreed: 'At Randwick, Sydney, and Flemington, Melbourne, racing is carried on in a way that would astonish English race-goers.'[14] So did Bob Sievier: 'The accommodation and comfort afforded to the public at Flemington, Randwick, and Caulfield, put in the shade the stands and space allotted in England. . . . I know of no stand in any part of the world that can compare with that of Flemington.'[15] Adelaide's Morpethville and Brisbane's Eagle Farm are described in similar terms.

At the next level of prosperity and popularity were the suburban meetings of Melbourne and Sydney. There were 300 days' racing a year in the immediate area of Melbourne, as well as pony-racing three times a week. Typically these were proprietory courses, laid out by speculators seized with the 'craze for building racecourses'.[16] Some, like Sandown, were very good and well run. There were certainly too many of them. Mordialloc was started by a journalist 'Braddy' Bradshaw, who once kept a racehorse in his kitchen because he could not pay for stabling. Elsternwick was started on reclaimed swamp-land by the Victoria Trotting Club. American businessmen were the principal supporters. But the sport did not catch on. It was turned into a racecourse until the 'goody-goodies' opposed the renewal of its government lease. 'Never was a grosser breach of faith perpetrated by any Minister of the Crown.'[17] On one occasion Ernest Benzon, the 'Jubilee Plunger', rode in an amateur race specially got up for his benefit: six furlongs, flat: he rode very badly and fell. On another, the judge was thought to have made a mistake. 'The crowd gathered round the weighing-room and for a time ominous growling was indulged in.'[18] The man who ran the course said the judge really was wrong, and the crowd nearly pulled down the grandstand.[19]

Further out there were country-town meetings. The most important of many in Victoria were Ballarat, Bendigo, Geelong, and Kyneton, with good and well-managed racing. New South Wales had as many in the Sydney area.

Further out still, 'Every little bush township in Australia has its race-course, if one can dignify with that name the various tracks cut through scrub and bush, upon which the residents of the district gather once a year and hold high festival.' There was always a Race Ball afterwards: 'the high jinks carried on at these festivities are remarkable for their thorough abandon at night and prevailing headaches next day'.[20]

On a humbler level still, an Englishman wrote in 1879: 'I know no country where racing has been carried on so extensively in proportion to its population as New South Wales. In that district you cannot find a township where there are but half a dozen huts congregated together that does not boast its annual races – hardly a roadside bush public-house that has not its racecourse. I have seen races over stony ground, hilly ground, hard sun-baked plains rent with wide fissures, and over land heavily timbered.'[21]

Near Melbourne and Sydney there was a great deal of pony-racing. The three Melbourne pony tracks in the 1890s had the resounding names of Ascot, Richmond, and Fitzroy. 'They are a little world in themselves – owners, trainers, jockeys, bookies, and punters. . . . It is a well-known fact that there is a lot of crooked running at these pony gatherings.'[22] It is a less well-known fact that the starting-gate was originally used in unrecognized pony-races.[23]

In 1885 New South Wales, Victoria, and South Australia 'are well provided with blood-horses of the purest pedigree; and Queensland, the great island of Tasmania, and New Zealand (the Britain of the South) have race-meetings conducted with all the English forms and ceremonies'.[24] The forms and ceremonies may have been English; in many details Australian racing management was far ahead of England. Number-cloths were invariable. Scratching-boards informed the public the moment a horse was withdrawn, inhibiting further bets on it. The starting-gate was the first major improvement in this vexed area since Lord George Bentinck invented the flag start. The gate was introduced at Sandown Park, Melbourne, and instantly became general. Its value was such that 'owners and trainers were very chary about entering at a meeting where it was not in use.'[25] Australians thought the English crazy not to adopt it at once.

Another innovation urged on Ascot and Goodwood was the official fan. On Cup Day at Flemington vast numbers of small silk fans were printed with the official programme, and sold at half-a-crown. They were available in white, sky-blue, or pink, and could tone in with any costume. Thousands of ladies carried them.[26]

Finally, by the time Carbine won the Melbourne Cup (1890) it had £10,000 added: 'a prize which should make some of our racecourse company officials hide themselves'.[27]

## Australian Steeplechasing

In Melbourne jumping began almost as soon as flat-racing. It was also popular in Hobart. By both cause and effect, Victoria and Tasmania bred the best steeplechasers. On most

FLEMINGTON: THE GOVERNOR'S
BOX. This is about 1875; the gentlemen
are (from the left) Sir George Bowers,
Sir Hercules Robinson, and Sir Anthony
Musgrave. Robinson, later Lord
Rosmead, was a visitor from New South
Wales, of which he was Governor; he is
important in Australian racing history
as the man who cleaned up the dis-
reputable Sydney turf.

Victoria courses, there was a hurdle-race and a steeplechase on nearly every day's card, all the year round.

Thomas Haydon (who knew Aintree but not Maryland) said Flemington was 'the stiffest course in the world'.[28] The obstacles were solid timber up to five feet and massive stone walls. Sievier said the country races at Warrnambool were 'the most sporting in the land of the Southern Cross. . . . The steeplechase course was made up of solid log fences, and both horse and rider required their nerves in the right place successfully to negotiate the country.'[29]

Australian horses were fine natural jumpers like the Irish. The best of all was Redleap, 'the marvel of steeplechasers'. Their jockeys matched them. 'No more daring riders exist than the Australian cross-country jockeys', who suffered, somewhere in Australia, an average of one death a week.[30] The greatest was the Irishman Tommy Corrigan: 'I doubt if in England there is his equal.'[31] He was killed in a steeplechase at Caulfield. All this eye-witness evidence makes not impossible Kipling's description of 'the awful butchery . . . of the Maribyrnong Plate. The walls were colonial ramparts – logs of *jarrah* spiked into masonry – with wings as strong as church buttresses. Once in his stride, a horse had to jump or fall. He couldn't run out. In the Maribyrnong Plate twelve horses were jammed at the second wall . . . the space between wing and wing was one struggling, screaming, kicking shambles. Four jockeys were taken out dead; three were very badly hurt.'[32]

Caulfield was started for sporting amateurs (hence the inaugural race for bare-backed bullocks); amateurs continued daring. At Cranbourne there was a bareback amateur hurdle race, $1\frac{1}{2}$ miles, six hurdles; all the starters finished; it was a race 'which would have made some of our gentlemen jockeys, not sit up, but fall off'.[33]

## Betting and Bookmaking

'The English specific for the improvement of the horse races has not been neglected. Jockey Clubs in Sydney, Melbourne, and Adelaide, offered prizes for winners with no niggard hand. The betting rings were well attended, betting was brisk, black-legs became acclimatized and flourished.'[34]

The 'blacklegs' had a Tattersalls in Melbourne in the 1870s, but they quarreled with their committee (who tried to enforce a minimum degree of fair dealing) and started the Victoria Club in magnificent premises. The leading Melbourne bookies were influential citizens: any political candidate they backed was certain of election.[35] Sydney's club was called Tattersalls, using a single long room adjoining Adams' Tattersalls Hotel. The Sydney bookmakers then got their own superb building. Queensland's Tattersalls was in the Australia Hotel in Brisbane. Adelaide had a similar arrangement. Perth's betting and bookmaking fraternity was composed of immigrants from Melbourne.

Double-event betting was 'extremely popular throughout Australia. . . . "This and the next" is the prevailing cry of the penciller, or "The Two Handicaps", or "The Hurdle and Steeple I'll bet on." '[36] In fact it was extremely popular only with the bookmakers. Bob Sievier became the biggest bookmaker in the country, overnight, simply by laying bets on a single race, and by paying out immediately instead of next day. The rage of the others was unbridled.[37]

Big betting was 'the custom of the country'. Australians 'are the greatest gamblers in the world'. 'Sydney was long regarded as a bookmakers' paradise; the public gambled upon anything.'[38] The first betting-shop opened in Melbourne in 1884. It was widely copied and vastly profitable. 'In no other city in the world, considering the population, has so much cash been taken from the general public than in Melbourne from 1888 to 1893.'[39] The betting-shops, camouflaged with a few cigars in the window, were then closed down by the police. Sydney had lists of the 1851 London type, until they too were made illegal. Brisbane had heavy betting in the late 1880s with sweeps, private totes, and plunges on the Melbourne and Sydney races.[40]

This weight of gambling had its inevitable effect even on big races at big meetings. There was flagrant pulling and foul riding.[41] Sievier records 'a very fine game of hankey-pankey': Malua, the best racehorse in Australia after Carbine, was Tasmanian-bred by Archdeacon Reiby, and bought by an amateur jockey of dubious reputation called J. O. Inglis. The stable laid heavily against Malua in the Adelaide Cup. Sievier foiled them by laying a huge win bet to the jockey, who duly won.[42] (Not all Sievier's stories are to be believed.)

In the suburbs and out in the country it was worse. 'The most crude and barefaced malpractices' were committed.[43] If the public suffered, so sometimes did the book-makers. At Pakenham (only 20 miles from Melbourne) a winner was disqualified and the favourite made winner. The bookies refused to pay out, claiming they laid on the basis of 'first past the post'. They were assaulted by the infuriated crowd; 'one poor fellow, who was the possessor of a fine pair of whiskers, had them completely torn off'.[44]

A distinct form of betting was the Sweep. Tickets were bought all over Australia for the Melbourne Cup. It was big business, and completely honest. An anti-gambling crusade drove it to Sydney. A crusade there drove it to Brisbane. A crusade there drove it to Hobart. The Tasmanians welcomed it; it flourished, and benefited racing, with government backing.

Hobart also had the first mechanical totalisator, which few bookies were able to oppose. It surprised a visitor as much as did the pool-betting at Jerome Park, and for the same reason: 'Quite a holy calm pervades the course.'[45]

## Carbine

Lord Derby's Toxopholite was second in the Derby of 1858; his son Musket, out of a daughter of West Australian, was exported to New Zealand, where he was extraordinarily successful. His sons and grandsons won dozens of the most important Australian races.

The very greatest was Carbine (1885), out of Mersey, bred at Sylvia Park near Auckland. He ran for Dan O'Brien as a two-year-old in New Zealand, winning all his five races; he then went to Australia, aimed at the Victoria Derby and Melbourne Cup. He was scratched from the latter; in the former his jockey Derritt was outsmarted by the brilliant Tom Hales, riding Ensign. He did win other races at the meeting, and was bought by the Hon. Donald Wallace, of Sydney. For him Carbine won a total of 14 races at Randwick and 12 at Flemington; when he was beaten it was by prodigious lumps of weight, or a split hoof. As a mature horse he won over every distance from seven furlongs to three miles. He often ran every day of a four day meeting. His greatest single performance was in the Melbourne Cup of 1890, in which he gave 59 lb. to the second horse, a good one called Highborn. He won three other races at the same meeting.

He had one foible: he hated his ears getting wet. Before one damp Melbourne Cup his trainer Hickenbotham walked down to the start with an umbrella, not over himself, but over Carbine's ears. He won. Afterwards he had leather ear-covers built into his bridle.

In his first season at stud he covered only three mares, one being Melodius. She was sister to Melos, a very good horse unfortunate in being Carbine's contemporary. They were out of Melody, by The Barb out of Mermaid, she by Fisherman. By Carbine out of Melodius was Wallace (gracefully named), a sire as important as Musket himself. In 1897 the first three horses in the Australian Jockey Club Derby (Randwick) were by Carbine. The Duke of Portland had by this time bought him for Welbeck, for 13,000 guineas; he left Melbourne in April 1895. 'Hundreds and hundreds of people flocked down to the pier to have a last look at their old favourite.'[46] In England he sired Spearmint (Derby 1906) who sired Spion Kop (Derby 1920) who sired Felstead (Derby 1928).

He was badly ridden in his first Australian race. By most accounts, he was likely to be. Haydon said: 'I am not a great admirer of Australian jockeys as a rule; there is frequently too much of the butcher boy about them.'[47] Nat Gould said Queensland had good horses

CARBINE. The Melbourne Cup of 1890 is regarded as the greatest of all Carbine's victories. He carried a record weight of 10 stone 5 lb. (145 lb.), beat a record field of 39, clocked a record time, and won a stake with a record £10,000 added. The second horse Highborn, here receiving a monstrous allowance of weight, won the Australian and Sydney Cups, and in India three successive Viceroy's Cups; he must have been a very good horse.

and good owners, but very bad jockeys. They both made an exception of Tom Hales, 'the Archer of Australia, wonderful judgement, fine hands, and seldom made a mistake; moreover, there was not a blemish on his reputation.'[48]

## New Zealand

New Zealand was colonized by the New Zealand Company from 1840. Horses were brought from Australia at once. Wellington and Nelson, on opposite sides of the Cook Strait, had races on the first anniversaries of their settlement.

At Wellington they raced on the beach. E. J. Wakefield was Clerk of the Course: 'Here and there I had to get a large pebble or a glass bottle picked out of the sand; to beg Te Puni to have the natives' dogs carefully tied up, and to keep the pigs at home; to explain to a party of natives that they could not be basking in the middle of the course; to induce a party of whalers to push the nose of their boat off the beach, and finally to stop the persevering band as the horses were coming.'[49]

Nelson, three months later, had a hurdle race. Some years afterwards racing was started in Auckland by army officers, and about 1850 Canterbury racing was started.

Formal racing dates from 1855, when the Canterbury Jockey Club was formed. Its first meeting, over two days, was in March. There were five races, including a hurdle, a Galloway race, and a hack race.

The first thoroughbred arrived in New Zealand at the very beginning, in 1840. This was Figaro, by Theorem. His best son was Il Barbiere, out of an imported mare by Emilius. During the next 20 years 15 more thoroughbred stallions were imported from England and 29 from Australia. Two Arabs came from India. In 1862 Charles Elliott published his *New Zealand Stud Book*, which listed 58 covering stallions of reliable pedigree. Eleven were New Zealand bred.

The first exclusively thoroughbred races were at Christchurch in 1860: three days,

12 prizes. The best horses had been brought south from Nelson. The meeting included the first New Zealand Derby. The Wellington Cup was first run in 1874, and the Great Northern Derby, at Auckland, in 1875.

In the following years the half-bred racehorse disappeared, except for steeplechasers. Many more thoroughbreds were imported, many more studs established. The most successful importations were Musket and Traducer (imported 1863, by The Libel out of Arethusa) who in 1900 had 51 thoroughbred daughters at stud.

The Jockey Clubs of Canterbury, Dunedin, Wellington and Auckland organized themselves into the Racing Conference. All racing was as a result seemly and well-managed. The Australian totalisator was introduced and given a monopoly of betting; it was said that all New Zealanders bet, but none heavily. The excesses of Sydney and Melbourne were not committed: nor were the skulduggeries of the minor Australian meetings.

Steeplechasing was from the beginning part of New Zealand racing programmes, and it spread with the army. A New Zealand Grand National was run in Canterbury in 1876; Auckland and Wellington had Grand Nationals in 1885. The fences were not formidable by Australian standards. The best 'chasers were by thoroughbred stallions out of half-bred mares, the most celebrated being Moifaa, which was taken to England by Spencer Gollan to win the Grand National in 1904. He was an enormous horse, exceptionally powerful, with, to English eyes, an ungainly Waler head.[50] Lord Marcus Beresford bought him for Edward VII, but he went in the wind. He fell in the National of 1905.

Trotting, a failure in Australia, was highly successful in New Zealand. It was introduced (as on the Union Course, New York) as an added attraction to thoroughbred racing, in the early 1870s. It was popular, and in the 1880s a number of American trotters were imported to Canterbury and Nelson. Successful breeding of trotters depended on the importation of American mares, which had arrived in adequate numbers by 1900. The principal trotting centres were Christchurch and Auckland. Racing was informal and democratic, but efficiently run. A Trotting Conference, modelled on the thoroughbred Racing Conference, co-ordinated the sport. In Canterbury trotting was as popular as galloping.

FLEMINGTON. This is Derby day 1886, in the week before the Cup. The Victorian Derby was inaugurated in 1855; it attracted crowds only less great than those for the Cup, though in this privileged paddock area all is seemly and demure. The winner was Trident, centre (by Robinson Crusoe by Angler by Fisherman). Others in the picture include the Duke of Manchester and Miss Blair's Aboriginal, in the sailor-suit.

# 24  India

## The First Races

Army officers appear to have held races in Madras in 1780; they did not record them. In 1791 Dr Anderson's Arab The Boy was champion of the Presidency; he beat Captain Close's Lothario, another Arab. In 1793 country-breds were raced at Madras and Trichinopoly; there were a few Persian and Kabuli horses and four Arabs.

In 1794 Mr Manesty became Resident in Basrah, and over several years sent Arabs to Madras. In January 1795 there was a race of two-mile heats for maiden Arabs, worth 200 star pagodas, and in February a Give-and-Take Plate for £100. In 1799 the first English horse arrived, a mare called Brown Bess: but when in 1808 33 entries were measured for the Give-and-Take Plate they were almost all Arabs.

Calcutta had two races, which included no Arabs, in 1798. Benares started about the same time. Although Madras was 'the Newmarket of India',[1] racing grew much faster in the North-East. By 1806 there were four other regular meetings. In 1812 Calcutta had a new racecourse, and in the following years Arabs began to be imported in quantity.

Bombay's first recorded races were the same year as Calcutta's, a month later. There were 15 entries for three heat-races. Poona started in 1818 and by March 1819 had four races, all in heats. This suggests Arabs, since few country-breds had the stamina for heat-racing.

In 1825 James Barwell, a Calcutta merchant, invented the Great Calcutta Welter, called the 'Derby of Bengal', for maiden Arabs. This was the first race with substantial added money. Barwell won the first running, and later another.

By 1830 there were over two dozen regular racecourses in India, from the mouths of the Ganges to the mouths of the Indus, from the Himalaya to Madras. Upper India racing grew particularly fast, but Calcutta had become headquarters.

Climate imposed a special timetable. A bugle was sounded at sunrise for saddling, and the first runners were mounted a quarter of an hour later. If the sun got high and racing was unfinished, it was started again at sunset.

Distances varied between half-mile dashes and three mile heats. Participation was civil as well as military, but until the 1840s exclusively British.

One would expect steeplechasing. In fact 'Steeple racing is not much practised in India. The death of two fine young men from falls, cast a damper over this cruel and unsportsmanlike pastime.'[2] The officers went in for competitive hog-hunting. The hogs could outrun the best Arabs; the country was rough and included jumps. Everyone wanted first blood. These hunts were exotic and hazardous versions of Restoration hunting-matches.[3]

## Arabs, Thoroughbreds, Country-breds, Capers, and Walers

'It may readily be supposed that it was not long before races were established in the East Indies [*sic*], and that they were properly patronised by the government. They were, however, confined almost entirely to the Arabian horses, for those of half blood were manifestly inferior to them.'[4] This was 1830; 10 years earlier Arabs had arrived in sufficient quantity in Calcutta, Madras, and Bombay to elbow the country-bred off the racecourse.

The best Arabs racing in India in the 1820s were good horses. Barefoot, imported to Bombay in 1820, won there, and at Baroda, Meerut, and Cawnpore. His owner, Major Gwatkin, wanted to bring him to England as a stallion, and was only dissuaded by Mr Weatherby himself.[5]

In 1812 the first Caper appeared on the Indian turf: a roan pony which was beaten at Barrackpore. In 1815 Captain Christopher brought another roan Caper, the thoroughbred Escape, which won five out of seven races. In 1818 thoroughbreds were consequently penalized 7 lb., and in 1819 12 lb. Capers of any breeding were similarly penalized after Maid of Stellendam beat a horse called Mauritius, champion of Mauritius, at Ghazepore in 1823.

In 1821 Colonel (later General Sir William) Gilbert of the 13th Light Dragoons imported a thoroughbred from England: Cannonade, by Sir Charles Bunbury's Smolensko (Derby 1813), which won 17 out of 19 races. In 1828: 'Recruit, by Whalebone, a horse of some celebrity at the time, was sent out to Calcutta.' He very easily beat the champion Arab Pyramus over two miles, give-and-take weights with an additional 7 lb. allowance for the Arab, the actual difference being 37 lb.[6] In 1829: 'In our Indian empire . . . as might be expected, racing has become very extensive; and the horses

PIG-STICKING. This sport, known to 'Nimrod's' generation as hog-hunting, was dangerous however undertaken owing to the strength and courage of the quarry; it was made more so by intense competition among the riders to get first blood. This meant crossing rough country at a gallop. The excitement of such 'hunting-matches' made steeplechases unnecessary until the 1860s.

imported from England, maintain their superiority on the course; but it is said, not so in the stud, where the natural Arabs prove superior; probably from the debilitating effect of a tropical climate upon the constitutions of northern horses.'[7]

In 1830 a horse called Tumbler arrived in Calcutta: only 14.3 hands, Cape-bred, but an undoubted thoroughbred. He won the Bengal Cup easily in December. In 1831 he beat Francesco, the best sprinter in India, easily over half a mile. In 1833 he beat the Arab Hurry Scurry, winner of the Calcutta Great Welter of 1830, over a distance. Suddenly well-bred Capers were the best horses in India.

The country-bred was also reappearing (Francesco was one). Mr Hill, a Behar tea-planter, took the view that 'seven times out of ten a 2000 rupee Arab would be beaten by a 200 rupee country-bred'.[8] Hill's country-breds had Arab or thoroughbred sires.

In the 1840s, Walers began to arrive in quantity.

Weighing all these horses against each other was complicated. There were three distinct scales, all often used for the same race: give-and-take, weight-for-age, and weight-for-breed. The latter continually varied, according to the success of pressure-groups or of individual horses. For example, the Arab Elepoo won 20 races in succession, and was consequently awarded a special penalty. Even so he beat the good half-bred Caper Glengall in Radamandhub Banerjee's Plate at Calcutta in February 1844. Glengall, as a Caper, had a still heavier penalty. In the following season the Calcutta Stewards abolished the penalty for Capers. The importers and breeders of Arabs were dismayed. Their dismay became fury when the Caper Sir Benjamin beat Elepoo, who had beaten him at the old weights.

Broadly, country-breds were sprinters (they might be called Indian quarter-horses); thoroughbreds, Capers, and Walers middle-distance horses; and Arabs out-and-out stayers. The normal weight-for-breed scale of the time set an English thoroughbred to give one stone (14 lb.) to a 'colonial', two to a country-bred, and three to an Arab.

## Decline and Revival

In the 1840s racing continued to grow. Horses arrived from Basrah and Baghdad, from the Cape and Australia, and from England. New meetings started all over British India, and the existing courses built fine new grandstands.

Active participation was still largely British; but in 1845 H.H. The Nabob gave a 200 guinea cup for a race at Madras, and there were a few locally-endowed races at Calcutta.

Also in the 1840s professionals began to arrive from England and Australia. 'Lanky Will Hall' came out to train for General Showers; George Barker, apprenticed to Heseltine at Hambleton, came to ride for Sir Herbert Maddock; he later trained and owned horses.

In 1850 everything suddenly turned sour, and for 10 years there was very little racing. There were many reasons, unfortunately coincident: there was an embargo on the importation of Walers, the result of pressure from breeders and the Arab faction; Capers were not arriving because of horse-sickness; people stopped importing thoroughbreds; and Arabs had deteriorated. More serious, a ban on jockeys, stable-keepers, and dealers being owners of racehorses was lifted in Bombay and Calcutta. This, according to the leading Indian sporting writer of the time, allowed a flood of undesirables into racing, which at once became crooked.[9]

More serious still, gambling grew. It was worst at Calcutta, bad at Barrackpore.[10] Lord Dalhousie disapproved. Senior civilians could no longer act as racing officials. Little men were left, powerless or venal. A newspaper said of Benares: 'The heads of society instead of being the first and staunchest supporters of any amusement likely to create good feeling are its strongest opponents, and they formed a family party acting in concert, in the same way as is practised in Calcutta to put racing down there.'[11]

The result was that the many dozens of meetings shrank to a surviving dozen.

Recovery began in 1855, when Walers were allowed in again. Delhi racing restarted in November, then Lahore and Lucknow. Bombay opened the new Byculla course in February 1856; the Aga Khan sent 16 horses to run, and raiders came from Mysore and Madras. An Arab called Lucifer ran in nine races and won them all. There were Galloway and pony races (the limits being 14 and 13 hands respectively). Lord Canning, more sporting than his great but prim predecessor, gave a Governor General's Plate to Calcutta: St Leger distance, weight for age and breed. The first running was in December 1856. In the Calcutta Derby of the same meeting Parsee jockeys made local history by riding two of the 13 runners. This race ended in scandal, because the best horse was pulled in order to enable the owner's second string to win.

Lotteries were meanwhile becoming the major betting medium, increasing rapidly from 1855 and becoming very valuable. There was up to £10,000 on a single race.[12]

In May 1857 the Mutiny began. 'I fear', said a letter to a Calcutta newspaper, 'this little disturbance will have some effect on racing next season.'[13]

Things were peaceful enough by August 1858 for garrison racing at Lucknow and Dehra, and Calcutta had a few races on 1 January 1859.

1860 saw a tremendous renaissance. In Mysore the Maharajah gave a 5000 rupee Gold Cup. The Calcutta Turf Club restarted and built a new grandstand. East in Dacca, west in Karachi, and at Bombay and Poona the courses reopened. Credit for strong leadership in Calcutta was given to Mr Beckwith, 'the Nestor of the Calcutta turf', and Lord Ulick Browne, 'the most remarkable Irishman ever known, because he had more ballast than impulse.'[14]

By 1862 there were 100 racecourses in India. Some owners had strings of 50. In Calcutta racing was supposed to begin at 7 a.m., but they often had to wait until nine because of fog. Bombay had four to six races in the afternoon; the jockeys, formerly Mahratta, were now (according to 'Druid', who was surely wrong) all English.[15]

In 1867 the biggest lottery of all started, the Calcutta Turf Club Sweep. Three years later the Irish Lord Mayo turned the Governor General's Plate into the Viceroy's Cup; it was the most important race in India. That year Lucknow had five days' racing, with 37 entries and seven professional European jockeys (the word included Australian). These allowed native jockeys 3 lb., which caused some dispute about the proper allowance for half-castes, a logical view being that it should be $1\frac{1}{2}$ lb.

In 1871 rough riding in the Viceroy's Cup caused a multiple disqualification, and the case was referred for the first time by the Calcutta Turf Club to the English Jockey Club. The Jockey Club replied that the Turf Club had made fools of themselves and their rules were wrong.[16]

In 1874 the Gaekwar of Baroda entered a number of horses at Bombay; he could not, however, attend, as he was being tried for attempting to murder his British Resident with a mixture of arsenic and diamond-dust. In that year, for reasons which are obscure, Calcutta racing once again almost died. Less than 200 people came to the races, most of whom were the police.

In 1875 The Prince of Wales visited Calcutta with Lord Marcus Beresford. He came to the races, which were thronged. Beresford's brother, Lord William, arrived the same year with a commission in the 9th Lancers. A new epoch dates from these events.

## Indian Steeplechasing

In 1858 hurdle-racing was introduced by the Upper India garrisons of Jullundur, Meerut, and Cawnpore. There were many falls.

The first steeplechases were at Rawalpindi in 1865. The obstacles were mixed – ditches, hedges, post-and-rail, hurdles, wall. The races were popular and caught on at

BRITISH RACING IN BENGAL. This watercolour, *c*. 1830, is the work of a Kalighat painter of Bengal. Racing was by now widespread and popular, and Calcutta was its headquarters. No doubt the artist saw it, but his design is said to owe as much to English prints as to observation; there is certainly a strong look of John Nost Sartorius and even James Seymour in the stylized positions of the horses.

once. Steeplechasing spread everywhere except Calcutta and Bombay. It was dominated by two professionals, Tingey and Dignam, for many years from 1866. In 1871 Calcutta tried it. In 1872 a rider was killed in the Bengal Annual Steeplechase; there was also an acrimonious volume of objections. The Lieutenant Governor forbade jumping. But elsewhere in the 1870s it was consistently more popular than flat-racing. Bombay – joining in at last – called it *Jungli* racing.

Apart from the Australian professionals, two of the most notable figures in the sport were Captain Horace Hayes, who was training and riding from 1868, and who was later Secretary at Cawnpore; and Bertie Short, who started riding 'chases in 1871. He had one hand bitten off by a savage country-bred; two months later he was riding with a hook.

## The Beresford Period

From the late 1870s Indian racing surged in success and popularity. By 1880 there were meetings everywhere, revived or new. The race-weeks of even the smallest stations were the social high times of the year. The big meetings were supported by Maharajas and other rich Indians, by sporting Armenian businessmen, by Arab horse-dealers in the west, and by the highest-ranking officials and British merchants. Some of the Maharajahs – Mysore, Cooch Behar, Patiala, and the Aga Khan – had enormous strings and English or Australian jockeys and trainers. (A lot of jockeys arrived from both countries in the 1880s. Many took to the bottle. The best became leading trainers.)

The pattern of racing changed. Polo had come down out of South China into Assam, and the first British Polo Club was founded at Manipur in 1859. It came to Calcutta in 1862. A great number of polo-ponies (averaging 12 to 13.2 hands) were imported, and pony racing much increased. At the same time General Parrott and others were breeding better country-breds, which won a lot of prizes in pony and Galloway events. The number of imported English thoroughbreds declined because of the excellence of the Waler for Indian conditions; from 1872 Walers gave Capers 8 lb. The occasional outstanding Caper was a good horse to have.

Organization was strengthened. In 1886 the Calcutta Turf Club framed new rules; all racing was run under them which was not controlled by the Western India Turf Club.

In 1890 Calcutta's Maidan course was gay, rich, and fashionable; the high point was Viceroy's Cup Day, in December. The racing world then moved to Lucknow, equally fashionable, for the Civil Service Cup meeting; and on to Bombay in early March. The

Maharajahs were most in evidence at Calcutta; Bombay depended on Arabs, both horses and men. Ballygunge, near Calcutta, was the top steeplechasing meeting. Nearly all the good professional jump jockeys were Australian; the meetings up-country continued to be dominated by amateurs.

In the new rules and tighter organization of Indian racing Lord William Beresford was the most important man. He was also a leading owner. Hayes described him as generous and efficient, but on the racecourse 'thick': he was 'apparently apt to take the readiest means to be first in every contest in which he engaged'.[17] He was less the Bunbury than the Bentinck of the Indian turf. In 1891 he went into partnership with the Maharajah of Patiala; they were overwhelmingly successful. The 'Beresford Confederacy' was only seriously challenged by the Maharajah of Cooch Behar.

Growth thereafter was on predictable lines, though interrupted to an extent by the Chitrah and Swat troubles, and the Boer and Boxer Wars. The culmination of the small Tibet expedition of 1906 was a race-meeting at Lhasa, on 26 August, which included a steeplechase and an Army Cup. The Nepalese Resident and four leading lamas were present; the Tibetans were puzzled by the racing, but enjoyed it.

As in every other country, modernity meant centralization, uniformity, and professionalism. Nearly 90 courses in 1900 shrank to two dozen which could maintain good tracks, provide good amenities, and attract good horses with good prizes. Uniformity was achieved in 1899, when the Calcutta and Western India Turf Clubs adopted common rules and full reciprocity. By this time the Australian starting-gate was in general use. In 1894 the Calendar listed 50 'European' professional jockeys and 135 registered Gentleman Riders. By 1914 there were many more of the former than the latter.

## Up-Country Racing

To the main professional circuit was added a large, and largely separate, racing world up-country. Owners toured miscellaneous strings from meeting to meeting. Racing was amateur-dominated, but the richer men had 'riding-boys' from Australia. Regiments as well as individuals owned and entered horses.

It should have been the cleanest and most sporting racing in the world. In fact, according to Kipling, it had 'the merit of being two thirds sham; looking pretty on paper only'.

In order to get fields, stewards framed races to accommodate almost every possible kind of horse: handicaps, sellers, races for Arabs, country-breds, Galloways, ponies, polo-ponies, and maidens of all these classes. A lot of the racing ponies were imported English or Australian, thoroughbred or nearly. Most of the races were middle-distance; Arabs raced up to two miles, country-breds down to half a mile. The smallest ponies (13 hands) had quarter-mile races. The courses were sand, tan, or 'litter' from the elephant-lines. They were apt to be brick-hard or deep mud.

For steeplechases, 'Stewards', said Kipling, 'build jumps to suit their own stables.'[18] Walls were a particular hazard because, being made of mud, they toned in with the prevailing mud-colour and became invisible.

For up-country owner-trainers Captain Hayes recommended this string: one or two second-class Walers which could stay $1\frac{1}{2}$ miles; two Arabs, most useful if Galloways; one fast 13.2 Arab; a country-bred, preferably able to stay half a mile; and one good steeplechaser. A top-class horse was useless: it emptied fields, prevented betting, and got weighted out of handicaps. The exception was in steeplechasing, where 'a good nailer is a real Eldorado'.[19]

The owners Kipling knew went 'jugging about the country with an Australian larrikin; a "brumby" with as much breed as the boy; a brace of *chumars* in gold-laced caps; three or four *ekka*-ponies with hogged manes, and a switch-tailed demi-rep of a mare called Arab because she had a kink in her flag'.[20]

## Betting

High betting aroused the official disapproval which almost killed Indian racing in 1850. Then lotteries grew, especially the Calcutta Turf Club Sweep from 1867. In 1872 the pari-mutuel was introduced at Calcutta. At small meetings the sweeps (properly auction-pools) were the major medium. They were run by the Race Club, who took 10 per cent; the draw was usually in the officers' mess.

In 1881 the first bookmakers appeared. 'Having confidence in the capacity and rectitude of the stewards, the public used to attend the meetings with all their spare cash in their pockets to back their fancy. To supply this demand, men like Bob Topping, Miller and Brittain, Archer, Crouch, and several of the "layers", used to go to Calcutta for the racing season, which begins about 1 December and finishes about the end of February. Miller and Brittain used to field during the summer in Italy, and Crouch was well known on French racecourses.'[21]

In the 1880s the bookmakers made a great deal of money, especially in Bombay. They were accommodated in little wooden houses like church pulpits, so that each bookie appeared to be preaching a sermon. In the 1890s their lot was less happy. The mechanical totalisator competed with them at every sizeable Indian meeting. They were subjected to levies and harrassment. Worse, India was 'the happy hunting-ground for the professional backer . . . the professional backer in India seldom puts his rupees on a "stiff-un". They are up to all the tricks of the trade; in fact, they live on the game.'[22]

There were a lot of *coups*. Not all came off. A well-known amateur, a soldier, was riding in a three-horse race against two Australian professionals. His horse stayed well but was certain to be beaten for speed by the favourite. He set off in front, and to his amazement was never passed. After the race he changed out of silks into uniform. The two professionals were chatting in the paddock; they did not recognize him, and his hearing was exceptionally keen. The rider of the favourite, which was third, said he could easily have won, but he had been told to stay behind the second. His employer was extremely angry, having backed the second to win.[23]

There were also a lot of bad debts and slow payers. Young English officers were the slowest: 'the native Baboo or Parsee set them an example in this respect'.[24]

## Burma, Ceylon, Darjeeling

Racing began in Burma, at Moulmein in the far south, in 1828. It grew steadily. There was successful racing at Rangoon, Mandalay, and a number of other places by mid-century. The horses raced were tiny Burmese ponies (11.1 to 13.1 hands) of the Shan or Pegu type: slow, hardy, good natural jumpers, half-breds of an ancient breed predominantly Mongol.

Ceylon had unrecorded racing early in the century: recorded from 1850. The pattern was much like India's: country-breds giving way to Arabs, with a later influx of Capers, Walers, and better country-breds. Late in the century and early in the next there was up-country racing of the Indian type in the highlands in the middle of Ceylon: 'any amount of racing' at Badulla, Uva Province. There were always 'Planters' Hack Races' on the card, in which the horses were not hacks at all, but good-class Walers. They also raced 'griffins', small imported ponies. At Nuwara Eliya on the Horton Plains there was excellent racing in a perfect climate at 7000 feet.[25]

Far to the North, in sight of Kanchenjunga, there was regular racing at Darjeeling. They raced Bhutan ponies, much like those of Shan, with mouths like iron.

# 25 The Rest of the World in the Nineteenth Century

## European Racing in Far Places

The British raced horses wherever the map was coloured red, or where they had a commercial and diplomatic community.

When the Calendar stopped reporting American racing in 1771 it reported Jamaican instead. All the larger Caribbean islands which were or became British had intermittent racing, put on by garrisons or plantation-owners. The waxing and waning of racing depended on the tastes of successive governors, the atmosphere in officers' messes, and the price of sugar.

In a surprising number of hot places, horses were successfully bred. Jamaica was notable for exceptionally close inbreeding: perhaps less a matter of deliberate policy than of the small number of blood-lines available.[1]

Programmes were mixed so that any quadruped and its owner could join in: the 13 prizes at the December meeting of 1841 at Kingston included the Jamaica Jockey Club Stakes and the Kingston St Leger at one end, a pony-race in the middle, and a mule-race at the other end of the spectrum.[2]

Almost everywhere racing came with the flag: in India, South Africa, Canada, Mauritius, St Helena, and Gibraltar. In St Helena the programme was varied. In about 1828, when a ship called the *Lowther* had arrived with provisions, a trotting-match was fixed between 'one of those immense dray horses which are made use of in London, and which had been brought out in that ship for the purpose of drawing the stores up the beach, and an ambling nag of the island, whose favourite pace was a canter'. The dray-horse was slow to get going, but at last accelerated enough to win 'amid the loud laughter and acclamations of nearly all the population of the island'. The winning jockey was an officer of the *Lowther* dressed in a white frock coat and a huge white hat.[3]

Gibraltar racing started about 1830. In the spring of 1841 there were nine prizes. There were two steeplechases, one rider being killed.[4] The horses were English or 'Moorish'. Lord Poulett, later eminent in English steeplechasing, rode his first winner at Gibraltar in 1845.

In the Far East the commercial involvement was strong: in Hong Kong and Singapore, and later Shanghai and Peking. Robert Sherwood, who won the 1855 Derby on Wild Dayrell, went to Hong Kong as racing manager to Gardiner, Mattheson and Company. Horses came from Australia, India, and Mongolia. In China, merchants, diplomats, and soldiers – predominantly English – raced 'griffins', imported in herds from the north, arriving unbroken and without pedigrees; 13.3 hands was the largest allowed by the Turf Club rules. There was formal and informal racing: the former of the familiar European type but with amateur jockeys; the latter, borrowed from India, called paper-chasing, although no paper was involved; it was in fact cross-country racing, the line

HONG KONG. Mr John Peel was a
dominant figure in Hong Kong racing
about 1900; this is part of his string.
The grey is an Arab called Leap Year,
winner of the Hong Kong Derby. It
probably came from India. Walers,
'griffins' and polo-ponies were also
raced.

being picked by the previous winner.[5] The French colonies of South-East Asia had
racing similarly supported by commercial and military gentlemen, but the direct links
to French racing were stronger.

Nowhere in Asia, except Mongolia, the southern steppes, and North-West India, does
racing seem to have been a significant part of local tradition. It was imported by Euro-
peans. It is not easy to say to what extent this was true of the Middle East. On the whole
the Arabs, like their equestrian heirs the Spanish, competed with their horses in games
rather than races. Racehorses were exported, as such, from Arabia to India from the
14th century, but there is little evidence of their being raced at home.

In the early 19th century the Egyptians did race. In 1849 Abbas Pasha, by way of the
Consul General Murray, challenged the Jockey Club to a race over the desert between
an English thoroughbred and one of his Arabs. Charles Greville, in the columns of *Bell's
Life*, asked a number of cautious questions about the challenge. Murray's reply sheds
light on Egyptian racing of the time. The Pasha was a sportsman. Fair play would be
done. Races were 10 or 12 miles over soft, stony ground. The horses wore all-over plates
(the normal Arab type) instead of European shoes, because of the stones. The best horses
were all imported from Arabia. The jockeys were Wahabees from Mecca, light men, good
riders, bad judges of pace.[6] It appears that the Egyptians raced regularly, but Arabians
had to go to Bombay for their racing.

Later in the century Egypt took to modern racing with enthusiasm. The model was
England. The Khedivial Sporting Club (Cairo) held a Spring and the Alexandria Sporting Club a Summer meeting. The courses were excellent, the rules shared, many of the
officials English. Towards the end of the century there were also 'sky' (or 'Skye') steeplechase meetings. The trainers were English, and most of the jockeys, although by 1900
there were good Egyptian riders. The G.R.s were all English. Four classes of horses
were raced: English and other European thoroughbreds; imported Arabs; part-Arab
country-breds; and country-breds with no Arab. All the top prizes were limited to Arabs:
the Khedivial Sporting Club's Eclipse Stakes, the Grand Prix of Alexandria, and Alexandria's Derby, St Leger, and Grand Annual Handicap. All the good Arabs came from
Arabia, and were much better than those in India.[7] Except for the breeds raced, the
sport was entirely European in character.

French North Africa began racing about 1900. Morocco, Algeria, and Tunisia all had
ancient traditions of horsemanship, but not of racing. Modern racing went first to
Morocco, and grew there fastest. There and in Tunisia there was a mixture of breeds
raced, as in Egypt: 'In North Africa a merciless struggle is going on between the devotees
of Arabs and the no less keen admirers of the English thoroughbred.'[8] Algeria – with the

271

largest population nominally, if not ethnically, French – concentrated on the thorough-bred. All three countries had trotting-races.

The French also took racing to Madagascar, whose steeplechasing was, like Tonkin's, affiliated to Auteuil.

The one other African country with recognizable racing was Kenya. This was started not by residents or officials, but winter visitors: notably the Duke of Westminster, Lord Howard de Walden, and Sir Claude Champion de Cespigny, who laid out the Nairobi racecourse. The first meeting – local hacks and ponies – was in July 1900. It was so popular that the East African Turf Club was formed. The first proper race-meeting was in July 1901, with racehorses from England. They ran under Calcutta Turf Club rules; in 1906 the East African Turf Club was recognized by Calcutta. Thereafter thorough-breds were imported from England, the Cape, India, and Australia, and successfully bred in the highlands, which were free of tse-tse fly. Horse-sickness remained a problem. Cards were filled, as in India, with races for ponies.

## Latin America

Spanish America in the 19th century had an ancient tradition of racing and fine native horses. The important breeds were: the Peruvian *Costeña*, a big, beautifully-gaited pony with Barb characteristics; the *caballo Chileno*, a burly, short-running Andalusian com-parable to the quarter-horse; and above all the *Criollo* (*Crioulo* in the Rio Grande do Sul of Brazil) of the Pampas.[9]

All these breeds were raced. In Argentina, time out of mind, 'every little store posses-sing its own racecourse'.[10] The races were matches of 600 to 1000 yards.

Modern racing and the thoroughbred horse were introduced to 'Chili' about 1835 by Balie Peyton of Tennessee, Minister to the Country. He was not impressed by the *caballo Chileno*, sent home for two horses, and issued a general challenge. It was taken up by an official known as the Secretary, said to be the Napoleon of the Chilean Turf. Balie Peyton rode his own, a son of Leviathan. He won easily. There were a lot of foreign ships in Valparaiso at the time; a big crowd; and heavy betting.[11] The first thoroughbred stallion to stand in Chile arrived in 1845 from Australia; but Chilean breeders rejected this contribution, preferring to keep their breed pure and their racing traditional.

Elsewhere the change was much greater. In the third quarter of the 19th century Argentina and Brazil had considerable programmes of improving the size, speed, and stamina of their horses with imported thoroughbreds. The first thoroughbred in Argen-tina was Bonnie Dundee (by Bay Middleton) imported in 1850, the second Elcho (by Harkaway). Many more came in the next 30 years. In the same period the *Crioulo* of Southern Brazil was being crossed with imported stallions, nearly all English. By 1880 almost every ship to Buenos Aires had an English thoroughbred aboard.[12] The purpose was specifically racing.

Modern racing began in 1881 with the foundation of the Argentine Jockey Club. Its rules were copied from England and France; its first President was Carlos Pellegrini, its course Palermo at Buenos Aires. There was a Premio Jockey Club in 1883 and a Gran Premio Nacional (Argentine Derby) in 1884.

In April 1888 Admiral Kennedy reported: 'Horse-races are held in the vicinity of the city, usually on Sundays, when good sport may be seen and some English thorough-bred horses also. The weak point seemed to me to be the jockeys, who looked too heavy and clumsy, and rode badly. . . . A nigger hunchback jockey, of most diabolical appear-ance, created much amusement when he came onto the course, but he had an impudent, self-satisfied air – and he came in first.'[13]

This view contrasts with another English comment of 20 years later: 'The native jockeys are natural horsemen, and are gifted with remarkably good hands, but are not

DONKEY-RACES IN ALEXANDRIA. The British raced wherever, whenever, and whatever they could. Before the Egyptians embarked on modern racing in Cairo and Alexandria this meant donkeys in the streets. There are precedents in colonial America; urchins are galloping alongside as at Newmarket; a rider crosses the course as at Epsom; a man clears the way as at Smithfield; accidents seem inevitable as in Rome.

particularly distinguished for judgment of pace.'[14] Locally they were much more highly esteemed than English jockeys. There were in fact two distinct schools of race-riding in South America, both derived from country match-riding of the old type, *linea reta*, still widespread and popular and virtually identical to American quarter-racing. One was the Chilean *bridòn*, snaffle, school; the other the Argentine *freno* (Brazilian *freio*) school. *Freno* means curb; for racing they used a short curb with a jointed bit. Both methods were quite different from American and European race-riding.[15]

The thoroughbred blood was mostly English. The breeders wanted the best and could afford it. In 1888: 'Within a league of Las Lamas is the beautiful estancia of Las Rosas, where Captain Kemmis has raised some of the finest horses in South America. . . . Three magnificent thoroughbred horses, Phoenix, Blair-Adam, and Whipper-In, each of them worth at least £5000, were trotted out for my inspection. I never saw more beautiful creatures. I fancy the climate must have brought out their perfections to the very highest point; their coats shone like satin. . . . Several young English gentlemen were staying in the house, learning the art of scientific horse-breeding on a large scale.'[16] Orbit (by Bend Or) came the following year; and, most celebrated of all, Ormonde: but he was a sick horse and a bad roarer, and he was re-exported to California in 1894. Diamond Jubilee was only the best-known of many top-class horses imported later. There was also some excellent French blood, especially that of Dollar.

The Spanish Caribbean must have had racing when it exported racehorses north to Mexico and south all over the continent; it died. It was re-introduced speculatively in Cuba in the winter of 1842–3, by Americans; the speculation was abortive because the crowd became violent to the point of lynching when it lost its money. This has remained a hazard on the turf of all the smaller Latin American countries.

## *Persians, Tartars, and Mongols*

In Persian tradition hunting and polo were more important than racing, which is hardly recorded. There were however in the early 19th century some Persian races under the highest auspices: 'My curiosity was fully on the spur to see the racers, which I could not doubt must have been chosen from the best in the nation to exhibit the perfection of its breed before the sovereign. The rival horses were divided into three sets, in order to lengthen the amusement. They had been in training for several weeks . . . so much pains had been taken to sweat and reduce their weight, that their bones were nearly cutting the skin. The distance marked for the race was a stretch of four-and-twenty miles. . . . The different divisions arrived in regular order at the goal, but all so fatigued and exhausted, that their former boasted fleetness hardly exceeded a moderate canter when they passed before the royal eyes.'[17]

To the north-east, about the same time, the Tartars of the Southern Russian steppes held races of a special character. They were matches between a man and a girl. If the girl was beaten she married the man. An English traveller understood that the girls' horses were not always ridden out to the fullest.[18]

Further east still, the Mongolians were racing as, presumably, they always had. From May to August pony races were the greatest attraction of religious festivals and fairs: 'A racing-stud with dimension commensurate with his rank and wealth is the proper appanage of a prince or *Jassak*, and his "string" usually includes some of the fastest beasts of the district. The stud of the Tsetsen Khan is the most renowned in Mongolia. . . .

'This national sport is as little affected by money indelicacies, as any that I know of. I constantly heard of matches between rival owners proud of the reputation of their stock, but seldom of serious betting on the result. There are prizes to winners, rarely of tempting value. In the Chahar country the stakes are usually an ounce or two of silver (say 2s. 6d. or 5s.) for a race of 10 miles, but now and then an opulent magnate has occasion to be generous, and offers something exceptional – cattle, sheep, or ponies, silk, or clothes. The races are never under 10 miles. . . .

'The Derby of Mongolia is held near Urga under the direct patronage of the Bogdo and is over a course of 30 miles of rough steppe, and the winners are presented to the Bogdo, who maintains them for the rest of their lives in honourable idleness. The jockeys are the smallest boys capable of riding the distance, which the owners can secure. A saddle or seat aid in any form is not allowed; the jockeys simply roll up their loose cotton trousers as high as they can, and clutch the pony's ribs with bare legs, and all carry long whips. The bridles, single snaffles with raw-hide reins, have each a round disc of burnished silver attached to the headband.'[19]

## Racing in West Africa

Ibn Batuta reported horses on the Niger in the 14th century: the King of Mali had them.[20] They came down from Morocco or Tunis with the soldiers of Islam who converted the people without, however, persuading the women to wear clothes.

Whether racing came with the horses, or developed locally, it is impossible to say: but in the early 19th century the race-meeting was a high festival:

'At Kiáma, in the Kingdom of Borgoo . . . in the afternoon all the inhabitants of the town, and many from the little villages in its neighbourhood, assemble to witness the horse-racing, which takes place always on the anniversary of the "Bebun Sàlah", and to which everyone had been looking forward with impatience. . . . The race-course was bounded on the north by low granite hills; on the south by a forest; and on the east and west by tall shady trees, among which were habitations of the people.' The people were extremely gay and animated. The girls wore vividly-coloured cheap Manchester cottons, intended by their designers for furniture. The king made a circuit of the town and its environs, ostensibly to inspect the unfortunate, actually to enjoy adulation. Guards, tumblers, and clowns attended the king when he arrived, with great ceremony, on the course.

The jockeys wore loose 'tobes' and trousers of every colour, red leather boots, and white and blue turbans. The horses were caparisoned with bells, tassels, and charms. The saddles and stirrups were Arab. The jockeys carried spears, which they brandished madly.

The start was given, amid wild excitement, by a volley of muskets. The horses galloped off furiously. 'The race was terminated only by the horses being fatigued and out of breath; but though every one was emulous to outstrip his companion, horror [sic] and fame were the only reward of the competitors. A few naked boys, on ponies without saddles, then rode over the course, after which the second and last heat commenced.

'Young virgins, according to custom, appeared in a state of nudity; many of them had wild flowers stuck behind their ears, and strings of beads, &c., round their loins; but want of clothing did not seem to damp their pleasure in the entertainment. No less than 100 Mohammedan priests were among those present.'[21]

# 26 The Belle Epoque and the American Invasion

## England and Ireland in the Noughts

In 1900 the Prince of Wales's Irish-bred Ambush II won the Grand National, and his home-bred Diamond Jubilee won the Derby. In the next few years his Sandringham stud was less successful. In 1907 Colonel Hall-Walker, hearing of the despair with which the royal stable faced the coming season, offered to lease his yearling colts to the king.

Hall-Walker had ridden in Galloway races and steeplechases as a young man in the 1870s. He registered his colours in 1895, and in 1902 bought the Tully Stud on the Curragh. His very first year he bred Cherry Lass (by Isinglass out of a Bendigo mare) which won the 1000 Guineas and Oaks of 1905. He continued a highly successful breeder, in spite of (or because of) his reliance on the horoscopes of his horses. In 1904 his influence was crucial in persuading the Aga Khan (already a force in Indian racing) to race in Europe.[1] In 1915 he sold Tully and his training-stables at Russley Park, Wiltshire, to the nation, at the government's valuation, and gave his bloodstock – four stallions, 43 broodmares – as the foundation of the National Stud. He became in consequence Lord Wavertree in 1919.

Among the first draft he sent to Newmarket in 1907 was Minoru (by Cyllene out of Mother Siegal), which won the 1909 Derby for the king, trained by Richard Marsh and ridden by Herbert Jones. Minoru was sold to Russia in 1913. He was not in the class of the king's previous Derby winners, the great full brothers by St Simon; it is generally supposed that if Bayardo had been fit he would have won.

Bayardo was bred by A. W. Cox, who raced as 'Mr Fairie'. He had gone to Australia, aged 20, in 1877. On the ship he won a sheep-farm in New South Wales in a poker-game; silver was found there; it became Broken Hill. Cox sold out for a vast sum, came home in 1887, and started breeding. His horses were trained by Alec Taylor ('young' Alec, who succeeded his father at Manton in 1894 and took over full control from his brother in 1902; he was 12 times leading trainer, with over 1000 winners). Bayardo was 'Mr Fairie's' best horse: by Bay Ronald out of his home bred Galicia, by Galopin. He won the St Leger and the 1910 Ascot Gold Cup. His son Gainsborough was sire of Hyperion.

The year after Minoru's Derby, the king's Witch of the Air won a race at Kempton Park on 6 May. The king was dying; news of the race reached him on his deathbed; his last words, to his son King George V, were a comment on his victory. The new king was unhappily involved in the Derby of 1913; a militant suffragette called Emily Wilding Davison hurled herself under the feet of his Anmer. Miss Davison was killed, Herbert Jones slightly hurt, Anmer uninjured. This Derby was also disagreeable for the disqualification of the hot favourite Craganour, ridden by Johnny Reiff; the race was awarded to a 100 to 1 outsider Aboyeur.

Certain other racing empires were becoming of first-class importance.

The Stanley family had abandoned their ancient but intermittent racing tradition, until in 1893 the 16th Earl revived the stud at Knowsley, built training-stables at Stanley House, Newmarket, and recruited the brilliant but still inexperienced George Lambton. Lambton was diffident. The earl's son, Lord Stanley, persuaded him. The combination was one of the most successful in racing history. When Stanley became 17th Earl he won over 1000 races.

The 1st Viscount Astor was American ambassador to Rome, fell in love with Europe and out of love with Tammany, bought Cliveden, Buckinghamshire, from the Duke of Westminster, and became an Englishman. His son strained his heart rowing for Eton and Leander, and took to the turf. He started the Cliveden stud and sent his horses to Alec Taylor. He hardly ran a horse he had not bred, and he won 12 classics.

Tully, Knowsley, Cliveden, and Rosebery's Mentmore were all producing middle-distance horses of the utmost merit, dominating both turf and paddock. There was also a crucial new contribution to speed.

The Byerley Turk (Herod) male line was almost extinct in Britain, but strong in France. This was by way of Dollar and Atlantic. Roi Hérode (1904), Atlantic's great-grandson, was imported to Ireland by Edward 'Cub' Kennedy. He sired The Tetrarch (1911) out of Vahren by Bona Vista. The Tetrarch was bought by 'Atty' Persse – once a great amateur steeplechase jockey, who now trained at Stockbridge – for Major Dermot McCalmont. The 'spotted wonder' was a bizarre colour, but he was the best two-year-old of his time by an unprecedented margin. Leg-trouble prevented his running as a three-year-old; it is impossible to say if he would have stayed the classic distances. In spite of marked apathy in the presence of mares, he sired three St Leger winners: but his enduring importance is as a transmitter of phenomenal speed.

Among the greatest horses of these dozen years were two extraordinary fillies: Sceptre and Pretty Polly.

The Duke of Westminster's dispersal was held after his death in 1900. One of the most important lots was Orme's son Flying Fox, bought for France by M. Edmond Blanc; he was sire of Ajax and grandsire of Teddy. Another was Sceptre (1899) by Persimmon out of Ormonde's full sister Ornament. Sceptre was bought by Robert Standish Sievier, an aggressive bandit, difficult to dislike but impossible to deal with, with a murky past in Australia and a character full of courage and unwisdom. He deposited £20,000 in cash with a dismayed Tattersall, the night before the auction, in the latter's hotel room. He was mad to get Sceptre, 'a mass of perfection'.[2] He got her for 10,000 guineas – 4000 more than the then record price for a yearling. After predictable battles he trained her himself; she won four of the five classics of 1902. In competent hands she might have beaten Ard Patrick for the Derby, too: but in competent hands she might have done less racing.

Pretty Polly (1901) was by Gallinule out of Admiration by Saraband. This breeding seemed unglamorous at the time; in fact Gallinule turned out a successful stallion and Admiration a good broodmare. The breeder was Major Eustace Loder, who had bought Linde's Eyrefield Lodge on the Curragh. Besides Pretty Polly he bred Spearmint (by Carbine) to win the Derby of 1906; his son, Major Giles Loder, bred Spion Kop (by Spearmint) to win the Derby of 1920. Pretty Polly, two years younger than Sceptre, was comparable to her on the racecourse. Trained by the Irishman Peter Purcell Gilpin at Newmarket, she won the 1000 Guineas, Oaks and St Leger in 1904. She is on the bottom line of pedigrees of good horses all over the world.

## The American Invasion

In 1897 Tod Sloan visited England. A jockey who used his forward seat had appeared two years earlier: a Negro called Sims. He was quite unsuccessful. No-one was prepared

*Above*

SCEPTRE. One of the greatest half-dozen mares in racing history, bred 1899 by Persimmon out of Ornament, and changing hands surprisingly often. She ran 25 times. Her 13 wins included every classic, except the Derby, of 1902. Like her younger contemporary Pretty Polly she was a disappointment at stud in the short term, but an important influence in the long.

or *de clergyman*', broke into this charmed English circle. The methods of Chantilly changed even more sharply than those of Newmarket. An important result was that the French entered the profession; by 1912 there were as many French trainers as English. The analogy has been made with boxing: the French learned from the Americans, and were thus able to beat the English.[19]

The methods of the Americans included doping. The *Société d'Encouragement* forbade it, following England, in 1903, but the embargo had little effect. About 1906 French trainers took to it, not wishing to lose every race to the Americans. In 1910 the saliva test was invented by the Austrian Professor Fraenkel. In 1912 Bourbon Rose won the Gold Cup at Maisons Laffitte, but was disqualified after the first positive dope-test; the owner sued but lost.

Tod Sloan was brought to France by baron Schickler. Johnny Reiff and Milton Henry were the most successful of many other Americans. The very best jockey in France was generally considered, however, to be the English George Stern, who adopted the American style. He was extremely good, extremely rough, and at his best and roughest when riding to beat Americans.[20]

Steeplechasing was invaded to a negligible extent. French jumping was dominated by a small number of owners, such as Arthur Veil-Picard and Senator James Hennessy. The former won the Grand Steeple-Chase de Paris six times, the Grande Course des Haies five. The latter bought Lutteur III (grandson of St Simon by St Damien) from a third dominant figure, Gaston Dreyfus, and sent him to George Batchellor at Maisons Laffitte. After many wins in France he went to England for the 1909 Grand National. He won easily, ridden by Georges Parfrement, who was French but had a father from Yorkshire. Parfrement was later killed at Enghien. The greatest steeplechase rider in France was Alec Carter, who knew every inch of Auteuil; he was killed at the beginning of the war.

French trotting was greatly influenced by American. Driving grew at the expense of riding; because there were so few competent French drivers, Italians and Russians as well as Americans began to dominate Vincennes. A few American trotters had been imported for many years, largely by enthusiasts who were not breeders; in 1911 M. Rousseau imported Halifax and Fred Leyburn, which broke all records, driven by the Italian Tamberi. They went on to become influential stallions, standing at the stud which was later Marcel Boussac's. Both the horse and the sport became more and more derivative of America.

## Europe and the World

Racing was not on a scale elsewhere in Europe to attract the big American battalions.

In Italy, the most important event in the years before the war was the establishment by Frederico Tesio of the Dormello stud. As a young man Tesio rode in 503 steeplechases in various countries. In 1904 he owned a mediocre Hermit stallion called Melanion. Convinced of the merit of the Hermit-Isonomy nick, he went to England and bought a granddaughter of Isonomy. He thus bred Guido Reni (Italian Derby 1911), the first of his 20 Derby winners. Italian racing was expanding and prospering at this period. Prizes were good, especially at Milan, and the government was favourable.

The improvement in the German racehorse was also overwhelmingly the achievement of one man, Count Lehndorff. The Germans had efficient racing, good prizes, and a substantial export trade in thoroughbreds.

Austrian racing remained an unimportant part of the national life; Hungarian a very important one.

The tiny amount of Swiss racing was increased in 1906 by the invention of 'skijoring' at St Moritz, in which the horses pulled skiers for $9\frac{1}{2}$ kilometres over the frozen lake.

# THE HISTORY OF HORSE RACING

This developed into thoroughbred racing in 1909, and in 1913 there were runners from England, Germany, France, Italy, Austria, Hungary, and Holland.[21] The Swiss thoroughbred came from Germany.

South African racing was blacked out by the Boer War, but briefly and incompletely. The British army raced at the Cape throughout the war, and in 1903 racing was immediately revived at Johannesburg. The big race at the first meeting was won by Mr (later Sir) Abe Bailey, who by his own account brought off the biggest *coup*, in South Africa or England, in a career of formidable *coups*.[22] Recovery was general in 1904, in the Cape, Natal, and the Orange Free State. Influential breeding was confined to a few great studs; some of these were very successful. Southern Rhodesia emerged as a racing province of South Africa; Kenya paid fealty to Calcutta.

In Australia and New Zealand racing continued to develop in scale, wealth and popularity. The money bet was tremendous. In 1907 Sol Green laid £10,000 to £1000 against the Melbourne Cup–Caulfield Cup double; he paid in cash next morning in the Victorian Club, Melbourne.[23]

Indian racing at the highest level was increasingly dominated by the wealth and enthusiasm of the Maharajahs. Up-country there were still officers managing to supplement their pay by winning little races on their own ponies. In between there was a stratum beginning to be known, throughout British India, as the 'racing swine'. Some potentates were starting to enjoy racing in England and France.

Egypt, Latin America, Scandinavia, the English Far East, French Indo-China, Imperial Russia – everywhere that racing was established it continued to grow. This was the *belle époque*. Nothing would change except to improve.

TARPORLEY RACES. Tarporley, Cheshire, is a small town near Chester. It followed its pioneering neighbour with a racecourse in 1622. It never achieved importance, and was an unrecognized 'flapping' meeting most of its long life. This scene, delightfully remembered from an Edwardian childhood, includes a man running away with a bookmaker's satchel.

# 27  1914 and After

AUGUST BELMONT II. Known as the Major, the younger Belmont (1852–1924) succeeded his father in 1890 as leader of the New York turf as a crown prince succeeds a king. At his inherited Nursery Stud he bred the superb Fair Play (1905), sire of Man o' War and Display, the best sire in America since Lexington, and of special interest as a representative of the Matchem male line. Belmont was also first Chairman of the Jockey Club's Board of Stewards, a position he held for 30 years. Provincial resentment of his 'dictatorship' had a good deal to do with the decentralization of American racing after 1918.

## North America

The First World War made no great difference to American racing. The major tracks stayed open and their major events were run.

In 1917 the most important man on the American turf sold one of the greatest horses in history. August Belmont II, though 65, enlisted. He sent all his foals to the sales. One was by Fair Play out of Mahubah by Rock Sand. (Rock Sand, English triple-crown winner of 1903, by Sainfoin out of a St Simon mare, had been imported by Belmont.) This colt was proudly named My Man o' War by Mrs Belmont. The auctioneer dropped the 'My'.

Man o' War was bought by Samuel D. Riddle of Glen Riddle, Pennsylvania, for only $5000. The horse was trained by Louis Feustel. He won 20 races in 21 starts, running only as a two- and three-year-old. His only defeat was by the Whitneys' Upset; he was incompetently ridden. His last race was against Sir Barton, the first winner of the American triple crown (Kentucky Derby and Preakness and Belmont Stakes).

Man o' War was too good to stay in training as a four-year-old. He went to stud, where he sired such tremendous horses as War Relic and War Admiral, who won the triple-crown. His stud-groom, Will Harbutt, described him as 'de mostest hoss dat ever was'.[1]

An older contemporary of 'Big Red' was 'Old Bones': Exterminator, bought as lead horse for Sun Briar when the latter was being trained for the Kentucky Derby. Sun Briar contracted ringworm; Exterminator won the Derby. He went on to win 50 races from 100 starts: the greatest Cinderella in racing history.

After the war racing was dominated by Harry I. Sinclair, who bought Lorillard's Rancocas Farm. Sinclair's horses were trained by Sam Hildreth; they made him leading owner in 1921, '22, and '23. His best horse was Zev (by The Finn out of Miss Kearney), the best three-year-old in America in 1923. August Belmont II arranged a $30,000 match between him and Papyrus, winner of that year's English Derby. Papyrus's trainer, Basil Jarvis, has left a full account of the match,[2] which Zev won easily, in dreadful sloppy going, in a slow time. Papyrus ran unfit in unfamiliar surroundings, but Jarvis records the hospitality and sportsmanship of the Americans and the desirability of this kind of event.

Following the 1923 initiative, M. Pierre Wertheimer brought Epinard from France in 1924. Epinard failed to win, but ran some extremely good races; the whole attempt was much appreciated in America. Further attempts would have been popular with the public, but European owners lost heart. The appearance of European-trained runners had to wait until Mr John D. Schapiro's Washington International in 1952.

Epinard was also beaten in France in 1924, by Teddy's son Sir Galahad III. The winner was imported to America, by Arthur Boyd Hancock (Senior) – who founded

Claiborne Farm, Kentucky – and William Woodward. Sir Galahad sired Gallant Fox (1927), trained for Woodward by James Fitzsimmons ('Sunny Jim' or 'Mr Fitz'), the first triple-crown winner to sire a triple-crown winner: Woodward's Omaha, foaled in 1932. Omaha was sent to England, and was second in the Ascot Gold Cup of 1936 to Quashed. But he won twice and was twice second in England in four starts. Bull Dog, another son of Teddy, was also imported; his son Bull Lea was sire of Citation. Teddy himself followed, a horse deprived by the First World War of the chance to prove what many people believe: that he was the best horse ever bred in France.

Middle-Western racing was slow to recover from the blackout, but by the late 1920s it was going strong in Missouri and Illinois. Chicago had Washington Park and a new Lincoln Fields in 1926; in October 1927 Arlington Park was opened by the American National Jockey Club, a title evidence of the decentralization of the 1920s. The leading owner was Mr Hertz, an Austrian immigrant who built up the 'Yellow Cab' fleet.

Florida racing began at Hialeah, Miami, in January 1925. Hialeah had 51 days' racing in that year; in 1926 it was joined by three more tracks in the state. Florida's racing was so successful so quickly that it remains remarkable that it started so late.

California continued obdurate. In the south of the state people flooded across the border to Tijuana, which was very prosperous. Tijuana's course was replaced by the nearby Agua Caliente in 1929. In the North, Tanforan was started hopefully near San Francisco, but without betting it lasted for only two years.

Another rich state continued to refuse to countenance thoroughbred racing: Texas. In 1929, the year of Harry Payne Whitney's dominance of the turf in happier areas, there was a strenuous campaign to legalize racing in Texas. This was mounted by William T. Waggoner, who had oil-wells on most of his 600,000 acres; he spent $2 million on a private track on his land. Racing was legalized in 1933: but only briefly. Texas had to wait almost another 40 years for thoroughbred racing.

The Great Depression lowered purses and yearling prices; it was nevertheless good for racing because impoverished state budgets needed the revenue of the pari-mutuel. In 1933 10 more states overcame their scruples: California, Michigan, New Hampshire, New Mexico, North Carolina, Ohio, Oregon, Texas (momentarily), Washington, and West Virginia.

California's renaissance was much the most spectacular. Tanforan, reopened, had 122 days' racing in 1933. In 1934 Santa Anita, Los Angeles, was opened on part of Lucky Baldwin's estate. It was an immediate success. As long before, California attracted Eastern horses with enormous prizes, and public interest with glamour and lush facili-

*Above left*

MAN O' WAR. Man o' War (1917) first ran on 6 June 1919 at Belmont Park, ridden by John Loftus and winning by six lengths. He ran nine more times as a two-year-old, at Belmont, Jamaica, Aqueduct and Saratoga, winning all except when second to Upset at Saratoga in August (Loftus left his challenge too late). He is here at Belmont for the Futurity (13 September), again ridden by Loftus. He won from John P. Grier and eight others. He ran and won 11 times as a three-year-old, twice beating Upset and both times giving him weight.

*Above*

NATIVE DANCER. Native Dancer (1950) was a great-great-grandson by Polynesian of Phalaris; his dam Geisha was a granddaughter of Display (by Fair Play). The blood is American to an exceptional degree, which may explain the success of his get, as an outcross, at stud in Europe. He first ran and won at Jamaica on 19 April 1952; he was always odds-on thereafter; he won the rest of his eight races as a two-year-old and all but one of his total of 22.

ties. With Aqueduct, Belmont, and Hollywood Park, Santa Anita was still in 1970 giving the largest total purses in America.

Important innovations date from these years.

Starting had been as much a problem as in every other racing country. The Australian barrier was not a complete answer. In the mid-1920s a gate with one stall for each horse was tried at Bowie. Gates of different types were tried at Lexington and New Orleans. In 1929 John Bahr invented a machine incorporating a new principle: the gates were held shut against a spring by electro-magnets; power-loss allowed the gates to open. This was tried in Chicago in the autumn of 1929, and became general within two years.

On 31 August 1931, at Saratoga, the stewards ordered Sinclair's Ladana to be scratched. The horse had been obviously and incompetently poisoned. The trainer was at no moment suspected of complicity, but his entries were not accepted for the remainder of the meeting. At the time there was an outcry against this manifest unfairness, but posterity has endorsed the stewards' decision.

In 1932, to deal with the same problem, the French technique of saliva-tests was introduced by Joseph E. Widener, heir of a fortune derived from the Philadelphia street-cars. Widener's family were horsemen; he had owned steeplechasers at college; he had raced in France and England during the blackout; he was the leading figure at Hialeah, where he introduced the Australian totalisator as well as the saliva-test.

1936 saw real recovery, with bigger purses and higher yearling prices. The photo-finish camera came into general use. Surprisingly it vastly increased the number of dead-heats: in 1933 there was one, in 1936 there were 115. The Keeneland track opened at Lexington in October: it was intended as an American Ascot, on land given by a Mr Keene who was no relation to J.R. and Foxhall; its yearling sales became as important as Saratoga's. And for the first time a woman was leading owner: Mrs Mars, widow of the candy-bar tycoon, with her Milky Way stable in Kentucky.

Besides Omaha, War Admiral, and Equipoise, the greatest horse was Seabiscuit (1933), bred in California by Hard Tack (by Man o' War) out of a Whisk Broom II mare. He won races all over America, and it became a matter of impassioned debate whether he was better than the triple-crown winner War Admiral. After months of negotiation, a match took place at Pimlico on 1 November 1938: $1\frac{3}{16}$ miles, $15,000, level weights. Seabiscuit won by a length.

The Second World War increased racing's popularity and prosperity. The best horse was Mrs John B. Hertz's home-bred Count Fleet (who had both The Tetrarch and St Frusquin in his pedigree), winner of the triple crown in 1943. When, at the end of the war, building materials became available, there were magnificent new plants all over the continent.

After the war there was a decade of superb horses, starting with Citation (1945), bred and owned by Calumet Farms, Kentucky. Citation was by Teddy's grandson Bull Lea out of Hydroplane II by Hyperion out of Toboggan by Hurry On. He raced for four years, as a two-, three-, five-, and six-year-old. He won the triple crown of 1948; what is extraordinary, to a European, is that in that season he also ran in 17 other races: a total of 20 of which he won 19. He was second in the other. In Europe in the 20th century this programme might fit a second-class sprint handicapper of exceptional toughness; for a classic horse it is inconceivable.

Five years younger was A. G. Vanderbilt's home-bred Native Dancer, by Polynesian out of Geisha. His only defeat in 22 starts, over three years, was in the Kentucky Derby of 1953, in which, ineptly ridden, he was second.

1952 was unique in seeing the foaling of two horses both in the Hall of Fame: Nashua and Swaps. Nashua, by Nasrullah out of Segula, was bred at Belair and owned by the Woodwards: a blend of Italian, Anglo-Irish, and French blood. He was second in the Kentucky Derby to Swaps; he won the Preakness, Belmont, and seven other races out of nine that year. Swaps, by Hyperion's son Khaled out of Iron Reward, a granddaughter of Son-in-Law, was bred by R. C. Ellsworth in arid, austere desert conditions in California. His second dam was by War Admiral, his third by Sir Galahad III: the cream of English, American, and French classic blood. He ran mostly in California, but raided far enough to win the Kentucky Derby and then the American Derby at Chicago. The only horse to beat him as a three-year-old was Nashua, in a match at Washington Park.

The year after their last races, Kelso (1957) was foaled, bred by Mrs DuPont and owned by her Bohemia Stable. Kelso was a great-grandson by Your Host of Hyperion. His sire's dam was by Mahmoud. His dam Maid of Flight was by Count Fleet out of a Man o' War mare. He was another mixture of the best of two continents. A gelding, trained by C. H. Hanford, Kelso ran for eight years. He ran mostly over a mile and a quarter or thereabouts, but he also won the two-mile Jockey Club Cup five years running (1960–4). He was second in the Washington International three times before winning it in 1964. He broke all records by winning just under $2 million.

As the breeding of these horses shows, America imported – before, during, and after the Second World War – some of the very best stallions Europe had. These included all the Aga Khan's five Derby winners, of which Blenheim, Bahram (probably), and Mahmoud were an appalling loss to Europe. Nearco's temperamental son, Nasrullah – also the Aga Khan's, out of Mumtaz Begum by Blenheim – was even more important, especially as sire of Bold Ruler, a wonderfully prepotent getter of speed and toughness. His brilliance derived in part from 'Boss' Croker's Americus. Nasrullah has nicked particularly well with another valuable import, Princequillo, by Prince Rose (sire also of Prince Chevalier and Prince Bio) out of Cosquilla by Papyrus. Princequillo was bred in Ireland and raced in America; like Nasrullah he went to stud at Claiborne. An example of the nick is Mill Reef.

More important yet is Ribot, the Italian champion leased for five years to Mr John Galbreath. At the end of the period he did not in the event go home, because he had become too valuable to be moved: it was impossible to negotiate insurance. Sea Bird II, possibly the best Derby-winner in living memory, also went to Mr Galbreath. As in the case of Nasrullah, there is some poetic justice in this, because Sea Bird is by Native Dancer's son Dan Cupid, imported to France by M. François Dupré.

American breeding at this highest level has produced several world champions. They have come and conquered Europe in increasing numbers: a few, such as Nasrullah's son Never Say Die, in the 1950s; more and more through the 1960s. Four English Derby winners in five years – Sir Ivor 1968, Nijinsky 1970, Mill Reef 1971, Roberto 1972 – are pulverizing evidence.

What is interesting is the preponderance of recently-imported European blood in these horses. Mr Raymond Guest's Sir Ivor, trained in County Tipperary by Vincent O'Brien, won the 2000 Guineas, Derby, and Washington International of 1968. His sire Sir Gaylord is by Nearco's imported grandson Turn-to, out of a mare by Princequillo. His dam Attica is by a son of Mahmoud. The late Mr Charles Engelhard's Nijinsky, also trained by O'Brien and ridden by the greatest living jockey, Lester Piggott, won the English triple crown in 1970. He is the first Canadian-bred (by Mr E. P. Taylor) of world class. His sire Northern Dancer – a great horse, also bred by Taylor – is by Nearco's imported son Nearctic; his dam Flaming Page is by a grandson of imported Bull Dog. His bottom-line traces to Sir Galahad III. Mr Paul Mellon's Mill Reef, trained by Ian Balding at Kingsclere and ridden by Geoff Lewis, won the Derby, Eclipse, King George VI and Queen Elizabeth Stakes, and Prix de l'Arc de Triomphe of 1971. His sire Never Bend, the best two-year-old and leading stakes winner of 1962, is by Nasrullah; his dam Milan Mill is by Princequillo.

America (the statistics for which include Canada) has by far the largest bloodstock industry in the world: well over 21,000 registered foals in 1968;[3] an estimated 30,000 in

1971: about four times more than Great Britain and Ireland, Argentina, Brazil, or Australia and New Zealand. This quantity implies a large substratum of low quality. Only the toughest reach the racecourse. The ruthless process of selection and elimination continues on the track because of the American pattern of long-meeting, year-round racing. The minority who survive can run repeatedly, over sprint distances, on identical dead-flat dirt-tracks.

Canada's pattern is similar. Though its origins were quite distinct, by 1914 the Canadian turf was becoming a province of the American. Its provincial organization is identical and it subjects itself to the Jockey Club. Eastern and Western Canada have about the same number of racing days, each a little more than Maryland, far fewer than California or New York. The climate is inhospitable to breeding, although Canada has always produced good trotters, pacers, and jumpers. Northern Dancer was nevertheless the top three-year-old of 1964 in the U.S.A.

Mexico had racing only at Agua Caliente (Tijuana) until 1943, known as Caliente since 1945. In March 1943 the Hipodromo de las Americas, near Mexico City, was opened. Each races solidly for about a third of the year. In April 1965 Juarez, just over the border from El Paso, Texas, was opened. Numerically, Mexican breeding has grown to a size approaching Venezuela or Germany.

Puerto Rico's single official racecourse, El Commandante, San Juan, was inaugurated in January 1957. As in other provinces of the American turf, a lot of the races are limited to local-breds; as in Mexico City, San Juan's programme includes quarter-racing.

In trotting, the moral pendulum has swung dramatically between extremes of clean and dirty. The sport thrust many of its malefactors into thoroughbred racing in the late 19th century; they oozed back, and it died of them. It recovered with changes in the law in some states, but in 1923: 'It is conceded that never since light-harness racing became organized as a sport has it been so honey-combed and demoralised by pernicious practises.'[4] One of the more obvious was stopped when classification by best times was changed to classification by money won.

While thoroughbred racing grew in the 1920s, trotting shrank. The movies, the radio, baseball, and the car have all been blamed. Its own 'pernicious practises' must also have contributed. A grave symptom was Wallace's *American Trotting Register* ceasing publication.

In the late 1920s recovery started, from a variety of directions.

KELSO. Kelso (1957) first ran, and won, at Atlantic City on 4 September 1959, and ran again on the same track twice in the same month, being second both times. At three he won eight out of nine, at four seven out of nine, at five six out of 12, at six nine out of 12, at seven five out of 11, at eight three out of six: a total of 39 wins and 12 seconds in 63 starts. As a three- and four-year-old he was ridden by Eddie Arcaro, thereafter almost always by I. Valenzuela, who won 22 races on him.

# THE HISTORY OF HORSE RACING

A group in Goshen, New York State, put on major new races with prizes big enough to encourage breeders. These included the Hambletonian Stakes for three-year-olds – trotting's Kentucky Derby – at Syracuse from 1926. The Grand Circuit was reorganized. The Trotting Horse Club and the American Trotting Horse Breeders' Association restarted the *American Trotting Register*.

All this was the work of a nostalgic older generation. But young men (and women), disenchanted with cars, became enthusiastic too, and in the early 1930s the amateur 'matinées' were restarted. The best were among polo-players at Mineola, Long Island, and among steeplechasers and hunting people at Aiken, South Carolina. At a different social level, trotting-races continued an important part of agricultural fairs.

The legalizing of pari-mutuel betting in so many states in 1933 helped trotting as much as thoroughbred racing. It grew rapidly at every level, from village to big city. Growth was particularly fast in Ohio and California.

Nearly all the best trotting-horses of this period were tail-male descendants of Peter the Great (a Boston horse who went to Kentucky), or Axworthy, a New York horse who got the fast, early-maturing stock which suited the times. Both were Hambletonians. The breed was thus so polarized that no high-quality outcrosses were available, the proportion of thoroughbred being at the optimum. The trotter of the 1930s could no longer stay four miles, but it still ran three one-mile heats.

In Canada the sport was also growing. In 1938 Ontario was more thickly dotted with trotting-tracks than any American state except Ohio. Many of the Canadian horses were natural pacers; it is not clear why. They were bred on normal trotting lines: Electioneer, Peter the Great, and Axworthy.

Probably the most interesting thing to happen in the quarter-century after the war was the Americanization of trotting all over the world. This process started in Russia in the 19th century, in France early in the 20th. The harness-racing of every trotting country has, latterly, more and more closely resembled the American in track, sulky, framing of races and programmes, and in the horses raced. Besides France, this is true of Belgium, Italy, Switzerland, Austria, Sweden, and New Zealand.

## *England*

In 1914 it looked a short war; racing was only slightly reduced. By the spring of 1915 the government faced reality. In May all racing was cancelled, except at Newmarket. There was a little more racing in 1916, at half a dozen courses, in the teeth of violent disapproval from the press and much of parliament. Racing's great men – Lords Jersey, Derby, Rosebery, and Durham – were fortunately influential with, or members of, the government. There was another complete ban in 1917, but a deputation to Lloyd George resulted in its slight lifting. In 1918 racing was back to Newmarket only. The post-war euphoria of 1919 filled racecourses with enthusiastic and free-spending crowds.

The greatest horse of the war years was Hurry On, by Marcovil out of Toute Suite, sold on the eve of the war to James Buchanan, a self-made millionaire distiller who became Lord Woolavington. Hurry On ran only as a three-year-old, in 1916: six races, including the substitute Newmarket St Leger and the Jockey Club Cup, all of which he won easily. He was an outstanding sire, getting three Derby winners. His most important son was Precipitation (Ascot Gold Cup), himself an influential stallion. This male line represents the only European remnant of the Matchem (Godolphin Arabian) line. After the Second World War this again looked doomed, but by 1970 it was more hopefully represented by the Derby-winner Santa Claus (who died in 1971), and Sassafras, Nijinsky's conqueror in the 1970 Prix de l'Arc de Triomphe.

In 1921 the Aga Khan decided to take up racing seriously. He asked George Lambton to train for him. Lambton's yard was full; the Aga went instead to the Irishman Dick

AGA KHAN. H.H. The Aga Khan (1877–1957) started racing in India. He began in Europe when he felt ready for success, in 1921. The scale of his racing and breeding grew until his operation was only approached in Europe by Marcel Boussac. He won two 2000 Guineas, one 1000 Guineas, five Derbys, two Oaks, six St Legers, and two Ascot Gold Cups. When offered a good price for a horse he always sold. Blenheim, Bahram, Mahmoud and Tulyar were his best horses, and Nasrullah his most influential.

Dawson at Whatcombe and then, after a terrible quarrel, to Frank Butters at New-market. Lambton did however buy yearlings for His Highness, including a filly bred by Lady Sykes at Sledmere, by The Tetrarch out of Lady Josephine, she by Sundridge out of Americus Girl by Americus. The filly was called Mumtaz Mahal; she was very fast indeed, as her breeding promised. Her daughters were marvellous broodmares: Mumtaz Begum, for example, by Blenheim, dam of Nasrullah, and evident source of some of the brilliance of that horse's descendants.

Breeding was dominated by the Aga Khan and Lord Derby. The influence of their stock remains prodigious all over the world.

The former won five Derbys, three before and two after the war. He was popular on English and French racecourses, but America owes him a golden statue. Ironically Bahram would almost certainly have been a stud success had he stayed at home; he bred Big Game for the National Stud before export, which won the 2000 Guineas in 1942 for King George VI.

HYPERION. A small, lazy, difficult horse of supreme quality and world-wide importance. America has had his sons Alibhai (grandsire of Kelso), Heliopolis, and Khaled (sire of Hillary and Swaps); Argentina has had Aristophanes (sire of Atlas, Forli and Tirreno) and Gulf Stream (sire of Ever Ready); Britain retained Aureole (grandsire of Vaguely Noble), Hornbeam (sire of Intermezzo) and Owen Tudor (sire of Abernant, Right Royal V, and Tudor Minstrel). Other sons of Hyperion have stood in France, Australia, New Zealand, and South Africa.

As important as the Aga Khan's horses was Lord Derby's Hyperion (1930) by the wartime triple-crown winner Gainsborough. From his dam Selene and her sire Chaucer he inherited his tiny size. He was taken out of the 2000 Guineas because of his great stamina and laziness; he won the Derby and St Leger. At the end of that season (1933) Lord Derby decided that George Lambton was no longer well enough to train his horses; Colledge Leader succeeded Lambton at Stanley House. He was thoroughly competent, but Hyperion was desperately difficult to get fit because of his idleness. He needed to be bullied more than anyone except Lambton realized. He was consequently a disappointment as a four-year-old. His stud importance is incalculable: in Britain, America, Argentina, Australia, New Zealand, and South Africa. He was also a great sire of broodmares.

Other great owner-breeders between the wars included the King, who besides his Sandringham and Hampton Court horses raced the National Stud products, exclusively so after Lord Lonsdale's death; and Lords Astor, Rosebery, Glanely, and Dewar. The Astor stud at Cliveden continued to aim at classic winners, and won the Oaks five times. Ironically, the most influential line is that of the fast Court Martial. Court Martial's grandsire was Lord Derby's St Leger winner Fairway, whose son Fair Trial was out of Lady Juror, daughter, like Mumtaz Mahal, of Lady Josephine, and transmittor of the

Americus speed. Court Martial went to America in 1958, having proved an outstanding sire of two-year-olds. Lord Rosebery's Mentmore stud had a consistent tradition of tough middle-distance horses. The very best was Blue Peter (by Fairway) who won the 2000 Guineas and Derby of 1939. He was to meet the French champion Pharis in the St Leger. Neither side believed defeat possible. But war was declared, Doncaster was cancelled, and both horses went to stud.

One horse, not of supreme class, and with no descendants, requires mention: Brown Jack: because he enjoyed the kind of popularity with which, in living memory, only that of Arkle can be compared. He was bred in Ireland in 1924, and after some minor races was bought by Aubrey Hastings of Wroughton, as a hurdler, for Sir Harold Wernher. He ran at Bournemouth (briefly the home of a National Hunt course): then won four hurdle-races in a month. As a four-year-old he became a very good hurdler – probably the best between the wars – his season ending with a win in the Champion Hurdle at Cheltenham. The leading jockey Steve Donoghue said he was too good for jumping, and must run on the flat. He did, and won the Ascot Stakes. Aubrey Hastings died, and was succeeded by Ivor Anthony, one of three famous brothers; in his patient care Brown Jack went on racing until he was 10, winning 24 races in all and the long-distance Queen Alexandria Stakes at Ascot six years in succession. Appropriately, Donoghue always rode him. He was a public darling, and did racing inestimable good.

Bookmakers, in the view of many people, were meanwhile doing it inestimable harm: not only living off a sport to which they were contributing nothing, but also profiting from, if not engineering, most turf fraud. The pari-mutuel in France and America was looked at with admiration and envy as early as 1914. In 1928 the Racecourse Betting Act set up the Racecourse Betting Control Board, and on 2 July 1929, at Newmarket and Carlisle, the Totalisator was tried. The result did not, however, revolutionize British racing to the extent its champions hoped.

Other reforms between the wars were that entries did not become void on the death of an owner; the starting-gate replaced the frail old tapes; dead-heats were mercifully not run off; and, in 1930, as the result of a race at Kempton Park, a horse was disqualified and its trainer lost his licence because the horse had been given a stimulant.

In 1939 racing was cancelled in September and half October. It started again in 1940; stopped when France fell; started again in a small way in the autumn. The arguments for and against were those of 25 years before. Feed was short, grazing ploughed up, racecourse buildings requisitioned, transport at a premium. Racing continued for the breed's sake, and substitute classics were run at Newmarket. Two of the best horses of the war were bred by the National Stud and raced by King George VI, who was consequently leading owner in 1942: Big Game (2000 Guineas), and Hyperion's wonderful daughter Sun Chariot (1000 Guineas, Oaks, and St Leger).

Racing restarted in 1945 with all the glee of 1919: but British bloodstock, suddenly exposed to foreign competition, was disastrously eclipsed. There was precedent for foreigners winning races: a number of French horses, and a few Italian and American, had done so in the 1930s. Bois Roussel (Derby 1938) ran in English colours only by dint of purchase a month before the race. But there was no precedent for 30 of the 100 British classics from 1945 to 1954 going abroad, as well as numbers of Eclipse and Champion Stakes and Ascot Gold Cups. Foreign supremacy was most crushing in middle and long distance races.

The reasons are complex. English racing had shrunk to a trickle during the war; France's had grown. The Jersey Act had for a quarter-century excluded 'half-breds' from English studs; a high proportion of the best American and European horses were thus not available in 1945 for English breeders who, financially, had to have their foals in the Stud Book. In a period of economic austerity, English breeders were compelled to go for the quick returns of precocity and speed.

Two outstanding English-breds were nevertheless foaled in this dim period: Alycidon and Meld. Alycidon (1945) was by the Tesio-bred Donatello II out of Aurora by Hyperion; he was trained by Walter Earl for Lord Derby. He was a lazy horse with great courage and stamina, and sire of the classic-winners Meld and Alcide. His particular importance is as the last pre-eminent cup horse. There have been great stayers since, but stayers are no longer important. It was once normal for a Derby winner to aim at the Gold Cup; but when the far more valuable King George VI and Queen Elizabeth Stakes was inaugurated as an international race in 1951 – a mile and a half, like the Prix de l'Arc de Triomphe – the supreme test for the supreme horse became this distance. In the early 1970s the argument has been heard that even the St Leger, at a mile and three-quarters, is irrelevantly long for a classic, and unlikely to be won by a horse breeders will care to use.

Alycidon's daughter Meld (1952), out of Daily Double by Fair Trial, was trained by Captain Cecil Boyd-Rochfort for Lady Zia Wernher. She was second first time out, then won five out of five, including the 1000 Guineas, Oaks, and St Leger. She was compared to Sceptre and Pretty Polly. Like many great race-mares – like Sun Chariot and Petite Etoile – she was a disappointment at stud until she threw Charlottown to win the 1966 Derby.

These natives were swamped by the exotics: Pearl Diver, My Love, Galcador, Never Say Die, Phil Drake. English recovery can perhaps be dated from the middle 1950s. The Queen's Aureole was second in the Derby of 1953 to Sir Victor Sassoon's Pinza, but became a much more important sire, transmitting Hyperion's excellence. Her Majesty also owned Carozza (Oaks) and Pall Mall (2000 Guineas). Pinza was the first of Sir Victor's four Derby winners. Much the best of them was Crepello (also 2000 Guineas, 1957), who beat Ballymoss comfortably. Leg-trouble removed Crepello, leaving Ballymoss the best horse in Europe. French raiders continued formidable in the 1960s – notably Relko and Sea Bird II – but the tables a good deal turned. Part of the answer lies in the decline of French bloodstock, part also in the sharp improvement of British.

Recovery was due to both private enterprise and official action. The former is exemplified by Crepello, bred by the Sassoons by an Italian-bred sire out of a largely French mare. This approach, on a wide scale, was made possible by peace, easy transport, and the abolition of the Jersey Act. At the same time the Norfolk and Porchester Committees put the emphasis where the French had it: on valuable middle-distance races, and especially those which bring the best three- and four-year-olds together. The Levy Board (1963) and the Turf Board (1964) could not only strengthen these policies but also finance them.

In a number of areas, in the 25 years after the Second World War, Britain followed the rest of the world at a respectful distance. But at last the photo-finish, the loudspeaker commentary, starting-stalls, patrol-cameras, the Tote 'jackpot', the commercial sponsorship of races for advertising purposes, television coverage, the licensing of women trainers, and other reforms or adventures succeeded in overcoming the most furious conservative resistance.

National Hunt racing – since it has virtually no breeding significance – stopped completely in both wars. When it started again in 1919 it was still a poor relation, dominated by sportsmen rather than racing men, and infested with crooks. The only really valuable race was the Grand National; its hurdling equivalent was Sandown's Imperial Cup, also a handicap. The only important conditions race was the four-mile National Hunt Chase at Cheltenham, for hunters and amateur riders.

Two important changes occurred in the 1920s. One was the foundation, at Cheltenham, of genuine championship races: the non-handicap Gold Cup in 1924 and Champion Hurdle in 1926. The other was the recruitment of a new sort of owner: the American J. H. Whitney, whose Easter Hero, trained by Jack Anthony, won the Gold Cup in 1929 and '30, and was one of the greatest horses never to win a Grand National; Lord Bicester; the flour-miller J. V. Rank; flat-racing tycoons like Lords Glanely and Woolavington; and above all Miss Dorothy Paget. Her father was Lord Queenborough, her mother a Whitney heiress. She jumped into racing about 1930. Her expenses were huge, her bets prodigious, her enthusiasm unlimited, her character eccentric and difficult. She was of great benefit to National Hunt racing, and got at least a partial return with Golden Miller.

Golden Miller won the Gold Cup five times – 1932–6. He fell in the National of 1933, and won it the following year. He was probably the greatest steeplechaser in history (certainly the greatest until Arkle, and Arkle never attempted Aintree). He was not at all a natural Aintree type, but it was inevitable that he should go for the National as it was the only considerable prize.

In the National of 1935 he fell again. Reynoldstown won, and won again the next year, ridden by Mr Fulke Walwyn, later one of the most distinguished of National Hunt trainers. He was lucky; Davy Jones should have won, ridden by Anthony Mildmay, but his reins came unbuckled between the last two fences. Mildmay succeeded as Lord Mildmay of Flete, and was, after the war, the leading amateur rider.

In 1938 the tiny Battleship won the Grand National, an American entire by Man o' War; the race was run in 1940, but not thereafter until 1946.

In steeplechasing generally amateurs were still important, the very best being Mr Harry Brown; officers kept up their traditional participation. The best horses were very good; races were run faster and faster, and (to simplify a large subject) racehorses which could jump replaced hunters which could gallop. The hurdlers were not good, being mostly rejects from flat-racing, but at least one hurdle jockey was very good indeed: George Duller, the first jump rider to adopt the forward seat.

In 1939 there were a great many National Hunt meetings, the majority having poor facilities, niggard prize-money, and dishonest racing. Five years' inaction killed 33, leaving a simpler problem of administration.

The hard spring of 1945 limited racing to four courses, but in the Autumn it came back with a bang. There were a lot of demobilized officers longing to ride races again, a lot of farmers with spare money and spare paddocks, and a public longing to be amused. J. V. Rank, Lord Bicester, and Miss Paget were as keen as ever. The honourable and popular Lord Mildmay played between 1945 and 1950 the role Lord Clanricarde had played 120 years earlier. Most important, the Queen owned Monaveen in partnership with her daughter Princess Elizabeth, and subsequently, as Queen Mother, became season after season one of the most devoted and successful National Hunt owners. Her Devon Loch (trained like most of her horses by Mildmay's friend Peter Cazalet at Fairlawne) ought to have won the Grand National of 1956; his fall on the flat after the last fence – jumping an imaginary extension of the water-jump? startled by the roar of the crowd? – remains inexplicable, even to his jockey, Dick Francis.

The Irish dominated National Hunt racing as much as the French the flat. This was partly because Irish horses had stayed in training in the war; it also had a great deal to do with one man, Vincent O'Brien. Cottage Rake (Cheltenham Gold Cup 1948) was his first big winner in England; he then dominated English jumping to an unprecedented extent. Cottage Rake won the Gold Cup again in '49 and '50, and Knock Hard in 1953. Hatton's Grace won the Champion Hurdle from 1949–52. Early Mist, Royal Tan, and Quare Times won the successive Grand Nationals of 1953–5.

The best 'chaser in Ireland during the war had been J. V. Rank's Prince Regent. He was still the best at the end. He was therefore given huge weights in the Nationals of 1946–8, under which he failed. Meanwhile the Cheltenham prize-money was much increased. During the 1950s other valuable non-handicap steeplechases were inaugurated. In 1957 the Whitbread Gold Cup at Sandown, and the Hennessy at Newbury were the first great sponsored 'chases. The consequence of all these events was that the jumping

ARKLE. Arkle (1957) was bred by Mrs Baker of Malallow, and foaled at Ballymacoll, Co. Meath. His sire Archive (by Nearco out of Book Law) was a failure on the racecourse and stood cheaply. His dam Bright Cherry was by Knight of the Garter, by Son-in-Law. He thus had much more blood of classic quality than most 'chasers, which showed in his finishing speed. He was also a wonderfully fast and fluent jumper; when he made a mistake he 'found an extra leg', in which he was helped by the horsemanship of Pat Taafe. The combination are here in the second of their three successive Cheltenham Gold Cups; in the third they started at 100 to 9 *on*. Arkle so dominated steeplechasing that any handicap in which he was entered had to be made twice: if he ran he had maximum weight and everything else was lumped together at the bottom.

*Above right*

'MASTERS AT WORK' – NIJINSKY,
LESTER PIGGOTT, VINCENT O'BRIEN
The horse was bred in Canada in 1967;
his pedigree is discussed on p. 284.
He was twice defeated at the end of a
long three-year-old season, by Sassafras
and Lorenzaccio, but he was a great
horse and full of the 'electricity'
characteristic of the best descendants of
Nearco. The jockey was born in
1936. He rode his first winner at 13; he
won the Derby on Never Say Die at 18,
and won it again on Crepello (1957),
St Paddy (1959), Sir Ivor (1968),
Nijinsky (1970), and Roberto
(1972). The trainer – christened
Michael Victor, born 1917 – graduated
from dominance of steeplechasing to
equal eminence on the flat, his greatest
successes having been for American
owners.

programme no longer hung on the National. Good horses could make a living without going to Aintree, and the best were not to be risked there.

It followed that a process visible before the war became more marked after it. Horses designed by nature for the National fences – Wyndburgh, Tiberetta, Freddie – remained the best each-way bets at Aintree; but for all other valuable steeplechases a racehorse with finishing-speed was needed. Many of the best were still half-bred, including Arkle, but they could not be confused with hunters. At the same time, the fences at Cheltenham and Sandown take jumping. The result is a specialized branch of the thoroughbred unique to England and Ireland. In all other countries, jumpers are failed flat horses; in Britain they are members of established jumping families.

Jumpers are exceptionally large and powerful thoroughbreds. At the other extreme there is the problem of exceptionally small ones. After the death of give-and-take races, the pony-sized thoroughbred – small by genetic accident, mishandling as a foal, or being a twin – was useless. The solution was pony-racing. Unrecognized and deeply dishonest meetings were held in all kinds of places, time out of mind. In 1923 pony-racing became respectable with the foundation of the National Pony Turf Club; Lord Derby was President in 1926. There were meetings in outer London and several in the West Country. The latter were dead by 1930, but meanwhile Northolt Park, in the western suburbs, had been opened. From the early 1930s the reconstituted Pony Turf Club ran Northolt Park as a centralized pony-racing headquarters, with 50–60 days' racing a season of otherwise valueless miniatures: 15 hands or under, 14.3 as two-year-olds.

The rules were virtually those of the Jockey Club, by which the Pony Turf Club was recognized, with added stipulations about measuring. Northolt was years ahead of its time, with full-course watering in 1934, a loudspeaker commentary and stipendiary stewards in 1937. It was a cradle of jockeys, trainers, and officials, many of whom went on to the flat. Like steeplechasing, pony-racing had no breeding significance, so it closed down during the war. Then in 1946 Northolt was compulsorily purchased by the local authority for building. Pony-racing re-emerged at Hawthorne Hill, but it never re-captured its pre-war success.

## Ireland

There was no great change in Irish racing in 1914–15. There were 95 meetings in the latter year. In 1916 the races at Fairyhouse and Cork began just as the Easter Rising started. It was put down; 86 meetings were held. In 1917 the government forbade all racing, and immediately relented. There were only five fewer meetings. In 1918 the Civil War started. The Sinn Fein sabotaged hunting and steeplechasing, the Curragh was full of the British Army, the 'Black and Tans' arrived in 1920. The pro- and anti-treaty armies of the Irish themselves had their own war in 1921–2. There were strikes, shortages and widespread violence and destruction. There were still 80 meetings in 1920 and 101 in 1922.

In 1923 there was peace. Punchestown was as much a state occasion for the new Irish Free State as the Prince of Wales described it in 1868. Harry Beasley rode a winner 44 years after his first.

Irish racing in the next 20 years showed little growth in scale, prize-money, or international prestige. The best Irish horses – especially steeplechasers – were sent to England to make money. They won the National from 1920 to 1924

Irish breeding began a growth which became spectacular. To the McCalmonts' Eyrefield and the (English) National Stud's Tully were added the Aga Khan's Sheshoon, also in Kildare. There were other new studs in Meath and Co. Dublin, and south-west in Limerick. The Tetrarch and Blandford both stood in Ireland; Blandford was the dominant sire in England in the decade before the Second World War, getting four Derby winners.

In 1939 Ireland expected a flood of English and French refugee racehorses, and races were framed to exclude them. The flood never came. There were shortages of oats and fuel, but Irish racing was scarcely touched by the war. From the point of view of the future, certain important things happened. In 1940 Joseph McGrath, one of the leaders of the Easter Rising and for a time imprisoned by the English, bought the Brownstone stud on the Curragh, to which he added Trimblestown in Co. Meath. His success was immediate and overwhelming: he was leading owner five times running, from 1942 6. His home-bred Windsor Slipper was the first Irish-bred to win the Irish triple crown. He imported Nasrullah, before selling him to America. In 1943 the English National Stud gave up Tully, which in 1944 became the Irish National Stud. In 1943 also the two most brilliant trainers in Ireland since Henry Linde took out licences: Vincent O'Brien and P. J. 'Paddy' Prendergast. As soon as conditions allowed them to raid England they did so with devastating effect.

From 1945 the growth of Irish breeding was enormous. Many new studs were started, with English and American investment as well as Irish. Mr McGrath bred Arctic Prince (by the imported French Prince Chevalier) to win the 1951 Derby, after which English royalty found itself congratulating an Irish rebel. McGrath also bred Le Levanstell, and by him Levmoss, the best horse in Europe in 1969; trained by Seamus McGrath, Levmoss came back from the Ascot Gold Cup distance to the Prix de l'Arc de Triomphe distance, winning both. After the English bred Vaguely Noble's Arc victory of the previous year, this was Anglo-Irish breeding reborn with a vengeance.

Vincent O'Brien's dominance of English National Hunt racing has been mentioned. In 1957 he also trained the Dublin-bred Ballymoss (by Nearco's son Mossborough) for the American Mr John McShain. Ballymoss emerged from the shadow of Crepello to be the best three and four-year-old in Europe. Like Mr Robert S. Clark's Never Say Die, Ballymoss went to stud in England; a decision by these American sportsmen greatly in contrast to the policy of the Aga Khan. Ballymoss's best get is Royal Palace (2000 Guineas and Derby 1967, Eclipse and King George VI and Queen Elizabeth Stakes 1968).

STEVE DONOGHUE. In the last 100 years only four British jockeys have become household names – Archer, Donoghue, Sir Gordon Richards, and Lester Piggott. The second was born in 1884 in industrial Lancashire, and after jobs in various English stables joined the American trainer Edward Johnson in France. He rode his first winner there in 1904. He rode in Ireland from 1906 to 1910, and joined 'Atty' Persse at Stockbridge in 1911. He won two wartime Derbys and four at Epsom. He was brave, skilful, popular, generous, rather casual about contracts, and very bad at saving money. He died in 1945.

*Overleaf*
'IMMORTALS OF THE TURF'. The artist has placed Mill Reef (third from the left, Geoff Lewis up) among some of his ancestors. From the left they are Eclipse, from whom Mill Reef descends via Pot-8-os in 18 tail-male generations; Gimcrack, grandsire of the third dam of Boston, from whom descends Lady Josephine, third dam of Mill Reef's grandsire Nasrullah; Diomed, Boston's great-grandsire; The Tetrarch, sire of Nasrullah's second dam Mumtaz Mahal; St Simon, tail-male ancestor of Princequillo, sire of Mill Reef's dam Milan Mill; Flying Childers, grandsire of Herod's dam Cypron, Herod being grandsire of Pot-8-os' dam Huncamunca; Voltigeur, St Simon's great-grandsire; and Hyperion, grandsire of Milan Mill's dam Virginia Water.

Painted in Chelsea today
before Donoghue left
for Kempton June 4 - 1921
Stephen Donoghue
rode the Derby Winner
1921.

In 1963, '64 and '65 Prendergast was leading trainer in England on the flat: an astonishing feat for a trainer based outside the country. In 1968 O'Brien trained Sir Ivor to win the 2000 Guineas, Derby, and Washington International, and in 1970 Nijinsky to win the English triple crown.

Irish-bred jumpers continued excellent. The very greatest was Arkle, bred in 1957 in Co. Dublin by Archive out of Bright Cherry, bought by Anne Duchess of Westminster in 1960, running for the first time in 1962, trained by Tom Dreaper and ridden – as always thereafter – by Pat Taaffe. Arkle's brilliance, especially at Cheltenham, and his sustained duel with the enormous Mill House, drew crowds and aroused passions as no other jumper in history.

Irish racing itself became of international importance for the first time in 1960, when the minor Irish Derby became the major Irish Sweeps Derby. In other respects also Ireland came up to date: photo-finish, commentary, television, sponsorship, starting-stalls. The patrol-camera used at the Curragh in 1958 was the first in Europe.

In spite of the new value and prestige of Irish races, Ireland's breeding-paddocks and training-gallops remained into the 1970s more important than her turf.

## France

In 1914 French racing was in a good position. The pari-mutuel financed big prizes and kept the turf honest; big owner-breeders raced for glory, not bets; there was a valuable contribution from North and South America; courses and stands were excellent; the established Dollar and the new Flying Fox lines helped make French bloodstock very good indeed.

For France and Belgium, however, 1914 was total war. Racing stopped. There were a few *épreuves de sélection*, the minimum number of tests for breeders, at Chantilly, Maisons Laffitte, and in the provinces. These were financed by the *Société d'Encouragement*. The best horse involved was Teddy, Flying Fox's grandson by Ajax.

Spain tried to profit from France's situation. Alfonso XIII established races at San Sebastian, in spite of a clear public preference for bullfighting. Frenchmen raced in Spain; a few Spanish aristocrats raced after the war in France; the government bought thoroughbreds annually from England. It all ended with the revolution.

In 1919 Longchamp reopened. A French journalist records the dismay of the establishment at the vulgarity of the crowd and, worse, the new owners: wartime profiteers, many notorious.[5] There were also a lot of foreigners: Lord Derby, the Aga Khan, Greeks, Americans, Argentinians.

In 1920 the Prix de l'Arc de Triomphe was inaugurated at Longchamp: a very valuable late season test for three-year-olds and upwards. It was a mile and a half; its value moved the emphasis away from the stayers' Grand Prix de Paris, Prix du Conseil Municipal, and Prix Gladiateur.

The same year Edmond Blanc died: the biggest and most successful owner-breeder in France before the war. Before he died he bought Ksar at the Deauville August sales of 1919. Ksar was by Brûleur out of Kizil Kourgan by Omnium II (most brilliant representative of the Dollar male line); both sire and dam had won the Grand Prix de Paris. Ksar won the Prix du Jockey Club in 1921, and the second and third runnings of the Prix de l'Arc de Triomphe. He was easily the best horse in France in those years. At stud he got Tourbillon (out of Durban by Durbar II), a great racehorse and sire – though half-bred according to Weatherby – with descendants all over the world. By this male line as by Flying Fox's, Edmond Blanc's influence continued half a century after his death.

His place was taken after the war by three new owner-breeders: baron Edouard de Rothschild, Marcel Boussac, and Léon Volterra. Each won every major French race

FRENCH TROTTING. These appear to record the same meeting, but at an uncertain place and date. In the harness-race the sulkies have the new small wheels, and Americanization is visibly far advanced. The ridden race is of a kind hardly seen in Britain after 1830, little in America after 1850, and seldom if ever in Italy or Russia, but which remained popular in France and Belgium. The riders resemble those of America in the 1840s – big men, riding long. The horses are quite different, strapping Anglo-Normans with far less thoroughbred blood than contemporary American trotters.

many times. Boussac also won the English 2000 Guineas of 1940 with Tourbillon's son Djebel, and the Derby of 1950 with Djebel's son Galcador. In that year he was the first Frenchman since Lagrange to be leading owner in England. His stud at Fresnay-le-Buffard (previously M. Rousseau's trotting-horse stud) was the most important in France from the 1920s until the 1950s; its failure thereafter was probably due to insufficient outcrossing.

Léon Volterra started a theatrical career selling programmes at Olympia; he finished it as king of the Paris music-halls. He began racing in 1919; in 1933 he took over the lease of the Bois Roussel stud, and bought its stock, from the Englishman Captain J. D. Cohn. He would have won the Derby of 1938 with Bois Roussel, but for selling the horse in May; he bred My Love and won the Derby of 1948 in partnership with the Aga Khan. His widow, Mme Suzy Volterra, won in 1955 with Phil Drake.

The most brilliant horse in France in the 1920s was Pierre Wertheimer's Epinard. Being by the unfashionable stallion Badajoz, he was entered in neither the French nor the English classics, but a French view is that he would have won them all.[6] He very nearly won the Cambridgeshire of 1923 as a three-year-old with an enormous weight; he was only just beaten by Lord Coventry's Verdict, the best filly in England, who was getting 18 lb. Verdict's daughter Quashed beat the American Omaha in the 1936 Ascot Gold Cup.

The other supreme French horse between the wars was Boussac's Pharis, by Nearco's sire Pharos out of Clarissima. He was not trained as a two-year-old. As a three-year-old he won the Prix du Jockey Club and the Grand Prix de Paris, brilliantly ridden by the

expatriate Charlie Elliott. In the latter race he stumbled, went on his knees, nearly threw Elliott, and won by a phenomenal burst of speed. This performance stamps him as a horse of the very highest class; it is impossible to say what would have happened had he met Blue Peter in the St Leger. The Germans took him prisoner from 1940–5, and though he covered many mares he was not a success: nor, by Boussac's request, were his German get admitted to the Stud Book. Back in France he was a success, used principally, like Djebel, for Boussac's own mares; probably overused.

The Act of 16 April 1930 legalized off-course betting; it set up the *Pari-Mutuel Urbain*, which allowed the racing societies to collect bets by way of authorized agents, usually tobacconists. The P.M.U. grew until, by 1950, it had twice the turnover of the on-course P.M.H. especially after the invention of multiple bets and the *tiercé*. Attendances did not suffer as the market was different. Repeated attempts to incorporate fixed odds betting into the pari-mutuel failed, although the French recognize that 'fixed odds satisfy one of the gambling needs most deeply ingrained in the turf'.[7]

1940 and the occupation had two opposite effects. Breeding stock was confiscated and taken to Germany, and Jewish-owned studs were expropriated or destroyed. Longchamp was bombed, though not seriously damaged, just before racing on 4 April 1943 (there was a German vehicle-park in the middle of the course; racing took place). The Hippodrome du Var at Nice was destroyed by bombs in 1944, and later became the airport. A number of studs were flattened in the Normandy campaign.

In spite of these misfortunes, racing in both occupied and Vichy France grew in attendance, prosperity, and pari-mutuel turnover. Breeding also flourished, which enabled the French to raid England so ruthlessly in the late 1940s and '50s.

A number of stallions were recovered in 1945 – Pharis, Bubbles, Brantôme – but many were never seen again. Some probably went to Russia. Volterra emerged from internment; baron Guy de Rothschild restarted his family's breeding; the Aga Khan transferred the whole of his stud empire to France, joined by his son Aly Khan. In the decade after the war Boussac's dominance, at home and in cross-Channel raids, was greater than ever.

In strong contrast to Boussac, M. François Dupré went in (like Tesio in Italy) for what came to be called the 'international outcross'. Most importantly, he imported Rhea II from Germany and Dan Cupid from America; the results were the two best French-breds in a quarter-century, Bella Paola and Sea Bird II.

Bella Paola was Dupré's own breeding and she was trained for him by François Mathet. She was by Ticino, one of the best horses of the war years, out of Rhea II. She won the Grand Criterium, and in 1958 the 1000 Guineas and Oaks, both easily, both from other French fillies. Sea Bird II, by Dan Cupid out of Sicalade by Sicambre, was bred and raced by M. Jean Ternynck and trained by Etienne Pollet. He was the best horse in Europe in 1965 by a margin perhaps unprecedented. In the Prix de l'Arc de Triomphe he beat with contemptuous ease the winners of the Irish, Russian, and American Derbys. Like Ribot he went to Mr John Galbreath in America.

In spite of Relko, Sea Bird II, Match III, and other successful raiders in England in the 1960s, there were clear signs by 1970 that the French thoroughbred had suffered a sudden and severe deterioration. In that year every French classic was won by a foreign horse. It is true that English and Irish horses had improved; also true that the munificent French prizes attracted some of the best of them. Nevertheless French middle-distance horses were not only comparatively but absolutely worse in 1970 than (say) 1955.

This deterioration has been, with the utmost indignation, ascribed to the following: a yearning for profit, on the part of a new generation of breeders quite unlike Volterra and Dupré, leading to the export of the best horses and to a search for precocity and speed; blind admiration of America, leading to the importation of second-rate American horses and the imitation of unsuitable American methods; the ignorance which this

BARON EDOUARD DE ROTHSCHILD. Rothschild was prominent both before and after the 1914 war. His best horses were Alcantara II, La Farina and his son Bubbles, and Blandford's son Brantôme. He had a 'bird-like profile, a disturbed and melancholy air.' His cousin Maurice owned Sardanapale, descended from Monarque. The family were the most successful owner-breeders in France until the period of Boussac's dominance. The jockey is P. Villecourt.

EPINARD. Epinard (1920) was descended from The Flying Dutchman's exported son Dollar. He was the outstanding two-year-old of 1922, said to be the best generation between the wars. His trainer Eugene Leigh decided he was a sprinter; for this reason he did much of his racing in England, France offering few valuable prizes for short races. He was said in 1923 to be the most popular French face in England after Georges Carpentier.

DEAUVILLE. Deauville was founded by Napoleon's friend the duc de Morny as a summer resort for the Paris racing establishment – a healthful change from Longchamp and Chantilly. Like most seaside courses it has excellent natural turf, and is convenient for the great studs of Normandy. Although 204 kilometres from Paris it has always been part of the metropolitan circuit.

implies; the professional incompetence of trainers, with the obvious exception of a few such as François Mathet; and the even greater incompetence of jockeys, with a few equally obvious exceptions.[8]

French racing has nevertheless continued prosperous: Paris (including Deauville) still overshadowing the rest. The provinces vary greatly in the quantity and importance of their racing. Marseille leads the south-east, followed by Avignon. The south-west has a long and vigorous racing tradition. The east centre, Lyon and its summer dependant Vichy, is the most visited by Paris horses. Nantes and the west have a lot of racing of small importance; the north-east little; Normandy and the north-west an immense amount owing to the Norman studs. A headquarters view is that of all the provincial courses, the only ones of sufficient status to tempt horses from Paris are Lyon, Vichy, Bordeaux, Marseille, and in the winter Pau and Cagnes.[9]

Steeplechasing has grown and prospered. In 1945 Auteuil's takings were bigger than Longchamp's. The large number of English and Irish raiders dried up almost completely between the wars and since. The most famous exception is Mme Kilian Hennessy's Mandarin, who in 1962, having won the Cheltenham Gold Cup, came over in June for the Grand Steeplechase de Paris. The course is a complicated, twisting four miles, with 30 fences of varied kinds unfamiliar both to Mandarin and his great jockey Fred Winter. At the fourth fence the rubber bit broke. Winter could only steer with his legs and weight. He won thanks to his own excellence as a horseman, Mandarin's sense and skill, and the sportsmanship of the French jockeys.

From 1919 trotting was the fastest-growing branch of French racing. Vincennes remained the headquarters of the *Société du Demi Sang*; from 1920 it had the international Prix de l'Amérique. Trotting stopped at St Cloud during the first war, but the *Société Sportive* added it to thoroughbred racing at Enghien in 1922. Between the wars there was also trotting at Caen, le Pin, all through the provinces (often on tracks inside the thoroughbred courses), and in North Africa. The saddled trot remained, but gave way more and more to the sulky. The Second World War saw redoubled growth; twice as many trotters were bred in 1950 as in 1938, and there were far more races on more tracks.

Belgium's growth was even faster. The *trotteur français* went also to Switzerland, Germany, and Scandinavia, where trotting grew at the expense of thoroughbred racing.

## Italy

Italy's bloodstock industry has always been tiny (only 360 registered thoroughbred foals in 1967), and its best races at Milan and Rome have scarcely attracted foreign runners. But the Italian thoroughbred has had a world-wide influence out of all proportion to its numbers, and one man has been overwhelmingly responsible.

Frederico Tesio founded the Dormello stud on Lake Maggiore in 1898. In 1923 he started raiding abroad – in France, Belgium, Germany, and England – sending only horses he was confident would win, and therefore having a high percentage of success.

Meanwhile the Gran Premio d'Italia was inaugurated at San Siro, Milan, in 1921, and the Premio del Commercio became the Gran Premio di Milano; with the Derby at Rome these were big prizes, and encouraged other breeders. They did so well that the Prix de l'Arc de Triomphe was won by Italian horses, not Tesio's, in 1929 and 1933. Tesio's pre-eminence thus threatened, he went into partnership with Marchese Mario Incisa, and Dormello became Dormello-Olgiata.

Tesio went everywhere for the blood he wanted. He sent his mare Delleana (by the French Clarissimus) to Blenheim, to breed Donatello II in 1934. Donatello sired Alycidon and Crepello.

Next year Tesio bred Nearco, by Pharos out of Nogara by Havresac II. Pharos was bred by Lord Derby; Havresac II was French-bred, by St Simon's English-bred son Rebellais; both were inbred to St Simon. Nearco won 14 races out of 14. He won the Grand Prix de Paris in 1938 only six days after winning the Gran Premio di Milano. Like Donatello II he was sold to England. His sons and daughters and their descendants have been mentioned enough, in connection with America and Britain, to show that he is a very Eclipse or St Simon in influence.

In the next decade Tesio bred the tough stayer Tenerani and the fast sprinter Romanella (granddaughter of Pharos). He sold Tenerani to the English National Stud, and then sent Romanella to him, this regard for speed close up on the dam's side being a consistent Tesio policy. The foal Ribot (1952) was so small that he was not entered in

any classics: nor was his breeding obviously of classic standard. He first ran in July 1954, sadly after Tesio's death. He had gentle two- and three-year-old seasons, ending with the Arc de Triomphe of 1955. As a four-year-old he won the Gran Premio di Milano, the King George VI and Queen Elizabeth, and the Arc again. He was trained by Ugo Penco and always ridden by Enrico Camici. He stood in England, Italy, and then America. His success has been enormous, although his stock are not always easy-tempered and they mature slowly.

Italy has produced good horses, but no world-beaters, since Ribot; and success in the great Italian races does not always convey international class. Italy's contribution to the thoroughbred, if she never does anything more, is nevertheless imperishable.

## Germany, Russia and Eastern Europe

The German turf was soundly based, in 1914, on well-run racing and good studs. From 1919 it continued efficient, clean, and prosperous, and the German thoroughbred much improved owing to high-quality imports.

The best horse of the 1920s was Oleander (1924), bred at baron Oppenheim's Schlenderhan stud near Cologne. He was by the Schlenderhan-bred Prunus, by the English Dark Ronald, out of Orchidee II by Galtee More, who had come to Germany from Russia. Oleander won twice as a two-year-old, then broke his pelvis. He recovered, miraculously, and got better and better as he aged. As a stallion he was marvellous, leading sire in 1935, then 1937–45. His second crop included Sturmvogel, who won the German Derby of 1935 and then beat Volterra's Admiral Drake (winner of the Grand Prix de Paris) in the Grosser Preis von Berlin. In 1936 Oleander's daughter Nereide beat Corrida, one of the best horses in France and winner of the Arc de Triomphe in 1936 and '37, at Munich. In these years the best German horses were up to international competition of the highest class.

Racing continued gaily all through the war, all the big events being run. German bloodstock was presumably enriched by the horses removed from France. The Schlenderhan stud, however, was one of those confiscated by the S.S. as the Oppenheim family were Jewish.

In 1945 some French horses went home. Many German horses went to Russia. Graditz was in East Germany and the Hoppegarten course in East Berlin. Breeding and racing were in shambles. Recovery started, and proceeded steadily. The Oppenheims got Schlenderhan back in 1947, and they and other breeders began importing stallions and broodmares. The government supported and subsidized this operation. A few German horses ran in France in the 1960s, and a very few in Britain. German prizes were often, however, won by French and English-breds. Germany had not succeeded by the early 1970s in becoming a major racing power.

Russia had made strenuous and expensive efforts, in the last years of the old régime, to improve its bloodstock, as also its trotters. War and revolution destroyed everything. In 1924 some cavalry generals persuaded the government to reopen a few courses. For the next 10 years thoroughbreds were imported from Hungary and then from all European sources. There was regular racing at Moscow and various provincial centres, with trotting and troika racing. Once again war destroyed courses and studs, and exterminated most of the bloodstock.

1945 saw a rebirth based largely on looted German and Hungarian horses. A few pre-war families may have survived. Courses were reopened and studs refounded. Racing now takes place all the year round (packed and raked snow, as in Switzerland, is a good racing surface) all over Russia. The champions of each area meet in Moscow. There are no handicaps, horses being divided into categories as in harness-racing. The horses are nearly all owned by their government breeding establishments, although Stalin is said to have had two of his own. Programmes still mix thoroughbred racing, trotting, and troikas.

Russia and her satellites have internationalized their own racing. There is a Thoroughbred Breeding Association of Socialist Countries; and in 1967 the centenary of the Hoppegarten course was celebrated with a series of international races for Russians, East Germans, Poles, Hungarians, Bulgarians, and Czechs.

The best iron-curtain horses are very good, the Russians having made respectable showings in the Washington International. Anilin (1961) is the best. He raced in West Germany, France, and America, as well as East Germany and Hungary, and won 22 of his 28 races.

## South America

Argentina, Brazil, Venezuela, Columbia, Chile, Peru, Uruguay, and Panama (in approximately that order of importance) all probably have ancient racing traditions. Most have bred thoroughbreds for a long time. Brazil's industry may be numerically the largest; Argentina's is easily the most important.

Several things contribute to the success of Argentine racing and breeding. Throughout this century the pattern followed France rather than America, with an emphasis on middle-distance horses. There is a quadruple instead of a triple crown: races over a mile, 1.2, 1.4½, and 1.7: the first three at Palermo and the last, on grass, at the other Buenos Aires track, San Isidro. During this century there have been many quadruple-crown winners, which demonstrates the toughness of the Argentine horse. Argentine breeders have brought this about by wealth and skill. Ormonde, Diamond Jubilee, Bahram, Gulf Stream and very many others stood in the Argentine for all or part of their stud careers. Argentine horses are apt to be the champions of other Latin-American countries. Many go to the U.S.A. to race (in 1970 they won more stakes than all other foreign-breds put together) and to breed. For example Forli, quadruple crown of 1966, went to Claiborne; Forli is by Hyperion's imported son Aristophanes.

America also imported during the 1960s from Brazil, Chile, and Uruguay. The most important influence in Brazil was King Salmon; (the Herod male line is consequently strong). King Salmon's son Treble Crown (1941) went to Chile, where he was of great value as a sire of broodmares.

South American racing is rich, even in the poorer countries. Venezuela is said to have the highest prizes and heaviest betting. Argentine stake-money was effectively doubled, across the board, with effect from 1 October 1967.

## Australia and New Zealand; India and the Far East

Australian racing continued enormous and popular. Big owner-breeders in Victoria and New South Wales maintained breeding continuity. Betting continued heavy and remained the reason for public interest. Stallions were still imported, and new blood was still necessary (as in the Argentine, and for equally obscure reasons) to maintain the quality of the breed. Australian horses remained tough, running for their keep like Americans.

Two changes were the withering away of steeplechasing, and the growing value and importance of sprints and two-year-old races.

New Zealand racing has centralized itself on the North Island (as has the population), with Wellington the most important course. The South Island has remained a major breeding area, although in Canterbury trotting has become more popular than thoroughbred racing. New Zealand has maintained a traditional emphasis on middle-distance races. English staying blood (especially that of Son-in-Law and Hurry On) is therefore of special importance. New Zealand-bred horses are for this reason prized in Australia for the cup races. This cuts both ways. Australian money has enriched the New Zealand breeding industry, but robbed its turf.

The outstanding example of a New Zealand stayer in Australia between the wars was Phar Lap (1926), bred in New Zealand by imported Night Raid out of Entreaty by imported Winkie. He was leased and trained in New South Wales by H. R. Telford, a small man struggling against the giants. Phar Lap was exceptionally big, and therefore gelded. This did not debar him from the Australian classics, of which he won five as well as eight other races as a three-year-old. As a four-year-old he won 14 races running, including the Melbourne Cup under a weight only less than Carbine's. Before this race, for which he was odds-on, some persons unknown tried to shoot him. Early in 1932 his owners took him to California to run over the border at Agua Caliente. After a brief preparation, locally considered eccentric, and in utterly strange conditions, he won very easily and in record time. Two weeks later he was accidentally poisoned. His carcase was stuffed and macabrely displayed in the paddock at Belmont. The great jockey Eddie Arcaro is one of the authorities to say that Phar Lap was the best thoroughbred ever to run in America.[10]

A commentator said in 1950 that the Australian breed was deteriorating. Stallions continued to be imported after the war, but no longer good ones. Individuals could only afford second-raters. The solution – syndication – was thought unlikely to work owing to the Australian character.[11] New Zealand did import good horses, and made good use of them. In 1954, for example, Mr D. H. Blackie bred Tulloch, by imported Khorassan (by Big Game) out of Florida, whose sire was English. Tulloch was another supreme example of the New Zealand middle-distance horse. Bought and trained by Tommy Smith at Sydney, and ridden by George Moore, he was the first horse for nearly a century to win the three Derbys of Sydney, Melbourne, and Brisbane; at Randwick he broke Phar Lap's record.

Tulloch had a contemporary, the Australian-bred Todman. He was just about as good, but a sprinter. These two horses neatly exemplify the difference between Australian and New Zealand thoroughbreds.

The antipodes have exported few horses to Europe since Carbine, but many to India and the Far East. They have also exported jockeys, notably to England, Ireland, France, and India. Before the war, Australian riders were not committed to extremely short leathers, but rode somewhere between the old and the Tod Sloan styles. Latterly they have looked, at Longchamp and Ascot, like the rest. They have been respected particularly as judges of pace, and for their gentle handling of two-year-olds. By 1950 they were said to be more honest than they used to be.[12]

Indian racing continued between the wars substantially on its pre-1914 lines: Calcutta and Bombay the headquarters of the two great Turf Clubs; other major courses in each area; and up-country racing of a widely-varied character in which the army remained prominent. In a country without thoroughbred breeding, the turf depended entirely on imports. This meant maharajahs and the richest bankers and merchants. Since the Second World War, modern communications have meant that some English jockeys habitually spend the winter riding in India, as others in Jamaica and Trinidad.

English racing was flourishing in China, and French in Indo-China, between the wars. The turf of these places is dead. In Singapore and Malaysia it is greatly improved; mixed programmes of polo-ponies and the like have given way to thoroughbred racing, and it is no longer assumed that all races are fixed beforehand for the benefit of the stewards of meetings.

PHAR LAP. The best Antipodean horse since Carbine, Phar Lap (1926) was by the very moderate imported Night Raid (by Bend Or's good son Radium) out of Entreaty, by the equally moderate but well-bred imported Winkie. The excellence discernable in his pedigree missed a generation on his sire's side and two on his dam's. Like most big stayers Phar Lap was slow to develop, winning one maiden in five starts as a two-year-old. But at three, four and five he became supreme. In all he ran 50 races and won 36, usually ridden by the brilliant Jim Pike.

### South Africa

Since the end of the Boer War, South African racing has made steady rather than spectacular progress.

The years during and after the first war were dominated by the get of imported Greatorex (by Carbine out of a St Simon mare), who was leading sire 10 times and second twice from 1910–22. After his time a spate of inferior animals was imported, to race as well as to breed. Good horses were also imported between the wars, and most successful stallions were English. The best home-breds were the sons of Greatorex.

1940 saw the first real growth for 40 years. The breeding industry particularly benefited since no horses were imported. This meant many new studs and high yearling prices. It also meant many extremely bad horses. Not only does the South African breed, like the others of the Southern Hemisphere, apparently need regular infusions of fresh blood from the North: but also stud management has never been (with certain honourable exceptions) a strength of the Afrikaner.

In 1945 importing began again after the war, mostly from England and France. It was high time. Many of the new imports were good, though few excellent. The South African racing programme had meanwhile adjusted itself into a pattern of sprint handicaps and two-year-old races, which made specific demands on breeders of a kind repugnant to much opinion. The South African bred was judged in 1950 not as good as between the wars.[13]

There were major exceptions to this process of deterioration. Heavy investments were made by certain knowledgeable racing men and breeders, notably Mr Harry Oppenheimer, Mr Charles Engelhard, and the Birch brothers. They produced horses of a class entirely new to South Africa: Colorado King, Sea Cottage, Hawaii. The first and third were by imported Italian sires. Colorado King won in America. Hawaii was second to Karabas in the 1969 Washington International. Sea Cottage (1962) by imported Fairthorn by Fair Trial, is said to be the best horse ever bred in South Africa; it is the greatest pity he never ran elsewhere.

### Japan

In 1895 Japan imported 14 thoroughbreds from America. This started a tiny bloodstock industry, which grew slowly and tentatively until 1939. In 1945 there was not much left of the little there had been. Since the war, growth has been faster than in any country in any period.

The Japan Racing Association was set up by statute in 1955 as a non-profit-making authority. It runs the dozen major courses. Another 40 minor courses are run by local authorities. They have a lot of racing each, like those of America and the Argentine. The programme is comparable to the English. The prizes are big, and subsidised by the pari-mutuel. The courses, grandstands, and all facilities are modern and expensive. In technical matters (starting, timing, cameras) Japanese racing is as advanced as any in the world.

The Japanese public, hardly exposed to racing before the 1950s, has taken to it with passionate enthusiasm, as to such other Western oddities as golf and skiing. This has made the sport extremely prosperous. As the public have taken to racing, so millionaire industrialists have taken to breeding, importing expensively and on a large scale. They have been particularly glad to get English stayers – stout horses, short of brilliant speed – which English commercial breeders have not patronised. By 1971 Japan had imported seven English Derby winners. The most influential import was Hindostan, bred by the Aga Khan, by Bois Roussel, imported in 1955 as the whole process really began.

A typical recent importation – typical, indeed, of modern racing – is Celtic Ash. He was bred in Ireland in 1957, by the French sire Sicambre out of an Anglo-Irish mare. He raced in America, winning the Belmont Stakes. He stood for a time in England before going to Japan. Now that he is no longer available to European breeders he is, by an increasingly common irony, sire of the 1971 St Leger winner Athens Wood.

## Internationalization

There are four aspects to the internationalization of the turf: horses in training racing in other countries; the export of horses for breeding, or the sending of mares abroad to be covered; the movement of people; and the sharing of rules and growth of international authority.

The journey is easy from Newmarket to Longchamp, or Hialeah to Mexico City. But from Europe to Kentucky is a long and expensive journey, and European horses are not likely, without prolonged acclimatization, to be happy on dirt. The *va et vien* is therefore now limited to horses of the highest class, and to races which, like the Washington International at Laurel Park, are a compromise between the conditions of all competing nations. But international competition is necessary to establish the real champions and so guide breeders; it must increase. A trend that seems sure to help is the growing popularity of grass-racing in America.

The breeding thoroughbred can adapt itself to astonishingly varied conditions of heat and cold, lushness and desert. Large parts of the world are totally unsuitable because of the absence of calcium and other minerals in the grazing; other large parts produce a coarsening and degeneration of the breed unless it is continually topped up from the cisterns of Western Europe. This done, the English thoroughbred can contentedly reproduce itself. In different environments it changes: either because of climate and geology, or because different patterns of racing cause different policies of breeding. It is valid, as a broad generalization, to point to the soundness of wind and legs of successful American horses, the stoutness of Argentine, the stamina of New Zealand. These qualities can become intensely desirable to breeders in other countries, who may also want particular blood-lines, not available at home, to cross with lines they have. This situation produces the 'international outcross', which is the major new breeding phenomenon.

All racing progress in the last hundred years has spread by people going to and fro: by Englishmen bringing back reports of Flemington and Randwick, by Jerome and Belmont reorganizing American racing on the basis of what they had seen at Newmarket and Longchamp. European training and riding were transformed by the Americans who arrived in the first decade of this century. To an extent, the boot should now be on the other foot: Lester Piggott was contemptuously criticized in America for his riding of Sir Ivor in the 1968 Washington International; the critics revealed their ignorance of the way in which a mile-and-a-half race can be won by a mile-and-a-quarter horse. The racing communities of all countries become provincial and introverted unless they expose themselves to the world: trainers, jockeys, stud-managers, racing officials, and journalists. It would be a good thing if some French jockeys were apprenticed in England, English trainers in America, American officials in Australia, and Australian breeders in France.

Rules of Racing are largely, and increasingly, standard throughout the world. Their enforcement varies considerably, in regard to such things as medication and rough riding. Standardization ought to be as complete, as universally accepted, as in tennis. We shall not see this until we watch Flying Childers, Lexington and Sea Bird II contest the Prix du Styx on the turf of the Elysian Fields.

# Notes to the Text

**Note** References to the notes are indicated in the text by a superior figure immediately after the relevant passage. Where a sequence of references comes from one work, the superior figure is at the end of the sequence. The first mention of a work gives its author, full title, and where known, the publisher and the date published; subsequent references give simply the author's name and, where necessary for clarity, a shortened form of the title.

## 1 THE ANCIENT WORLD

1 Homer, *Iliad* xv. 625 sq.
2 Ibid. XXIII. 241 sq.
3 Herodotus IV. 189
4 Xenophon, *Art of Horsemanship*, Ch. X
5 Diodorus Siculus, XIII. 82
6 Pindar, Pythian Ode V. 32, 45, 100
7 Sophocles, *Electra*, III. 2. 660–803
8 Plutarch, *Lives* ; tr. J. & W. Langhorn, W. Scott, undated, p. 8
9 Aristophanes, *The Clouds*, 1225 sq.
10 Xenophon, *Agesilaus*, IX. 6–7; tr. Rev. J. S. Watson; Bohm 1857
11 Plato, *Republic*, I. 328 sq.
12 Xenophon, *Anabasis*, IV. 8. 28
13 Plutarch; tr. and ed. cited, p. 154
14 Xenophon, *Art of Horsemanship*, tr. M. H. Morgan, J. A. Allen 1962; text of 1894
15 I Kings, 10:28
16 Strabo, *Geography*, XI. xiii, ch. 7
17 The comparison is made by Strabo, III. iv. ch. 15
18 Aelian, *Characteristics of Animals*, XIII. 9
19 *Rig-Veda*, X. 75. 8, tr. F. Max Müller 1883
20 Herodotus, VII. 84 sq.
21 Arrian, *Anabasis of Alexander*, V. 15
22 Herodotus, V. 9
23 Caesar, *Gallic War*, IV. 2
24 Ibid. IV. 4
25 Tacitus, *Germania*, 32
26 Livy, XXI. 46
27 Strabo, III. iv. ch. 15
28 Oppian; tr. Thomas Blundeville *c.* 1580
29 Pliny, *Natural History*, VIII. 67
30 Ibid. VIII. 64
31 Athenaeus *Deipnosophists*, XII. 16
32 Tacitus, *Annals*, XIV. 21
33 Strabo, V. iii. ch. 2
34 Apollodorus, II. 3
35 Livy, I. 35
36 Pliny, XXXVI. 24
37 Burton, *Antiquities of Rome*, Rivington 1828, Vol. 2, p. 8
38 Suetonius, *Lives of the Twelve Caesars : Julius Caesar*, XXXIX
39 Varro, *The Latin Language*, V. 153
40 Ovid, *Tristia*, V. ix. 29
41 Evelyn, John, *Diary*, 20 Nov 1644, 23 Feb 1645, ed. William Bray, new edition, 1850
42 Varro, VI. 61
43 Suetonius, *Claudius*, XXI
44 Livy, XLI. 27
45 Suetonius, *Caesar*, XXXIX; *Augustus*, XLIII; *Caligula*, XVIII; *Nero* XVI
46 Suetonius, *Caesar*, XXXIX
47 Juvenal, *Satires*, XI. 195
48 Suetonius, *Caligula*, XVIII, LV; *Claudius*, XXI, XXXIII; *Nero*, IV, XII, XXI, XXIV, XXV; *Domitian* IV, V

49 Evidence in *Revue Archéologique*, 1903
50 Strabo, V. i. ch. 4
51 Pliny, VIII. 65
52 Bury, J. B., *History of the Later Roman Empire*, Macmillan 1923
53 Listed in detail in Holmes, W. G., *The Age of Justinian and Theodora*, G. Bell 1905, pp. 63–67

## 2 THE MIDDLE AGES

1 Procopius of Caesaria, *De Bello Gothico* ; there is alleged to be a reference, but the writer has not been able to find it.
2 Bruce, Rev. J. C., *The Roman Wall*, Smith 1853, pp. 329 sq.; and Tozer, Basil, *The Horse in History*, Methuen 1908, p. 76
3 Villemarqué, Hersart de, *Les Chants Populaires de la Vieille Armorique* ; cited Royer, E. de, in Darley, Godolphin, *Racing in France*, Paris 1950, p. 87
4 Bede, *Ecclesiastical History of England*, III. ch. ix, xiv, xxii.
5 Bede, V. ch. v
6 Malmesbury, Gilbert of, *De Gestibus Regum Anglorum*, Rolls Series, 90, i (1887), Vol. 1, p. 150
7 Johnson, R., *Kingdom and Commonwealth*, 1630, cited Oxford English Dictionary
8 *Táin Bò Cúalnge* (Saga of Cuchulain); tr. Joseph Dunn, Nutt, 1914, II p. 5, IV p. 17
9 Joyce, P. W., *Social History of Ancient Ireland*, Longmans Green 1908, pp. 38 sq.
10 *Cuchulain*, II, III, IV, VI, VIII B. etc., pp. 5, 11, 13–14, 27, 70
11 Qu. Joyce, p. 490
12 Ibid., pp. 498–510
13 Brehon Law Tracts, H.M.S.O., Ireland 1901, Vol. 5, p. 485
14 Stories and poems cited Joyce, p. 509
15 Herodotus, VII. 87
16 Strabo, XVI. iv. ch. 26
17 Blunt, Lady Anne, *Bedouin Tribes of the Euphrates*, John Murray 1879; Appendix by W. S. Blunt, Vol. 2, pp. 265 sq.
18 Upton, R. D., *Newmarket and Arabia*, Henry S. King 1873, pp. 108 sq.
19 Blunt, Vol 2, pp. 255, 263
20 Tesio, Frederico, *Breeding the Racehorse*, ed. and tr. Edward Spinola, J. A. Allen 1958, p. 52
21 Anglo-Saxon Chronicle, A.D. 1087, ed. J. A. Giles, Bell 1900, p. 462
22 Giraldus Cambrensis, *Itinerary of Baldwin Archbishop of Canterbury through Wales in the year 1188*, ch. XII; tr. Sir R. C. Hoare, William Miller 1806, Vol. 2, p. 173
23 Fitzstephen, William, Monk of Canterbury; tr. and qu. Stow, John, *Survey of London*, 1598, Everyman 1912, p. 505
24 Qu. Strutt, Joseph, *Sports and Pastimes of the People of England*, 3rd ed., Thomas Tegg 1838, p. 44
25 *The Romance of Sir Beues of Hamtoun*, ed. Eugen Köbling, Kegan Paul for E.E.T.S, 1885, lines 3261 sq., pp. 165–69. The earliest text is 1327.
26 Saluces, Thomas marquis de, *Le Chevalier Errant*, 1395, ed. Legrand d'Aussy, Bibliothèque Nationale, 'Notices et Extraits des Manuscrits', Institut Nationale de France, 7me année de la République, Vol. 5, pp. 564–80
27 Shakespeare, *Richard II*, V. iv. 75 sq.
28 Qu. Laffon, F., *Moeurs Actuelles du Turf*, Rothschild 1896, p. 83
29 Froissart, Sir John, *Chronicles*, IV. ch. X, Vol. 2, pp. 424–25 in ed. of 1855
30 Evidence qu. Jusserand, J. J., *Les Sports et Jeux d'Exercice dans l'Ancienne France*, Plon 1901, p. 403
31 Sidney, S., *The Book of the Horse*, Cassell, undated; French sources; qu., p. 114
32 Marco Polo, *Concerning the Kingdoms and Marvels of the East* ; tr. Col. Henry Yule, John Murray 1875, II. xlix
33 Constituto of 1262; qu. Heywood, William, *Palio and Ponte*, Methuen 1904
34 Dante, *Paradiso*, Canto XVI. 40–42
35 Dati, Goro di Stagio, *Storia di Firenze* ; qu. Heywood, pp. 8–9
36 Dante, *Inferno*, Canto XV. 121–24
37 Burckhardt, Jacob, *The Civilization of the Renaissance in Italy* ; tr. S. G. C. Middlemore, Kegan Paul 1878, Vol. 2, pp. 176 sq.
38 Machuca, Capt. Bernardo de Vargas, *Libro de Exercicios de la Gineta*, Madrid 1500; qu. Denhardt, R. M., *The Horse of the Americas*, University of Oklahoma Press 1949, p. 18. Oxford English Dictionary notes: 'other conjectures have been made'.
39 Tombstones of *caballeros* ; qu. Denhardt, p. 17

40 Bourgoame, Chevalier de, *Voyages*, ed. Paris 1803
41 Inca Garcilaso de la Vega, *La Florida del Inca*, late 16th century, pub. 1723; qu. Denhardt, p. 43
42 Polo, III. xxxvi
43 Ibn Batuta, *Voyages ;* tr. H. A. R. Gibb, Hakluyt Society 1958, Vol. 1, p. 224
44 Polo, III. xxxvii
45 Batuta (Gibb), Vol. 2, p. 383
46 Usama Ibn Munquidh, 12th-century Syrian; qu. Chenevix-Trench, Charles, *History of Horsemanship*, Longman 1970, p. 88
47 Polo, I. xv
48 Mainwaring, George, *Journey into Persia ;* qu. Chenevix-Trench, pp. 208–9
49 Batuta (Gibb), Vol. 2, p. 478
50 Polo, II. iii, lxv
51 *Asva-Sastra ;* qu. Chenevix-Trench, p. 304
52 Ibn Batoutah, *Voyages ;* tr. C. Defrémery & B. R. Sanguinetti, Société Asiatique, Imprimerie Nationale, 4th ed. 1914, 1922, Vol. 3, pp. 119–20
53 Polo, III. xvii
54 Batuta (Gibb), Vol. 1, p. 224; Vol. 2, p. 479

## 3 THE 16TH CENTURY

1 Berners, Dame Juliana: *The Boke of St Albans*, printed by the schoolmaster-printer 1486; facsimile ed. Elliot Stock 1881
2 11 Henry VII, ch. 13
3 Letters from Mantua's agent Ratto, Henry VIII, Peter Martyr, Cardinal Campaggio, Ferrara, Bishop Hooper; qu. Hore, J. P., *History of Newmarket and Annals of the Turf*, Baily 1886, Vol. 1, pp. 71–80 and nn.
4 Archaeologia, *Miscellaneous Tracts relating to Antiquity*, Soc. of Antiquaries of London, Vol. 3, pp. 157–59
5 Harrison, William, *Description of Britaine ;* incorporated in Holinshed, Raphael, *Chronicles, now newlie augmented to the yeare 1586*, ed. J. Johnson 1807, Vol. 1, p. 371
6 Nicholas, N. H., *Privy Purse Expenses of King Henry the Eighth*, Pickering 1827, pp. 11, 19, 23, 25, 29, 31, 133, 199, 224
7 MS in P.R.O.; qu. Hore, Vol. 1, p. 61
8 Rodgers, Rev. Robert, *Certayne collections of Anchiante times*, ed. his son of the same name, died 1595; qu. Lysons, Daniel, *Magna Britannia : a topograph account of the counties of Great Britain*, 1806, Vol. 2 (Cheshire), pp. 570 sq.
9 Acts of Assembly of the Mayor and Council of Chester, 10 Jan 3 Henry VIII; qu. *Horse Racing* (Anon.), new ed. Roche 1865, p. 108
10 Wardrobe Accounts; qu. Hore, Vol. 1, p. 86 n.
11 Hoare, Sir R. C. (ed.), *History of Wiltshire*, Nichols 1843, Vol. 6, pp. 294, 306
12 Camden, William, *Britannia*, 1st ed. London 1594; tr. P. Holland 1610
13 Gilbey, Sir Walter, *Racing Cups 1559–1850*, Vinton 1910, p. 1
14 Corporation Order; qu. Hore, Vol. 1, p. 95
15 Anonymous Diary; qu. Hore, Vol. 1, p. 96
16 Qu. Tesio, pp. 2–3
17 Harrison in Holinshed, Vol. 1, p. 371
18 Blundeville, Thomas, *The fower chiefest offices belonging to Horsemanshippe. That is to saye, the office of the Breeder, of the Rider, of the Keeper, and of the Ferrer*, first part 1565
19 Markham, Gervase, *Cavalarice, or the English Horseman*, 1607
20 Markham, *How to Chuse, Ride, Traine and Dyet* etc., 1599
21 Markham, *Masterpiece*, ed. of 1680, ch. cx
22 Hall, Joseph (later Bishop of Norwich and Exeter), *Virgidemiarum*, 4th Book, 3rd Satire. Actually a free translation of Juvenal.
23 Markham, *The Complete Jockey or the most exact Rules and Methods to be observed for the training up of Race-Horses* etc., ed. of 1680, ch. iii, v., xv
24 Markham, *Masterpiece*, ch. ix, cii
25 Accounts of the Lord High Treasurer; qu. Fittis, Robert Scott, *Sports and Pastimes of Scotland*, Alexander Gardner 1891, p. 109
26 Records of the Burgh; qu. Fittis, p. 110
27 Lindsay of the Mount, Sir David, *The Complaynt of Schir David Lyndesay to the Kingis Grace ; Poetical Works*, ed. David Laing, Paterson 1879, Vol. 1, p. 50, lines 177 sq.
28 Chalmers, Robert, *Domestic Annals of Scotland*, Vol. 1, p. 103
29 Council Books; qu. Fittis, p. 112
30 Hume (or Home), David, *History of the House of Wedderburn*

31 Carve (or Carue, Carew, O'Corrain), Thomas, *Lyra, seu Anacephalaeosis Hibernica*, Vienna 1651
32 Blundeville, *The fower chiefest offices* etc.
33 Harrison in Holinshed, Vol. 1, p. 371
34 Major, Joannes, *History of Greater Britain*, 1521; tr. A. Constable, Scottish Historical Soc. 1892
35 Ewart, Prof. J. C., *The Multiple Origin of Horses and Ponies*, Transactions of the Highland Soc. 1904
36 Anonymous Priest; qu. Camden, p.1047 in ed.of 1695
37 Lisini, A., *Relazione fra Cesare Borgia e la Republica Senese*; qu. Heywood
38 Carnessecchi, *Storia Senese*; qu. ibid.
39 Ratto to Mantua; qu. Hore, Vol. 1, pp. 71–73
40 Grisone, Frederico, *Gli Ordini di Cavalcare*, 1550; *see* Chenevix-Trench, pp. 104–22
41 Letter from English Ambassador; qu. Hore Vol. 1, pp. 80–81
42 By J. P. Hore, most surprisingly
43 French account qu. and tr. Hore; no source named, but authenticity undoubted
44 Castañeda de Nagera, Pedro de; qu. Denhardt, p. 27
45 Burton, Robert, *Anatomy of Melancholy*; 16th ed. from ed. of 1651, Blake 1838, I. 2, 4, 6, p. 231
46 Acosta, José de, *Historia Natural y Moral de las Indias*, 1590; qu. Denhardt, p. 33
47 Dìaz del Castillo, Bernal, *La Conquista de Nueva-España*; qu. Denhardt, p. 50
48 By Tesio, pp. 45–46

### 4 EARLY STUARTS AND COMMONWEALTH

1 Burton, *Anatomy*, II. 2, 4, pp. 341–42, 343
2 Sir Thomas Lake to Lord Salisbury, 15 Nov 1609; qu. Hore, Vol. 1, p. 152
3 Camden, William, *Annales*, 1639; tr. Bishop Kennet, ed. of 1719
4 Lysons, Vol. 2, pp. 584 sq.
5 MS qu. *Horse Racing*, p. 110
6 Corporation Records; qu. Cook, Sir T. A., *History of the English Turf*, H. Virtue 1901, Vol. 1, p. 60
7 Nichol, *Progresses of James I*, Vol. 2, p. 265
8 Prior, C. M., 'Early Records of the Thoroughbred Horse', *The Sportsman* 1924, pp. 110, 164
9 Butcher, *Survey and Antiquity of the Towne of Stamford*, 1646, p. 39
10 Burton, William, *Chronology of Stamford*, 1662, p. 243
11 Municipal Register; qu. Cook, Vol. 1, p. 80
12 Baker, George, *History and Antiquities of the County of Northampton*, 1822–41, Vol. 1, pp. 171, 573
13 Surtees, Scott Frederick, *History of Durham*, 1864, Vol. 3, p. 332
14 Webbe, Edward, *His trauailes* etc., ed. 1868
15 Heywood, Thomas, *English Traveller*, 1620
16 Dodsley, *Collection of Old Plays*: 'Merry Beggars, or the Jovial Crew', 1641
17 State Papers; qu. Cook, Vol. 1, p. 66
18 Full documentation qu. Hore, Vol. 2, pp. 130–42
19 State Paper; qu. Fittis
20 Printed in *The Yorkshire Newspaper*, 26 Aug 1837
21 The cup examined and descr. Fittis, pp. 115–16
22 Lodge, Edmund, *Illustrations of British History*, 2nd ed. 1838, Vol. 3, p. 53
23 Privy Seal Brevia; qu. Hore, Vol. 1, p. 303
24 Sign Manual Grants; qu. Hore, Vol. 1, p. 304
25 Birch, Thomas, *Court and Times of James I*, ed. R. F. Williams 1848, Chamberlain to Carleton, Vol. 2, p. 53
26 Dean Lockier to Alexander Pope, letter qu. Dictionary of National Biography
27 Young, William, *Diary*, 1 Aug 1621
28 Graham MS; qu. Muir, J. B., *W. T. Frampton and the 'Dragon'*, Sporting Fine Art Gallery 1895, pp. 101–3
29 Ibid, pp. 106–9
30 Qu. Banks, Sir Joseph, in *Archaeologia* Vol. XIII, p. 236
31 Reresby, Sir John, *Memoirs*, 1634–1698, ed. J. J. Cartwright 1875, p. 10
32 Burton, *Anatomy*, I. 2, 2, 1, p. 140
33 *Archaeologia Aeliana*, Vol. 1, p. 4
34 A. Deleto to Earl of Rutland; qu. Prior, C. M., '*History of the Racing Calendar and Stud Book*', Sporting Life, 1926, p. 13
35 Pelham MS; qu. Muir, pp. 113–16
36 Birch, Vol. 1, p. 71
37 Harrington, Sir John, *Nugae Antiquae*, ed. of 1804, Vol. 1, pp. 210, 220
38 Hinde, Rev., *Biography of Bruen*; qu. Tozer
39 Burton, *Anatomy*, I. 2, 3, 13, p. 191

40 Warton, Thomas, *History of Poetry*, ed. of 1824, Vol. 2, p. 316, *Of Covetice*
41 Buckingham's stable accounts; qu. Muir p. 109
42 Letter qu. Hore, Vol. 2, p. 148
43 Herbert of Cherbury, Lord, *Autobiography*, ed. of 1870, p. 37
44 Jonson, Ben, *Alchemist* 1610, I. i
45 Shirley, James, *Hyde Park* 1632, IV. iii
46 Records of the Burgh; qu. Fittis
47 State Papers; qu. Hore, Vol. 2, p. 206
48 Hoare, Vol. 6, p. 416
49 Letters of Dorothy Osborne to William Temple, ed. E. A. Parry; new ed. 1888; 25 May 1654
50 Dorothy Osborne to William Temple, 6 June 1654
51 Evelyn, 20 May 1658
52 *A character of England as it was lately represented in a letter to a Nobleman of France*, 1659; qu. Parry, notes to Dorothy Osborne, p. 272
53 Evelyn, 22 April 1655, 18 Oct 1664, 25 July 1650
54 Hore, Vol. 2, pp. 170 sq.
55 Italian source; qu. Tesio, p. 3
56 Pelham MS; qu. Muir, p. 116

### 5 RESTORATION AND LATER STUARTS

1 Evelyn, 13 March 1650
2 Newcastle, Duke of, *La Méthode et Invention Nouvelle de dresser les chevaux*, Antwerp 1657
3 Pepys, Samuel, *Diary*, 5 Oct 1663, 22 and 23 May, 18 July 1668, 7 and 8 March 1669
4 Tuscany, Duke of, *Journal of his Travels in England*, 9 May 1669. Manuscript in the Laurentian Library, Florence
5 Evelyn, 22 July 1670
6 Ibid.
7 Evelyn, 9, 10, 21 Oct 1671
8 Despatch to Whitehall from Sir Robert Carr, March 1675; qu. Prior C. M. & F. M., *Stud Book Lore*, F. M. Prior 1951, p. 63
9 Pope, Alexander, *Imitations of Horace*, Poetical Works ed. Herbert Davis, O.U.P. 1966, Bk II, Epistle 1, lines 139 sq., p. 365
10 Evelyn, 23 Sept 1683
11 Hatton Correspondence, 5 Sept 1682; qu. Siltzer, Frank, *Newmarket*, Cassell 1923, p. 239
12 John Baylor to Thomas Hales; qu. Harrison, Fairfax, *Equine F.F.Vs*, Old Dominion Press, Richmond, Va 1928; p. 99
13 *London Gazette*, Sept 1699
14 Qu. *Annals of Sporting*, Vol. 10, p. 269
15 Qu. Prior, *Early Records*, p. 110
16 Despatch from Lord Conway, 5 April 1682; qu. Tozer, pp. 254–55
17 Lawrence, John, *The Horse in all his varieties and uses*, Arnold 1829, p. 292
18 Pepys, 27 May 1663, 26 July 1663, 14 July 1667
19 *London Gazette*, May 1684
20 MS qu. *Horse Racing*
21 E.g. *London Gazette*, Easter Wednesday 1688
22 Evelyn, 21 Feb 1689
23 Municipal Records of Bristol; qu. Hore, Vol. 3, p. 288 n.
24 Macaulay, Lord, *History of England*, ed. of 1906 Longmans Green, Vol. 5, p. 482
25 Sessions Order, 14 Jan 1695; qu. Sykes, John, *Local Records*, ed. 1886–1876; Vol. 2, p. 370
26 Council Records, 16 April 1706; qu. Fittis
27 Chafin, Rev., *Anecdotes of Cranborne Chase*; qu. Muir, p. 16
28 Accounts of the Master of the Horse; qu Muir, p. 21
29 Parsons, P. *Newmarket, an Essay on the Turf*, 1771; qu. Siltzer, p. 170
30 *Adventurer*, No. 37, 13 March 1752
31 E.g. Whyte, J. C., *History of the British Turf*, Colburn 1840; and Lawrence, *The Horse*
32 Tennant, Richard, MS at Sledmere; qu. Prior, *Stud Book Lore*, p. 105
33 9 Anne, ch. 14, sec. 3
34 Tennant; qu. Prior, loc. cit., p. 101
35 Declared Accounts of Charles Duke of Somerset; qu. Cawthorne, G. J. & Herod, R. S., *Royal Ascot*, Treherne 1902, p. 18
36 Swift, Jonathan, *Journal to Stella*, 10 and 13 August 1711; ed. Frederick Ryland, Bell 1922, Vol. 2, pp. 220 sq.
37 Manx Museum MS; qu. Megaw, B.R.S., 'Mount Strange and the "Manx Derby" Races', *Journal of the Manx Museum*, Vol. VI, No. 74, 1957, p. 9
38 *Intelligencer*, 15 May 1665

39 Qu. Hore, Vol. 3, pp. 111–14
40 Clarendon to Rochester, 1 and 4 May 1686, *Correspondence and Diary*, ed. S. W. Singer, Vol. 1, pp. 370–73
41 Pepys, 11 Nov 1661, 21 Dec 1663
42 Evelyn, 6 Jan 1662, 8 Jan 1668
43 Pepys, 14 Feb 1668
44 Evelyn, 18 Sept 1683
45 16 Charles II, ch. 17
46 Evelyn 28 Feb 1699
47 Qu. Prior, *Stud Book Lore*, pp. 61 sq.

### 6 CREATION OF THE THOROUGHBRED

1 His own words: preface to *The Horse*, p. iii
2 Lawrence, p. 264
3 Rous, Captain Hon. Henry, *Laws and Practice of Horse Racing*, Baily 1850, Introduction, p. vi
4 Collins, Digby; qu. Sidney, p. 65
5 E.g. Cook, *History*, Vol. 1, pp. 20–21
6 Pepys, 26 Oct 1661, 29 April 1667
7 Pepys, 24 June 1663
8 Commission qu. Prior, *Early Records*, p. 162
9 Evelyn, 17 Dec 1684
10 For this interesting but discredited classification see Lowe, Bruce, *Breeding Race Horses by the Figure System*, 1895; and Allison, William, *The British Thoroughbred Horse*, Grant Richards 1901
11 Thomas to Richard Darley; qu. Willett, Peter, *The Thoroughbred*, Weidenfeld & Nicolson 1970, p. 29
12 Duke of Devonshire's Trial Book; qu. Orchard, Vincent *The British Thoroughbred*, Ariel Press 1966, p. 1
13 Evidence assembled by Miller, Sir Mordaunt, in *The British Racehorse*, Vol. XIV, No. 2, Summer 1962, pp. 188–91
14 The legend originated with Sue, Eugène, who serialized a novelette about the Godolphin Arabian in *La Presse* about 1825. See Rice, James, *History of the British Turf*, Samson Low 1879, Vol. 1, pp. 188–89
15 Rous, p. viii
16 Osmer, William, *A dissertation on Horses*, 1756; qu. Miller, loc. cit.
17 Upton, pp. 201 sq.
18 Pick, William, *The Turf Register and Sportsman and Breeder's Stud-Book*, 1803
19 Mr Peter Willett's figure: *Introduction to the Thoroughbred*, Stanley Paul 1966, p. 21
20 Muir, p. 80
21 Osmer; qu. Sidney, pp. 55–56
22 Lawrence, *History*; qu. ibid
23 Upton, p. 95
24 Especially that of J. B. Robertson ('Mankato') and C. M. Prior
25 Earl of Bristol to his son Carr, 17 July 1713; qu. Prior, *Stud Book Lore*, p. 79
26 Becker, F., *The Breed of the Racehorse*, B.B.A. 1935, pp. 137 sq.
27 Earl of Bristol to Duke of Bolton, 22 April 1737; qu. Prior, *Stud Book Lore*, p. 80

### 7 17TH-CENTURY EUROPE

1 Heywood, pp. 233 sq., quotes various 17th-century writers
2 Evelyn, 27 Feb 1645
3 Evelyn, 25 Oct 1644, 31 Jan, 6 Feb 1645
4 Burton, *Anatomy*, II. 2. 4
5 Evelyn, 7 Oct 1644
6 Ménétrier, le Père, *Traité des tournois, joutes, carousels et autres spectacles publics*, Lyon 1669; qu. Jusserand, p. 385
7 Thétard, Henry, *Histoire et Secrets du Turf*, Robert Laffont 1947, 13th ed., p. 335
8 Bassompierre, Maréchal de, *Memoires*; qu. Tozer
9 Buisson d'Aubenay, *Diary*; qu. and tr. Black, Robert, *Horse-Racing in France: a History*, Samson Low 1886
10 Carlyle, Thomas, *Speeches of Cromwell*, ed. of 1880, Vol. 3, p. 194
11 *Gazette*, 27 Feb 1683; qu. Jusserand; and Macaulay, loc. cit.
12 Dangeau, *Journal*; qu. Jusserand
13 Fourches, Marquis de, 'Mémoires,' *Le Sport*, January 1877
14 *Mercure Gallant*, 1700; qu. Jusserand, p. 405
15 Ibid., pp. 406–7
16 Ibid., p. 409
17 Verney, F. P., Vol. 1 of *Memoirs of the Verney Family*, Longmans Green 1892; pp. 182–94

## 8 GEORGIAN BRITAIN: HORSES AND RACES

1 Accounts of the Master of the Horse; qu. Muir, pp. 35–36
2 *Whitehall Evening Post*, 26 March 1719
3 Frampton's will; qu. Muir, p. 38–39
4 Drake, *Eboracum*, 1736, p. 241
5 13 George II. ch. 19
6 18 George II. ch. 34
7 Rous, pp. 7–8
8 *Post Boy*, 11 Sept 1711
9 *Sporting Magazine*, Nov 1827
10 Rous, p. x
11 *Horse Racing*, p. 340
12 Lawrence, p. 295
13 Ibid.
14 *Westminster Journal*, 23 June 1744
15 Stone, *Year Book*, p. 538
16 *Sporting Magazine*, May 1804
17 *Sporting Magazine*, Jan 1792
18 Horace Walpole to George Montagu, 20 July 1749; ed. W. S. Lewis & R. S. Brown, O.U.P. 1941
19 Walpole, Horace, *Memoirs of the Reign of King George the Second*, ed. Lord Holland 1847, Vol. 1, p. 402
20 Lawrence, p. 286
21 Lawrence, *History*; qu. Sidney, p. 58
22 E.g. St Bel, Vial de, *Essay on the Geometrical Proportions of Eclipse*; *see* Rathbone, George, 'Reconstruction of Eclipse' *The British Racehorse*, Vol. XV No. 5, Dec 1963, pp. 546–47
23 Lady Sarah Lennox to Lady Susan O'Brien (Fox-Strangways), 9 Jan 1766, *Life and Letters*, ed. Countess of Ilchester & Lord Stavordale, John Murray 1901
24 Ibid. 12 July 1765
25 Rous, Admiral: evidence before the Committee of the House of Lords on Horse Breeding, 1873
26 Rous, *Laws and Practice*, p. ix
27 Corporation Order, 6 June 1615; qu. Fletcher, J. S., *History of St Leger Stakes*, Hutchinson, undated, p. 37
28 Toland, John, *Letter to Eudoxa*, c. 1730
29 Lysons, Vol. 5, p. 377
30 *Morning Post*, 23 Oct 1776
31 Bath, Earl of, in *The World*, Vol. 1, No. 17, 1753

## 9 GEORGIAN BRITAIN: CONTROLS AND PEOPLE

1 Cheny, volume of 1731
2 Sir William Musgrave to Lord Carlisle, 11 Dec 1767, Earl of Carlisle MSS, H.M.C.
3 Lady Sarah Lennox to Lady Susan O'Brien, 12 May 1768
4 *Post*, 24 Oct 1776
5 Qu. Black, Robert, *Horse-Racing in England, A Synoptical Review*, Richard Bentley 1893, pp. 11 sq. Rice, Vol. 1, pp. 103–4, quotes a slightly different version; he gives the author as M. Grossley, the book as *Tour to London; or, New Observations upon England*, and the date as 1800.
6 Lawrence, p. 270
7 Ibid., p. 77
8 Chifney, Samuel, *Genius Genuine*, 1804, pp. 52–53
9 Greville, Charles, *Memoirs*, 12 Jan 1829, ed. Henry Reeve, 5th ed. Longmans Green 1875
10 Chifney, p. 79
11 Qu. Prior, *Stud Book Lore*, pp. 111–18
12 Lawrence, p. 295
13 See Dupont, Richard J. M., 'Equestrian Painting', *The British Racehorse*, Vol. XV No. 2, Summer 1963, pp. 152 sq.
14 Mirabeau; qu. Black; but see note (5) above
15 Berenger, *History and Art of Horsemanship*, 1771
16 Lawrence, p. 268
17 Lady Sarah Lennox to Lady Susan O'Brien, 16 Oct 1763, 11 Oct 1674
18 Horace Walpole to George Montagu, 2 June 1759
19 Lady Sarah Lennox to Lady Susan O'Brien, 16 Oct 1763
20 *Morning Chronicle*, 11 Sept 1776
21 *Morning Chronicle*, 5 Aug 1791
22 George Montagu to Horace Walpole, 9 Oct 1759
23 Anon.; qu. Rice, Vol. 1, p. 106
24 D'Urfey, *Pills to Purge Melancholy*, 4th ed. 1719, Vol. 2, p. 53
25 Toland, *Eudoxa*
26 Anon.; qu. Cook, Sir T. A., *Eclipse & O'Kelly*, Dutton 1907, pp. 108–9
27 Chifney, pp. 64, 69
28 *Public Advertiser*, 1 and 9 July 1791; *Morning Chronicle*, 6 July 1791

## 10 18TH-CENTURY EUROPE AND RUSSIA

1 Toland, *Eudoxa*
2 Mirabeau; qu. Black; *see* note (5) to Ch. 9
3 Eyewitness qu. Youatt, William, *The Horse*, Chapman & Hall, 1st ed. 1831, pp. 45 sq.
4 Piozzi, Mrs Gabriel (Hester Lynch Salusbury); qu. Youatt, pp. 46–47
5 Barbier, Edmond, *Chronique de la Régence et du Règne de Louis XV*, 17 Aug 1722; ed. Charpentier, Paris, 1806
6 Voltaire, F. A. de, *Essai sur les Moeurs, Oeuvres Complètes*, Garnier Frères 1879, Vol. 12, ch. xcix, p. 445
7 Horace Walpole to George Montagu, 17 May 1763
8 Horace Walpole to Rev. W. Cole, 28 Feb 1766; to George Montagu 20 June 1766
9 Lawrence, p. 273
10 Mercy-Argenteau, comte de, *Lettres à Marie-Thérèse*, ed. comte de Pimodan, Plon 1911, Feb to Nov 1776
11 Contemp. qu. Laffon, pp. 82 sq.
12 Mercier, Louis-Sebastien, *Tableau de Paris*, ed. of 1783–88; and 'Nimrod', *Nimrod Abroad*, Colburn 1843, Vol. 1 pp. 180–83
13 Bath, Earl of, in *The World*, Vol. 1, no. 17, 1753
14 Buc'Hoz, *Amusements des Français*, 1798; qu. Jusserand, p. 426
15 Castéra, *Histoire de Cathérine II*; qu. Hayes, Capt. M. H., *Among Horses in Russia*, Everett 1900, p. 66
16 Blundeville, Thomas, op. cit.
17 Hayes, *Russia*, p. 70
18 Strachof & Jacharef; qu. Hayes, *Russia*, p. 72

## 11 COLONIAL AMERICA

1 Denhardt, pp. 178, 225
2 Act of Assembly; qu. Harrison, Fairfax, *The Equine F.F.Vs*, Old Dominion Press 1928, p. 38
3 Established by Hervey, John, *Racing and Breeding in America* in Richardson, Charles (ed.), *Racing at Home and Abroad*, London & Counties Press Association 1923–31, Vol. 3, p. 8
4 Court Records; qu. Robertson, William H. P., *History of Thoroughbred Racing in America*, Prentice-Hall 1964, p. 8
5 Court Records; qu. Harrison, Fairfax, *The Roanoke Stud 1795–1833*, Old Dominion Press 1930, Appendix 2, p. 67
6 Qu. Robertson, p. 8
7 Act of General Assembly; qu. Robertson, p. 10
8 Contemp. qu. Robertson, p. 24
9 Qu. Hervey, p. 6
10 Contemp. MS; qu. Denhardt, p. 179
11 Qu. Hervey, p. 5
12 Engraving qu. Robertson, p. 10
13 Qu. Harrison, *Roanoke*, Appendix 13, p. 204
14 *New York Gazette*; qu. Robertson, p. 12
15 Contemp. qu. Robertson, p. 16
16 *Virginia Gazette*; qu. Robertson, p. 16
17 *Virginia Gazette*; qu. Harrison: *Equine F.F.Vs*, p. 56
18 *Maryland Gazette*, 23 April 1761
19 Smith (or Smyth), J. F. D., *American Turf, c.* 1765; qu. Hervey, p. 16
20 Ordinance; qu. Hervey, p. 16
21 John Baylor to Thomas Hales; qu. Harrison, *Equine F.F.Vs*, p. 99
22 One of the many advertisements qu. ibid.
23 By Allison, p. 150
24 *Maryland Gazette*; qu. Robertson, p. 19
25 *New York Gazette*; qu. Robertson, pp. 13–14
26 Advertisements in *South Carolina Gazette*; qu. Harrison, Fairfax, *The John's Island Stud 1750–1788*, Old Dominion Press 1931
27 *South Carolina Gazette*; qu. Robertson, p. 23
28 Engraving qu. Robertson, p. 12
29 Contemp. qu. Hervey, p. 14
30 Ibid.
31 By R. L. Gerry; qu. Robertson, p. 13
32 Dispersal Sale Advertisement; qu. Harrison, *Equine F.F.Vs*, p. 98
33 *Virginia Gazette*, 9 May 1771
34 Smith, op. cit.; qu. Allison, p. 144
35 *American Turf Register*, III, 193, 419
36 Contemp. qu. Denhardt, p. 146

## 12 19TH-CENTURY BRITAIN: BENTINCK AND BEFORE

1 Royal Archives: Georgian Papers 40449–50
2 Greville, 16 March 1827; 29 June, 6 Aug, 25 Aug, 21 Dec 1828; 11 June, 24 June 1829; 18 Sept 1830

3 An old *bon vivant's* definitive account is qu. Rice, Vol. 1, pp. 126–7
4 Greville, 18 July 1830
5 'Druid', *Post and Paddock*, 1st ed. 1856; 5th ed. Vinton 1912, p. 101
6 Greville, 5 June 1831; 17 May, 25 June 1832
7 'Nimrod', *The Chase, The Road, and The Turf*; orig. *Quarterly Review* 1835 sq.; Sportsman's Library, Edward Arnold 1898, p. 131
8 Kent, John, *Racing Life of Lord George Bentinck*, William Blackwood 1892, p. 349
9 'Druid', *Post and Paddock*, pp. 166–67
10 Raikes, *Diary*; qu. 'Druid', *Post and Paddock*, p. 106
11 'Druid', *Silk and Scarlet*; 1st ed. 1858; 5th ed. Vinton 1912; p. 87
12 Egan, Pierce, *Book of Sports*, Tegg 1832, p. 177
13 'Sylvanus', *Bye-Lanes and Downs of England*, Richard Bentley 1850, pp. 76–86
14 'Druid', *Post and Paddock*, p. 48
15 Day, William, *Reminiscences of the Turf*, Richard Bentley 1886, p. 72
16 'Sylvanus', pp. 91–92
17 Greville, 17 Dec 1832
18 Day, p. 63
19 Ibid. pp. 74–75
20 'Sylvanus', pp. 67–68
21 Qu. 'Druid', *Silk and Scarlet*, p. 6
22 'Nimrod', *Chase, Road and Turf*, p. 154
23 Kent, *Bentinck*, pp. 278–79
24 *Sporting Magazine*, Sept 1806
25 'Sylvanus', pp. 7–8
26 Greville, 28 Sept. 1848
27 Greville, 25 Oct 1830
28 Day, pp. 105–6
29 Greville, 28 Sept 1848
30 Kent, *Bentinck*, pp. 64 sq.
31 Disraeli, Benjamin, *Lord George Bentinck: A Political Biography*, 5th ed. Colburn 1852, p. 348
32 Remark made to Sir William Gregory; qu. Kent, *Bentinck*, p. 452
33 His betting-book; qu. Newmarket, 'Chapters from Turf History'; *National Review*, 1922, p. 74
34 Day, p. 87
35 Day, pp. 91, 126–27
36 Kent, *Bentinck*, p. 170
37 Greville, 6 June 1843
38 Greville, 25 Nov 1843
39 Greville, 5 June 1844
40 'Nimrod' in *Quarterly Review*, 1841
41 Disraeli, *Bentinck*, p. 347
42 Day, p. 128
43 Greville, 23 March 1847
44 Disraeli, *Bentinck*, p. 539

## 13 19TH-CENTURY BRITAIN: ROUS AND AFTER

1 Lawrence, p. 295
2 'Nimrod', *Chase, Road and Turf*, p. 180 n.
3 'Druid', *Post and Paddock*, p. 58
4 Rous, p. 45
5 'Nimrod', *Chase, Road and Turf*, p. 178
6 'Druid', *Post and Paddock*, p. 170
7 Rice, Vol. 2, p. 213
8 Day, pp. 250 sq.
9 'Druid', *Post and Paddock*, p. 60
10 Ibid. pp. 49–50, 56
11 Correspondence qu. Willett, Peter, 'Admiral Rous', *The British Racehorse*, Vol. XIV, no. 4, Sept 1962, p. 417
12 *The Times*, 5 April 1825
13 Lawrence, p. 291
14 Rous, pp. xi–xii, 124, 125
15 Qu. Bird, T. H., *Admiral Rous and the British Turf*, Putnam 1939
16 Day, p. 25
17 Mostly in the editorial and correspondence columns of *The Times*, 1869–70
18 'Druid', *Silk and Scarlet*, pp. 186–87
19 See Anstruther, Ian, *The Knight and the Umbrella*, G. Bles, 1956
20 'Newmarket', p. 54 n.; Fairfax-Blakeborough, J., *Northern Turf History*, J. A. Allen, Vol. 1, 1949, p. 272 n.
21 Eye-witness qu. Fletcher, p. 205
22 Galopin may have been sired by Delight; *see* Mortimer, Roger, *History of the Derby Stakes*, Cassell 1962, p. 248
23 Lambton, Hon George, *Men and Horses I have Known*, Thornton Butterworth 1924, p. 100

24 Ibid., p. 104
25 'Druid' *Post and Paddock*, p. 119
26 *See* Fawcett, William, *Turf, Chase & Paddock*, Hutchinson 1932, pp. 49 sq.
27 Disraeli to Lady Londonderry, 7 Aug 1854; qu. Moneypenny, W. F. & Buckle, G. E., *Life of Benjamin Disraeli*, John Murray 1914, Vol. 3, pp. 546–47
28 Day, pp. 35, 37
29 Lehndorff, Count G., *Horse Breeding Recollections*, Horace Cox 1883, pp. 15 sq.
30 Qu. Welcome, John, *Fred Archer, his Life and Times*, Faber 1967, p. 135
31 Lambton, p. 109
32 'Thormanby', *Kings of the Turf*, Hutchinson 1898, pp. 307–8

### 14 19TH-CENTURY BRITAIN: COURSES, JOCKEYS, TRAINERS, MARGINALIA

1 Contemp. qu. 'Druid', *Scott and Sebright*, 1st ed. 1862; 5th ed. Vinton 1912, p. 6
2 Greville, 10 Aug 1830
3 Corbet, Henry, *Sporting Life*, Rogerson & Tuxford 1864, p. 121
4 Sidney, p. 89
5 *Sporting Annals*, Vol. VIII, p. 239
6 Sidney, p. 90
7 Lambton, p. 175
8 The late Sir Jack Jarvis, Godding's grandson, told the writer this story in 1965
9 'Druid', *Scott and Sebright*, p. 6
10 Cawthorne & Herod, pp. 61–62
11 Sidney, p. 89
12 Brayley, Edward Wedlake, *Topographical History of Surrey*, 1850, Vol. 4, p. 372
13 *Household Words*, 7 June 1851
14 Disraeli, Benjamin, *Sybil, or the Two Nations*, 1st ed. 1845, World's Classics, O.U.P. 1926, p. 6
15 Sidney, p. 89
16 *New Sporting Magazine*, May 1824
17 'Sylvanus', p. 123
18 Lawrence, p. 294
19 Bates, Sir Loftus, who was Clerk of the Course, in intro. to Fairfax-Blakeborough Vol. 2
20 *New Sporting Magazine*, Feb 1832
21 Surtees, R. S., *Plain or Ringlets*, Bradbury Agnew 1860
22 Surtees, R. S., *Mr Sponge's Sporting Tour*, Bradbury Agnew 1852
23 Surtees, *Plain or Ringlets*, p. 62
24 Rous, p. 51
25 Qu. *Morning Herald*, 16 Aug 1817
26 *The Courier*, 5 June 1837
27 *The Sunday Times*, 4 June, 1837
28 *The Sunday Times*, 25 June 1837
29 'Nimrod', *Chase, Road and Turf*, p. 165
30 Lawrence, p. 274
31 'Druid', *Scott and Sebright*, p. 156
32 'Druid', *Saddle and Sirloin*, 1st ed. 1870; 5th ed. Vinton 1912, p. 261 n.
33 Rutland MS; qu. Prior, *Racing Calendar and Stud Book*, p. 220
34 Lawrence, p. 273
35 Corbet, p. 37
36 Especially 'Druid', *Saddle and Sirloin*, passim
37 Grimshaw v. Lomax, King's Bench, 12 Feb 1825
38 *Stockport Advertiser*, 1 April 1825
39 Snowy, J., *The Stanley of the Turf*, Chapman & Hall 1896, p. 45
40 Acton, C. R., *Silk and Spur*, Grant Richards 1935, p. 92
41 Qu. Rice, Vol. 1, pp. 308–310
42 Descr. Lambton, pp. 70 sq.
43 Contemp. qu. Corbet, pp. 177–78
44 Kent, *Bentinck*, pp. 143, 148
45 'Druid', *Scott and Sebright*, p. 60
46 Lawley, Hon. Francis, Appendix to Kent, *Bentinck*, pp. 383–85
47 'Druid', *Scott and Sebright*, p. 52
48 'Druid', *Post and Paddock*, p. 32
49 'Sylvanus', p. 26
50 'Nimrod': *Nemrod, ou l'Amateur des Chevaux de Courses*, Arthur Bertrand 1838, pp. 208 sq.
51 'Druid', *Scott and Sebright*, p. 31
52 Lawrence, pp. 277–78
53 Lambton, p. 42
54 Qu. ibid., p. 38
55 Welcome, John, *Fred Archer, his Life and Times*, Faber 1967

56 'Druid', *Silk and Scarlet*, p. 128
57 Kent, *Bentinck*, p. 261
58 Day, p. 362
59 E.g. Black, *England*, p. 237
60 'Druid', *Post and Paddock*, pp. 22, 24
61 Kent, *Bentinck*, p. 87
62 'Sylvanus', pp. 26 sq.
63 'Druid', *Scott and Sebright*, p. 170
64 Rice, Vol. 2, p. 225
65 'Nimrod', *Chase, Road and Turf*, p. 207
66 Day, pp. 371 sq.
67 Corbet, p. 23
68 Rice, Vol. 2, p. 273
69 'Nimrod', *Nemrod*, p. 204
70 'Nimrod', *Chase, Road and Turf*, p. 173
71 'Sylvanus', p. 26
72 'Druid', *Post and Paddock*, p. 25
73 Corbet, pp. 19–20
74 Ibid., p. 19
75 Snowy, p. 9
76 Qu. Fawcett, William, *Racing in the Olden Days*, Hutchinson, undated, p. 187
77 Rice, Vol. 1, p. 252
78 Qu. 'Druid', *Post and Paddock*, pp. 170–71
79 Surtees, *Plain or Ringlets*, p. 63
80 Snowy, pp. 14, 18, 35, 37
81 'Druid', *Post and Paddock*, pp. 177–82
82 Snowy, p. 30
83 'Druid', *Post and Paddock*, p. 183
84 Surtees, *Plain or Ringlets*, p. 82
85 *Yorkshire Gazette*, 17 Sept 1836
86 Fletcher, p. 125; Rice, Vol. 2, p. 34
87 Kent, *Bentinck*, p. 122
88 'Druid', *Post and Paddock*, p. 175
89 Haydon, Thos., *Sporting Reminiscences*, Bliss, Sands 1898, p. 10
90 Surtees, *Plain or Ringlets*, p. 81

### 15 BRITISH STEEPLECHASING

1 Berenger, *History and Art of Horsemanship*, 1771
2 Baret, Michael, *Hipponomania, or the Vineyard of Horsemanship*, 1618
3 E.g. used by Corbet, p. 161
4 Pepys, 11 Aug 1661, 25 Aug 1663, 11 Aug 1664
5 Allegedly MS in possession of O'Briens of Dromoland; qu. Blew, W. C. A, *History of Steeple-Chasing*, Nimmo 1901, p. 4
6 Lawrence, p. 229
7 Prior, *Racing Calendar and Stud Book*, pp. 145–47
8 Lawrence, p. 234
9 Ibid., p. 230
10 Youatt, p. 105
11 Qu. 'Druid', *Silk and Scarlet*, p. 23
12 Ibid., p. 26
13 'Druid', *Post and Paddock*, p. 343
14 Taplin, *Sporting Dictionary*, 1803
15 'Druid', *Silk and Scarlet*, p. 1; *Post and Paddock*, pp. 336 sq.
16 'Druid', *Silk and Scarlet*, pp. 9, 22
17 Dick Christian; qu. 'Druid', *Post and Paddock*, p. 357
18 'Druid', *Scott and Sebright*, p. 282
19 Egan, dedication of *Book of Sports* to Osbaldeston
20 Dick Christian; qu. 'Druid', *Silk and Scarlet*, pp. 57, 59
21 Correspondence, Bentinck to Coleman; qu. Blew, pp. 20–21
22 'Druid', *Scott and Sebright*, p. 296
23 Egan, pp. 161 sq.
24 'Druid', *Scott and Sebright*, p. 295
25 Qu. Eliot, Elizabeth, *Portrait of a Sport: A History of Steeplechasing*, Longman 1957, p. 43
26 'Druid', *Scott and Sebright*, p. 304
27 Corbet, p. 69
28 Letter qu. Seth-Smith, Michael, in Part I of *History of Steeplechasing*, Michael Joseph 1966, p. 27
29 'Druid' *Scott and Sebright*, p. 295
30 Ibid., p. 317
31 Dick Christian; qu. 'Druid', *Silk and Scarlet*, p. 11
32 Blew, p. 62
33 'Druid', *Post and Paddock*, p. 356
34 Qu. Seth-Smith, p. 39
35 Lawrence, pp. 238–39, 256
36 *Liverpool Mercury*, 27 Feb 1839
37 'Nimrod', *Chase, Road and Turf*, pp. 292–93
38 *New Sporting Magazine*, April 1840

39 'Nimrod', *Nimrod Abroad*, Vol. 2 repeatedly
40 Surtees, *Sponge*, p. 429
41 Ibid.
42 Both qu. Seth-Smith, pp. 43, 61
43 Surtees, *Sponge*, p. 435
44 *Sporting Review*, 1863; qu. Seth-Smith, p. 61
45 Surtees, *Sponge*, p. 441
46 'Druid', *Post and Paddock*, p. 294
47 Anonymous amateur rider; qu. Acton, pp. 76–77
48 Ibid., p. 78
49 Lambton, pp. 24–26
50 Blew, p. 249
51 Qu. Willett, Peter, Part II of *History of Steeplechasing*, p. 99
52 W. E. Oakeley M.F.H.; qu. Arthur Coaten; in turn qu. Williams, Michael, *The Continuing Story of Point to Point Racing*, Pelham 1970; p. 23
53 Eye-witness qu. Williams, p. 26
54 Smith, Vian, *Point to Point*, Stanley Paul 1968, pp. 20–21

### 16 IRELAND

1 Dickson, *Dublin Intelligencer*, 11 Aug 1731
2 Oliver Goldsmith to Daniel Hodson, 27 Dec 1757; qu. Foster, J. *Life and Times*, Bickers, 6th ed. 1877, Vol. 1, pp. 125 sq.
3 Goldsmith, Oliver, *Citizen of the World, Letter V*, ed. of 1785, Vol. 1 p. 25
4 Pue, *Occurrences*, 7 Sept 1751
5 Robinson, J. R., *Old Q*, Samson Low 1895, pp. 26–28
6 Documents qu. Healy, Thomas E., in Richardson, Vol. 2, p. 200
7 Letters and newspapers qu. Watson, S. J., *Between the Flags: a History of Irish Steeplechasing*, Figgis 1969, pp. 38–41
8 MacCabe, F. F., in Richardson, Vol. 2, pp. 235 sq.
9 Ibid.
10 Ibid., pp. 239–40
11 Snowy, pp. 47, 206
12 Correspondence qu. Hore, Vol. 3 pp. 349–53
13 Horace Walpole to George Montagu, 12 April 1762
14 'Nimrod', *Nimrod Abroad*, Vol. 2, p. 237
15 *Sporting Magazine*, April 1819
16 Egan, p. 167
17 Letter to *Sporting Magazine*, Feb 1833
18 *Letters to Queen Victoria 1862–1878*, ed G E. Buckle 1926, 11 March 1862
19 *Irish Sportsman and Farmer*, 10 Jan 1874

### 17 19TH-CENTURY FRANCE

1 Qu. Laffon, p. 148
2 Castelbajac, M. de, 27th Director of le Pin; qu. Thétard, p. 337
3 'Nimrod', *Nimrod Abroad*, Vol. I, pp. 184–85
4 Ibid. p. 186
5 Royer, Jacques de, officier des Haras, in Perrin, Olivier (ed.), *Encyclopédie Française du Cheval de Sang*, O.P. Paris 1951, p. 7
6 Karle, P. in Darley, Godolphin, *Racing in France*; tr. Roland Atkinson, H. Dupuy 1950
7 'Nimrod', *Nimrod Abroad*, Vol. 2, pp. 256, 258 sq.
8 'Nimrod', *Nemrod*, pp. 15–16
9 Minutes of 2 Aug and 18 Dec; qu. Stern, Jean, *Courses de Chantilly sous la Monarchie de Juillet*, Calmann-Levy 1913, pp. 10–11 nn.
10 Contemp. qu. Stern, p. 44
11 'Nimrod', *Nimrod Abroad*, Vol. 2, pp. 256–57
12 Qu. Stern, pp. 41–43
13 'Nimrod', *Nimrod Abroad*, Vol. 2, p. 274; and *Nemrod*, p. 238
14 Listed Laffon, pp. 86–92
15 Letter of Madame de Girardin; qu. Black, *France*
16 'Nimrod', *Nimrod Abroad*, Vol. 1, pp. 13, 120, 169
17 *Paris Elégant*, 16 May 1838
18 'Nimrod', *Nimrod Abroad*, Vol. 2, p. 175
19 Qu. Thétard, p. 207
20 Laffon, p. 283
21 'Nimrod', *Nimrod Abroad*, Vol. 2, p. 177
22 Moscowa, prince de; pamphlet qu. 'Nimrod', *Nimrod Abroad*, Vol. 2, p. 251
23 Ibid., pp. 239–40
24 *L'Illustration*, 25 May 1844
25 Black, *France*, p. 83
26 French contemp. qu. and tr. Black, *France*, p. 150
27 Jennings, Thomas Junior, *Journal*, ed. Rickman, Eric, 'Gladiateur and the Jennings'; *British Racehorse*, Vol.

Dixon, W., see 'Thormanby'

Drayson, Capt. Alfred W., *Sporting Scenes among the Kaffirs of South Africa.* Routledge 1858

'Druid, The', *The Post and the Paddock,* 1st ed. 1856; 5th ed. Vinton 1912

'Druid, The', *Silk and Scarlet,* 1st ed. 1858; 5th ed. Vinton 1912

'Druid, The', *Scott and Sebright,* 1st ed. 1862; 5th ed. Vinton 1912

'Druid, The', *Saddle and Sirloin,* 1st ed. 1870; 5th ed. Vinton 1912

Egan, Pierce, *Book of Sports.* Tegg 1832

Eliot, Elizabeth, *Portrait of Sport: A History of Steeplechasing.* Longman 1957

Evelyn, John, *Diary;* ed. William Bray; new ed. Colburn, 1850

Fairfax-Blakeborough, J., *Northern Turf History.* Vol. 1; *Hambleton and Richmond,* 1949; Vol. 2, *Extinct Race Meetings,* 1950. J. A. Allen

Fawcett, William, *Turf, Chase and Paddock.* Hutchinson 1932

Fawcett, William, *Racing in the Olden Days.* Hutchinson, undated

Fittis, R. S., *Sports and Pastimes of Scotland.* Gardner 1891

Fletcher, J. S., *History of the St Leger Stakes.* Hutchinson, undated

Gianoli, Luigi, *Horse and Man,* tr. Iris Brooks. Allen & Unwin 1969

Gilmour, Col, see 'Ubique'

Gould, Nat, *The Magic of Sport.* Long 1909

Greville, Charles, *Memoirs,* ed. Henry Reeve, 5th ed. Longmans Green 1875

Harrison, Fairfax, *The Equine F.F.Vs.* 1928

Harrison, Fairfax, *The Belair Stud 1747-61.* 1929

Harrison, Fairfax, *The Roanoke Stud 1795-1833.* 1930

Harrison, Fairfax, *The John's Island Stud 1750-1788.* 1931

Harrison, Fairfax, *Background of the American Stud Book.* 1933

All privately printed by Old Dominion Press, Richmond, Va.

Haydon, Thomas, *Sporting Reminiscences.* Blair, Sands 1898

Hayes, Capt. M. H., *Among Horses in Russia.* Everett 1900

Hayes, Capt. M. H., *Among Horses in South Africa.* Everett 1900

Hayes, Capt. M. H., *Training and Horse Management in India.* 6th ed. Longmans Green 1905

Herbert, Ivor & Smyley, Patricia, *The Winter Kings.* Pelham 1968

Heywood, William, *Palio and Ponte.* Methuen 1904

Hore, J. P., *History of Newmarket and Annals of the Turf,* 3 vols. Bailey 1886

*Horse-Racing; its History and Early Records of the Principal and Other Race Meetings,* Anon., new ed. J. Roche 1865

Jarvis, Sir Jack, *They're Off.* Michael Joseph 1969

Jayne, Leonard, *Pony Racing.* Hutchinson, undated

Jusserand, J. J., *Les Sports et Jeux d'Exercice dans l'Ancienne France.* Librairie Plon 1901

Kennedy, Admiral W. R., *Sporting Sketches in South America.* Porter 1892

Kent, John, *Racing Life of Lord George Bentinck.* Blackwood 1892

Kent, John, *Records of Goodwood.* Samson Low 1896

Kock, Victor de, *The Fun They Had!* Timmins, Capetown 1955

Laffon, F., *Moeurs Actuelles du Turf,* 3rd ed. Rothschild 1896

Lambton, Hon. George, *Men and Horses I Have Known,* new ed. J. A. Allen 1963

Lawrence, John, *The Horse, in all his Varieties and Uses.* Arnold 1829

Lehndorff, Count G., *Horse-Breeding Recollections.* Cox 1883

Leslie, Anita, *The Fabulous Leonard Jerome.* Hutchinson 1954

Leicester, Sir Charles, *Bloodstock Breeding,* new ed. J. A. Allen 1964

Lonsdale Library, *Flat Racing.* Seeley Service 1940

Markham, Gervase, *How to Chuse, Ride, Traine and Dyet* etc. 1599

Markham, Gervase, *Cavalarice, or the English Horseman.* 1607

Markham, Gervase, *Country Contentments.* 1631

Markham, Gervase, *Masterpiece,* new ed. 1680

Markham, Gervase, *The Complete Jockey,* new ed. 1680

Moorhouse, Edward, *The Romance of the Derby,* 2 vols. Biographical Press 1908

Mortimer, Roger, *The Jockey Club.* Cassell 1958

Mortimer, Roger, *The Derby Stakes.* Cassell 1962

Mortimer, Roger, *Twenty Great Horses.* Cassell 1967

Mortimer, Roger, and Willett, Peter, *Great Racehorses of the World.* Michael Joseph 1969

Muir, J. B., *W. T. Frampton and the 'Dragon'.* Sporting Fine Art Gallery 1895

Newcastle, William Cavendish, Duke of, *La Méthode et Invention Nouvelle de dresser les chevaux.* Antwerp 1657

Newcastle, William Cavendish, Duke of, *A General System of Horsemanship,* 2 vols. (bound together), ed. J. Brindley 1743

'Newmarket' (Rt Hon. J. S. Saunders), *Chapters from Turf History.* National Review 1922

'Nimrod' (Charles James Apperley), *Nemrod, ou l'Amateur de Courses.* Arthur Bertrand 1838

'Nimrod', *Nimrod Abroad,* 2 vols. Colburn 1843

'Nimrod', *The Chase, the Road, and the Turf,* new ed. Arnold 1898

O'Leary, Con, *Grand National.* Rockliff 1945

Orchard, Vincent, *Tattersalls.* Hutchinson 1953

Orchard, Vincent, *The British Thoroughbred.* Ariel Press 1966

Orton, J., *Turf Annals of York and Doncaster.* 1844

Perrin, Olivier (ed.), *Encyclopedic Française du Cheval de Sang.* Paris 1951

Pepys, Samuel, *Diary,* ed. Lord Braybrooke, 6th ed. Bohn 1858

Pick, William, *Authentic Historical Racing Calendar.* 1786

Pick, William, *Turf Register and Sportsman and Breeder's Stud-Book.* 1803

Prior, C. M., *Early Records of the Thoroughbred Horse.* The Sportsman 1924

Prior, C. M., *History of the Racing Calendar and Stud Book.* Sporting Life 1926

Prior, C. M., and Prior, F. M., *Stud Book Lore.* F. M. Prior 1951

Rice, James, *History of the British Turf,* 2 vols. Samson Low 1879

Richardson, Charles, *The English Turf; A Record of Horses and Courses,* ed. E. T. Sachs. Methuen 1901

Richardson, Charles, and others, *Racing at Home and Abroad,* 3 vols. London and Counties Press Association 1923-31

Ridgeway, Prof. William, *Origin and Inflence of the Thoroughbred Horse,* Cambridge Biological Series. Cambridge University Press 1905

Robertson, William H. P., *History of Thoroughbred Racing in America.* Prentice-Hall 1964

Robinson, J. R., *Old Q.* Samson Low 1895

Rodrigo, R., *The Racing Game; a History of Flat Racing.* Phoenix 1958

Rous, Capt. Hon. Henry, *Laws and Practice of Horse Racing.* Baily 1850

Saunders, J. S., see 'Newmarket'

Seth-Smith, Michael; Willett, Peter; Mortimer, Roger; Lawrence, John, *The History of Steeplechasing.* Michael Joseph 1966

Sidney, S., *The Book of the Horse,* 1st ed. 1875; new ed. Cassell undated

Sievier, R. S., *Autobiography.* The Winning Post 1906

Siltzer, Frank, *Newmarket.* Cassell 1923

Smith, Vian, *Point to Point.* Stanley Paul 1966

Snowy, J., *The Stanley of the Turf.* Chapman & Hall 1896

Stern, Jean, *Courses de Chantilly sous la Monarchie de Juillet.* Calmann-Lévy 1913

Strutfield, G. H., *Tattersalls Rules on Betting.* Horace Cox 1888

Strutt, Joseph, *Sports and Pastimes of the People of England,* 3rd ed. Thomas Tegg 1838

'Sylvanus' (Robert Colton), *Bye-Lanes and Downs of England.* Bentley 1850

Tesio, Frederico, *Breeding the Racehorse,* tr. Edward Spinola. J. A. Allen 1958

Thétard, Henry, *Histoire et Secrets du Turf,* 13th ed. Laffont 1947

'Thormanby' (W. Dixon), *Kings of the Turf.* Hutchinson 1898

Tozer, Basil, *The Horse in History.* Methuen 1908

Trevathan, C. E., *The American Thoroughbred.* American Sportsman's Library 1905

Tweedie, W., *The Arabian Horse.* Blackwood 1894

'Ubique' (Col. Gilmour), *Gun, Rod and Saddle.* Chapman and Hall 1869

Upton, R. D., *Newmarket and Arabia.* Henry S. King 1873

Watson, S. J., *Between the Flags: A History of Irish Steeplechasing.* Allen Figgis 1969

Welcome, John, *The Cheltenham Gold Cup.* Constable 1957

Welcome, John, *Fred Archer: his Life and Times.* Faber 1967

Welcome, John, *Neck or Nothing: the Extraordinary Life and Times of Bob Sievier.* Faber 1970

Whyte, J. C. *History of the British Turf.* Colburn 1840

Willett, Peter, *An Introduction to the Thoroughbred.* Stanley Paul 1966

Willett, Peter, *The Thoroughbred.* Weidenfeld & Nicolson 1970

Williams, Michael, *The Continuing Story of Point to Point Racing.* Pelham 1970

Woodruff, Hiram, *Trotting Horse of America,* 1st ed. 1867; 18th ed. Porter and Coates, Philadelphia 1876

Wykes, Alan, *Gambling.* Aldus 1964

Wyndham, Hon. H. A., *Early History of the Thoroughbred Horse in South Africa.* Humphrey Milford 1924

Youatt, William, *The Horse.* Chapman & Hall 1831

# Notes on Illustrations and Acknowledgments

Note. Where the following abbreviations appear in the notes, they are intended to acknowledge permission to reproduce photographs that museums, art galleries, other institutions (or specifically their governing bodies), private collections and photographic libraries have granted where they hold copyright; and, in the case of museums, other institutions and private collections, to indicate the location of the pictures.

Ackermann: Arthur Ackerman & Son Ltd, London

*BM*: The Trustees of the British Museum, London

*BN*: Bibliothèque Nationale, Paris

Jockey Club: The Stewards of the Jockey Club, Newmarket

Fores: Fores Ltd, London

Mellon Collection: From the Collection of Mr and Mrs Paul Mellon

*RTHPL*: The Radio Times Hulton Picture Library

Saratoga: The National Museum of Racing Inc., Saratoga Springs, NY

Tryon: The Tryon Gallery Ltd, London

The pictures illustrated on pages 26–7, 31, 45, 48, 50, 51, 61, 66–7, 74, 93, 114, 122, 149, 151, 152, 156, 157, 163, 172–3, 174, 177, 267, 272–3, 276–7 (above) were photographed by John R. Freeman.

The research in connection with the pictures illustrated on pages 102, 176, 178–9, 180, 183, 184, 187 was carried out by Mme Marianne Dumartheray.

Note. Where illustrations are across two pages, only the number of the left-hand page is listed.

11 Greek amphora. *BM*
12 Macedonian coin. *BM*
14 Terracotta relief, 1st century AD *BM*
17 ABOVE Mosaic. Bardo Museum, Tunis. *Photo: Michael Holford Library*
17 BELOW Mosaic. Museo Argeológico, Barcelona.
18 Mosaic. Museo Nazionale delle Terme, Rome. *Photo: De Antonis*.
21 ABOVE Mosaic. *BM*
21 BELOW Decoration in *The Book of Kells*, c. 800. The Board of Trinity College, Dublin. *Photo: Green Studio*
22 Detail from the Bayeux Tapestry, c. 1070. *Photo: Mansell Collection – Giraudon*
26 ABOVE Engraving in *Arte da Cavalleria de Gineta e Estradiota* by Antonio d'Andrade, 1678. *BM*
26 BELOW Decoration in *The Shah Namah*, 1340. Chester Beatty Library, Dublin. *Photo: Rex Roberts*
29 Drawing, artist unknown, 1511. *Photo: RTHPL*
31 Engraving by Stradanus in *Equile Joannis Austriaci Caroli V*, 1570. *BM*
33 Portrait, artist unknown. *Photo: RTHPL*
35 ABOVE Painting copied by Lorenzo Fratellini from the original by an unknown artist. By courtesy of the Azienda Autonoma di Turismo, Siena
35 BELOW Detail from a painting by Giovanni di Francesco Toscani. The Cleveland Museum of Art, Holden Collection.
36 Detail from a fresco by Francesco del Cossa, 1469. Palazzo di Schifanoia, Ferrara. *Photo: SCALA*
38 Drawing in the *Historia de Indias* by Diego Duran. *Photo: Federico Arborio Mella*
40 Portrait by Sir Anthony Van Dyck, c. 1637–40. National Gallery, London
42 Portrait 1625. *Photo: RTHPL*

43 Engraving in *A General System of Horsemanship* by William Cavendish, Duke of Newcastle, 1743
45 Portrait. National Portrait Gallery, London
48 Engraving by Francis Barlow. *BM*
50 Engraving by R. Blome, 1686. *BM*
51 Portrait after John Wootton. *BM*
53 Detail from a painting by Peter Tillemans. Mellon Collection.
54 Painting by James Seymour, 1740. *Ackermann*
57 Portrait after Sir Godfrey Kneller. *Photo: RTHPL*
59 LEFT and RIGHT Engravings after John Wootton. Fores
61 Mezzotint after George Stubbs, 1704. *BM*
62 Painting by John Wootton. Mellon Collection
65 Engraving by Vincenzo Pazzini Carli. By courtesy of the Azienda Autonoma di Turismo, Siena
66/67 Engravings in *L'Instruction du Roy en L'Exercise de Monter à Cheval* by Antoine de Pluvinel, 1627.
71 Portrait by Thomas Beach. Tattersalls, London
72 Painting by Benjamin Marshall. Mellon Collection
74 Stipple after J. N. Sartorius. *BM*
75 Painting by John Wootton. Mellon Collection
81 ABOVE and BELOW Engravings after Thomas Rowlandson, c. 1789. *Photos: Mansell Collection*
82 Painting by George Stubbs, 1770. Jockey Club
84 ABOVE and BELOW Paintings by James Pollard, 1833. Mellon Collection. *Photos: Ackermann*
86 Painting by John Boultbee. Tattersalls, London. *Photo: The British Racehorse, London*
87 Detail from a painting by George Stubbs. Jockey Club
90 Engraving after Thomas Rowlandson. Jockey Club
92 Painting by Francis Sartorius, 1766. Ackermann
93 Painting after Thomas Rowlandson, 1791. *BM*
95 Aquatint after H. Alken, 1821. *Photo: Mansell Collection*
96 Painting by Benjamin Marshall. Ackermann
100 Engraving by M. Gaiel. *Photo: RTHPL*
102 Engraving by J. M. Moreau le jeune. *BN. Photo: Collection Viollet*
104 Painting by N. G. Sverchkov, 1871. Equestrian Museum, Moscow
107 Silver Porringer. Saratoga
108 Detail from a portrait by John Wollaston the younger. The Tayloe Family of Virginia
109 Detail from a portrait by Gustavus Hesselius. Collection of John Baylor, Carnegie Institute, Pittsburg
110 BELOW Engraving. By courtesy of the Jockey Club, New York
111 LEFT Detail from a portrait copied by Mrs Samuel Evans Jr. from the original by an unknown artist. The Tayloe Family of Virginia. Saratoga
111 RIGHT Detail from a portrait by Gilbert Stuart, c. 1790. Collection of George DeLancey Harris.
113 Detail from an engraving. *Photo: Maurice Michael*
114 Aquatint after James Pollard. *BM*
116 Painting by J. F. Herring senior. Ackermann
119 Detail from a portrait after Samuel Lane. Jockey Club
120 Painting by Abraham Cooper. Welbeck Abbey. By courtesy of the Duke of Portland
122 Engraving after J. F. Herring senior. Fores
126 Detail from an engraving. Jockey Club
127 From *The Laws and Practice of Horse Racing* by Admiral Rous, 1851
128 Painting by J. F. Herring senior. Jockey Club
130 Painting by Harry Hall. Mellon Collection
133 Detail from a painting by William Powell Frith. Tate Gallery, London
134 Engraving after Anson. A. Martin. Jockey Club
136 ABOVE Painting by J. F. Herring senior. Jockey Club
136 BELOW Painting by Lynwood Palmer. Jockey Club
138 Painting, artist unknown. *Photo: RTHPL*
140 Painting, artist unknown. *Photo: RTHPL*
142 Engraving. By courtesy of the Parker Gallery, London
145 Painting by J. F. Herring senior. Mellon Collection
146 Pastel drawing by 'C.W.S.'. National Portrait Gallery, London
149 Mezzotint by C. Turner, 1807. *BM*
151 Painting by J. Brown, 1862. *BM*
152 ABOVE and BELOW Engravings by J. Doyle, 1823. *BM*
156 Painting after H. Alken, 1839. *BM*
157 Aquatint after H. Alken. *BM*
159 Aquatint after F. C. Turner. *BM. Photo: Elek Books Ltd*
163 Detail from an aquatint after F. C. Turner. *BM. Photo: Elek Books Ltd*
164 Painting by J. F. Herring senior. Mellon Collection
166/167 Frontispieces in *Bailey's Magazine: Sports and Pastimes* Vols 12 & 21, 1867 and 1871. *Photos: RTHPL*
172 Engraving after Henry Barraud. Fores
174 Engraving after John Sturgess, 1872. Fores
176 Portrait, artist unknown. Société d'Encouragement, Paris. *Photo: Roger Schall*
177 Engraving after E. Lami. Victoria and Albert Museum, London
178 Engraving by H. Delamarre. The Jockey Club, Paris. *Photo: Giraudon*
180 LEFT Engraving after Barennes, 1865. *Photo: Collection Viollet*
180 RIGHT Portrait in *Le Monde des Courses*, 1896. *BN*
183 Engraving by Princeteau, c. 1885. *BN*
184 Engraving, 1870. *BN*
187 Engraving. *BN*

189 Painting by Henri de Toulouse-Lautrec. Private Collection. *Photo: Giraudon*
190 Painting by Jean-Louis Forain. Mellon Collection
192 Painting by Edgar Degas, c. 1889. Mellon Collection
194 Engraving. *Photo: RTHPL*
198 Lithograph after Franz Kruger, Cohn 84, p. 90, 356–114. Staatliche Museum, Berlin
199 Engraving. By courtesy of the Hungarian Jockey Club
200 Engraving. By courtesy of the Austrian Jockey Club
202 Painting by A. O. Orlovsky, 1810. The Equestrian Museum, Moscow
203 Painting by N. G. Sverchkov, 1876. The Equestrian Museum, Moscow
206 Painting by Francis Sartorius. Jockey Club
207 ABOVE Detail from a portrait copied by Mrs Samuel Evans Jr. from the original by Gilbert Stuart. The Tayloe Family of Virginia. Saratoga
207 BELOW Detail from a portrait by John Wesley Jarvis, 1811. New York Historical Society
208/9 Engravings. By courtesy of the Jockey Club, New York
212 Painting, artist unknown. Saratoga
217 Painting by Edward Troye, c. 1856. Saratoga
218 Portrait copied by Charles Baskerville from the original painting by Reinhart, c. 1850.
220 Engraving after Lady Alexander, 1843. From *Racing and Breeding in America and the Colonies* Vol III, by Charles Richardson, the London and Counties Press Association, 1931
222 Portrait, artist unknown, c. 1869. Saratoga
223 Portrait copied by Charles Baskerville from the original by an unknown artist. Saratoga
224 Lithograph by Nathaniel Currier & James Ives. *Photo: Elek Books Ltd*
225 Lithograph by Nathaniel Currier & James Ives. Saratoga
227 Detail from a portrait by R. L. Seyffert, c. 1900. Saratoga
230 Water coloured photograph. Saratoga
232 Detail from a lithograph by Nathaniel Currier & James Ives. By courtesy of the Old Print Shop, New York
235 Painting by L. Maurer. Saratoga
236 Lithograph by Nathaniel Currier & James Ives, after J. H. Wright, 1865. (See *p. 236 for acknowledgment*.)
240 ABOVE Detail from a lithograph by Nathaniel Currier & James Ives, after Robert A. Clarke. (see *p. 240 for acknowledgment*.)
240 BELOW Detail from a lithograph by Nathaniel Currier & James Ives. (see *p. 240 for acknowledgment*.)
242 Lithograph by Nathaniel Currier & James Ives. *Photo: Elek Books Ltd*
244 Lithograph by Nathaniel Currier & James Ives, 1890. (See *p. 244 for acknowledgment*.)
247 Lithograph by Nathaniel Currier & James Ives, after J. Cameron. (See *p. 247 for acknowledgment*.)
249 Portrait copied by Jan Veth, 1898, from the original painting attributed to D. Craey. The Library of Parliament, Cape Town
251 Engraving, 1811. Africana Museum, Johannesburg
255 Engraving. *Photo: Mary Evans Picture Library*
258 Engraving in the *Illustrated Australian News*, 1876. The State Library of Victoria
260 Painting by Martin Stainforth. *Photo: Mansell Collection.*
262 Lithograph after Carl Kahler, Brasmere Collectors series, Melbourne 1970. Reproduced in *First Tuesday in November* by D. L. Bernstein
264 Engraving after Samuel Howett from *Oriental Field Sports* by Capt. Thomas Williamson, 1805. The India Office Library and Records, London
267 Water Colour, artist unknown. Victoria and Albert Museum, London
271 Engraving. *Photo: Mansell Collection*
272 Engraving in the *Illustrated London News*
276 ABOVE Engraving after A. C. Harvell, 1903. Fores
276 BELOW Painting. *Photo: RTHPL*
278 *Photo: RTHPL*
280 Painting by Helen Bradley, reproduced in *And Miss Carter Wore Pink*, Jonathan Cape Ltd, 1970
281 Detail from a portrait by Chartran, 1893. Saratoga
282 LEFT Painting by F. B. Voss. Saratoga
282 RIGHT Painting by Allen Brewer, 1954. Saratoga
285 *Photo: The New York Racing Association Inc.*
286 *Photo: RTHPL*
287 Painting by Sir Alfred Munnings. Mellon Collection
290 *Photo: W. W. Rouch Ltd*
291 Painting by Susan Crawford, 1971. Collection of Mr Vincent O'Brien. *Photo: Tryon*
293 Portrait by Sir Alfred Munnings, 1921. Mellon Collection
294 Painting by Leesa Sandys-Lumsdaine, 1971. Tryon
296 ABOVE and BELOW Paintings ascribed to Izta Ruibas, c. 1900. Tryon
298 ABOVE *Photo: Collection Viollet*
298 BELOW *Photo: The British Racehorse, London*
300 Water Colour by Raoul Dufy, 1939. By courtesy of Wildenstein & Co Ltd © by SPADEM, Paris 1972
301 LEFT *Photo: W. W. Rouch Ltd*
301 RIGHT *Photo: Sport & General*
304 *Photo: The British Racehorse, London*

# Index

**Note.** Figures in **bold** type refer to illustrations; those in *italics* to captions. Illustrations across two pages are indexed to the left-hand page only or to that on which the caption appears.